Knowledge Democracy

Roeland J. in 't Veld
Editor

Knowledge Democracy

Consequences for Science, Politics, and Media

Springer

Editor
Prof. Dr. Roeland J. in 't Veld
Waterbieskreek 40
2353 JH Leiderdorp
Netherlands
roelintveld@hotmail.com

ISBN 978-3-642-11380-2 e-ISBN 978-3-642-11381-9
DOI 10.1007/978-3-642-11381-9
Springer Heidelberg Dordrecht London New York

Library of Congress Control Number: 2010921154

Cover design: WMXDesign GmbH, Heidelberg

Printed on acid-free paper

Springer is part of Springer Science+Business Media (www.springer.com)

Preface and acknowledgements

This volume is devoted to an important and challenging idea: knowledge democracy. It will mobilise the necessary attention for the emerging threats and opportunities of relationships between science, media and politics, we hope. The book was inspired by the more than 200 contributions from scientists, policy-makers en media representatives who participated in the international conference Towards Knowledge Democracy which was organised by the Netherlands Advisory Council for Research on Spatial Planning, Nature and the Environment (RMNO) in co-operation with many other organisations on 25–27 August 2009 in Leiden, the Netherlands.

We asked twenty of the most interesting paper givers to compose their contribution into a chapter. They, as the authors of this book, are the first I would like to thank.

Moreover, I am very grateful to the members of the scientific advisory board for reviewing the draft chapters. Their comments were very valuable. They have improved the arguments in this book. Therefore I want to thank Prof. Dr. Frans Berkhout (VU University of Amsterdam), Prof. Dr. Herman Eijsackers (Wageningen University and Research Centre), Prof. Dr. Rudy Rabbinge (among others chairman of the Science Council of the Consultative Group on International Agricultural Research) and Prof. Dr. Julie Thompson Klein (Wayne State University).

And finally, without the enormous enthusiasm and endurance of the RMNO team that organised, edited, formatted and proof-read the book contributions within tight time constraints, this publication would have never been possible: Madelon Eelderink and Sophie Jongeneel who did most of the organising and editing work, Louis Meuleman, Bert de Wit and Martijn Ligthart, who commented and brought in their extensive experience.

Roeland Jaap in 't Veld

Scientific Advisory Board

Prof. Dr. Frans Berkhout is Professor of Innovation and Sustainability, and Director of the Institute for Environmental Studies (IVM) at the VU University in Amsterdam, The Netherlands. Until 2004 he was a Senior Fellow at SPRU (Science and Technology Policy Research), University of Sussex (UK) and Director of the UK Economic and Social Research Council's (ESRC) Sustainable Technologies Programme.

Prof. Dr. Herman Eijsackers is currently chairman of the Scientific Board of Wageningen University and Research Centre, which advises the Board on the direction and quality of research and education. He was scientific director of the Environmental Sciences Group, department Alterra at the Wageningen University and Research Centre. He is extraordinary professor at the VU University in Amsterdam.

Prof. Dr. Rudy Rabbinge is among others chairman of several national and international organisations. He is deputy chairman of the Netherlands Commission for Environmental Assessment (MER), chairman of the Science Council of the Consultative Group on International Agricultural Research (CGIAR, Rome/ Washington DC, Italy/USA).

Prof. Dr. Julie Thompson Klein is Professor of Humanities at Wayne State University and has been a Visiting Professor in Japan, a Fulbright professor in Nepal, a Distinguished Visitor at the University of Auckland in New Zealand, and a Senior Fellow at the Association of American Colleges & Universities.

Contents

1 Towards Knowledge Democracy

Roeland Jaap in 't Veld

Abstract

The concept of knowledge democracy is meant to enable a new focus on the relationships between knowledge production and dissemination, the functioning of the media and our democratic institutions. The emerging concept of knowledge democracy moreover obliges us to realise that the institutional frameworks of today's societies may appear to be deficient as far as the above mentioned undercurrents, trends and other developments demand change. We explored the directions for institutional change during the conference.

Democracy is without a doubt the most successful governance concept for societies during the last two centuries. It is a strong brand, even used by rulers who do not meet any democratic criterion. Representation gradually became the predominant mechanism by which the population at large, through elections, provides a body with a general authorisation to take decisions in all public domains for a certain period of time. Representative parliamentary democracy became the icon of advanced nation-states.

The recent decline of representative parliamentary democracy has been called upon by many authors. On the micro-level the earlier consistent individual position of an ideologically-based consistent value pattern has disappeared. The values are present but the glue of a focal ideological principle is not any longer at stock. Fragmentation of values has lead to individualisation, to uniqueness but thereby also to the impossibility of being represented in a general manner by a single actor such as a member of parliament. More fundamentally media-politics destroy the original meaning of representation. On the meso-level the development of political parties to marketeers in the political realm destroys their capacity for designing consistent broad political strategies. Like willow trees they move with the winds of the supposed voters' preferences. And on the macro-level media-politics dominate. Volatility therefore will probably increase.

The debate on the future of democracy in advanced national societies has not yet led to major innovations. Established political actors try to tackle populism with trusted resources: a combination of anti-populist rhetoric and adoption of the populist agenda. Some of the media have responded by attempting to become "more populist than populists themselves", almost always at the expense of analytical depth.

Meanwhile, the worldwide web provides for a drastic change in the rules of the game. A better educated public has wide access to information, and selects it

R.J. in 't Veld (ed.), *Knowledge Democracy*, DOI 10.1007/978-3-642-11381-9_1,

by itself instead of by media filters. Moreover citizens themselves have become media. They may produce world-famous YouTube pictures.

The crucial combination of a network society and media-politics provides new problems and tensions. The political agenda is filled with so-called wicked problems, characterised by the absence of consensus both on the relevant values and the necessary knowledge and information. Uncertainty and complexity prevail.

Advanced societies are characterised by an increasing intensity and speed of reflexive mechanisms. Reflexive mechanisms in a more or less lenient political environment cause overwhelming volatility of bodies of knowledge related to social systems. As all available knowledge is utilised to facilitate reflexive processes, the result of such processes might establish new relationships that undermine the existing knowledge. Social reality has then become unpredictable in principle.

The relationships between science and politics demand new designs in an environment of media-politics, wicked problems and reflexivity. The classical theory on boundary work in order to master the existing gaps between science and politics is nowadays widely accepted among experts. The underlying insight is that scientific knowledge by its very structure never directly relates to action, because it is fragmented, partial, conditional and immunised. This observation is valid for both mono- and multi- disciplinary knowledge. So translation activities are always necessary in order to utilise scientific knowledge for policy purposes.

The literature on transdisciplinary research is dominated by process-directed normative studies. It appears clear to me that the core concept of transdisciplinarity is to be defined as the trajectory in a multi-actor environment from both sources: from a political agenda and existing expertise, to a robust, plausible perspective for action.

In this volume 20 selected and carefully edited essays represent the harvest of the international conference "Towards Knowledge Democracy" which took place on 25–27 August 2009 in Leiden, the Netherlands. The introduction to the harvest is presented in Chap. 2.

The final part of our study is devoted to observations on quiet and turbulent democracies as very different typologies of potential evolutionary patterns of knowledge democracy.

1.1 The overwhelming success of democracy

Democracy is without a doubt the most successful governance concept for societies during the last two centuries. It is a strong brand, even used by rulers who do not meet any democratic criterion. Democracy according to Abraham Lincoln is a very broad concept:

> government of the people, by the people and for the people.

Some centuries later Schumpeter however defines it in a minimal manner:

....the democratic method is that institutional arrangement for arriving at political decisions in which individuals acquire the power to decide by means of a competitive struggle for the people's vote.

From Plato onwards, the continuous debates on the relative merits of democracy versus aristocracy, of consensual versus majoritarian typologies of democracy, of unicentric versus pluricentric concepts of democracy enrich our thinking.

In the course of the last two centuries, a group of related types of representative constitutional democracy became the predominant format of the nation-state. It enjoyed unheard popularity, and still does, all over the globe. All Western and most Southern political leaders preach democracy as an all-healing recipe. Representation gradually became the predominant mechanism by which the population at large, through elections, provides a body with a general authorisation to take decisions in all public domains for a certain period of time.

State, sovereignty, society and territory became intensely related with democracy: the formation of the nation-state was territory-oriented by nature, its violence monopoly became legitimated by representative democracy, and the population to be represented was the stable population of that same territory, gradually evolving into a society with a degree of cohesion that justified sovereignty. Of course the dynamics of this development were far more complicated than indicated here so far.

1.2 The curse of success

The cognitive and emotional investments into the present democratic institutions have been large. As a consequence the stability of these institutions is embraced. However, exogenous as well as endogenous developments threaten the continuation of success of representative parliamentary democracy.

The recent decline of representative parliamentary democracy has been called upon by many authors. Both Castells (1998, 2009) and Dahrendorf (2002) explicitly refer to the rise of media-politics as a threat to democracy. The reciprocal structural dependence of politicians and media then becomes the focal determinant of political action. Their explanations are related to the waning role of political parties and the migration of the political forum from parliaments to television studios. As a result of the disappearance of compelling political ideologies, political parties have started to behave like economic actors striving to maximise the number of future voters: following sole economic marketing theory for as far as their position on the political spectre is concerned. In the absence of consistent ideologies, the main parties choose a position very close to their competitors, shrinking the programmatic space dramatically. So voters complaining about the diminishing choice options are right.

Three intertwining simultaneous developments have taken place on the macro-, meso- and micro-level of societies, with important effects. On the micro-level the earlier mentioned consistent individual position of an ideologically-based consistent value pattern has disappeared. The values are present but the glue of a focal ideological principle is not any longer at stock. Fragmentation of values has lead to individualisation, to uniqueness but thereby also to the impossibility of being represented in a general manner by a single actor such as a member of parliament. None of the values cherished by an individual may be unique, but the combination probably is. The preference on behalf of individuals for partial representation by an NGO per value-domain therefore is no mistake, but a logical evolution. On the meso-level the development of political parties to marketeers in the political realm destroys their capacity for designing consistent broad political strategies. Like willow trees they move with the winds of the supposed voters' preferences. And on the macro-level media-politics dominate. As a consequence the epicentre of politics is shifting from parliament to the media.

Personalities in stead of programmes become the most important discriminating factor and therefore the voters choose personalities. In the attempt to maximise the number of voters, political parties are keen to use the media, as it is merely possible to actually "sell" personalities through mass media. This of course significantly increases the structural dependence of politicians on the mass media. Media and politics, a relationship based on mutual interest as on the other hand the media equally need politicians in order to produce news, one of their main products. So this dependence is reciprocal. The central position of the media – networks in themselves – with their natural focus on the production of news, causes the political debate to become superficial and short-term oriented. The classical function of democracy to protect the people against tyranny and random or arbitrary action by rulers is endangered by the stress on personalities in stead of programmes. More fundamentally media-politics destroy the original meaning of representation.

As Castells points out,

> It is not improbable that people will utilise their vote at general elections to show disgust or disapproval, more than revealing their preference for the favourite representative.

To his judgement, representation does not any longer produce a sustainable mandate for the representative. It does merely register an instantaneous picture of disgust at the moment of elections, timeless, without any meaning for future trust, and certainly not for a longer time span. Volatility therefore will probably increase.

The arguments in some attempts to gain insight in the consequences of the decline of democracy, point at the under-institutionalised global developments characterised by the increasing predominance of global economic conglomerates and accompanied by the rise of a new global elite. Other comments indicate that new communication technologies create virtual worlds and weaken the relevance of a physical stable territory. The notion of state, of territory, of society, of sovereignty and therefore of democracy appear to be endangered. ICT and mass media are identified by the above-mentioned analysts as threats for the political realm with a specific negative influence on political representation as media-politics develop. All these trends appear to cause the gradual disappearance of checks and balances, among which adequate protection against arbitrary or random political action. We will digress upon these options later. Another group of far more optimistic experts indicates that ICT enables new types of democracy that could prove to deliver adequate countervailing powers against the just listed threats.

The debate on the future of democracy in advanced national societies has not yet led to major innovations. Established political actors try to tackle populism with trusted resources: a combination of anti-populist rhetoric and adoption of the populist agenda. Some of the media have responded by attempting to become "more populist than populists themselves", almost always at the expense of analytical depth.

1.3 Wide access to information for everyone

Meanwhile, the worldwide web provides for a drastic change in the rules of the game. Acts of harassment on weblogs become political facts; virtual allegations become unchecked urban myths and pressure groups design increasingly easier ways to find endorsement on the internet. Obama's campaign was trendsetting for the latter.

Internet, better education and other societal changes have made knowledge accessible to many more people than in the past. This leads to an abundance of knowledge that needs to be interpreted. It also leads to different types of knowledge: not only scientific knowledge but also citizens' knowledge. This is a huge challenge for policy-makers, for scientists and for the media. Politics is not just about how knowledge can be selected for political decisions, but also about how democratic decision-making processes should change in order to incorporate the different types of knowledge adequately.

Moreover citizens themselves have become media: any citizen may produce a YouTube picture that is world-famous in 2 days: icons in political turmoil with great political momentum may be created by amateurs, as the recent events in Iran showed us. The classical media suffer from the new ones: not only in a commercial sense, but also because of the influence of the new media. We call the new media the bottom-up media in order to distinguish them from the classical media, the top-down media. Many of the new media do not know an editing function: nobody accepts the obligation to select the rubbish from the trustworthy materials. This results in very high costs for the recipient of the information in order to make the aforementioned selection. The developments in and with the media are confusing. Our capacity to observe appears deficient.

The wicked character of many problems on the political agenda sheds a fascinating light on the complexities caused by the interaction of top-down and bottom-up media.

Inclusion and exclusion get new dimensions: while the official Dutch authorities promoted a campaign of vaccination in order to protect young girls against future cervical cancer in the official media, the target group itself communicated on MSN Messenger, including series of very negative rumours. As a consequence a considerable part of the target group refused vaccination. Like ships in the night, the different streams of information passed each other.

As mentioned above, we distinguish "top-down media" and "bottom-up media". Both contribute to the agenda-setting of politics. The top-down media operate in structural interdependency with politics. The expression "media-politics" is devoted to this interdependency. The bottom-up media are to a considerable degree independent from both the top-down media and politics. Participation in decision preparation and – making may be invited by public authorities, but uninvited participation takes place too, in particular with support of bottom-up media.

1.4 From knowledge economy to knowledge democracy

During the last decade, an influential debate was conducted on the "knowledge-based economy". This concept even became the main policy objective of the European Union, the Lisbon Strategy. However, there are signs that the strength of the argument for the knowledge-based economy is weakening rapidly.

The current worldwide economic crisis leads to new, very challenging questions. These questions refer mainly to the institutional frameworks of today's societies. It is therefore time for a transition to a new concept that concentrates on institutional and functional innovation. As the industrial economy has been combined with mass democracy through universal suffrage and later by the rise of mass media, one might suggest that the logical successor of knowledge economy is a new type of governance, to be called "knowledge democracy".[1]

Which challenges and threats will we be facing? How will the respectable parliamentary and new direct forms of democracy mix, and which roles will knowledge play in the transition towards a knowledge democracy? The crucial combination of a network society and media-politics provides new problems and tensions. During this conference we concentrated upon the roles of knowledge and information in today's democracies. We further developed the concept of knowledge democracy in order to analyse whether we might be able to deal with these problems and tensions.

Today policy-making in many instances is evidence- or knowledge-based, providing both legitimacy and effectiveness, according to the supporters. Effectiveness is assured as the knowledge concerns true statements on the relationships between political interventions and their societal effects. Legitimacy is furthered when the policies are based upon the "objective" truth. As Silvio Funtowicz has explained over and over again, this image of knowledge is not adequate according to the modern science model. We will elaborate upon this later.

The political agenda is filled with so-called wicked problems, characterised by the absence of consensus both on the relevant values and the necessary knowledge and information. Uncertainty and complexity prevail.

---

[1] This concept was already formulated in the 1990s (Gaventa 1991) and since then survived on a moderate level. Only recently it emerges as a focal point of scientific and societal debate (Cohill 2000, Brown, 2003, Biesta 2007, Ober, 2008).

1.5 Reflexivity

Advanced societies are characterised by an increasing intensity and speed of reflexive mechanisms. We define reflexive mechanisms as events and arrangements that bring about a redefinition of the action perspectives, the focal strategies of the groups and people involved, as a consequence of mindful or thoughtful considerations concerning the frames, identities, underlying structures of themselves as well as other relevant stakeholders. Defined in this manner, reflexivity has to do with a particular kind of learning potential. Reflexive systems have the ability to reorientate themselves and adapt accordingly based on available self-knowledge.

Reflexive mechanisms in a more or less lenient political environment cause overwhelming volatility of bodies of knowledge related to social systems. As all available knowledge is utilised to facilitate reflexive processes, the result of such processes might establish new relationships that undermine the existing knowledge. Social reality has then become unpredictable in principle. The efficacy of reflexive mechanisms is furthered by institutional arrangements that enable individual liberty and tolerance.

In a tyrannical environment reflexive learning may take place, but it is not transformed into a change in behaviour because that change probably is illegal, and severely punished. Insofar as tyranny is negatively correlated with democracy, a democratic environment will prove to be apt for reflexivity.

It is necessary to develop this notion further because it is of utmost importance for the design of an advanced way of thinking on policy-making: we should realise that a social theory of any kind may never be used to create policy measures without an earlier research effort on the specific issue. Such an effort should include the question whether it is probable or plausible that the theory is already undermined by reflexive reactions in or around the target group of the measure. This latter effort will never deliver results with an absolute truth claim. So uncertainty is overwhelmingly present there too. The policy dialogue will then be characterised by different layers of uncertainty, and so by a discussion on the impact of the different layers of uncertainty too.

Evidence-based policy-making as a normative concept probably bears some relevance when it concerns the application of a physical, chemical or biological scientific theory. But it becomes a hazardous pretention if the decision support comes from a theory in the social sciences for the reasons just explained. In particular the claims of economics in important fields as education and health are sometimes preposterous. More modesty would fit once the complexity jump that results from reflexive systems is internalised by the expert.

Knowledge democracy could become an emerging concept with political, ideological and persuasive meaning. The analogy with the concept of knowledge economy is clear: the latter brought political attention for the economic meaning of research and development, a focus on the quality of education and political support for larger public budgets for the domains under consideration. The human capital theory – although deficient from a scientific point of view – became the predominating policy paradigm in educational policies.

The concept of knowledge economy has developed as a rather vague persuasive notion concerning the relationships between advanced research and education on one hand and economic prosperity on the other. The "container"-character of the concept has not prohibited favourable effects. It has proven to cause a more conscious approach to the relationships between knowledge production and dissemination on one hand and economic innovation on the other.

The concept of knowledge democracy is meant to enable a new focus on the relationships between knowledge production and dissemination, the functioning of the media and our democratic institutions. The emerging concept of knowledge democracy moreover obliges us to realise that the institutional frameworks of today's societies may appear to be deficient insofar as the above mentioned undercurrents, trends and other developments demand change. We explored the directions for institutional change during the conference.

In the perspective of new relationships between politics, media and science also classical problems demand new solutions: the concept of knowledge democracy concerns a *problematique* that relates to the intensification of knowledge in politics. We developed earlier a heuristic scheme in order to think properly about the bottlenecks that threaten optimal trajectories between the realm of politics, policy-making and useful research (Figure 1.1):

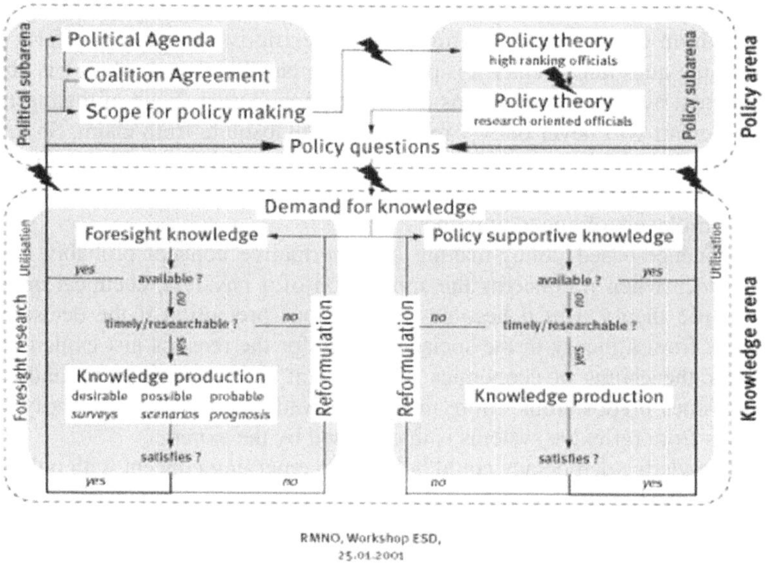

Fig. 1.1 Bottlenecks between the realm of politics, policy-making and useful research.

The thunderbolts show possible bottlenecks in the processes of articulation of the demand for knowledge, as well as the utilisation of knowledge, for instance:

- The actual political agenda may not correspond with the existing policy theories that are either laid down in existing policies, legal systems budgeting rules etc. or/and are embraced by the top civil servants.
- The translation of policy questions in knowledge demand may prove to be extremely difficult, for instance because the policy objectives bear a symbolic character, or because the policy questions are wicked in nature, lacking underlying consensus on values.
- Inconvenient truth, newly produced knowledge that attacks the existing policy theories, will probably not be applied in policy-making.
- Research will produce knowledge in the future but the need is urgent, and the political agenda is slightly volatile so there is a general problem of timeliness. In order to recognise the time lags just described on one hand and the legitimate demand for useful new knowledge on the other we should attempt to design the policy agenda in the near future in stead of only the present one, but that is a dangerous activity.

The aforementioned bottlenecks can be reformulated as problems that demand a solution or at least improvements.

The trajectory between science and politics however is only one of the relevant relationships in the triangle that was used as the basis of the 2009 Leiden conference on knowledge democracy which triggered this book (Figure 1.2):

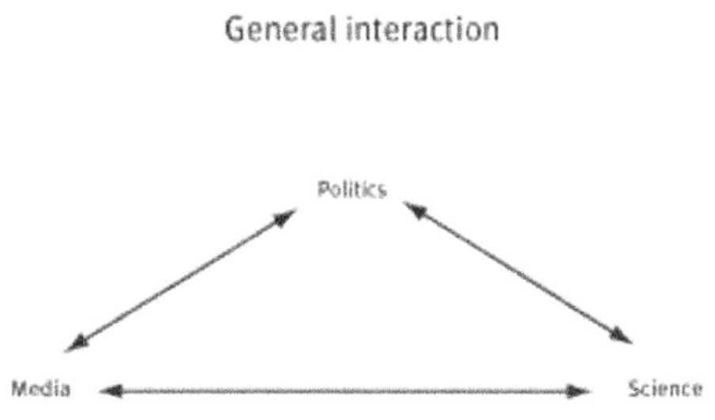

Fig. 1.2 The "Towards Knowledge Democracy" conference triangle.

The media are far from neutral or passive. The illusion that they are a neutral mirror of reality belongs to a forgotten past. We have already shed light on the relationships between politics and media. Media create realities, they also produce knowledge, and moreover report on citizens' knowledge. They are the reporters on scientific findings but also competitors of scientists. The same goes for the relationships between media and citizens. This increasing complexity demands efforts in order to gain insight. Other important questions are for instance:

- How do media deal with scientific knowledge, and in particular how do they select the new knowledge to be reported on from the vast supply of new knowledge?
- How can scientific knowledge and citizens' science both be utilised in processes within politics?
- How can conflicts between both types of knowledge be solved?
- How do supervisors and regulators deal with citizens' science?

A number of questions concerning the functioning of the democratic institutions themselves as far as application of knowledge is concerned are very relevant:

- How do parliaments deal with different types of knowledge?
- How do parliaments not only use e but also produce knowledge?
- Is parliamentary research to be trusted since parliamentary research committees never lose their power orientation?
- How do parliaments deal with their dependence on information from ministries?
- Which challenges and threats will we be facing? How will parliamentary and new direct forms of democracy mix, and which roles will knowledge play in the transition towards a durable and sustainable knowledge democracy?

We will deal with some of these questions in this volume.

1.6 Transdisciplinarity

Much valuable scientific work has been performed on the relationships between science and politics, in order to answer the last question partially. Jasanoff and others have argued that it would be wise to design an independent boundary function in order to foster the quality of the translation. The classical theory on boundary work in order to master the existing gaps between science and politics is nowadays widely accepted among experts. The underlying insight is that scientific knowledge by its very structure never directly relates to action, because it is fragmented, partial, conditional and immunised. This observation is valid for both mono- and multi-disciplinary knowledge. So translation activities are always necessary in order to utilise scientific knowledge for policy purposes. Pohl, Scholz, Nowotny, Regeer and Bunders, and many others have explored this vast domain and developed the concept of transdisciplinarity in a number of variations.

The literature on transdisciplinary research is dominated by process-directed normative studies. It appears clear to me that the core concept of transdisciplinarity is to be defined as the trajectory in a multi-actor environment from both sources: from a political agenda and existing expertise, to a robust, plausible perspective for action. Funtowicz's later models contain both solutions and caveats on this thorny road. The terminology of the main authors is still more hesitant and still bears the word "research" in the title. It appears fair however, to acknowledge that the core activity of transdisciplinarity is design, more than research. Researchers of course may contribute to design.

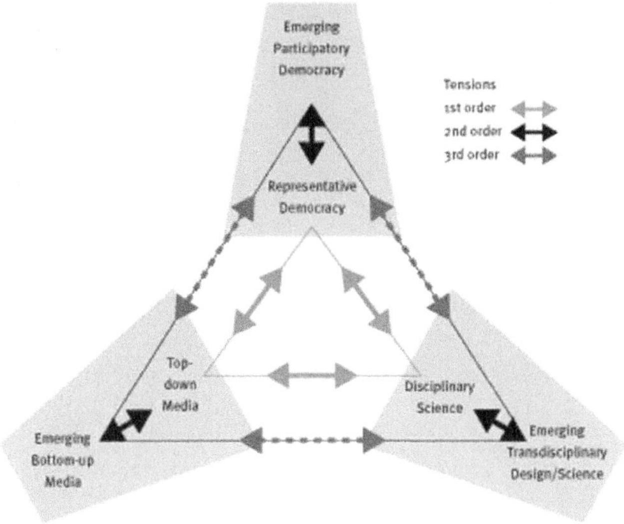

Fig. 1.3 The emergence of the knowledge democracy concept.

This scheme (Figure 1.3) illustrates the emergence of knowledge democracy. The original institutional framework was fit for the application of the fruits of disciplinary science, in order to solve rather simple policy problems within the framework of representative democracy. Society was ordered clearly in terms of ideological patterns and classical top-down media fulfilled their roles. The first-order relationships show this picture. Each of the corners in the triangle is prone to profound change, indicated in the second-order relationships:

- The bottom-up media do not only supplement the classical media, but also compete with them.
- Participatory democracy is complementary to representative democracy but is also considered as a threat to the latter.
- Transdisciplinary design or research is not only a bridge between classical science and the real world but also produces deviant knowledge and insights.

As a consequence we are confronted with tensions, threats and opportunities that are indicated in the third-order relationships.

2 The harvest of the "Towards Knowledge Democracy" conference

Roeland Jaap in 't Veld

Abstract

The harvest of the conference "Towards Knowledge Democracy"[1] is only partially collected in this volume. We have selected the most promising contributions that illustrate aspects of knowledge democracy. Of course, this selection is not objective at all. We will introduce the selection in this chapter in a more or less neutral manner, and draw some conclusions in the final chapter.

We did not attempt to introduce the concept of knowledge democracy as either a consistent theoretical framework or as a closed well-defined concept at the conference nor in this book. Our objective was to focus on a group of crucial relationships, in order to draw attention.

2.1 The character of the knowledge democracy concept

We consider the concept of knowledge democracy as an inspiring normative notion that indicates, integrates and summarises emerging phenomena. *Esther Turnhout* points out that this type of concept is neither riskless nor without dangers. She ranks knowledge democracy in the range of concepts dealing with the relationships between the production of knowledge and its use. She discusses at first the traditional speaking truth to power model and the information-deficit reasoning. She considers both to be simplistic and unsatisfactory concepts that cannot any longer be upheld in a world that is characterised by "scientisation of politics and politisation of science". Therefore a need for new visions on the relationship between knowledge production and use exists. The analysis of written statements during the Knowledge Democracy Conference in August 2009 leads her to the assumption that the concept of knowledge democracy should be interpreted as an enriched speaking truth to power model, as a model supplemented with a participatory ideal. Moreover she interprets knowledge democracy as a utopian concept. Following Achterhuis, she points at the potentially totalitarian character of utopian concepts.

---

[1] Leiden, the Netherlands, 25–27 August 2009.

R.J. in 't Veld (ed.), *Knowledge Democracy*, DOI 10.1007/978-3-642-11381-9_2,

The aforementioned participatory ideal is her next concern. Like many other authors, she criticises the assumption that the participatory processes could be constructed by process architects in each relevant case according to standardised protocols prescribed by a or "the" theory on knowledge democracy. She points out that the public is brought into being in the context of participation. She shares this viewpoint with Floor Basten, who also argues that the public is an event-bound phenomenon that can only be observed ex post. She fears technocratic applications of knowledge democracy concepts.

2.2 The institutional context of knowledge democracy

Voters are also citizens and clients. Public authorities deliver services to clients, who earlier decided upon the service deliverance indirectly in their quality as voters.

We depart from an institutional framework characterised by the classical representative democracy that produces collective goods and merit goods with classical instruments like standardised regulation and standardised subsidies, in order to provide equality and justice. The complexity of the relationships between public authorities and citizens however, cannot be met adequately any longer by standardised arrangements only. Values are more fragmented than ever before. More flexible systems should be introduced.

Dirk Wolfson digresses on the concept of "situational contracting". To his opinion, the application of this type of contract would fit the demand for organisation of a properly informed democracy. It appears that equal and standardised provision of services by public authorities causes injustice because under the surface, equal cases are unequal. The available knowledge and information are insufficient for the purpose to meet variety in a just manner. Public failure is the consequence. Being a self-critical economist, Wolfson concludes from an overview in social theories that a new institutional design is needed which modernises the "contractarian" conception, and among other things does justice to the growing fragmentation of values in a pluralistic society.

Departing from principal-agent theory, he moves to situational contracting. This concept is characterised by the discretionary authority of public service deliverers to offer facilities customised to differences in the counterparts' abilities to perform. Value convergence is revealed in relationships characterised by empathy and the expectation of reciprocity, both essential components of the concept of trust.

Situational contracting rests on the firm base of value patterns of public officials that are not only restricted to the pursuit of self-interest, but also contain altruistic parts. Application of the concept is, according to Wolfson, a manner to deal adequately with the flow of information as well as to introduce elements of deliberative and direct democracy. The crucial factor is the way in which information is revealed and the interactions that take place between stakeholders throughout the entire chain of policy-making and implementation.

2.3 The constitutional values in a knowledge democracy

Freedom of choice and equality belong to the most important constitutional values to be realised by democracy. The majority rule is one of the least deficient methods to take collective decisions while respecting these values, as was explained in the previous chapter. These constitutional values are in general not related to a certain substance. Equality is a relational value.

Klaus Töpfer and *Günther Bachmann* introduce a substantial constitutional value: the fundamental idea of environmental justice in the formulation "one man, one vote, one carbon footprint". They consider this idea as a contribution to knowledge democracy. According to them, the sustainability challenge adds a normative, political challenge to justice. The classical democratic concept should be broadened to the idea – based upon the precautionary principle – of concretising the individual environmental space into "one carbon footprint". The necessity of such a concept is based upon the empirical observation that an overwhelming amount of available scientific evidence on the threatening ecological disasters so far has not led to adequate political action.

They argue, in analogy to "the one man, one vote" adagium that was meant to avoid civil wars, that the introduction of a restricted individual claim on ecological damage could avoid ecological disasters.

2.4 The people

In classical democracy the population of a certain territory is the "logical" electorate. In the previous chapter we already pointed at the consequences of ICT and the existence of virtual communities as a complicating factor. Moreover people are absent from their homes more than ever before. The notion of a steady electorate fits in schemes of representation, but far more complex considerations are at stake in participatory collective decision-making. The question: "Who are the stakeholders that should participate?" is sometimes answered by the public authorities themselves, but in less orthodox cases groups of citizens themselves decide to utter themselves. ICT plays an important role here also in the creation of communities by bottom-up media. Masses, crowds and publics are well-known concepts in sociological theory. But they are hard to handle in prescriptive theory on participation.

Analysing roles of citizens in participatory processes we often tend to speak about either civic society at large or about inhabitants of a certain territory. However, citizens manifest themselves collectively in many shapes and formats. We deal here with masses, crowds and publics. Floor Basten deals with publics in the context of the crisis in social sciences as she experiences it. Her first insight relates to Baudrillard's description of the mass as a highly implosive phenomenon, a "black hole", "that does not think, but is researched". "Nothing can represent the silent majority and that is its revenge" (Baudrillard). Masses are cemeteries for the dying social. Information produces still more masses.

The inertia of masses is absent in the term "publics". Publics are defined by and after events. They must become involved when existing institutions do not (any longer) provide an adequate framework to settle issues. The outlines of a public are defined by the people involved in an event. A public has no central intelligence, but may act consistently. Recognising and involving publics may create "democratic spaces" that produce knowledge under democratic conditions. Event-oriented decisions are taken more and more as the media create agendas and hypes. Hypes are events that enable publics to constitute themselves.

The crowd is a somewhat vaguer notion. *Maurits Kreijveld* attempts to reduce the applicability of insights into the potential wisdom of crowds by describing far more accurately the series of circumstances that enable the emergence of wisdom to be produced by crowds. He also indicates the potential wisdom of process-bound groups of participants in interactive decision preparation.

Of course more in general the interaction of different stakeholders with different interests and varied types of knowledge is at the heart of all participatory processes in decision-making. We will deal with this later on.

2.5 The political process: agenda-setting

The theoretical viewpoint that considers the policy process as a life cycle indicates agenda-setting as the initial phase.

Agenda-setting is a crucial process in the political realm. The selection of agendas is usually based upon the objectives of the actors involved: politicians will select agendas that may produce success. The citizen who might have thought that societal agendas have to cover the most serious societal problems will be disappointed, but the logic of politics is irresistible in itself. Unsolvable problems do not appear on political agendas because success is impossible. The construction processes of political agendas by cabinet formations and the like are well-described in political science literature. Media play an active role in agenda construction.

Politicians rely upon participation by citizens and other relevant actors if they are uncertain about future success. *Anders Jacobi* et al. analyses in particular the combination of foresight and citizen participation. The CIVISTI project specifically deals with seven smaller European nations, where citizen panels were constructed in a comparative approach. The character of the approach is iterative: at first well-informed citizen panels design long-term visions, subsequently experts and stakeholders transform these visions into research agendas, followed by the final step where citizens set priorities on the expert designs and policy options. The project is underway.

Tjard de Cock Buning describes an actual case which involved citizen participation in policy-making on biotechnology and food in the Netherlands. A constructed societal agenda was produced by iterating classical approaches with participative tools. According to the author, this societal agenda serves as a reflective mirror, and illustrates the development that the focus of power on innovation is shifting from an elitist mode to a democratised mode in which concerns of society are analysed and transformed into the content of research policies.

Civil society is organising itself, but also has to organise itself because the traditional institutions do not function properly any longer so that one might speak about an institutional void, in the terminology of Hajer (2003). Also in De Cock Buning's approach iteration between revealing preferences and priorities on one hand and the formulation of expert judgements, report and designs on the other hand is furthered. The result of the approach described by him is the concrete identification of a number of areas where research efforts should be intensified.

2.6 Wicked problems and configurations

Wicked problems dominate political agendas nowadays. We speak of wicked problems if dissensus exists regarding both the relevant values and the necessary knowledge and information. Multiplicity and plurality of knowledge are essential characteristics of these problem domains. Transdisciplinarity is the concept that covers processes and trajectories that lead to robust plausible action perspectives for wicked problems. Configuration theory sheds an interesting specific light on the complications that can be found in the amalgamation of knowledge and preferences in transdisciplinary processes. Configuration theory explains "organising" as a process of gradual construction of meaning, of a common view on reality, in two dimensions: the social and the cognitive dimension. "Organising" is then realised by communication and argumentation. Configurations gradually acquire a specific identity, close themselves, and become "fixed", both in the cognitive and in the social dimension. They often experience the utterings of other configurations as lies, as hostile opinions that should be mistrusted.

*Katrien Termee*r and others analyse the issues around the revolutionary agricultural idea of mega-stables in terms of configurations. They try to explain why this creative idea was not accepted by majority coalitions. They clearly demonstrate how fixations in different configurations that are rooted in self-referentiality and revealed in convictions of self-evidence, hamper fruitful communication between configurations and produce mistrust and still deeper dissensus.

The understandable but wrong approach to overcome this bottleneck on behalf of the process architecture is to conduct more research in order to strengthen the cognitive basis of the proposal. The recommendations from the authors to the process architecture are: identify the relevant configurations, avoid fixations by maintaining reflection, and try to return from fixation to reflection by the variation of context.

The authors were not successful as consultants in the real case in proposing variations of context that overcame the fixations in the real case. They suggest an incremental "small step" approach as desirable. We might also explore other approaches, aiming for instance at "revelation". This quest for effective interventions is the continuous assignment of process architecture around wicked problems.

2.7 Media

Miguel Goede attempts to present a conceptual framework describing the interrelated functioning of the media, democracy and governance. The classical top-down media have changed the character of politics profoundly. The media frame the societal debate in which politics function like a television reality show. The classical media impose their specific logic upon the political process. The structural mutual dependence of politicians and media leads to an unholy alliance. Representation in its original meaning disappears, so democracy itself is threatened. Hypes prevail.

New bottom-up media however reveal preferences of until now inaudible groups. Bottom-up media may also exercise political influence. As a consequence, the media logic changes dramatically. Mediacracy is no longer a top-down affair only. Classical media-politics are sometimes overthrown by bottom-up media. But one may also observe that either classical media or politicians attempt to incorporate bottom-up media. Goede concludes that the convergence of politics and the media towards a reality show is now irreversible. The notion of reality show may bear a negative connotation, but Goede argues that it may also hold the promise of a direct or participative democracy in which people play an active role in their own government.

2.8 Transdisciplinarity

Transdisciplinary research is a process that is meant to amalgamate different types of knowledge on one hand and values and preferences on the other.

Joske Bunders et al. answer the question how transdisciplinary research may contribute to knowledge democracy. They compare the historical developments in Switzerland and the Netherlands, followed by the design of a typology of transdisciplinary research styles in two dimensions: the degree of involvement of non-dominant groups and the degree of lay knowledge input. A low score on both dimensions illustrates a self-referential knowledge production style, a high score on the first dimension and a low score on the second describes a knowledge dissemination style, while a low score on the first and a high score on the second dimension is named mutual learning between scientists and dominant societal actors, and a high score on both dimensions is named a broad process of co-creation. The Transdisciplinary Case Study Approach as applied by Scholz and some other approaches are described. The upheld pretention is, that the architecture of transdisciplinary research (should) hold(s) an unbiased position. The authors' conclusions are that the mutual learning (for knowledge between scientists and dominant actors) style aims at enriching the decision-making process. This type of research can be exercised within the boundaries of the classical representative democracy. The co-creation style fits in deliberative democracy, and causes potential tensions with classical representative political bodies.

Jurian Edelenbos et al. analyse the synchronisation of knowledge. They focus on the interplay between experts, bureaucrats and stakeholders in the production of knowledge for decision-making. Their case studies relate to water management. In general they distinguish scientific or expert knowledge, bureaucratic knowledge and stakeholder knowledge. The latter is often grounded in experiences, and often is location- or context-oriented. It may be lay knowledge. As the cases show, sometimes the non-dominant stakeholders have to fight for influence, while the other two groups acquire influence more or less automatically. The roles of experts and bureaucrats differ, but they understand each other relatively well because of a common scientific background. The interplay between experts and stakeholders may appear to be more problematic, because models and instruments are expert-driven, and the application of these methods is often very rigid. In both cases the civil servants are not receptive to or responsible for the knowledge provided by stakeholders. Already available new approaches for process management leading to negotiated knowledge were neither accepted by the civil servants nor by the political principals. Experts and bureaucrats – because of common background – do cooperate better. More in general, according to Edelenbos – and contrary to conclusions by others – experts and bureaucrats do not acknowledge that stakeholder knowledge has the potential to improve either the identification of problems or the search for feasible solutions.

One may conclude that both in literature and in reality it is possible to distinguish between believers and non-believers in the "wisdom" of communicative and argumentative processes. The believers think that processes may enrich the solution of problems, and may produce results that no single participant could have come up with. The processes have added value. The non-believers are only willing to accept that processes may produce compromises.

2.9 Boundary work

So far we spoke about process architecture. Do we have to think about a specific process architect or just about a method? Jasanoff and others have argued that the communication between experts and bureaucrats should be furthered by boundary workers who speak the languages of both groups and understand the differences in roles and responsibilities. Some European nations have created public advisory organisations that play the role of boundary worker.

Rob Hoppe describes the recent development of the predominating political doctrine in the Netherlands leading to the destruction of boundary work organisations that aimed at bridging science and policy-making. The ministries themselves will from now on assign advisers and experts. Destroying these boundary organisations is based upon a simplistic view on their functions. The result is according to Hoppe "anorexia consulta", because impact of advice is defined on the basis of unidirectional transfer of knowledge. A closer look into the internal structure of the advice process reveals that it is a myth that politics would only be concerned with values and interests, and scientists or expert advisors would only occupy themselves with facts and causality. The traffic of information moreover proves to be not unidirectional at all, but reciprocal. Policy-makers and experts negotiate tensions and disconnects between the political-administrative worlds and academic-professional worlds. One part of boundary work is continuous demarcation, and the complementary part is coordination. Mutual dependence is the consequence. Hoppe distinguishes seven types of boundary workers and relates them to a 2×2 diagram describing problem structures. He introduces "policy politics" describing the combination of the types of cognitive processes (puzzling) and the types of competitive interaction (powering).

Successful arrangements for boundary work are identified: double participation, dual accountability, choice of boundary objects, co-production and last but not least metagovernance and capacity building. From Hoppe's combination it becomes crystal clear, that a certain amount of boundary work may be found to be necessary in any high-level policy-making process but that the organisational shapes as well as the division of roles and tasks may vary considerably.

2.10 Roles of creativity and knowledge

Stella van Rijn and *René Tissen* have a thorough look at the roles of knowledge in decentralised government, in regions and cities. They concentrate on ideas and creativity as the crucial factor in regional economies almost immediately and therefore consider the viability of the ideas of Richard Florida. They interpret his theory in such a manner that businesses follow knowledge and therefore cities should attract creative citizens, the Creative Class being a super-creative core who realises meaningful new forms of living and working. Creative professionals combine with the just mentioned core. Knowledge becomes a competitive advantage. According to Florida the world consists of twelve mega-regions with powerful centripetal forces. The advanced city is concentrating on accumulating creative people and businesses. Departing from Tissen's organisational design theory with respect to a threefold notion of necessary space, physical, virtual and mental space, the authors argue whether city governments should provide space to knowledgeable citizens. Participatory democracy might provide space in some respect. The authors try to define satisfactory conditions for a knowledge society and appear to accept transdisciplinarity as a natural way of life. So the traditional roles citizens play in city planning needs to change in the direction of much more participation.

2.11 Unwelcome knowledge

In the absence of boundary work many "traffic accidents" may happen in a system that is populated by scientists and bureaucrats. It is well known that policy-makers will hardly accept new knowledge that does not fit into their core belief systems, for instance their policy theory. But also other bottlenecks may become visible.

Louis Meuleman and *Henk Tromp* write two connected essays on the end-of-pipe bottlenecks after knowledge production. Of course the whole concept of "usable knowledge" is now well known since Cohen and Lindblom (1979). Louis Meuleman sums up many of the reasons why knowledge may not be usable for policy-makers. He applies the variety of governance styles – hierarchy, market, and network – to find different notions of usability. He recommends metagovernance: a conscious combination of styles. The framing of the policy problem under consideration is a crucial matter. The sense of urgency is a determining variable: the more urgent the problem, the more hierarchical the knowledge governance. Governance styles may also vary in different phases of the knowledge production process. Henk Tromp tells us about experiences with cases of unwelcome knowledge. The different techniques practised by policy-makers in order to neutralise unwelcome news are: to silence the messenger – who pays the piper, calls the tune – to distort the conclusions and recommendations, to put sanctions on the utterings of the researchers, etc. This author recommends among other things the build-up of a system of jurisprudence on the compromises reached in the cases of unwelcome knowledge.

2.12 Future research

Reflexivity, the predominant characteristic of all social systems, prohibits forecasting. The future cannot be known. However other forms of future research than forecasting are possible. One of the most promising activities is the design of a Horizon Scan.

Victor van Rij describes the exercise in the Netherlands – other programmes were developed in Great Britain and later in Denmark. Horizon Scanning has been developed upon a tradition of foresight. A Horizon Scan contains a large collection of feasible threats and opportunities for the next half century or so. Each of them gets a mark for probability, seriousness of impact, and/or desirability. This exercise is extremely fit to enable wide participation by stakeholders and citizens. The exploration of threats and opportunities, but also the indication of impact, plausibility and desirability could be fascinating elements of interactive processes between different types of experts, bureaucrats, politicians and citizens. Moreover the results of Horizon Scans are valuable tools in strategic political decision-making.

2.13 Long term decisions

Louis Meuleman and *Roeland in 't Veld* concentrate on the specific characteristics and peculiarities of long-term decisions. A general observation shows that politicians are often very competent in designing long-term visions, while hesitating at the same time to take decisions with benefits on the long term while sacrifices have to be made today. The explanation for this hesitance generally is given in terms of a nearby political time horizon. The next elections necessitate producing political success beforehand. Disasters around PCBs and asbestos show the abovementioned hesitance to take adequate action. The authors define two types of long-term decisions:

- Cases with a relatively long period between the policy intervention and the intended effects: a long lead time.
- Cases that demand a long-lasting series of interventions that as a whole is necessary to cause a favourable effect, following the "drop in the bucket" metaphor.

The first type demands firm leadership in order to collect sufficient momentum for the focal decision, the second type asks for perseverance and consistency.

As to long-term futures uncertainty and complexity prevail. In some cases we are able to forecast to a considerable degree, then we may anticipate. In the majority of cases we have to meet the existing uncertainty by concentrating on the acquirement of resilience.

The authors deal extensively with the roles of knowledge in long-term decisions and in particular formulate recommendations for sensible processes in order to integrate values, knowledge and political preferences in long-term decision-making.

2.14 Knowledge governance

The institutional framework of today's societies consists of complex combinations of hierarchy, markets and networks, as Meuleman (2008) has pointed out. Within this framework crowds, publics and citizens may exercise influence, while top-down as well as bottom-up media enable and hamper nearly all functions in public decision-making. In this volume Wolfson has formulated a proposal for an institutional innovation leading to knowledge democracy by situational contracting.

Arwin van Buuren and *Jasper Eshuis* propose to introduce an additional fourth institutional arrangement, to be called knowledge governance. This arrangement is about purposefully organising the development of knowledge in order to deal with societal problems. The paper analyses the situations in which knowledge democracy may be a viable alternative for the traditional arrangements in order to provide adequate coordination.

Coordination is, according to the authors, the essential condition for collective action. Sometimes the three classical coordinating mechanisms fail. A case study illustrates this, in which the production of new knowledge served as a catalyser to reach consensus on a solution for a water management problem. The involvement of all actors in the design of an innovative research programme enabled them to learn collectively, and to redefine their framing of the problem. The voluntaristic character of the common efforts – no relation with future action or implementation was visible in the beginning – appeared to accelerate the birth of consensus. Sharing ideas gradually enabled all parties involved to share initiatives for action later on.

2.15 Commissions as innovative boundary organisms

Boundary work is necessary in order to reconcile the paradigms and approaches of different scientists on one hand and the values and convictions of policy-makers on the other hand in an adequate manner. Boundary work may be performed by intermediate organisations indicated as such, but also by other organisms. *Martin Schulz* and *Mark van Twist* deal with commissions. A commission is a group of people with origins outside of government, which is set up to consider a matter of some kind within the public service. The core function of commissions may be advisory, but commissions may reach authoritative conclusions, may break taboos, and may find new solutions. Schulz and Van Twist discover three perspectives on changing roles and positions of commissions in a knowledge democracy. They had an almost exclusive role in the development of knowledge for policy until the sixties, and are gaining a position in power games and checks and balances since the 1980s.

Schulz and Van Twist observe that the boundaries between domains and between societal actors are fading, and as a consequence the role of commissions is fading. The authors indicate four major transitions in the functioning of commissions:

- From a "flat" structure to a multi-layered structure, to be called cascade commissions, provided with many sub-commissions that reach into the capillaries of society.
- From commissions of inquiry to citizens' assemblies where citizens' knowledge is appreciated besides scientific knowledge.
- From evaluation commissions to policy hubs, with the assignment to create new knowledge, and to establish connections across organisational boundaries.
- From political commissions towards conventions and network consultations, where citizens reveal preferences on government policies, creating "living documents" similar to a wiki.

Schulz and Van Twist define the future challenge for commissions as finding the balance between opposing values on the interface of organised relationships.

2.16 Political networks

Commissions consist of experts. New technologies enable every one to communicate, also politicians and citizens. One may attempt to define networks that stimulate rich communication.

We indicated above in a general manner that the so-called bottom-up media are in full development. *Chris Aalberts* and *Maurits Kreijveld* analyse the knowledge exchange through online political networks. The relationships between politicians and citizens may change as a consequence of the application of Web 2.0 networks. The case the authors deal with, concerns the Dutch social network Hyves. Hyves can be compared with Facebook or MySpace. More and more politicians attempt to utilise Web 2.0 applications for communication with citizens.

The majority of the members of Hyves is sleeping, never visits the hyve. The hyves of politicians show only moderate participation by citizens. The membership of the hyves of two right-wing politicians is the most numerous. It appears that unless the discussion is very well-structured, the communication on Hyves tends to degenerate into small talk.

2.17 Knowledge democracy, innovation and sustainability

The final chapter is devoted to the relationships between knowledge democracy and sustainable development, the most focal global political issue.

Bert de Wit concentrates on the design of a societal innovation system that produces more sustainability. Having declared linear innovation models obsolete, he deals at first with innovation on the micro-level. He follows the suggestion of the Netherlands Scientific Council for Government Policy to create hybrid spaces for interaction between scientists, entrepreneurs and societal groups. On the meso-level De Wit has in the past analysed a number of sectors – food, energy, water – and concludes that the innovation system for sustainability within these sectors is deficient.

On the macro-level De Wit concludes that both government and the powerful intermediate research organisation, the Royal Academy of Science and the Netherlands Organisation for Scientific Research in the past have failed to produce either consistent viewpoints or courses of action regarding sustainability.

Klaus Töpfer and Günther Bachmann departed from the basic democratic principle “one man, one vote” and formulate an argument in favour of the recognition of “one carbon footprint”. De Wit recommends the above mentioned hybrid spaces and moreover “bypasses” in order to overcome the failures of the official organisations. These bypasses should be specific programmes directed at innovation in sustainability.

3 Heads in the clouds: knowledge democracy as a Utopian dream

Esther Turnhout

Abstract

Knowledge democracy serves as an inspiring new vision for the relationship between knowledge production and use, to replace the old and discarded speaking truth to power and information deficit models. However, a closer look at what is envisioned makes it clear that knowledge democracy has a problematic Utopian character. Knowledge democracy is based on technocratic and scientific Utopian ideals complemented with Utopian governance and participation ideals. It refers to a society with empowered, competent citizens and public actors who: (1) have unrestricted access to scientific information; (2) contribute to its production and/or assessment and (3) utilise it to make informed and rational decisions. This chapter uses two examples in environmental governance (the Water Framework Directive and sustainability certification) to argue that – as has been demonstrated for many other Utopia – putting knowledge democracy into practice may have undesirable technocratic and anti-democratic implications.

3.1 From "speaking truth to power" to knowledge democracy

The relation between the production of knowledge and its use, is a contentious issue. In much of the literature on this topic, the current state of affairs is characterised as one in which a gap exists between the production of knowledge and its use (Meffe 1998, Bradshaw and Borchers 2000, Lawton 2007, Pohl 2008). Either because – and this is a common statement among policy actors – science does not produce the right kinds of usable knowledge, or – and this is the complaint of many scientists – because knowledge is wrongly or insufficiently used in decision-making. To remedy this, many experts on the subject seem to envision a speaking truth to power model to produce more and better knowledge which is fully utilised for rational decision-making and effective policies.

This chapter was written with financial support from the NWO Contested Democracy programme. It has benefitted from discussions with Sonja van der Arend, Jelle Behagel and several participants of the 2009 knowledge democracy conference during which an earlier version of this chapter was presented.

R.J. in 't Veld (ed.), *Knowledge Democracy*, DOI 10.1007/978-3-642-11381-9_3,

The speaking truth to power model is a linear model that assumes one-way traffic of truth from science to policy and separate domains of production and use of knowledge. Under this linear logic, deviations are often considered as resulting from a lack of information and communication – referred to as the information deficit model (for example Bulkeley and Mol 2003, Wynne 2006). If only producers and users of knowledge would communicate better, scientists would be more able to produce relevant knowledge and policy-makers would have a better understanding of this knowledge and would be more able to translate it into well-founded rational decisions and policies.

The information deficit model and the speaking truth to power model have both been criticised for being idealistic, unrealistic and politically naive. Firstly, studies of the history of science have shown that science is a cultural, social activity permeated with values and preferences (for example Shapin and Schaffer 1985, Collins and Pinch 1993). Thus, science is not essentially different from other cultural practices – including policy – and has no privileged, unmediated access to the truth. Secondly, Jasanoff (2004) states that science and policy are not separate domains but continuously influence and shape each other in dialectical processes of coproduction. Thirdly, difficulties in the relationship between production and use of knowledge are not due to a lack of information and communication. Potential knowledge users can have well-grounded and justified reasons to reject scientific knowledge. Scientific controversies are often characterised by competing knowledge coalitions that use and reject knowledge based on vested interests (Turnhout et al. 2008a). Wynne's (1996) publication on Cumbrian sheep farmers explains how lay publics distrust scientific knowledge not necessarily on methodological or epistemological grounds, but on the basis of a justified lack of trust in the knowledge-producing institutions. Obviously, a better understanding of science or its methods, will do little to remedy this.

Despite these criticisms, the two models have not disappeared. Speaking truth to power still functions as a powerful ideal to describe how science, policy and society should interact and simplistic information deficit models continue to influence the way in which problems in the relationship between knowledge production and use as well as suggestions to overcome them are framed (for example Vaes et al. 2009). For example, a study on the Dutch Environmental Assessment Agency, shows that all respondents used these models to describe their role and position as a translator of scientific knowledge into usable knowledge, thereby enhancing knowledge utilisation (Huitema and Turnhout 2009).

However, the increasing entanglement of science and policy – in particular in the environmental domain (for example Turnhout 2009) – makes clear that the dual processes of scientisation of politics and politicisation of science (Weingart 1999) are likely to continue. This means that the speaking truth to power and information deficit models will become even more problematic. Because the separation between knowledge production and use, which is an important source of science's authority and credibility, will be increasingly difficult to uphold, science is in need of a new legitimacy and requires a new appealing vision for the relationship between knowledge production and use. Hence the call for a knowledge democracy. However, what exactly does knowledge democracy mean and what are its democratic implications?

In this chapter I will first sketch the contours of the concept of knowledge democracy (Sect. 3.2). Subsequently I will use relevant literature on Utopia to demonstrate the different Utopian characteristics of knowledge democracy (Sects. 3.3 and 3.4). Section 3.5 will offer some examples of knowledge democracy in practice and I will then finally discuss the concept of knowledge democracy and its possible undesirable consequences (Sect. 3.6).

3.2 Dreaming of knowledge democracy

The first chapter of this book offers an outline of the ambitions of knowledge democracy. The main suggestion is to move beyond a narrow focus on "knowledge economy" to a more reflexive and less simplistic conception of the importance of the advancement of knowledge – and its wise use – for functioning democracies. While this is inspiring and provocative, it remains rather abstract in terms of it possible meanings and practical implications.

A good way to start the further exploration of the meaning – or meanings – of knowledge democracy is to look at the Knowledge Democracy Conference website (www.knowledgedemocracy.nl, accessed 13 October 2009). The collection of statements of the different participants that can be found there offers a wealth of ideas, concerns and outlooks which together serve to substantiate the concept.

Several statements emphasise the importance of ensuring optimal utilisation of knowledge:

> We have to be sure that policy-making is based on well-tailored, validated information;
> Efficient utilisation of different types of knowledge;
> Responsible use of knowledge;
> Knowledge democracy is the ambition to have decisions based on [...] science for the good of the people.

These statements clarify that the concept of knowledge democracy does not explicitly reject the speaking truth to power model. The aim is to improve knowledge utilisation without addressing how this knowledge should be produced. Furthermore, many of the suggestions indicate a belief in the information deficit model in the sense that better interaction and communication will achieve a better knowledge utilisation:

> Bridging the gap between science and policy-making is the never-ending challenge in a knowledge democracy;
> An open, honest and timely exchange of facts and figures;
> Communication;
> We need dialogue and reflection for using knowledge effectively.

Many statements explicitly address the public. It is considered important to improve public access to information because using this information will empower citizens:

> When knowledge is democratic it means that it is free, that everybody can access it;
> Open access to knowledge for capable citizens;
> Improving access to and use of knowledge allows people become more empowered;
> Knowledge democracy is sharing information and [...] transparency in decision-making.

Again, this is very much in line with the speaking truth to power and information deficit models. Access to information will ensure its use and enable science to speak the truth to power better. However, power is now extended to include citizens.

Finally, many statements indicate that sharing or access to knowledge alone is not enough. They are concerned with changing the way knowledge is produced to involve stakeholders:

> Acknowledging the value of different kinds of knowledge;
> The ability to draw on multiple sources of knowledge is of crucial importance;
> Knowledge is produced as a joint effort between practitioners, scientists, lawyers, and policy-makers;
> Accepted, feasible and legitimate knowledge is produced only in interaction among professionals, experts, and citizens.

This deviates from the speaking truth to power model because it explicitly addresses knowledge production and is no longer concerned with truth per se. The idea is that legitimate, trustworthy and useable knowledge about current complex and uncertain issues can only be achieved when stakeholders are involved in its production. The objective to improve knowledge utilisation is very much part of this, but not according to the information deficit model. Knowledge utilisation by the participants is expected to be guaranteed because they helped to produce it.

The statements are representative of the current literature concerned with this issue. A first strand of this literature makes ample use of the "boundary" metaphor – in a rather instrumental, managerial and interventionist way – to describe ways to improve interactions between producers and users of knowledge. Such an "interventionist turn" is clearly visible in the use of the concept of boundary object (Zeiss and Groenewegen 2009). Boundary objects – for example science-based policy-relevant tools such as scenarios, models or indicators – are being promoted as tools able to bridge the gap between science and policy, thus improving knowledge utilisation (Turnhout 2009). Furthermore, the literature on boundary organisations is quite explicit about this. Sarewitz and Pielke (2007) use a market transaction logic to explain what is meant by this. Boundary organisations are able to "bridge the gap" between science and policy by "reconciling supply of and demand of science" (Sarewitz and Pielke 2007). The notion of boundary work, which started out as a concept to describe how science is defined in practice and demarcated from other social domains (Gieryn 1983, 1995, 1999), is increasingly being replaced by concepts such as boundary management or spanning, both of which emphasise the importance of overcoming or managing rather than drawing boundaries and designing effective strategies to do so (for example Cash et al. 2003).

The second strand of literature explicitly takes up the participatory element of knowledge democracy. It is captured by concepts such as post-normal science (Funtowicz and Ravetz 1993), Mode-2 science (Gibbons et al. 1994) and transdisciplinarity (Thompson Klein 2001, Regeer and Bunders 2009). What these new modes of knowledge production have in common is that they emphasise the importance of so-called lay or local knowledge next to scientific knowledge. They argue that, in order to address current post-normal science – to use Funtowicz and Ravetz's terms – complex and uncertain problems, it is crucial that lay knowledge is taken into account. Stakeholders should be allowed to have a say not only in decision-making processes but also regarding the knowledge relevant to those processes, for example by participating in extended peer review processes or by engaging in joint knowledge production processes. Participatory knowledge production produces knowledge that is seen as legitimate by all involved and that is more likely to be used (Ballard et al. 2008, Fernandez-Gimenez et al. 2008). This also links up well with current debates about the democratisation of science and expertise (Jasanoff 2003, Liberatore and Funtowicz 2003).

So, what the concept of knowledge democracy does is supplementing the speaking truth to power model with a participatory ideal. When put together, the statements envision a society with empowered, competent citizens and public actors who:

- Have unrestricted access to knowledge and information;
- Are involved in the production and/or assessment of knowledge;
- Utilise knowledge to make informed and rational decisions.

This makes clear that knowledge democracy deviates only slightly from the old speaking truth to power model and replaces it by "speaking truth to democracy". Instead of solely considering sites and actors of power as recipients of knowledge, the concept of knowledge democracy requires science to speak to the public as well. The suggested way forward complements the information deficit-inspired suggestions of improving access to information, communication and interaction with stakeholder participation as a new way to improve knowledge utilisation. Below, I will demonstrate that the image of knowledge democracy as outlined here has a problematic Utopian character.

3.3 Political, scientific, technological and governance utopia

The ideal of knowledge democracy as outlined above is a complete, holistic, integrated and internally consistent image of what could be. Knowledge democracy concerns society as a whole and argues for its transformation. This gives it a dream-like or Utopian character. Based on Achterhuis (1998), the following characteristics of Utopia can be outlined:

- They are "makeable", or at least, they are considered makeable.
- They are holistic or totalising, aiming towards the transformation of society as a whole.
- There is no room for individual deviations as these would endanger the project as a whole (Achterhuis 1998).

A particularly well-known Utopian ideal that is relevant for the knowledge democracy concept is Bacon's New Atlantis. New Atlantis is an island with a technologically advanced society able to cure all sorts of diseases and extend life expectancy. The scientists of Salomon's house play a central role by developing scientific and technological innovations to benefit all inhabitants of the island. This central role of science suggests a technocratic form of governance in which questions of *what is*, are smoothly and unproblematically transformed into issues of *what should be (done)*. Politics has become obsolete and science serves as the basis for optimal decisions and choices. New Atlantis is based on a singular view of knowledge; there is no room for disputes about what knowledge is, what it means to use it and how to decide what kinds of decisions and choices should be made based on that knowledge.

Achterhuis (1998) is deeply critical of Utopia because behind their "good intentions", they are intrinsically absolutist, totalitarian and violent[1]. Indeed, the negative consequences of actually putting them into practice have been widely reported. For example, J. Scott's book *Seeing like a State* (1998) offers important analyses of a wide variety of such Utopian projects, from the design of the city of Brasilia, to the Soviet agricultural collectivisation.

In light of the many Utopia-inspired failures[2] that have characterised the twentieth century, it is surprising to find that we have not seen the end of them yet. De Wilde (2000) demonstrates how old style political Utopia have been replaced by equally optimistic technological ones in which technology will create new and better ways of living. What is envisioned is nothing short of a paradise in which technologies will extend our capacities infinitely and take over all the boring and tedious chores of life. Again, societies are seen as makeable, although this time not through revolutions but through technological innovations. The Utopian character of

---

[1] Achterhuis is relatively mild about Bacon's New Atlantis. In his view, this utopia is less totalitarian than others and the exertion of violence is largely restricted to the conquering of nature by science and technology.

[2] Such as those described in Scott (1998) and Achterhuis (1998).

technological images of the future lies in the little room they offer to reflect on the desirability of technological innovations and in the way that these innovations and their inventors exert power over their potential users.

I argue that currently we are witness to the emergence of yet another Utopian ideal, which goes by the name of governance. Governance implies a trend away from hierarchical command and control modes of steering towards civil society participation and the use of voluntary and market-based instruments. Governance Utopia refer to societies with full citizen participation, fully transparent and accountable policy processes and maximum efficiency and legitimacy. Participants engage in Habermas-inspired deliberations and achieve communicative rationality. Instead of hierarchies, societies are characterised by horizontal networks of connected, free and equal actors.

However, governance Utopia have been criticised as well. Cooke and Kothari's (2001) book *Participation, the new Tyranny* shows clearly how participation has served to strengthen vested interests and reinforce existing power relations rather than empower the poor and powerless. Studies in critical geography have demonstrated the drawbacks of introducing assumingly efficient market mechanisms (for example Robertson 2006). Critical management and science studies have made clear how systems of performance measurement or evidence-based policies are prone to all sorts of perverse effects and have not improved the transparency of policy processes (De Bruijn 2007, Turnhout et al. in prep. a).

Regardless of these criticisms, it appears that governance remains an attractive ideal, perhaps because it is a-political. Two factors contribute to this. Firstly, power is usually lacking in discussions about governance and participation (Van der Arend 2007). Secondly, governance and related notions of participation, transparency and efficiency are matters of implementation, dealing with the how rather than with the what. They aim at "making things better", which entails the promise of optimal solutions while at the same time side-tracking the political issue of what constitutes better and who decides that.

3.4 Knowledge democracy as a utopian dream

Utopian thinking has been present throughout history. Utopia have been criticised but so far, it appears that this has mostly resulted in the emergence of new ones. The ideal of "makeability" (in Dutch: maakbaarheid), which was criticised in the 1980s, has not been discarded but replaced by different ones (for example related to innovation, see Duineveld et al. 2007). Knowledge democracy is the newest member of the extended family of Utopian makeability ideals.

Linking the different Utopian ideals described above to the concept of knowledge democracy it becomes clear that it has several Utopian characteristics. Similar to New Atlantis and the speaking truth to power model, knowledge democracy aims to increase knowledge utilisation in order to improve the rationality of policies and decisions. This is a technocratic form of rule that neglects power and politics. Knowledge democracy is also inspired by governance. It envisions knowledge as freely circulating in networks of connected, free and equal actors. In addition, it incorporates the participatory ideal of governance by promoting stakeholder participation in knowledge production. Also here, the neglect of power and politics is striking. It appears that there is very little recognition of the performance aspects of participation (Hajer 2005). However, the public is not a pre-existing entity waiting to be involved; it is brought into being – performed – in the context of participation. Participatory initiatives are sites of power in the sense that they create their own participants in ways that fit with the objectives and expectations of the initiators (Turnhout et al. in prep. b). Using the three characteristics of Utopia outlined in the previous section, it is clear that knowledge democracy has a problematic Utopian character:

- It is considered to be makeable by means of organising interaction and communication between knowledge producers and users and involving stakeholders in knowledge production.
- It involves society as a whole, existing of competent public and private actors who have complete access to knowledge and utilise it to make rational and informed decisions.
- There is little room for deviation. Actors who do not fit the requirements or expectations, who lack the skills and competences to use information or participate in knowledge production, or who wish to refrain from involvement will become effectively marginalised. Also, to a large extent, knowledge democracy depends on a singular and unproblematic view on what knowledge is leaving little room for contesting knowledge claims. The ideas of speaking truth to power, increasing knowledge utilisation by improving communication, and participatory knowledge production are based on the possibility of achieving consensus on what knowledge is, what it means to use it effectively and how it should be transformed into action.

3.5 Knowledge democracy in practice: two examples from environmental governance

This section will give two examples from environmental governance to give an illustration of the kinds of practices and activities that could sail under the flag of knowledge democracy.

A first example is taken from water governance. In the framework of the Netherlands Organisation for Scientific Research (NWO) "Contested Democracy"-programme, I[3] am involved in a study about the democratic implications of the EU

[3] The project involves a cooperation between researchers from the Forest and Nature Conservation Policy Group, Wageningen University and the Policy, Organisation, Law & Gaming Section, Delft University of Technology.

Water Framework Directive (WFD). The WFD, has two important objectives: getting Europe's waters cleaner[4] and getting the citizens involved. Although the WFD at first sight presents these two objectives as separate and equally important objectives, the following quotation from the WFD website (http://ec.europa.eu/environment/water/water-framework/info/intro_en.htm, accessed 22 September 2009) demonstrates that it in fact relates and integrates the two:

> The greater the transparency in the establishment of the objectives, the imposition of measures, and the reporting of standards, the greater the care member states will take to implement the legislation in good faith, and the greater the power of the citizens to influence the direction of environmental protection.

This is very much in line with knowledge democracy. Participants are involved in knowledge production in the sense that they are involved in making decisions about water quality objectives and about indicators and monitoring parameters to measure water quality. The measurement of water quality achieves transparency about the efficiency and effectiveness of policies. This knowledge is used by the participants to hold decision-makers accountable and speed up the implementation of the WFD. The WFD involves participatory knowledge production, unrestricted access to information and complete knowledge utilisation. However it is also clear, that participation is a means rather than an end. The WFD's guidance document on public participation openly admits this:

> A well-managed public participation process is not free of costs and demands time and energy, but it will pay off in the end. Public participation is not an end in itself but a tool to achieve the environmental objectives of the Water Framework Directive. Trust, transparency of process and good management of expectations will help to achieve good participation. Now just do it! (CEC 2003: 6).

Participation is intended to increase knowledge utilisation, which enhances the achievement of the WFD's ultimate objective of cleaner water (for a detailed argumentation see Turnhout et al. in prep. a).

A second example is certification. Certification initiatives worldwide gain growing attention as promising instruments for promoting sustainability (Cashore et al. 2004). Certification is a voluntary market-based instrument. Producers who decide to join a certification scheme have to meet the standards and requirements prescribed by the scheme. In return, they earn the right to put the certificate on their product. Certified products offer potential consumers transparent information about that product thereby enabling them to make informed decisions about which products to buy. The website of the Forest Stewardship Council (www.fsc.org/about-fsc.html, accessed 12 October 2009) phrases it as follows:

---

[4] Bouleau (2008) considers this objective to be an ecological dream that may be difficult to achieve thereby indicating the Utopian character of the WFD.

> The FSC label provides a credible link between responsible production and consumption of forest products, enabling consumers and businesses to make purchasing decisions that benefit people and the environment as well as providing ongoing business value.

By making information about the environmental effects of products available, certification is seen as a way to counter market failures due to incomplete information and environmental externalities. Citizens are invited to express their political preferences by making responsible consumption decisions. According to the Fair Trade website (www.fairtrade.nl/653/Introduction/, accessed 12 October 2009):

> Modern consumption is responsible consumption. Fair Trade Original offers you the easiest and most agreeable way of making your contribution to changing the world.

Certification is in line with knowledge democracy because it offers knowledge and transparency which is used by the public. However, the public only has limited possibilities for engagement. The scope of their actions is restricted by the market in which the only possible choice is to buy or not to buy.

The two examples presented here share the problematic characteristics of knowledge democracy. They are based on a technocratic ideal in which knowledge is fully used and unproblematically translated into action and they assume a singular view of knowledge. Both the WFD and certification require consensus about knowledge – about what counts as clean and sustainable an about how it can be measured – and contestations of the knowledge claims pose a serious threat. In the case of the WFD, competing claims about how clean waters are or how effective and efficient policies will restrict the capacity of citizens to hold government accountable and might endanger the WFD as a whole. In the case of certification, competing claims about the merits of the scheme in terms of ensuring sustainability will harm the trustworthiness of the scheme thereby endangering its competitiveness in the consumer market. Both examples are inspired by governance Utopia. Certification is a voluntary instrument and the public can freely join the initiative by using the information offered by the scheme to decide on whether to buy certified products. The WFD is based on an ideal of stakeholder participation in which stakeholders take responsibility for the implementation of the WFD by producing and using knowledge about the environmental status of water and about policy-effectiveness and -efficiency.

3.6 Utopian dream or totalitarian nightmare?

So far, this chapter has argued that knowledge democracy is a new Utopian dream about the relationship between production and use of knowledge. It does not reject the old speaking truth to power model, but complements it with a governance inspired participatory ideal. It is a totalising vision of society with a technocratic a-political form of rule that is based on a singular view on knowledge and that leaves little room for power or for deviations. In contrast to the argument made in In 't Veld (2009), knowledge democracy may serve to strengthen, rather than criticise, neoliberal and technocratic notions of evidence-based and efficient policies.

The examples given in the previous section serve to illustrate this. The point is not to argue that the WFD is a bad policy or that certification should be abandoned. They – and other initiatives to increase access to information, improve communication between knowledge producers and users or organise participatory knowledge production – can be very productive and lead to desirable outcomes. However, knowledge democracy entails the promise of being democratic and it is this explicit link to democracy – and the idea of the public implicit in this – that makes it vulnerable for criticisms.

For the concept of knowledge democracy to work, it needs a vision of a general public or citizenship. The view of the public that is implicit in knowledge democracy is a homogeneous one that consists of engaged, competent, empowered and knowledge using citizens. Importantly, this public is not merely reflected on or imagined. It is, as was also briefly touched upon in Sect. 3.4, brought into being; it is performed. The WFD assumes and performs a public that consists of engaged citizens who participate in (knowledge production for) water governance and certification performs a public that consists of informed consumers. The homogeneity of these performed publics is at odds with views of democracy that emphasise plurality and diversity (for an interesting analysis of DNA bar coding with a similar argument, see Ellis et al. in press).

Authors such as Mouffe (2005), have emphasised that democracy should not be conceived as an end-state or horizon. They argue that harmony, completeness and consistency can only be obtained at the cost of exclusion and oppression. The paradoxical conclusion is that when democracy is obtained – that is, when understood as potentially complete –, it ceases to exist. The project of democracy will always fail to meet its own objectives. In Laclau's (2005) terms: it is a failed totality. According to this view, democracy should ensure space for "the political"; foster diversity and open up possibilities for struggle and contestation of competing values and claims. The totalising aspect of knowledge democracy – and Utopia in general – and the homogeneity of the public that it performs, sits uncomfortably with this view of democracy.

Thus, what is envisioned under the label of knowledge democracy is not necessarily democratic. Rather, it is inspired by technocratic ideals about science-based decision-making and by neo-liberal or managerial governance ideals about transparency and efficiency (see Maasen, and Lieven 2006 for a similar argument). As such, it is not necessarily about ensuring space for political struggle and contestation but about strengthening the power and position of actors involved in measuring, accounting and controlling (including managers, scientists, accountants and bureaucrats). Attempts to make the dream of knowledge democracy real, run genuine risks of ending up with technocratic, totalitarian, exclusionary and anti-democratic nightmares.

Laclau's (2005) notion of a failed totality already points to the impossibility to achieve Utopian ideals. Attempts to put Utopia into practice will never succeed completely (as also demonstrated by Scott 1998) and this may lead to the undesirable consequences outlined above. However, the same is true for knowledge democracy's dystopian twin: the technocratic, totalitarian exclusionary nightmare. While elements of the nightmare might emerge as a result of knowledge democracy put into practice, it will not be realised completely. Both can only be imagined with our heads in the clouds, but while for knowledge democracy these clouds are white and fluffy, the dystopian nightmare involves dark thunderclouds. What knowledge democracy will be made to be in practice is shaped by the continuous interaction between Utopian dreams and dystopian nightmares.

4 Dreaming about a properly informed democracy

Dirk J. Wolfson

Abstract

The present paradigm shift away from *laissez-faire* creates a window of opportunity to improve the flow of structured information or knowledge by making individual access to excludable public benefits conditional on ascertainable efforts to limit claims, as agreed upon in situational contracts. Contracts are *situational* when agents in delivery are mandated to allow for differences in ability to perform of beneficiaries and to offer customised enabling facilities to improve their capabilities, in line with the vision on fairness of the government in charge. Degrees of freedom and transaction costs are controlled through political guidance in protocols and mandates, on the basis of apply-or-explain. Mutual adjustment in situational response reveals individual preference in direct democracy, improves goal convergence and the fit between supply and demand, reduces opportunism, furthers trust and induces open innovation. The chapter reports on a successful application in The Netherlands.

4.1 Introduction

Knowledge democracy is a blissful state in which people are well-informed about social problems and politicians behave as honest brokers of individual preference. Real life is different. This chapter explores the tenuous relationship between information, ideology, governance, innovation and accountability, and shows how the present paradigm shift away from *laissez-faire* creates a window of opportunity to improve targeting and revitalise democracy. Section 4.2 introduces "knowledge democracy" as a properly informed mode of achieving ends; Sect. 4.3 deals with a missing link between theory and actual practice in ordering values, and Sect. 4.4 introduces a new mode of situational contracting, reporting on a successful experiment in social security reform.

R.J. in 't Veld (ed.), *Knowledge Democracy*, DOI 10.1007/978-3-642-11381-9_4,

4.2 An analytical framework of democratic coordination

4.2.1 Precepts for living together

The democratic state has a basic responsibility to order values for society, establishing a system of human rights, property rights and user rights that enable people to live their own life in safety and security. Ordering values requires institutions, as collective constraints structuring economic, social and political interaction, and so the question arises how institutions come about. Buchanan and Congleton (1998) present two contrasting views on this: a "truth judgment conception" and a "contractarian conception". In a truth judgment conception, the basic system of cultural values is autonomous and autocratic, interpreted and applied top-down by a ruling political or religious elite. In other words, precepts for living together are handed down unilaterally from on high. In the contractarian conception, value systems are endogenous and democratic, derived bottom-up, based on mutual dependence and compromise between, or on behalf of, individual citizens. "The metaphor is that of a social contract. And agreement itself serves as the criterion for goodness or truth" (Buchanan and Congleton 1998: 4). In modern democracies, the contractarian conception dominates. While there are still traces of truth judgment in the way traditions and elites influence the institutional environment, the contractarian conception explains how "constitutional" arrangements are reviewed under pressures and experiences from the bottom up, in learning loops of institution building.

Institutions provide guidance on goals and the use of instruments in implementation. Following Lindblom (1977) and Thompson et al. (1991), three basic categories of means to achieve ends may be distinguished: authority, in hierarchies harnessed by law or convention; horizontal coordination in voluntary exchange, in markets offering quid pro quo; and persuasion in networks pursuing communicative strategies. These means may be seen as legal, economic and sociological instruments respectively, and interact with one another; mutual adjustment and evidence from implementation may lead to a reconsideration of both ends and means. In actual practice, further specification of the policy toolkit is needed to deal with flaws in information, the meaning of rationality, the nature of motives and the unintended consequences of ideologies and incentives.

4.2.2 Asymmetrical information, rationality and motivation analysis

Information may be costly, unreliable or even unavailable. In judging the feasibility of policies, transaction costs – the costs of negotiating and monitoring agreement on ends – are difficult to asses if the relevant information is distributed asymmetrically – if "different people know different things", as Stiglitz (2002: 469) puts it simply in his Nobel Lecture. Things get even worse when problems are "wicked", or intractable, and there is no consensus about their causal structure and solution.

Simon (1976) taught us to model rationality as a *procedural,* not a substantive concept, meaning that individuals, when dealing with choice under a constraint of time or money, are generally capable of ordering their preferences in appropriate deliberation. Obviously, lapses of judgment will occur (Akerlof and Shiller 2009, Kahneman et al. 1997) but, on the whole, mistakes in individual choice tend to cancel out; hence, assumptions about appropriate deliberation are validated in empirical testing. Moreover, as Simon points out, appropriateness also means that satisfying behaviour (developing routines) may be a socially efficient way of limiting transaction costs. As Hirschleifer (1985: 59) elaborates,

> in the light of one's goals [...], if the means chosen [...] are appropriate the individual is rational; if not, irrational.

"Appropriate" here refers to method rather than result. Rational behaviour is action calculated on the basis of rules of logic and other norms of validity. Owing to chance, good method may not always lead to good result".

A similar reservation applies for the popular misconception of self-interest as the exclusive driving force in economic analysis (Sen 1977, 1987). In modern behavioural economics, self-interest serves as a benchmark from which to consider deviations for a wide range of alternative motivations (Sent 2004), from altruism, compassion and commitment to egoism and malevolence. Empirically, people are observed to care about what other people have, and about what is left for future generations. They actually vote for programmes of income redistribution or environmental sustainability. So, if rational people can be wrong, and economics can accommodate whatever motive inspires us, where does that leave the intellectual basis of economic and social policy? With the need to distinguish economic *theory,* as an analytical tool to diagnose scarcity relationships and the way people actually deal with scarcity, from economic and social *policies* as a set of value-loaded and political tools providing guidance on how people *should* deal with scarcity.

4.3 Mediating ideology and information in public governance

4.3.1 Goal formulation

In public governance, formulating goals requires that policy-makers reconcile refutable principles of efficiency with normative considerations of fairness, sustainability and individual freedom, as basic values of good governance that generally pull in different directions. When they do, economic analysis contributes the insight that the scarcity of resources makes ambitions interdependent (Hennipman 1995). Hence, it needs to be judged to what extent the attainment of each of these values or ends is worth the commensurate sacrifice (the "opportunity costs") of other objectives. That judgment, however, is a *political* valuation. As long as opportunities are indeed appraised to reflect scarcity relations, a comparison of costs and social benefits can indicate, for instance, what it *costs* – in terms of alternatives sacrificed – for society to provide in vitro fertilisation as a social benefit, or to build a new subway-line in Amsterdam. As the latter example already suggests, economists may make mistakes in costing – or may be *pressured* to make mistakes by politicians dreaming of cutting ribbons – but costing is what they do, and analysing how people respond to opportunities and incentives, while warning against unintended consequences that decisions may have. *Valuating* benefits, however, and comparing them with alternative uses of public resources is a political responsibility.

4.3.2 Unintended consequences of ideologies and incentives

How does political theory deal with the evaluative part of paradigms and research programmes? It formulates ideologies. For brevity's sake, I'll demonstrate this with the dilemmas involved in balancing fairness and individual freedom. In continental Europe, political liberalism, christian-democracy and social democracy may be distinguished as the major ideologies, focusing on individualism, community and solidarity respectively, as dominant perspectives. Liberal philosophers, from Hayek (1960) to Rawls (2001) and Dworkin (2002), stress individual freedom and responsibilities, and plead restraint in government intervention. In their vision, concerns with fairness can be limited to creating equal opportunity in terms of *inputs.* The christian-democratic vision is more communitarian, keen on self-organisation and emphasises *process*; it places man in the context of his community (Etzioni 1993, Cohen and Rodgers 1995). Individualism is toned down and fairness and solidarity are believed to belong essentially to the realm of the civil society; the state is kept at bay, but allowed to subsidise. Social democracy, finally, identifies with the vulnerability of man (Vandenbroucke 2001). It strives to equalise *outcomes* by compensating differences in needs, capabilities and access to social networks, for which it turns to the state, rather than the civil society.

Values are non-refutable. Yet, their treatment in theories of justice raises some very hard questions that are all too often side-stepped. Is freedom *from* paternalism, as an aspiration of individual liberty, equivalent to freedom *to* participate, as long as new social risks – such as deficient capabilities to deal with rapid technological change, or single parenthood – are unevenly distributed? Should policies cater to new social needs, such as the need to reconcile work, family life and education? Is responsibility of the have-nots to make use of the opportunities on offer – a attribution put forward by Dworkin as well as Vandenbroucke – not a figment of the imagination of the have's, as long as differences in access to networks and ability to perform are not addressed?

On the latter question, Granovetter (1985), Sen (1985, 1999) and Nussbaum (2006) argue convincingly in seminal contributions that cognitive, psychological and social capabilities as well as embeddedness in the relevant networks to make use of the opportunities on offer vary widely within ostensibly homogeneous social groups. Hence, whatever a society's vision on fairness, it would seem that the traditional canon of equal treatment needs to be modified so that comparable differences are dealt with in a comparably different way. This tallies, incidentally, with a finding of welfare economics that matching a fixed packages of public services with individually diverging needs requires that conditions for access are customised accordingly. In other words, when content is fixed and indivisible – as with an educational qualification, or with granting a voluntary association access to a policy arena – an optimal solution requires that demand (access) is "priced" according to ability to deliver on an obligation in kind. Yet, the consideration required is not necessarily a price, but may be a cooperative relationship as well (Weber 1979: 114, Arrow 1985: 44; more on this in Sect. 4.4). As noted before, economics as such cannot judge values, as its methodology uses the preferences of consumers in the market place and of citizens in the public space as independent variables. Yet, economists can point out inconsistencies and unintended consequences in dealings with scarcity. They may warn against penny-wisdom and pound-foolishness, for example when an ill-advised efficiency measure as asking a fee for seeing a general practitioner would result in a reduction of early detection of serious and very costly problems later on, or they may show how failure to make polluters pay may lead to costly environmental crises over time. Furthermore, they may remind policy-makers that any policy-mix chosen needs to be supported by appropriate incentives, a point that leading scholars of distributive justice – all of those mentioned here, as a matter of fact – tend to disregard (Wolfson 2008).

4.3.3 Knowledge democracy: a tenuous relationship in an operational void

In short, there seems to be a lot of unfinished business in the intellectual underpinnings of governance and in the distribution of responsibilities. Theories of justice, whether right- or left-leaning, show a surprising resilience to findings of the social sciences that refute predilections about motives and capabilities of man, a benign neglect of problems in implementation, and little reflexivity in dealing with feed-back. Economists all too often play the guru, entertaining biased views on what ought to be done, rather than sticking to their trade: presenting options for politicians to choose from, and warning for presumably unintended consequences of political intentions. And politicians have a way of presenting valuations as beliefs, or even facts (Myrdal 1969), and of obfuscating responsibilities.

Where does all this leave knowledge democracy, as a grand ideal that presumes all relevant parties well-informed and politicians to behave as honest brokers of individual preference? Nowhere, as long as it operates in an institutional void. What is needed is a new institutional design that modernises the contractarian conception, recognises findings about motives and capabilities of men as identified in the behavioural sciences, does justice to the growing diversity of needs and the fragmentation of values in a pluralistic society, leaves scope for self-organisation and reintroduces political guidance in public administration, now that the limits of the market mode have been rediscovered the hard way. In short, a design that redecorates decision trees with the relevant hypotheses regarding the responsibilities and behaviour of people in relation to their institutional environment, to further goal convergence on the basis of "negotiated pictures of reality" (Klein and Snellen 2009). Against this background, it will be shown how situational contracting provides a substitute for the glue of a focal ideological principle that In 't Veld finds lacking in Chap. 1 of this book.

4.4 Pulling things together: what makes institutions tick?

4.4.1 Principal-agent theory

The flaws in information and reciprocity, and the need to specify and enforce acceptance of responsibilities identified in Sects. 4.2 and 4.3 may be analysed in terms of principal-agent relations in which agents are typically better informed about possible solutions than principals, but dependent on – or interested in – the principal's resources (Breton 1995). Hierarchies, markets and networks may be seen as chains of supply and demand, in which parties have something on offer that other parties want. Yet, although mutually dependent, actors are faced with information asymmetry at every step of public governance. Ministers for example, supply resources and demand solutions from senior civil servants who, in turn, depend on ideas from their staff. At the end of the line, caseworkers, as principals in the delivery of benefits, may have difficulty in appraising the willingness of individual agents – the claimants of public support – to make an appropriate effort to limit claims to what is necessary. Hence the need for institutional arrangements that clarify and enforce responsibilities and reveal information throughout the chain of policy-making and implementation.

Differences between models of coordination remain, however, in that hierarchies are based on authority, markets deal on the basis reciprocity and the distribution of property rights, and networks need to secure cooperation. Note, moreover, that democracy itself may be interpreted in terms of principals and agents as well, with the citizen as the sovereign principal and the government as his agent. What unifies the analysis is that real life is characterised by information asymmetry, mutual dependency and the need to specify rights and responsibilities. Principal agent theory highlights the full circle from power to the people to the citizen as a loyal subject.

4.4.2 Situational contracting

Mutual dependency in principal-agent relationships may be institutionalised by making individual access to benefits conditional on ascertainable efforts to limit claims on public support, as agreed upon in situational contracts with caseworkers. Contracts are situational when staff in delivery systems are mandated to allow for differences in the ability to perform of their counterparts and to offer customised facilities to improve capabilities. Situational contracts differ from New Public

Management (Pollitt et al. 2007) and from "contractualism" as developed elsewhere (Le Grand 2007, Halligan 2007, Steane 2008) in sensitivity for differences in capabilities to deliver on obligations and in scope for mutual adjustment and bottom-up inputs in networks of policy-making and implementation. Transaction costs are controlled through protocols and mandates, on the basis of apply-or-explain. Mutual adjustment in a situational response to demand and supply in public intervention reveals individual preference, reduces opportunism, furthers trust and goal convergence – an alignment of the frames of reference with which problems are perceived (Van Buuren et al. 2009) – and induces open innovation.

As a mode of governance, it is based on reciprocity, bonding and accountability. Reciprocity between rights and obligations binds, and demands accountability. Customising on the basis of ability to pay or to perform (to deliver in kind) bonds; it nurtures individual involvement while allowing for diversity in preference and differences in circumstances and capabilities. It allows, moreover, for an intelligent and adaptive order of self-organisation and bottom-up initiatives that lies at the basis of trust in democracy (Van Gunsteren 2006). Conditionality of access – the strong point of markets, but here remodelled in terms of willingness and ability to perform – reveals preference and reduces opportunism. Without it, asymmetric information makes disciplining the "non-deserving" difficult and performance hard to control. Effectiveness, finally, is monitored in accountability in independent peer reviews, to assess satisfaction on the demand side and to control managerial efficiency on the supply side.

Situational contracting creates a dialogue in which stakeholders in complex networks swap information, resources and commitments in recognition of their mutual dependency, investing in an organisational culture of citizenship and deliberate moulding of a shared fate (Van Gunsteren 1998). Recognising that there cannot be inclusion without exclusion, access to networks, discretionary powers and individual benefits of all participants depends on willingness and ability to perform. Self-organisation, reflexivity and bottom-up policy initiatives are encouraged, but policy capture and emergent patterns of strategic behaviour are constrained by maintaining political responsibility for protocols and mandates. In short, situational contracting endeavours to fill the operational void in the modern writing on complexity in public administration (Teisman et al. 2009).

4.4.3 Contributions from the behavioural sciences; stewardship

The situational approach is deduced from empirical findings that distrust breeds distrust, that trust depends on empathy, identification and the expectation of reciprocity (Nooteboom 2004), and that professionals in public service are motivated by more than self-interest alone (Bénabou and Tirole 2006). They want to heal, to teach, to design policies, to serve the common good, or whatever it is that motivated their choice of profession. They are – up to a point – prepared to trade leisure or pay for professional satisfaction, recognition, or career concern (Tirole 1994), but feel constrained in settings of command and control. For many of them, a bureaucratic environment crowds out intrinsic motivations (Fehr and Falk 2002,

Frey and Stutzer 2002, Fischer and Huddart 2008). Surveying the evidence, Le Grand (2003: 64) concludes that the incentive structures of professional workers in the public sector should "nurture individuals" non-material concerns". That is what situational contracting does: bonding with counterparts, shaping rather than steering performance, and guiding behaviour in a situational response with tailor-made solutions and incentives (Wolfson 2010). It makes principal-agent relationships, originally perceived as self-interest driven, develop into principal-*steward* relationships, in which a higher value is placed on goal convergence than on self-interest (Van Slyke 2007) and, more generally, re-specifies models of mutual adjustment on the basis of findings from the behavioural sciences.

Traditionally, professionals in areas such as public health have considerable degrees of freedom to cater to the needs of patients, and educators are entrusted to pass judgment on the ability to perform of students. Empowering professionals in other areas as well helps to adjust agendas to specific needs, ranging from the deployment of police protection to urban renewal. It reduces the risk of shirking and rent seeking, formulates policies with bottom-up inputs, and grants professionals operational degrees of freedom on the basis of the mantra apply-or-explain. In short, it relies – within boundaries of political guidance – on professional ethic and experience to help overcome the asymmetries in information that are at the core of modern theories of incentives.

4.4.4 Scope and limitations

In appraising the scope for situational contracting, transaction costs are the easiest part, as cost-benefit analysis can approximate whether the marginal transaction costs remain below the marginal social cost of regulation superseded. Yet, there are other limitations as well, such as the possibility of exclusion – a condition of contractibility (Shleifer 1998) – and the unconditional delivery of entitlements when recipients cannot influence eligibility, or are not supposed to (primary education). Access to non-excludable public goods remains open, and in authoritative routines, such as grading papers or upholding traffic regulations, there may be scope for appeal, but not for negotiation.

Within these limitations, there is considerable scope to improve the targeting of public services and to further citizenship and public service motivation. Conditionality of access reveals individual preference, reduces information asymmetry, improves the match between demand and supply and constrains uncooperative behaviour, not just in the delivery of individual social services, but also in general government (allowing police regions to develop their own mandates, for example), and in relations with network partners. Internationally, recent reforms have made IMF-conditionality more sensitive to differences in ability to perform, and the European Union has introduced a mode of situational contracting with farmers to improve environmental sustainability, food safety and animal welfare which reduces payments to farmers who fail to respect EU-standards.

Yet, the cultural change required to introduce situational contracting requires a step-by-step approach and appropriate resources of time, money and continuity to develop a bonding between principals and agents. Getting used to an interactive regime calls for gradual realignment of responsibilities and incentives, starting out with management-by-speech to prepare for cultural change, and with getting safeguards in place, such as exit and voice options and contestability. Initially, management-by-mandate, deregulation and the devolution of responsibilities might increase transaction costs but, over time, new and more open routines in communication will develop and mandates will prove an efficient mode of communication. Finally, shifting the balance between rules and discretion raises the question of safeguarding propriety, and calls for exit- and voice options and contestability of service providers as checks and balances against harassment.

4.4.5 Applications, empirical results and points for further research

In recent years, The Netherlands introduced situational contracting to deal with a number of public concerns. It all started with a parliamentary enquiry into the performance of the social security system. The parliamentary committee documented an unsatisfactory situation in which employers and unions controlled access and used public insurance benefits as an exit route for surplus labour. Subsequently, the government commissioned the Scientific Council for Government Policy, a public but independent think tank, to develop suggestions for a fundamental reform, with a view to reducing unintended use of benefits and increasing labour participation. In consultation with academic specialists and resource people in the field, the Council developed three options for a new institutional design, from which the government selected the mode here identified as situational contracting for a step-by-step introduction over the period 1998–2002.

To initiate the actual reform, an inclusive community of political participation was put together in the Dutch tradition of consensual democracy. Roles were redefined to achieve goal convergence in a common strategy to promote employability. Employers, labour, manpower brokers, health management agencies (HMAs) and the Ministry of Social Affairs agreed on best practices in prevention and reintegration, which were then formalised in a protocol. An understanding was reached, for instance, to appraise the risk of disability in the first week of sickness, and to forthwith involve an HMA in developing and monitoring a plan of action for reintegration.

As of 2002, all the necessary legislation had passed and a mode of situational contracting was fully operational. Public agencies now provide social insurance and take decisions on eligibility. Moreover, they classify individual cases in four broad categories of employability, as a base for a selective awarding of customised reintegration programmes. Individual employers and employees are held accountable for prevention and reintegration. As an incentive to outplace or reintegrate employees, employers have to pay 70 % of the last wage during the first two years of sickness, as long as the public agency sees reasonable prospects for employability; that period that may be extended if efforts to further participation are considered inadequate. Moreover, employers have to contract private and competitive manpower agencies and HMAs to provide a facilitating interface serving three different stakeholders: customers (employers), clients (workers on sick leave) and political principals (who retain responsibility for the way the system works). Employers and HMAs are to keep logs of actions undertaken – to be validated by the employee – for submission to the public "gatekeeper" if reintegration efforts are unsuccessful and a disability benefit is to be considered. Uncooperative employees may see their benefits discontinued, but are protected by exit- and voice options. In short, the new approach replaces a rule-based but asymmetrically informed bureaucracy by a mode of well-informed discretion. It introduces customised conditionality of access to reveal preference, induce cooperative behaviour, enable a situational response to perceived needs and ability to perform, and provides a documented basis for decisions by a public gate-keeper.

4.5 Empirical results

The reform has a significant impact on participation. Over the period 2000–2008, the employment rate increased from 72.9% to 77.2%, in the EU second only to Denmark (Eurostat 2009). In a recent study the Central Planning Bureau concludes that the reforms in the disability case here selected "are considered successful as the inflow in the disability schemes for workers declined from almost 120,000 persons in 2000 and 2001 to less than 25,000 persons in 2006 and 2007" (Euwals et al. 2009: 36). There are more direct pointers of success as well: between 2002 and 2004, the number of employees on sick leave – in the past all too often leading to claims on disability insurance later on – dropped from 5.4% to 4.6%, and the inflow in disability insurance from 87,000 to 60,000 per annum (Hoogtanders et al. 2006: 20 and 23). The most dramatic result, however, is that undue entitlements granted, before 2002 estimated at 38%, were virtually eliminated by 2003 (Euwals et al. 2009).

As far as the *outflow* from disability insurance is concerned, Kok (2006) estimates the social costs and benefits of reintegrating disabled workers at about € 100 million and € 350 million per annum respectively, suggesting a substantial yield. Note, however, that there is some skimming involved here, as younger workers or those with lesser disability have a better chance of getting enrolled in a reintegration programme (Kok and Hop 2008). As for the immaterial rewards of participation, reintegrated employees cite the social benefits, such as having regained social contacts on the job, slightly more often than financial considerations.

Although the programme as a whole is undeniably successful in raising the employment rate and reducing the reliance on benefits, it is hard to establish to what extent results are attributable to its constituent components, such as the new reintegration programmes, the better hands-on monitoring during periods of sick-leave, the clarification of responsibilities, or the more appropriate incentives for both employers and employees that were all introduced at the same time. The empirical snag, of course, is that in complex reforms results are obtained through a "common funnel" of inputs, and are hard to decompose ex post. Although detailed evaluations are still going on, the cabinet was sufficiently convinced to commission a follow-up study to explore options for a wider use of situational contracting (Wolfson 2005). Following its recommendations, the new mode was, as of 2007, introduced in supporting personal care for the non-working handicapped, with a first evaluation to be completed in early 2010, and elements of a principal-steward relationship were further developed in such areas as deregulating education en police deployment.

An example of situational contracting under advisement is the Common Agricultural Policy of the EU, where income support is gradually decoupled from production. Efforts are induced to improve environmental sustainability, food safety and animal welfare through a system of conditionality or "cross-compliance", which reduces payments to farmers who fail to respect EU-standards (European Commission 2007). Here again, uniform regulation is not feasible. Hence, following recommendations from the Social and Economic Council (SER 2006, 2008), The Netherlands is now proposing to mandate member countries to deal with diversity, engaging farmers in situational contracts for the delivery of "green" (environmental) and "blue" (water management) services.

4.6 Discussion

In the social security case discussed above, the main players for a long time pursued diverging goals. Employers and unions wanted easy access to benefits, while the government wanted a least-cost solution, but was held hostage in the corporatist tradition of the original arrangement. The story highlights how collective action problems in networks of horizontal relationships might lead to self-interested actions and sub-optimal results that are difficult to manage. Over time, however, a prospect of full employment or even labour shortage resulting from demographic developments opened a window of opportunity, and goal convergence could be achieved in a new deal that rearranged responsibilities and competences.

The point to grasp is that situational contracting introduces conditionality of access to the resources of principals at all levels in the chain of command, and horizontally as well. Willingness to make a credible effort to limit claims reveals the urgency of a need and avoids complexity in detailed categorisation – citizens and other agents classify themselves, as it were, for entitlements or resources, while customising efforts required takes care of differences in ability to perform. At the meso-level, access of professionals to policy arenas and degrees of freedom in delivery are conditional on making a constructive contribution, and delivering on responsibilities. Summing up, conditionality reveals preference, takes the guile out of self-interest and leaves scope for more empathic and cooperative motivations.

4.7 Conclusions

This chapter claims that goal convergence and effectiveness of public intervention crucially depend on the ways in which information is revealed and the interaction between stakeholders is coordinated throughout the entire chain of policy-making and implementation. To that effect, the basic elements of governance – agenda-setting, policy-making, implementation and accountability – are brought together again, in a format that deals with information asymmetry and diversity, on the basis of new insights from the behavioural sciences and theories of justice that have been ignored too long in public administration. Situational contracting bonds by nurturing non-material concerns, in reciprocity and accountability, making access to policy networks and benefits conditional on a credible and ascertainable effort to limit claims, but allowing for differences in preference and capabilities. Reviving intrinsic cooperative motivations, it creates ownership, tapping new ideas and spreading the right to define and judge the value of what is being produced across legitimate stakeholders (Moore and Hartley 2008, Van Gunsteren 2006). It is argued that this will create a better fit to individual preference and a better over-all performance than traditional hierarchies or networks.

Note again that conditionality depends on excludability. Non-excludable goods remain provided in top-down modes of command and control, although the consultative element of situational contracting in preparing legislation described in the case study may prove a useful innovation here as well. Exclusion and monitoring requires an initial investment, and so there are transaction costs to be considered. Yet, costs are reduced by diffusing best practice in peer reviews, protocols and mandates. More important is that situational contracting is indeed *situational* in that it introduces the option to make access to policy arenas and public benefits conditional on the basis of ability to perform, rather than on an equivalent quid pro quo as in the market mode.

Where – I am asking again – does all this leave knowledge democracy? Situational contracting provides a format to make ideologies operational, but disciplines a world of make believe, shirking, rent seeking and populist grandstanding by holding politicians, partners in implementation and individual citizens accountable for mutual obligations. It will not solve all the wicked problems of modern governance, but it improves the flow of information and introduces elements of deliberative and direct democracy, reducing the wicked problem of aggregating individual preference as the driver in policy-making.

5 One Man – One Vote – One Carbon Footprint: Knowledge for Sustainable Development

Klaus Töpfer and Günther Bachmann

Abstract

"One man, one vote" is the core idea of modern democracy. It is a slogan that has been used in many parts of the world, and in many public campaigns for universal suffrage. It became particularly prevalent during the period of emerging parliamentarism, and later during the phase of decolonisation and the global struggles for national sovereignty. Today, while modern societies are being challenged by non sustainable developments, the concept of knowledge democracy is emerging. This concept emphasises direct, participative forms of coping with challenges of increasing knowledge production and of applying this knowledge to solve problems of very long term and fundamental characteristics. With this, the slogan "one man, one vote" gets a new connotation and gains renewed relevance for societies in dealing with their debt to the future. In this chapter we will argue that it will even expand its relevance if combined with the fundamental idea of environmental justice as expressed by the idea of "one man, one vote, one carbon footprint", and that this also requires that the debate on sustainable development will be better informed.

5.1 Democracy in a challenging time

In many countries around the world the principles of democracy are not yet fully established, and the democratic countries display a huge variety of how democracy is being practiced, be it in different voting systems, employee participation in enterprises, or public participation. All this alone gives enough reason to discuss the perspectives of democracy. But there is much more. After the first decade of the 2000s, the world is troubled by a double crisis, one being perceived as financial meltdown and subsequent economic crisis of 2008/2009, the other known as an environmental crisis with the global warming at its heart. They are challenging the way our society debates the future and the way knowledge about risks and opportunities is dealt with. Scientific research on the loss of biodiversity, the dynamics of climate change and resource depletion, has made quite plausible that the world as we know it, will change. Greed, subprime mania, risk without responsibility and smug thinking are building up a crisis-affine mindset and, thus, lead to

R.J. in 't Veld (ed.), *Knowledge Democracy*, DOI 10.1007/978-3-642-11381-9_5,

deficits in market behaviour and policy formulation. Purposely, no thought is given to the consequences of unrealistic and unreasonable growth. The "buy now and pay later" mentality and the notion that we can neglect the costs of environmental damage and pass them to future generations are both attitudes that fuel short-term thinking in the green-house. The unbridled nature of this crisis is endlessly annoying. It breeds doubt about how knowledge, responsibility, and liability are shared today. Yet the worst annoyance, comes from those who are not at all annoyed by this crisis.

The economic crisis in 2008 and 2009 is a "short wave and high tide" type, and this is worrying enough. But the climate crisis is a long wave, which may develop into a tsunami. There is increasing evidence that the global greenhouse will put our societies at risk, ecologically, economically, and certainly regarding the social impacts that climate change will have on the quality of life, culture and people's prosperity (Leggewie and Welzer 2009, Friedman 2008, Diamond 2005). With climate change at its core, the global challenge is therefore broader: it is a challenge of development and of how pathways could be designed in the transition to a sustainable development.

The question is how to shape the direction of change and how to get people involved: What are the challenges of the sustainability crisis to our democracies? The state, nationally and in multinational agreements, will have to play an important role, but the state alone will not be apt to avoid climate disruptions and environmental depletion. The state will not just regulate society onto more sustainable pathways. There are also other trends that influence the functioning of democracies, like globalisation of production chains, individualisation of lifestyles and behaviour, the demo-graphic change in ageing societies, food safety and security, and the Internet and how it influences our communication skills and other soft skills in dealing with knowledge.

The sustainability challenge, however, adds a normative, political challenge: The extrapolation of the democratic concept of "one man, one vote" to include the environmental justice concept of "one carbon footprint" will be a crucial part of climate solutions, together with other instruments targeting to adjust market behaviour and political commitment. This makes the relation of knowledge and democracy an interesting feature and it renders it clear enough that new ideas are needed to make knowledge work for sustainable development.

The case for global warming

Increased greenhouse emissions have already warmed the planet by 0.8°C and even with a zero additional emission policy enacted right away, the planet will experience the "fat tail" of greenhouse impacts, and will warm another 0.5°C to 1.5 or 2°C, or even to 2.5°C, given the long standing warming potential of greenhouse gases. Whether this "fat tail" will come out closer to the minimum or the maximum depends on how serious carbon mitigation policies will be implemented and, to a substantive part, on whether and how aerosol emissions of "black carbon" are being cut down.

The role of atmospheric brown clouds for the dimming of climate forcing and the role of aerosols in processes that may accelerate climate impacts on for example glacier systems is only recently being targeted (Ramanathan 2007) and has lead to a rethinking of the strategies for climate research (Ramanathan et al. 2009).

The major impact of climate forcing threatens the vulnerability of human habitats. The real extent of those threats becomes clear on the regional and local level, and cannot be deducted from global average warming figures alone. Given the fact that any heating of the atmosphere basically means to power up the physical reactivity of the earth system it is understood that extreme events will be triggered. Those events may be for example glacier melting, ocean-weather interfaces, sudden effects of soil deterioration, droughts and water flooding respectively, food chain disruptions, and the melting of soil-permafrost, or the release of hitherto accumulated and bound residues with green house gas potential such as for example benthos bound methane or carbon stored away in peat reservoirs. Neither the UN Framework Convention on Climate Change nor the Kyoto Treaty considers the need for immediate measures that would gain time and hedge against climate forcing.

Politically far reaching commitments have been negotiated in the frame of the G8 and G20 summit meetings in L'Aquila, Italy. They are displaying a roadmap for implementing an internationally shared way to combat climate change. The main action point to note is that industrialised countries are committed to put in place a major transition to reduce carbon emissions by 80% in 2050, therefore sending strong signals along midway from now to 2050. Scientific advice provided by the Intergovernmental Panel on Climate Change, IPCC, goes even further. In order to have a higher probability to avoid worse climate change impacts industrialised countries should reduce greenhouse gas emissions 80–95% as part of global effort to reduce emissions by 80% by 2050 as concluded by the IPCC Fourth Assessment Report 2007 (IPCC 2007). Time is of the essence, noting the need to peak global emissions in the next 10–15 years if we are to avoid the most disruptive impacts. IPCC introduces the concept of a climate emergency for the chance that the peak carbon point would not be met, global temperature rises more than 2°C, and major tip-ping points of the earth system would be triggered.

CO_2-emissions account for only about half of the global warming story. Ground-level ozone (from transport and biomass burning), black carbon (aerosols from motor vehicles and households) and me-thane production (from agriculture, cattle) also play roles. While mitigation of CO_2 is mostly a case for high tech clean energy generation from renewable sources, energy saving appliances, retrofitting buildings, the other greenhouse gases and black carbon substances require some very different sets of measures. Mostly, they require changes in land use methods in forestry and agriculture, a transition of consumption patterns (in particular meat consumption). Above all, they are caused by all kinds of wood-fired domestic heating and cooking. Whereas the first may be targeted by industrial policies and innovation, the latter require decentralised action on the ground.

5.2 Making democracy work for sustainability

With a large part of the scientific community in broad agreement over the climate change challenge, one might expect the democratic political system to take immediate and thorough measures. It seems, however, that there is no automatic response and that a closer look into the mechanics of decision-making is necessary. When the world leaders gathered for the UN Summit on Environment and Development, in 1992 in Rio de Janeiro, and processed the Rio Agenda 21 all aspects of stakeholder involvement, public sharing of experience and knowledge, informed debates and access to sound information have been covered as a centrepiece of sustainable development (Brundtland 1987). The last two decades have significantly added more weight to this.

The UN Framework Convention on Climate Change (UNFCCC) is the legal framework for multinational efforts to curb greenhouse gas emissions and has even been ratified by the US. In particular, it is one sentence that turned out to be of crucial value for any activity following up, be it on the international or the national level:

> Human activities have been substantially increasing the atmospheric concentrations of greenhouse gases (…) and that this will result on average an additional warming of the Earth surface and atmosphere and may adversely affect natural ecosystems and humankind.

Ever since, the central open question is to what extent do we have to limit the increase in greenhouse gases concentration in order to avoid unacceptable or even dangerous impacts on nature and for mankind? This triggered intensive discussions in science, and it still does. The Intergovernmental Panel on Climate Change, IPCC, has become a successful mechanism for the creation of collectively shared scientific findings. A key conclusion on the basis of this body of scientific evidence is that the increase of average global temperature must not surpass 2°C; otherwise it seems to be most probable that the earth system reacts and irreversible changes will be tipped off. It is widely shared knowledge that the 2°C threshold translates into a maximum concentration of greenhouse gases in the atmosphere well below 450–500 ppm. With today's 380 ppm we therefore know that we have to take serious action urgently. Give and take, there are only six years to go until we have to reach the "carbon peak" (the point in time when the maximum carbon load will be emitted into the atmosphere starting then a period of ever decreasing emissions). That is a tremendous challenge that almost seems out of reach given the experience the world shared in respect of the time it took to internationally negotiate the Kyoto Protocol, to bring it into action and then to realise that, to a large part, reality is counteracting commitments even of a number of signatory states. The message of scientific knowledge suggests that another such time gap is not affordable.

After 1992, it took climate diplomacy altogether 13 years for getting a legally binding Kyoto Protocol entered into force. And still, large emitters such as the United States of America and Australia did not ratify, other big emitters are not subject to the obligations of the protocol that is nearly without any "teeth" and lacks a reasonable enforcement and compliance instrument. It is not surprising that global green house gas emissions increased instead of decreased.

To make matters worse, in the last two decades the world has changed profoundly. This change makes the case for rethinking knowledge, democracy and sustainability an intriguing one. Today, the knowledge about climate change is overwhelmingly concrete and convincing: we can calculate the point in time by which we have to manage the carbon emissions to peak (very soon), and how much carbon tonnes remain to be emitted without increasing the possibility of climate disruptions (very few), and we can even design options of how this remaining emission could be allocated and how the burden of emission reduction could be shared (for example very asymmetric taking into account that the most competitive economies should accept the most extensive burden; and more symmetric in the sense of suggesting the global equal per capita emissions rights).

The lesson to be learnt is that knowing this evident information does not automatically bridge the gap to political knowledge, not to speak of the societal wisdom to take appropriate action.

5.3 Co-evolution and knowledge workers

Judging from long standing experience in environmental decision-making there is no point in waiting for scientific knowledge to just drop into society. Neither is it reasonably possible to deliberately boost up the process of dropping knowledge. And what is frequently referred to as "knowledge society" is a construction as diffuse as possible that rarely leads to concrete measures.

Instead, we suggest exploring a new approach. It builds from the observation gained in the efforts such as the control and reduction of long range transport of acid pollutants, the reduction of airborne heavy metals, ozone and sulphur according to so-called critical loads and levels, or the cleaning up of contaminated land: Science and policies are being co-produced, and the value of scientific evidence comes with the process of negotiating find-ing, measures and means (for example Lidskog and Sundquist 2002).

In general, environmentalism may generate a special brand of mentality and governance (governmentality, according to Sutton 2004: 171), but it sometimes seems to be useful with respect to other policies as well. One example is the conceptual framework for the establishment of the Intergovernmental Panel on Climate Change. This concept reacts to the increasing need to generate additional knowledge on climate change and the mutual reaction of the earth system and society. It also reacts to the problems of society and decision-makers to keep track of scientific progress.

IPCC was deliberately designed as an intergovernmental panel and not just as a scientific panel, the latter being state of the art at that point in time. This has been an innovative feature. Another innovation was the concept of webbing the IPCC deep into the scientific community, rather than just appointing a number of eminent members to form a panel body. Those two social innovations proved successful in helping to create informal knowledge networks and fostering a community of specialists and officials (Enders 2008, Schneidewind 2009).

The co-evolution of science and policy-making does not go without all sorts of frictions, of course. On the contrary, those frictions purposely be-long to the social dialogue and ask for new forms of dialogue (see below). There is, however, another impact of co-evolution, and that is the concept of a knowledge worker. Co-evolution needs a new brand of intellectual thinking and it creates a new type of intellectual: the knowledge worker. They would work within diverse organisational schemes inside and outside of the "silos" of disciplines and departments, at the same time. Also, their work should address highly complex issues encompassing technical and scientific issues as well as the social learning and transition management. They perceive reality as room for possibilities. For them the opposition of being a realist versus thinking more fundamental or creative is outdated. Instead, this new brand of knowledge working would ask for critical analysis, co-operative networking plus the ability to create a momentum and to make use of it in a way that allows continuing progress. Mutius (2008: 24) proposes to qualify this type of intellectual a "constructive intellectual" as opposed to the conventional approach to the role of intellectuals in European societies (also: Minx and Preisler 2008). That is why we suggest advancing the discourse on science, society and role of knowledge in democracies.

5.4 Democratic climate futures

In almost every aspect the climate change poses problems that are asymmetric in time and place. Climate change requires a "drop in the bucket" type of long-term decision-making: a continuous series of interventions during a long period is necessary to cause favourable effects (Chap. 18 by Meuleman and In 't Veld, in this volume). Those who did not cause climate change are most likely the ones that have to carry the biggest climate change impacts. Obviously, the developed countries have been and continues to be the basic cause of the problem. In the developing countries the conclusion is obvious: rich nations must take on the basic burden of mitigation, consume less of the world's resources and absolutely reduce their contribution to global warming. That is why attempts to declare flat goals of emission reduction across all countries have not been achieved so far and are seen as unequal and unfair.

While the developing world did not create the problem, they now clearly add to it significantly. Between 1980 and 2006, per capita carbon emissions doubled in developing countries as a group, and nearly tripled in China. And the people from the developing countries have a real stake in global action on this front, for they are already the worst affected by the growing incidence of climatic change – temporary or not -, especially in tropical and semi-tropical zones.

However, from an ethical standpoint, one may not expect people who are annually emitting a per capita amount of one tonne carbon dioxide to reduce their share of emitted green house gases – as long as in other parts of the world people are emitting 10, 20 ton and more. On average, carbon emissions per capita in the developed countries are about five times higher than those in developing countries. Between some countries the differences are even starker, and a closer look into the carbon divide within the (US-)American, the Indian and any other society will most likely reveal a social differentiation in carbon emissions between the rich and the poor that is of no less significance than the social divide in terms of income or life expectancy is.

The problem is that the sustainability project, in terms of ensuring basic needs to the whole population without compromising the way future generations will decide to meet their needs, is still far from complete in many parts of the world. Worse: Mankind seems to be heading north on a southbound track, with all indicators of greenhouse gas emissions pointing constantly that mankind is moving in the wrong way.

Even without trying to replicate western standards of living, by just trying to provide every citizen with the minimum decent standards of living that contemporary technology can offer, such as permanent housing, electricity, access to clean water, sanitation and sufficient food, emerging countries necessarily require more natural resource use which results in more carbon emissions than the planet may carry in the long run without tipping the line that may cause major disruptions for people and prosperity.

Therefore the concept of environmental justice may become a necessary addition to the "one man, one vote" claim of democracy. Such a plea is not new. In the 1970s the precautionary principle was introduced in environ-mental policies. For long-term decision-making this was rephrased into a version of Kant's categorical imperative: "We have no right to make decisions which would, according to our present knowledge and values, impose on future generations such costs and risks as we would not be willing to assume by ourselves" (Meuleman and In 't Veld 2009). In 1990s the economic term "environmental space" was introduced (Weterings and Opschoor 1994), as a measure for how to utilise the environment without compromising future uses. The concept considers environment and nature as "resources" which can be "consumed" by people. The consumption should not exceed a certain amount, expressed as quota. The problem was and is that this idea is quite difficult to quantify. Nevertheless, the concept merged into new forms that try to footprint the per capita consumption of ecological resources, water, or fish stock. They all present figures that explain reasonably well the social divide in threats to environment and our societies (source: Worldmapper). For the time being, the so-called carbon footprint may serve as a catch-all. A carbon footprint relates to the amount of greenhouse gases produced in our day-to-day lives through burning fossil fuels for electricity, heating and transportation. The carbon footprint is a measurement of all greenhouse gases we individually produce and has units of tons of carbon dioxide equivalent.

This is why, today, the principal claim of democracy "one man – one vote" has to be amplified: "one man – one vote – one carbon footprint". This would help in making concrete the individual "environmental space"; it would stimulate public consciousness about the impact of the use of natural resources and of environmental pollution. Finally, it would also stimulate the design of democratic decision-making procedures for the exchange of individual quota, a "cap and trade" system on an individual basis.

5.5 Governance of climate emergency?

Mitigation of greenhouse gases is – and will stay – the best option for any serious global change approach in politics and for economies. In terms of scientifically describing ways and means to cope with the climate challenge, we have to ask what happens if mankind is crossing the red-tape line of 2°C average global warming. To trespass this limit is often said to run the world into a climate emergency situation, because impacts of all sorts are to be expected and might endanger flood control, food security, urban development or cause climate-caused migration. If they do, this of course would very profoundly impact every aspect of global interaction, both ecologically and economically. It would possibly destabilise the whole of society and add to the rundown of democratic and institutional power, known as failing state syndrome.

There is, however, no political idea of how to react to a climate emergency and its impact on the decision-making system, not to speak of democracy. During the whole of human history, the concept of emergency used to be a national feature, or in some worst cases of wartime and negligence of human rights, a regional one. It has certainly never been a global one, fortunately. The international decision-making practice is suited to respond to genocides by taking action in the name of human ethics against national sovereignty. This alone poses humanitarian and political questions sometimes difficult to resolve. A climate emergency would go even further and raise all kind of issues of how to institutionalise any significant, reliable (accountable, transparent), reversible and controllable emergency response.

The decision capacity as institutionalised today is not prepared to fulfil this task. The UN was established as a multinational reaction to the threats of the World War II, which, at that point in time, definitely was an emergency response. In order to face the challenges of modern societies, multi-lateral institutions and the national level, even the self-regulated civil society, have to merge into a new state in order to meet the challenge of democratic decision-making in the realm of climate change, or, positively put: in the upcoming area of a sustainable development. This leads to important questions:

- Can this be conceived in a way that makes full use of democratic comforts?
- Can we leave the decision whether a country will adapt to rapid climate change to the respective government, or must we perceive this a decision that needs more than just one voice because the adaption itself is imposed or will have to be enforced rather than being just a free will "take it or leave it" option?
- Do we already understand the dimension of democratic challenge involved here for the multinational governance system and for the way modern societies deal with expanded knowledge about self-destruction?

These are fundamental issues. For the modern knowledge society their role might be comparable to the one the worker's participation and codetermination once had for the establishment of democracy and a democratic self-understanding of society. In more concrete and focused on the above mentioned governance issues of climate emergency terms the following questions are of prime importance:

- Who would be de facto and legally capable to assess which impact may be reversible or irreversible – given the fact that measures to adapt to climate change may display both of these properties?
- Who would be legitimised to provide and prepare decision tools taking into account assessments of impacts on food supply, arable land, water accessibility and the land use in coastal areas where the majority of population is living and working now, worldwide?
- Who would be held liable in case of enforced climate adaptation costs imposed to regions that clearly have only a minor share in causing the climate change?
- Who would act as clearing house once benefits need to be shared between regional communities, or asymmetric disparate time-bound impacts have to be implemented in a fair way?

Whatever the political choice will be in the end, this is a topic for advanced thinking along the science-society interface. The aim is to provide society with an informed debate about climate change policies on mitigation and adaptation clearly asking for answers that go beyond what seems economically feasible today.

5.6 Metaphors for the yet untold

Assuming there is enough political will and economic power to trigger major transitions towards sustainability the other key question is: Where do we get the metaphoric images for the Great Transformation? What kind of symbolic pictures and mythological images human culture needs for awareness-building processes?

Collective awareness for the Earth's environment system was first catalysed by the image of the planet Earth taken by the "Man to the Moon"-missions. However, today we experience a revolution in communication techniques from internet to all features of individualised and easy-access-telecommunication, but for the Earth-Man-Interface we still have no up-to-date cultural features. This is obviously a serious setback for the communication of science results.

With the means of basic math that explain threats of global warming to the broader public. Graphs, tables, stats indicators and figures are building the information that is expected to advance the public debate into an informed debate. The success remains disputable.

All past major societal transitions have produced symbols, mostly embedded in a complex system of symbols. They process pure data into information, information into knowledge, and knowledge into what finally serves as the groundwork of judgment. Icons and iconic forms are an important tool with the help of which humans communicate reality. Reality might even be perceived with the help of certain iconography. It might be created through linguistic, scholarly, scientific, and artistic thoughts and concepts; they might be coming up through societal sharing of experiences, and they might be remodelled through permanent communication, individual understanding, legislation and politics itself. They use, of course, cultural archetypes such as rituals, myths, imagination and routine narratives. In particular in the arts they might make additional use of manifestos and social practice.

If it is seen as a given that the universe of symbolic meaning and semiotics created by man structures and shapes the way we perceive reality and what is accepted as information and knowledge, then, we have to ask what this observation does tell us in respect to climate change and unsustainable developments?

5.7 From access to information to informed debate

To improve “sustainability literacy”, free and unrestricted access to information is needed. This is the starting point. The protection of the environment and public health depends on scientific information that is reliable and impartial. Citizens and policy-makers rely on the most current scientific knowledge and technologies to make wise decisions. The “right to know” is helping people push for improved access to information on the environment, health, and safety held by government or also by private parties. In addition, one of the signs of an emerging knowledge democracy is that citizens, better educated and informed than ever, produce knowledge themselves. Such “citizen’s knowledge” may be an enrichment of the total body of knowledge available for democratic decision-making, but can also be in competition with scientific knowledge. New mechanisms are needed to combine scientific and lay knowledge into productive combinations (see also Bunders, this volume).These requirements are widely accepted in politics although they are not sufficiently implemented and lacking political stomach.

Since the UN Summit 1992 in Rio de Janeiro the agenda of sustainable development is programmatically linked to the inclusive and consensus-orientated decision-making that gets people involved as actors rather than only as voters, and that gets sustainability thinking mainstreamed in parliaments, the private sector, and science and humanities. In general terms (the whole of society including politics and business) we are far from achieving an informed debate about what is not sustainable and what are positive options to get ourselves out onto the sustainable pathway. The task at hand is to bring life to the concept of informed debate by continued efforts to stimulating knowledge support and sustainability action. However, there is a need for stocktaking and new action to recombine economy and ecology, to improve sustainability governance, to sharing knowledge in eco-innovation, resource efficiency and green growth, adaptation to climate change, food security, land use, public financing and benefit sharing.

Already existing instruments play an important role and should be implemented more often and more effectively. Those instruments such as impact assessment, open coordination, technology assessment, risk prediction and risk management, however, are designed to sort out what should better not be done. New thinking is required to scout out new ways and options for sustainable development.

5.8 Organising informed debates

The broader normative conception of democracy that includes environ-mental justice in the form of the "one carbon footprint" statement requires a broad societal consciousness of the responsibility we have, as individuals and as nations, for a sustainable future. A crucial factor is that the societal debate on this subject must be well-informed. National Councils for Sustainability are designed to take part in such an informed debate, and to stimulate this. They advise national governments on all items of the national sustainability strategy, propose action and projects, and communicate the aspects of sustainability in the public. They include in their debate science, society and the media. This implies leadership in setting the agenda and designing possible solutions. Meaningful contents will mostly be only provided if processes of participation, empowerment, capacity building, and cooperation are being successfully triggered.

In Germany, the Council for Sustainable Development is a body of eminent persons mandated to advise the Federal Chancellery on the sustainability strategy (Bundesregierung 2008, Rat für Nachhaltige Entwicklung). The council developed a line of instruments and formats that are functional to qualify up the sustainability debate:

- Expert dialogues on certain issues (fact finding and scouting for new frontiers);
- Leadership fora with industrial and commercial leaders on Corporate Social Responsibility (action-orientated);
- Mission Sustainability (best-practice forum for social practice);
- "Citizens engaged in generational dialogue and sustainability" (award scheme fostering a "culture of acknowledgement");
- "Carl von Carlowitz Lectures" (high-end scientific lectures covering the society-sustainability interface starting November 2009 with a lecture on

ecology and sustainability given by Professor Wolfgang Haber);

- In collaboration with other institutions the Council contributes to developing new evidence-based formats such as "Ranking of Sustainability Reports of large and medium-sized industries", German Sustainability Award;
- International Peer Review on German sustainability policies (Stigson et al. 2009).

In a number of other European countries, such councils have meanwhile been established.

5.9 Completing the knowledge grid

Computing a maximum of bits does not sum up to active thinking. The number of bits processed does not by itself make software smart. There has to be more. Knowledge-based debates are as good as they may be in the position to hook up with the scientific high-end thinking. Regarding the sustainability thinking this is a severe shortcoming.

For designing and applying political choices towards sustainable development advanced thinking is important. It needs a special brand of sustainability knowledge brokers that would manage the interface of advanced knowledge on the part of science and, on the part of society, of the processes needed to prepare for decision-making. Ideally, this would be embedded in or related to practical and complex processes of change and transition, be it technically, economically or socially. For this purpose, the European Union Sustainable Development Strategy introduces the buzz word "informed debate about sustainable development" (European Union 2007).

In order to decide what actually makes a debate an *informed* debate measuring appears to be necessary. This is a lesson learnt: the concept of democracy would have remained a lifeless token as long as people did not start to measure the democratic process. Metrics alone would not guarantee substantial progress, but without it there might be no option at all.

"Informed debate" must not be misunderstood as being a limited debate. Informed debate does not reduce the debate to those who are informed, excluding others. In addition, the involvement of stakeholders in sustainable development debates is essential, because what is thought of as "sustainable" is often dependent on assumptions and values. Judging from the example of ongoing debates on climate strategies, land consumption, or carbon capture and storage, it seems questionable whether a debate is "informed enough". Deficits or shortcomings of this kind only give reason to empower integrative thinking. In dealing with complexities of all sorts we have to think big about the concept of thinking, and we have to start thinking about changing the knowledge grid.

5.10 A duty-to-know

We suggest that there is also a duty for everybody to impart and acquire sustainability literacy. This duty might be conceived as "must be known"-duty, or as "duty to know". It would add to what we until now know as in-formation right. It would make the pathway data take in order to become societal knowledge a two-tier-way, finally leading to a knowledge grid.

Both the (already mostly understood) "right to know" and the (new and suggested) "duty to know" are essential for informed debates around sustainable development. Frequently, decisions have to be taken under the precondition of asymmetric knowledge: scientific evidence is available, but political consequences are unclear (for example some aspects of climate change policies), knowledge is incomplete or no full knowledge can ever be achieved, but political consequences are quite clear (for example the financial meltdown in 2008).

The public is reluctant to accept enormous and "out of the norm"-threats. The prospect of possible emergencies related to climate forcing, the un-abated species extinction, asymmetries in food security, safety, poverty and health are indeed threatening human existence in some regions of the earth. Gloom and doom communication does not help, nor does an elaborated ignorance. The situation is similar to how democratic societies re-acted to the destructive potential of the atomic bomb in the 1950s and 1960s. The sheer dimension of potential destruction was so scary that people tended to lose the ability to feel sorrow and just decide to refrain from letting this dimension influence their way of living.

But averting dangers may turn out to be no less perilous than the dangers themselves if society finds the courage to collectively make tough decisions and embark on courses designed by vision and ambition to make the world a better place by combining democracy and sustainability. Critics who regard themselves as realist, may object. They may say that the virus of unattainability and delusion lurks in every hope. But there is also the opposite saying: the virus of hope lurks in every unattained reality.

6 Unlocking the full potential of the crowd – a government perspective

Maurits Kreijveld

Abstract

As a result of technological developments over the past two decades citizens have become increasingly connected, both socially and virtually. Now, more effective use of the collective knowledge and expertise of a group of citizens can be made in a way that improves knowledge and produces greater insight into information. This phenomenon is widely referred to as the "wisdom of crowds".

The experts interviewed in this study use "wisdom of crowds" to refer to a range of phenomena, with differing degrees of social interaction and different numbers of decision-makers. Their definitions do not necessarily, therefore, comply with the traditional definitions of "wisdom" and "crowds".

We developed a framework to map these phenomena in terms of numbers of decision-makers and amounts of knowledge. This involved identifying three stages of development, with interaction between governments and citizens increasing from Stage 1 to Stage 3. At the same time, decision-making processes are becoming more and more complex, and the traditional role of governments is increasingly being challenged.

More effective social interaction and greater involvement of citizens in decision-making processes are predicted to lead to more "wisdom of crowds". In order to unlock the full potential of this, more knowledge about social interactions in the "crowd" is needed, as well as progress in the technological tools available to facilitate coordination and collaboration.

6.1 Introduction

The technological developments over the past two decades have changed the societal playing field dramatically. Computers have become connected worldwide, while much more information is now available to every citizen. At the same time citizens have become connected in new ways and now have the tools to produce, share and distribute their own information, knowledge and opinions. Citizens all around the world have embraced these new opportunities enthusiastically, as the explosive growth in personal websites, blogs, social networking sites, YouTube and Twitter demonstrates. The Web has become a social Web.

R.J. in 't Veld (ed.), *Knowledge Democracy*, DOI 10.1007/978-3-642-11381-9_6,

This fully networked and global structure, with its huge range of many-to-many communication opportunities, has created a completely new set of dynamics, where citizens can raise their voice and group and regroup themselves ad hoc around the issues that matter to them. In this way, bottom-up and lateral initiatives can arise and rapidly grow in popularity. Citizens have become less dependent on and, therefore, less bound by traditional organisations, institutions and states. Initiatives such as Wikipedia and Linux show some of the potential that citizens can create by working together enthusiastically, without the involvement of traditional organisations.

More and more organisations and governments have started to make use of these new opportunities in recent years. Companies such as Lego, Boeing and Dell have successfully involved their customers and harnessed their knowledge and expertise through online communities where consumers can send in and discuss ideas for new products and have the opportunity to influence the configuration of products being developed. Web 2.0 tools also played an important role in President Obama's election campaign. Indeed these tools are seen as the key to his success because they enabled him to engage citizens and mobilise them to play an active role in his campaign and fundraising (Harfoush 2009). Growing numbers of organisations have recognised the potential for involving citizens in developing and marketing their products and policies. The Netherlands has seen the following examples of such co-creation or crowd sourcing initiatives:

- the Battle of Concepts, an online idea contest where companies can put questions to students and young professionals about innovation and marketing;
- innovation 2.0, where companies can provide input for the Ministry of Economic Affairs' innovation policy;
- wijbouweneenwijk.nl, an online community where citizens and experts can meet to co-create a new residential area in the municipality of Smallingerland.

New technologies, such as augmented reality[1], sensor networks, mobile devices and advancements in artificial intelligence (including semantics[2] and swarm modelling), are being developed to provide greater insight into data and information and to improve interaction among people and between people and their surroundings. These technologies are expected to enable citizens to coordinate their efforts even better in the future and to collaborate more effectively than before. This will make citizens an even stronger force to be reckoned with.

---

[1] An augmented reality (AR) is created when data and information are merged with an image or view of the real world, for instance through a mobile phone camera or a TV screen. AR is seen as a powerful technique for contextualising data and information in a way that people can easily interpret and interact with.

[2] Technology that enables computers to understand and interpret human language and grammar.

These developments could fundamentally change our society and the way people coexist and collaborate (Shirkey 2008, Tapscott and Williams 2007). They could provide new ways to tackle organisational, social and societal problems by actively involving citizens and providing them with the tools they need to attune their behaviour to each other and to their environment.

At the same time, existing organisations and institutions, such as governments, political organisations and businesses, are all having to face the challenge of how best to respond to these developments. They may need to adjust and possibly even redefine their positions on citizens so that citizens can play an active role and create solutions of their own. All in all, therefore, decision-making processes are set to become much more complex than before.

In this chapter we analyse some of the implications for society of this wide range of current developments in ICT technologies so as to identify the main challenges and opportunities faced by policy-makers, politicians and governments.

6.2 Wisdom of crowds

Within the scope of these developments, the term "wisdom of crowds" (Surowiecki 2004) is often used to refer to the concept that the collective knowledge and expertise of a group of individuals, somehow connected through a network, can be larger than the sum of the individual contributions. Surowiecki argues that, under specific conditions, lay groups can take better decisions and make better assessments than experts. According to Surowiecki, wise crowds are characterised by diversity of opinion, independence from group thinking, the ability to preserve the richness of diversity, decentralised decision-making that allows for specialisation and local knowledge and by having a mechanism for aggregation that turns private views and judgements into a collective decision.

In this chapter we will discover that the term "wisdom of crowds" is used as a metaphor to describe a series of current and future developments, ranging from identifying citizens' preferences and opinions to co-creating policy, actively involving citizens in policy decisions and the self-organising of citizens. This extends Surowiecki's concept of crowds to areas in which diverse groups take decisions involving complex social interactions. But these groups do not automatically comply with Surowiecki's criteria for "wise crowds" in that they do not always demonstrate independence of opinion and decentralised decision-making. The "wisdom" of a crowd is the aggregation of individual contributions to information, experience and judgment that can lead to new or better knowledge and insight. Each contribution can be relevant and, thanks to ICT technologies, can be collected without citizens needing to be personally related or work together actively.

Mechanisms for aggregation can range from intelligent software (the Google search engine, for example, ranks web pages based on popularity, or book shopping suggestions on Amazon.com), wikis and economic markets to all sorts of internal coordination and collaboration between people, with and without the use of technology. ICT technologies can play a significant role in internal coordination within crowds, as in the case of peer-to-peer technology for free telephony

(Skype) or the TomTom car navigation software, which calculates the fastest route home for each individual, based on the amount of traffic (in other words, the collective behaviour of the crowd) measured by the Vodafone telecommunications network. These are just the first, very simple examples of what is likely to come when the web evolves into the Web 3.0 and 4.0 environments, where technology will understand human language (referred to as the "Semantic Web") and all objects will become connected to networks (referred to as the "Internet of Things").

Although technologies to improve insight and facilitate coordination are available, we still have to deal with social interactions that remain highly complex. The recent financial crisis has shown that psychological and social factors are very hard to grasp and can dominate the behaviour of crowds. These factors can lead to mass hysteria and blindness to risks. The balance between "wise" and "unwise" crowds can be very delicate, as Surowiecki (2004) acknowledges. To sum up, the "wisdom of crowds" can manifest itself in many different ways and has the potential to generate more and better ideas, increased commitment and involvement and the mobilising (or self-mobilising) of citizens into action. Technology has a major role to play in aggregating knowledge from crowds and facilitating coordination and collaboration.

6.3 Method

The aim of this study was to find out how the "wisdom of crowds" currently manifests itself and what future developments are expected to increase the use of this wisdom, as well as to establish how this will affect organisations and society as a whole. In order to get differentiated and wide-ranging views, 50 experts from different fields, including social sciences, computation, ICT, mathematics, biology, psychology, economics, politics and policy-making, were interviewed about their views on the "wisdom of crowds". These experts came from both public sector organisations (such as government departments and universities) and the private sector (multinationals, SMEs and self-employed people), as well as from both executive and operational levels. Their expertise and positions meant they could be expected to have a good overview of current developments in this respect.

These experts were asked to define both the phenomenon of the "wisdom of crowds" itself and the terms "wisdom" and "the crowds". They were also asked to give current examples of organisations using the "wisdom of crowds" and to explain their vision of the associated opportunities and challenges. We continued conducting new interviews adding new dimensions or details to the description of the phenomenon until, after 40 interviews, we considered that the data had reached saturation point (Glaser and Strauss 1967), with the results from the final ten interviews being consistent with the information from the previous interviews.

In this chapter we discuss the views and challenges that these experts identified for the public sector and political decision-making. In many cases these views were very similar to the opportunities and challenges identified in the private sector.

6.4 Results

After analysing the interviews we concluded that our experts did not define the "wisdom of crowds" in a single, consistent way. So, too, did their definitions of "wisdom" and "the crowd" differ. Rather than coming up with a consistent definition, they referred to a range of phenomena that varied both in terms of the kind of social interaction and the extent of interdependence between the members of a group. What these phenomena have in common is that the amount of knowledge of the group as a whole is seen as larger than the total knowledge of the group's constituent parts. In almost all cases "wisdom" was used to refer to "knowledge" and "insight" rather than to a higher form of contextualised knowledge. According to the experts, the complexity and challenges related to the phenomena are primarily determined by the number of members involved in decision-making. The trend seen is of growing numbers of decision-makers over the next few years because of the growing involvement of "the crowd" in innovation and policy-making processes.

Based on this analysis, we devised a framework to map the different concepts of the "wisdom of crowds" with respect to decision-making processes, as shown in Figure 6.1. The *x* axis shows the number of decision-makers, while the *y* axis shows the amount of knowledge generated by the group, reflecting the concept of wisdom. Firstly, three traditional types of decision-making were defined: decision-making by one individual person or organisation, decision-making involving multiple stakeholders such as in representative democracies and decision-making in large social groups such as societies and masses. These three types are shown in the lower half of Figure 6.1.

For each type, the group's total amount of knowledge can be increased by making more effective use of the information and knowledge of all the individual group members. This translates on the *y* axis into three types of "wisdom of crowds", which are described and analysed in more detail below. All the phenomena mentioned by the experts can be classified as belonging to one of these three types.

In this framework these types are considered to be three stages of "wisdom of crowds", with rising numbers of decision-makers and more social interactions within the group. According to the experts, social interactions between group members are essential for the creation of "wisdom". Greater social interaction is seen as having the potential to create more "wisdom of crowds" than groups of unrelated individuals, which seems to contradict the original concept of the "wisdom of crowds" introduced by Surowiecki. According to the respondents, the greater the number of social interactions between members of a group, the greater the challenges involved in using the available knowledge and interactions effectively and in unlocking the full potential of the "wisdom of crowds".

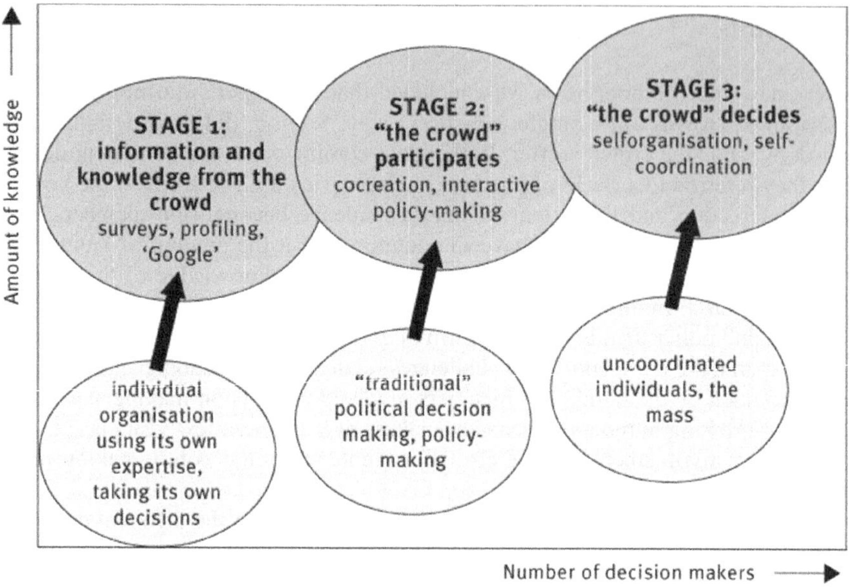

Fig. 6.1 Three stages of the "wisdom of crowds".

6.4.1 Stage 1: using knowledge and information from the crowd

The first stage represents the original concept of "wisdom of crowds" as used by Surowiecki (2004). In this stage, individuals and organisations tap into the knowledge of a large group of people consisting of independent members making decentralised, individual decisions. These organisations use the crowd to get extra information ("information intelligence") and new ideas. Organisations use the crowd to help them, for instance, to resolve difficult issues that require knowledge, insight and expertise. In this way, organisations gain access to the diversity of opinion among crowd members.

Input from the crowd can be obtained by using intelligent search engines such as Google, data mining and the profiling software used by online book stores such as Amazon and Bol.com. The experts consulted claim that this input can also be obtained more actively by setting up online questionnaires such as 21minuten.nl, a Dutch initiative launched by McKinsey and De Publieke Zaak that asks people for their opinions on, for example, the economy, the environment and the European Union. The government can then use this information to improve its policy. Other examples include internet forums and idea contests, such as Showusabetterway.com in the United Kingdom, which asks citizens to help develop better ways of publishing the vast amounts of non-personal information that the government collects, such as the location of state schools.

According to the experts, organisations are in the lead in this stage, and decide for themselves how they use the information from the crowd. There are no social interactions among members of the crowd, and there is almost no social interaction between the crowd and the organisation. The organisational structures are unchanged.

The respondents saw the main challenges in this stage as being how to:

- gather, filter, synthesise and contextualise relevant information so as to obtain greater insight and more knowledge from multiple sources of information and the crowd;
- improve current market research techniques (which use panels of up to one thousand respondents) and voting systems (approval voting: yes or no?) so as to make better use of the "wisdom of crowds" by obtaining better insight and higher-value information from the crowd;
- preserve the diversity of opinion while using statistical techniques that tend to reduce the amount of data.

6.4.2 Stage 2: co-creation between citizens and organisations

In the second stage, citizens' involvement has grown: organisations and citizens collaborate to solve problems. In this stage, there is interaction between organisations and citizens. There is scope for the crowd to modify and configure a public policy or public service, and this process is often referred to as "crowd sourcing".

An example that was mentioned is the Ministry of Economic Affairs' Innovation 2.0 community, where entrepreneurs can help shape subsidy schemes for innovation. Other common examples can be found in the decision-making processes involved in infrastructural projects and spatial planning. These processes already have a lot of experience with citizen participation and representation, while Web 2.0 has made it easier to reach and interact with even larger groups. Another example is Wijbouweneenwijk.nl, set up by the municipality of Smallingerland.

In many cases, citizens collaborating with such initiatives not only have contacts with the organisation, but also with other citizens and so are used to discussing ideas and proposals and reacting to each other's wishes and demands. To a certain extent these social interactions make these citizens interdependent. Decision-making becomes a group process rather than an individual one, as in Surowiecki's original model of the "wisdom of crowds".

Although organisations may have actively involved citizens in this phase, our respondents still see them as having a high degree of control over the decision-making process and the public products and services that are offered. Organisations are largely able to define the margins of input by citizens, who present themselves as players representing even larger groups of citizens.

The social web means citizens are increasingly becoming connected and collectively organised, and these collectives can come and go. These days, for example, citizens are less and less represented by traditional labour or other unions and associations, but are instead opting for self-representation. They choose on an ad hoc basis how to organise themselves so as to best defend their interests. In other words, an "adhocracy" (Mintzberg 1983). This puts pressure on the amount of control that organisations can have. According to our experts, organisations wanting to make optimal use of the wisdom of these citizens need to evaluate their decision-making processes and develop more sophisticated decision-making tools.

The other main challenges facing organisations in Stage 2, according to the experts, are:

- deciding the margins for input by citizens. Raising the margins could result in more innovative ideas, but also in less control for organisations;
- getting and maintaining citizens' commitment through the entire process of gathering ideas to taking decisions and action. Citizens who feel they are not being taken seriously may turn against the organisations;
- redesigning organisational structures and procedures. Working with groups of citizens requires openness, transparency and a more personal approach, which contrasts sharply with the way most bureaucracies operate.

6.4.3 Stage 3: self-organisation

In Stage 3, citizens have become even more self-aware and have taken the lead. Organisations have more or less dissolved into these groups of citizens. This stage can be described as a highly complex system, full of relationships and continual interaction between individual citizens or groups of them. It is characterised by self-organisation: initiatives are taken by citizens themselves, with no need for organisations to control them. One of the best examples of this is the Linux software, which was developed by a team of collaborating experts who distributed tasks among the group and were completely self-organised.

The respondents also interpreted this concept of self-organisation as a sort of "crowd", just like the other two forms. However, the high degree of social interaction in these groups means they cannot be seen as crowds consisting of citizens making independent decisions. In this phase, decisions are made by the group as a whole.

In this stage, wisdom is seen as a collective action of decision-making based on the collective awareness of the complex system. Instead of being able to control these citizens, organisations have now become part of the complex system in which both organisations and individuals can start initiatives and work together on a basis of greater equality. This seems to follow the trend, as predicted by our experts, of citizens becoming more empowered by social web tools and wanting being more involved, while also feeling more free to take action themselves (as a group) and to represent themselves rather than be represented by third parties.

Decision-making processes will consequently become much more complex and unpredictable, involving many players with no hierarchical structure and no-one in overall control. The experts predict that governments will also be less able to control and manipulate citizens and so may need to redefine their role, focusing on enabling citizens rather than controlling them. New organisational structures may also be needed.

Examples of self-organisation can already be seen in society. But, according to our experts, there do not yet seem to be many online examples other than Linux. More effective self-organisation may require more technological tools to support internal coordination and decision-making. The technological tools in use today, such as car navigation software, have been developed on the basis of the swarm models of ants and bees. We can certainly learn a lot from "swarms" of insects or the like seen among birds and fish. Indeed these swarms can achieve amazing things that go far beyond what one individual can achieve. Even simple rules of self-organisation and self-coordination can generate complex organisational structures (Kauffman 1995). However, although swarm models may provide a strong image for self-organisation, we also need to take account of the complexity of social interactions between humans.

The respondents see this final stage as involving the challenges of:

- unravelling animals' mechanisms for self-organisation and seeing whether they can also be applied to humans, as well as enabling self-coordination by using technologies to improve interactions and decision-making processes in large groups of citizens;
- redefining the role of traditional decision-making organisations and structures, such as parliaments, that will tend to be bypassed by groups of citizens acting and deciding collectively;
- predicting or detecting changes in sentiment at an early stage that might turn wise groups into unwise groups and trigger mass hysteria.

6.5 Conclusion

As a result of technological developments over the past two decades citizens have become increasingly connected, both socially and virtually. This provides opportunities to make more effective use of the collective knowledge and expertise of groups of people and to build public support for and public involvement in change. Citizens and organisations have taken the first steps to profit from what Surowiecki refers to as the "wisdom of crowds". At the same time this increases the complexity of decision-making processes and challenges the role of governments and politicians.

Our study involved asking experts from business, government institutions and universities to give their views on the "wisdom of crowds". This term was found to be used to describe three different phenomena, which do not always comply with the original concept of the "wisdom of crowds" introduced by Surowiecki. We built a framework to map these phenomena with respect to increases in knowledge and numbers of decision-makers. This resulted in our identifying three stages of "wisdom of crowds", with increasing degrees of social interactions in a group resulting in increasing complexity.

The experts referred to in this chapter see an evolution from Stage 1 towards Stage 2 and then on to Stage 3. While the interaction between organisations and citizens increases towards the third phase, groups of citizens in this stage are also likely to demand greater accountability and more involvement in the decision-making process. In increasing numbers of cases citizens will self-organise and even bypass current organisational structures in order to achieve their own goals and ambitions. In this way, existing organisations may completely lose the control they currently enjoy. In response they may need to redefine their role and facilitate citizens instead of trying to control them, while new organisational structures may also need to be developed.

The first stage of the process can be seen as the "wisdom of crowds" as described by Surowiecki. In other words, organisations and individuals using information from the crowd. These crowds consist of independent members making individual, decentralised decisions. In the second stage, citizens participate in the decisions taken by organisations, while in Stage 3 citizens organise themselves into complex systems that take the decisions themselves. Social interactions within these groups mean, however, that these groups do not automatically meet Surowiecki's criteria for a "wise crowd", characterised by independence and decentralised decision-making. The recent financial crisis has shown that social interactions can lead to mass hysteria and blindness to risks among large groups of people. If social interactions and individual contributions are not used effectively, the total amount of knowledge of "the crowd" may easily reduce. The balance between "wise" and "unwise" crowds can be very delicate, especially in Stages 2 and 3, as Surowiecki recognises.

Interestingly, the experts we interviewed saw social interactions as crucial for creating knowledge and wisdom in Stages 2 and 3. Indeed these interactions may provide even better ideas and more commitment for implementing these ideas, thus resulting in more "wisdom of crowds". In order, however, for these complex interacting groups to become "wise", the social interactions need somehow to be coordinated and to improve collaboration. This demands the development of more technological tools to enhance coordination and interaction among citizens. New technologies that are currently being developed are expected to stimulate this trend, while combining these new technologies with a better understanding of the social interactions and mechanisms could help us to progress to unlocking the full potential of the "wisdom of crowds".

7 Researching publics

Floor Basten

Abstract

The crisis of representation is felt in both social sciences and democracy. I describe the main features of this crisis and sketch the outlines of a possible way out. Starting from an optimistic viewpoint on what social sciences might accomplish once evolved to a next level, I present a scale for social research that facilitates new ideas about democracy and discuss the notion of "public" as a collection of people that can be identified after an event, because they share common experiences during the event. These experiences are expressed in narratives. The method I propose is based on narrative research and transdisciplinary processes to co-create knowledge and meaning. The research process is democratic and the outcomes offer opportunities for social change.

7.1 Crisis in social sciences

Founding father of sociology Auguste Comte was pessimistic about empiricism yet positive about social laws that explain continuity and development. As a result of this ambiguity, sociologists have followed two roads from then onwards.

The first path, characterised by the pessimistic viewpoint on empiricism, has encountered serious problems. For instance, as Denzin and Lincoln (2005) outline, a crisis of representation reoccurred in sociology in the mid 1980s. Academics from critical theory, feminist theory and post-colonial theory maintained that the neutrality of representation of the "other" was a fiction. They preferred theories that focus on patterns over theories that depart from causal loops and linear relations. This crisis continued throughout the 1990s, when post-structuralists and post-modernists criticised representation, legitimacy and the praxis of social sciences. Post-structuralists questioned the possibility of representing lived experiences without mediation. They claimed that these experiences came forth from the text of researchers and were therefore always mediated through their linguistic, social, cultural, ethnic and disciplinary background as well as their race and gender. Because they doubted the innovative potential of social research when society is only expressed in texts, they pleaded for action-oriented research. Post-modernists put aside the aspirations of *grand narratives* that try to offer all-embracing explanations for humanity, often mutually exclusive and oppressive. They turned to local, small-scale theories instead (Denzin and Lincoln 2005). The

R.J. in 't Veld (ed.), *Knowledge Democracy*, DOI 10.1007/978-3-642-11381-9_7,

road continuing from the flaws of empiricism and the embrace of the mediated gaze has led to a set of micro-sociologies and qualitative methods to accompany their followers.

The foundation of the other path was laid by Comte's positive conviction that social laws can indeed be discovered, but have not been discovered so far. This is a problem waiting to be fixed, be it not by sociologists alone. Sociologists' by far biggest problem is, according to Lopreato and Crippen (1999), that they fail to provide even one law or principle general enough to suggest a large number of logically interrelated hypotheses. This failure implies that social sciences also lack "the logic needed for coherent conceptualisation and operationalisation, appropriate methods for falsification, and hence the guidance toward a growing body of systematic, cumulative knowledge represented by a hierarchy of theoretical propositions cutting across the entire institutional framework" (p. xii). This road led some sociologists to seek rapprochement to natural sciences in order to borrow tools proven successful there. Lopreato and Crippen warn that, unless sociology wants to be cancelled out of the intellectual landscape in the next few decades, it will have to participate in the scientific revolution that evolutionary biology has started and that has infected so many other disciplines since: "Here, more than anywhere else, is where the action is today in behavioural science" (p. xiii).

7.2 Can the social be researched?

Both roads, divergent as they might be, are similar in one respect: they lead to research activities. The unspoken assumption is that society can be researched. For sociologists, this is not a strange assumption, for it is the legitimation of their activities. But some scholars have taken neither road. Baudrillard, for instance, doubts a legitimate ground for sociology. In his 1983 essay *In the shadow of the silent majorities* he calls the social a "spongy referent", an "opaque but equally translucent reality", a "nothingness" he sums up with "the masses" (p. 1). A mass is a highly implosive phenomenon that consists in its silence, a "black hole which engulfs the social" (p. 3). Understanding a mass as a black hole, Baudrillard says, is the opposite of sociological understanding, which has to rely on a "positive and definitive hypothesis of the social" (p. 4). He states that the silent majority of the masses as an imaginary referent does not mean it is not there, but that it is impossible to represent it. The masses are no longer referents, because they do not want to belong to the order of representation. They do not speak out, they are polled. They do not think, they are researched. The referendum has replaced the political referent. Opinion polls, questionnaires, referendums and the media are the operating parts that no longer belong to a representative dimension, but to a simulative one. The significance of the silence is paradoxical: it is not a silence that does not speak, but a silence that forbids that it is spoken for.

7.3 Fluid knowledge

There is another point to be made about researching the social. Giddens (1990) says that more sociological knowledge does not lead to more control of social development, because "the development of sociological knowledge is parasitical upon lay agents' concepts; on the other hand, notions coined in the meta-languages of the social sciences routinely re-enter the universe of actions they were initially formulated to describe or account for" (p. 15). Giddens calls this "double hermeneutics", to explain how no knowledge under conditions of modernity is knowledge in the sense of "to know". This reflexive relation actively constitutes behaviour and practices. As a consequence, knowledge of the social is fluid, dynamic, contingent and open for revision. In 't Veld (2008) stresses the reflexive character of social systems as well and hypothesises that human reflection can in effect lead up to the negation of knowledge about the social altogether. There is a paradoxical relationship between knowledge production about behaviour and the situation it produces. As knowledge production grows, society learns to respond more quickly with a potential negation of that knowledge as a consequence. Society can undo knowledge about itself.

The above can be seen as an indication for a crisis in representation. This crisis is not limited to the study of society, but is also felt in other domains where representation is sought after. In media, for instance, we see the cinematic self (Denzin 1999, in Holstein and Gubrium 2000) as an identity that is shaped or informed by Hollywood alongside the rise of platforms for self-representation. Holstein and Gubrium refer to an explosion of self-presentation in America at the turn of the twenty-first century, "where nothing holds selves in place for any length of time and all manner of self-definitions collide with each other" (p. 66).

In a world where the self is considered to be scattered and represented in multiple places, where is there room for the rationale of representation and democracy? Who do politicians represent, if they do so at all?

7.4 Crisis in democracy

Nothing can represent the silent majority and that is, says Baudrillard (1983), its revenge. For centuries it seemed that power rested upon the passivity of the masses, but the force of inertia which power has stirred up, now turns against it as a sign of its own death. Therefore, strategies are developed to reverse the process: from passivity to participation, from silence to speaking. But it is too late, says Baudrillard: the threshold of the critical mass, the involution from the social by inertia, is crossed. To prevent the mass to fall back into its silence and inertia, it is listened (in) to and questioned in order to worm out some oracle. Hence the universal predominance of information and statistics. But instead of energising masses, information produces only more mass. Masses absorb all signs, meanings and messages without beaming them back to a central intelligence: they consume them. Baudrillard defines the masses as cemeteries for the dying social.

7.5 Active citizenship

We recognise the strategy of energising the mass in new transactions politicians seek under the header of "active citizenship". As I demonstrated elsewhere (Basten 2002), this is a slippery term that depends on definitions of both "active" and "citizenship". People who are busy solving social problems do not refer to themselves in these terms. A lesson most politicians learn today, is that when calling upon "the masses" (and their call for active citizenship is an example of such a generic strategy), they get no response. Masses cannot be represented. Baudrillard stresses that the imperative of meaning production that is expressed in the constantly renewed imperative of moralising information (to inform better, socialise better, elevate the cultural level of the masses) is nonsense. None of the efforts has effectuated a conversion to the seriousness of the content, not even to the seriousness of the code. It is also nonsense, he continues, to claim that the masses are fooled. That the masses would spontaneously strive for the natural light of rationality has always been a hypocritical hypothesis to secure the intellectual peace of the producers of meaning and to avert the opposite: masses have always rejected meaning and satisfied their lust for spectacle in full freedom. The denial of this freedom is robbing the silent masses of their indifference; even their apathy cannot be theirs. Hence the increasingly louder cries for active citizenship. This appeal to a moral responsibility, however, is largely defined in terms of effectuating policies, not in terms of co-designing or judging them. Transactions are mere quasi-mutualities in giving and taking, new acts of sociality without genuinely sharing power. Ironically, activities from concerned citizens remain unnoticed or unwanted by politics (Basten 2002, Marres 2005, Verhoeven 2009).

7.6 Emotion and vitalism

Another approach to address masses is to appeal to emotions and dismiss knowledge or reason altogether. Seeking to represent *vox populi*, politicians reach out to tribes and try to establish an artificial sense of kinship. Maffesoli (1996) claims that mass culture has disintegrated and that social existence is conducted through fragmented tribal groupings, with a collective feeling of *puissance*. Puissance, as the inherent energy and vital force of the people, is opposite to *pouvoir*, the power of institutions. Like Baudrillard, Maffesoli does not see the twentieth century masses in terms of the proletariat or other classes, but as the people without a logic of identity or a precise goal (in fact, both say that sociology is unable to define masses, because the traditional categories for describing them have either become obsolete or proven inadequate to begin with). These masses are not subject to any historical movement and the tribes that crystallise from them are unstable. Maffesoli is interested in the untidy aspect of sociality and social configurations that go beyond individualism, "in other words, the undefined mass, the faceless crowd and the tribalism consisting of a patchwork of small local entities" (p. 9). He coins this most recent period the emphatic period, marked by the lack of differentiation and the loss in a collective subject. In this period we witness politicians becoming mediators of emotions, trying to connect to aesthetic tribes and tap into their vitalism. They happily join the self-representation circus one might even call hedonistic.

Political intellectuals who measure with the yardstick of the "project" will find the ambiguity and monstrosity of the masses always proof of their incapability of being something else. But masses, claims Maffesoli, are self-sufficient; they are not finalised, have no goals or projects, and do not even need political intellectuals. In fact, their "sole *raison d'être* is a preoccupation with the collective present" (p. 75).

7.7 Can the social be represented?

The problem of representation is also felt in democracy. As In 't Veld (2007) puts it, democracy suffers from its own success. Its representational form was useful in times when the scale of society was small, but it has currently become obsolete. Politicians who seek to represent a general public turn their backs on citizens who actively put forward their issues, arguing that these issues are particular (instead of general) and motivated by self-interest (as opposed to public interest). Indeed, as Mouffe (2007) points out, we live in a time that is characterised by our incapacity to think politically. This, she presumes, is due to the uncontested hegemony of liberalism. As she defines liberalism, it "is characterised by a rationalist and individualist approach which is unable to grasp adequately the pluralistic nature of the social world, with the conflicts that pluralism entails" (p. 2). In a rationalist belief in the availability of a universal consensus based on reason, the political dimension of choice and decision is naturally a blind spot. The liberal understanding of pluralism is that the many values and perspectives, although largely unknown due to empirical limitations, add up to some harmonious ensemble (Mouffe 2007). However, the political ambition to represent a general public that in turn represents this ensemble, is based on two dangerous abstractions, namely that of the general public and that of democracy.

Upscaling social groups to such a vague conglomerate as a "general public", has led to the creation of masses and the loss of the political. Masses do not make choices, Baudrillard analyses; they do not create difference, but indifference. And they have never consciously been politically or historically engaged, other than to leave everything in the lurch in full irresponsibility. A general public, in short, will not concern itself with anything other than the platitude of normal life. Addressing a general public equals setting this platitude as the standard and therewith making the stage for politics smaller. This is, however, not what politicians usually mean to do. In a Baudrillardian logic, they will make a comeback, but in grotesque forms. Masses do not reinterpret messages using their own codes: they simply do not care about codes. They accept everything and transform it *en bloc* into the spectacular, without needing a different code, a meaning or fundamental resistance. The masses display hyper conformity. They let everything slide into an undefined sphere. But our society is not ready to embrace its grieve over the loss of the real, of the power and, inherently, the loss of the social itself. We try to escape through an artificial revival of codes. This is a doubling of the representation: power survives only to conceal that it has vanished.

The second dangerous abstraction involves democracy. Marres (2005) wonders why political democracy is so often conceived of as an "architecture that remains unaffected by the issues that are processed in such a virtual edifice" and that it "is mostly assumed to be dedicated to the realisation of ideals … such as popular sovereignty, the inclusive community, or the public use of reason" (p. 136). Neglect of the effects of issues and consequent social reconfigurations results in poor handling of social concerns. In 't Veld (2007) analyses this poor handling as the lack of attention for the intensity of a preference and also as the outcome of Arrow's paradox which leads to decisions nobody understands, although they were based on rational arguments. This is in line with Mouffe's conclusion referred to above about liberalism's incapacity to think politically. What is at stake is what Mouffe labels an agonistic struggle between opposing hegemonic projects that can never be reconciled rationally, but that at the same time are contained in the belief that a democracy is the best choice. A democracy that does not deal with real people and real issues is a danger to itself, because disappointment in democracy will turn agonistic struggles into antagonistic ones, as people are either excluded or exit on their own choice.

7.8 Towards a knowledge democracy

A demos is understood to deliberate beforehand. Some say the demos has dissolved into masses that do not care for reasoning Others are more optimistic. They focus on new methods for knowledge production about the social and develop tools to analyse narratives as the action and reflection of meaning production. I am among them and I try to connect these new methods to democracy. If we compare social sciences with democracy, we see that democracy is a closed questionnaire from which citizens can choose one answer every once in a while. For a long time this was also the dominant method in sociology. But quantitative and qualitative methods are colliding, offering possibilities to engage larger amounts of participants in research with the same depth earlier reserved for small scale analysis (Thrift 2006). New research methods, so I claim, provide us with new building blocks for a knowledge democracy: they give us insight into degrees of involvement, ranges of meaning production on an emotional and interpretative level, and varieties of concepts of truth. New ways of knowledge production can lead to new decision-making rationales based on scales of involvement.

7.9 The public

The crisis in social sciences is largely due to the empirical practice of squeezing social reality into fixed entities with variable qualities. Causality is then attributed to variables instead of agents. On the contrary, various micro-sociologies have focused on social processes, and branchings and turnings of interactions, yet the main empirical traditions of sociology ignore process issues altogether (Abbott 1992). This is the heritage of the ambiguous origins of sociology. To bring the two roads together, I propose neither a micro-sociology nor a macro-sociology, but a meso-sociology based on the mediating level of a public (for example Dijstelbloem 2008, Marres 2005, Verhoeven 2009). Public, as opposed to private, means out in the open and involving more than one. As it is impossible for social sciences to describe "the public", I suggest a different scale and the possibility of multiple, coexisting "publics". A public is neither a demos nor a mass or a tribe. A demos is a predefined community that holds negotiating and decision-making powers. It depends on its scale for its success. A too large demos will lose its cohesive "us". A mass is not a community, it is an indefinable entity that represents nothing and cannot be represented. Its scale is endless because it relies on negative definitions (it is not a demos, nor a nation, a village, the Irish, the one-eyed, and so on). To define an appropriate scale, the notion of "publics" can be helpful. A public is not a demos, for it is defined after an event. It is not a mass either, for it can actually be defined. And it is not a tribe, for it has an action perspective. The notion of "public" is the outcome of a renewed interest in pragmatist thinking about democracy and is defined as: "all of those who are affected by the indirect consequences of transactions to such an extent that it is deemed necessary to have those consequences systematically cared for" (Dewey 1927, as cited in Verhoeven 2009: 73). Analysing the debate between Lippmann and Dewey, Marres remarks that for both of them it is "precisely when existing institutional forms do not provide an adequate framework for the settlement of issues that publics must become involved" (p. 165). She also observes that they appreciate the failure to contain politics in available democratic procedures and subject definitions positively, because these bring to light insufficiencies of current institutional arrangements. This means that an outburst of collective grief, for instance after the death of Lady Diana, can be interpreted as the formation of a public. It certainly gave rise to a debate about the British monarchy. However, a public has not been formed, since there was no public involvement in this debate. At most, some members of the royalty became worried, but in the end there was no insufficiency of institutional arrangements.

Complex issues enable public involvement in politics. But it does more, since it solves a sociological Ouroboros (the ancient symbol of a serpent swallowing its own tail and forming a circle). Traditionally, the matter of who is to be studied is decided at forehand and therefore also forms the focus and outcome of the analysis. People respond from the perspective they were invited to speak from. This is most visible in a priori categories, where race, social class and gender seem to explain or negate conditions rather than that they are assumed to be possibly affected by other variables. Persons do not seem to matter. The criterion for the selection of respondents to be considered representatives of a group is established before the actual group they are supposed to represent is defined. All boundaries we draw are artificial, prompted by our research interest. We therefore only find, as it were, the representatives we were looking for. This is a puzzle of circularity which a post-analysis of groupings in terms of publics can help us solve.

7.10 Researching publics

If we want to research a public, we need to establish what it is that connects people in a public. Our first task then is to identify a public. Some authors (Verhoeven 2009 for example) presume that a public is activated by collective actors. They suggest that the actors are not part of the same public and that publics are homogeneous as far as their choice of collective actor is concerned. Others (Dijstelbloem 2008 for example) consider that a public consists of all those involved in an event or issue, suggesting that a public can be very heterogeneous in background and level of involvement; the motives of all those who make up the public can also be very heterogeneous, up to a degree of inherent antagonism and mutual exclusion (Marres 2005 for example). I will use a general description of the public and take as my starting point that the outlines of a public are defined by the people involved in an event. This raises some methodological issues (for instance: what precisely is an event?) I will not discuss here. Suffice it to say that I suggest that patterns in narrative data can inform us of events, which in turn can be used as attractors to further investigate the public concerned.

7.11 Complex adaptive systems

A public is an entity without a central intelligence, that is: it is not created by a god, a manager or a demagogue. In fact, it is a temporary configuration of a contingent collection of possible complex adaptive systems (Mouffe 2007 for example). As Kurtz and Snowden (2003) state, empirical research into complexity is rather recent. The ontology of a known world results in best practices and handbooks. The ontology of a knowable world leads us to experts and consultants. Both ontologies depart from cause-and-effect-relationships that are known, either by everybody (the former) or by some (the latter). Opposite to these ontologies, they propose the ontologies of chaos and complexity. The former has no (perceivable) cause-and-effect-relationships; the latter does, but these relationships can only be constructed a posteriori. A major challenge is that humans are not limited to one identity. In a complex human system, Kurtz and Snowden write, an agent is anything that has identity. The multiplicity of identities in one agent, for instance individual identities that allow for contingent behaviour (as a parent, as a professional, as a citizen, as an inhabitant, et cetera) causes a problem for defining the unit of analysis. So do collective identities that allow us to be part of groups (for instance the Maffesolian tribes). This is what I referred to above as the crisis of representation and the problem of circularity in choosing the representatives of groups. I think this challenge can be faced using the concept of public, defined as the people involved in an event. Once we identify a public, we can map its inner logic in terms of arguments, issues and perspectives and thus get around the problem of multiple identities by making these the focus of our research.

7.12 Conditions for the next level

The strategy for sociological research I propose is identification of publics by way of narrative patterns and, once identified, engaging the public in research (or becoming engaged in the public's research). This strategy can bring us closer to a knowledge democracy for several reasons, because it is inclusive and agenda-setting.

A narrative approach is considered by many to be an approach that gives voice to those who have been silenced or silent. The travellers on the path that was guided by pessimism ended up gaining a better insight into the ordinary social. Their methods are designed to analyse discursive practices and to reveal how people construct their lives around and in the midst of events. The drawback of their work, however, is that their attention for the ordinary social is based on both a priori and small scale groupings. We learn how specific people, selected on the criteria of categories, construct their lives, but we are unable to connect different research outcomes into a meaningful network of knowledge. Knowledge of the social remains fragmented. I suggest using the event as a binding variable. Events create publics and these should be the object of our studies. Identification and analysis of narrative patterns teach us the events we live by, the way we make sense of these events and how we evaluate and value them. Patterns in complex adaptive systems and therewith identified publics guide the research agenda. Identifying patterns and publics is a political act in itself: it matters who identifies. It could be sociologists or the media, but in fact it could be anyone with access to data and skills in handling information and creating knowledge.

Moreover, publics can become events on their own, generating new publics. Whoever does not like to wait for evolution to take its course can actually create new patterns. The actions of many new social movements, politicians, and media can be understood in this light. We live, in fact, in a world in which event-making machines compete for our attention, aiming to change our daily patterns into a world in which these machines can become self-evident and legitimate (Thrift 2006 for example). Living in the discursive practices mentioned above, prefabricated narrative patterns are freely at our disposal. However, the patterns we actually live by and produce ourselves are largely matters of choice, although the price sometimes is extremely high. To be sure, our choices do not add up to a harmonious ideal. This is how publics can set the political agenda. In the knowledge democracy I envision, politicians do not address publics as much as publics address politicians. Representing publics demands a different set of political skills than just airing moral demands or co-opting tribal vitalism. It needs both recognising and being attentive to (that is researching) publics and acknowledging their agonistically unfolding (that is researching) meaning production. However, keeping the importance of real people and their events in mind, I do not propose a blueprint for future political behaviour, but I suggest a *modus operandi* will evolve as a result of learning from researching publics. If we want to take steps towards a knowledge democracy, we need to realise how intertwined sociological research and politics are and design a programme in which their inherent demands are settled. My guess is that the key to new political legitimation lies in facilitating spaces as in-between public locations for the mediation between an event and its handling, and in helping these spaces relate to each other while keeping in mind their agonistic nature (in short: boundary work).

7.13 Transdisciplinary research practices

The problem of representation in sociology can be tackled by opening up research for non-academics. As Thrift (2006) states, most methods are no longer the preserve of academic researchers: “To the extent that this has ever been true, it is quite clear that research methods now exist in a web of use which stretches from academe and government through to business and civil society” (p. 12–13). When these webs of use are heterogeneous in disciplines and knowledge sources, they are usually called “transdisciplinary practices”. In ’t Veld (2008) sums up four characteristics of this type of research: academic disciplines are integrated, knowledge production takes place in the context in which it will be used, the research team consists of all types of experiences and skills, and knowledge is produced in different sorts of organisations, not just universities. But, as Regeer and Bunders (2009) point out, as the term is derived from the substantive and organisational structure of universities, it is less meaningful for other organisations. The perspective of Regeer and Bunders remains scientific. This sounds reasonable considering my remarks earlier about who identifies patterns: access to relevant data and skills in handling information and creating knowledge are traditionally contained in science institutions. But with the widespread use of internet, access to relevant data does not have to form an obstacle to identify emerging patterns. Our empirical limitations do not preclude the possibility that there could be enough data to see the contours of a pattern arise. Individual abilities and a supporting infrastructure (Thrift 2006 for example) facilitate our awareness of large-scale patterns (Kurtz and Snowden 2003). Moreover, internet evolves to a space where individuals not only consult, but also deposit information. As a consequence, narrated events flourish and it will be easier to identify virtual publics. Furthermore, our current society is more highly educated than ever (Basten 2008) and skills in handling information and creating knowledge are more current than ever before. From a traditional point of view, I therefore believe it is legitimate to restrict transdisciplinary research to science, but I perceive this restriction to be unnecessary nowadays.

Events create publics and all those involved can initiate research, inviting others to join. Therefore I propose to rename transdisciplinary practices to "researching publics". If the pattern is that existing institutional forms do not provide an adequate framework for the settlement of issues and a public subsequently arises to remedy this failing, then there is no reason to limit this pattern to politics instead of extending it to science. In the latter case, one can think of science institutions that do not provide an adequate framework for understanding the social and a public that arises to correct conclusions that derive from categorical thinking and a priori groupings.

7.14 Public knowledge

Renaming transdisciplinary practices to "researching publics" is not just semantics. It is to stress that science does not hold a monopoly over knowledge and that research can be a democratic way of producing knowledge by solving the problem of the mediated gaze through the involvement of the "other" as co-researcher. Researchers, policy-makers, clients, professionals, and other stakeholders all become the "other" and can test and adjust their mutual assumptions. In a way, everybody is always researching. In the same manner as trained researchers construct meaning, laymen construct facts from interpretations and meanings (Olesen 2005). In most research academics do this solo, whereas in researching publics researchers and laymen construct knowledge together. This assures that the representations and constructs are co-products, but only under the condition of an equal contribution of all stakeholders (for example Regeer and Bunders 2009, In 't Veld 2008). Validity is then the agreed and preliminary truth that arises out of negotiations (Guba and Lincoln 2005), because the involvement of relevant actors in the process of knowledge co-creation ensures extended peer review (Regeer and Bunders 2009).

As it was conceptually developed by American pragmatists, publics are inherently tied to democracies. In fact, they arise when democracies fail to settle affairs. Traditionally, these affairs are of a political nature. In this chapter I propose they can be of an ontological nature as well. But the important part of the definition is the relationship to democracies. This relationship implies that publics consists of citizens. The notion of citizens' knowledge, however, can be too limited to cover the full potential of human experience. Today, the word "citizen" is used to refer to a human residual that is left once people are stripped of their academic, professional, governmental, personal, etcetera knowledge and experience. It is mostly used in negative terms (non-academic, non-professional, non-governmental, et cetera). But being a laymen in one field does not preclude being an expert in another. Especially when it comes to experience and meaning, it is hard to find people who are non-experts in their own lives. The complexity of the problem does not define the public, the level of involvement with an event and its characteristics does. The heterogeneity of publics assures that their participants (academics, professionals, volunteers, business people, parents, in short: all those affected by the event) are all experts in some field connected to the event, be it on an abstract level, a local level or even a tacit level. There is no room for arrogance or pessimism when it comes to non-academic knowledge about these events. Therefore, I prefer to speak of "public knowledge". This knowledge is brought about in a joint effort to make the affair manageable by politics.

To reach this goal and establish an equal contribution and fair negotiation, researching publics must be designed as democratic spaces. Elements for the design of transdisciplinary research can be helpful, such as their focus on learning and reflection from a contingent perspective and their experimental and innovative character, which requires both creativity and an action perspective.

7.15 Democratic spaces

Changing narrative patterns represent events that reflect (in both senses of the word) social practices and therewith present a challenge to the existing hegemony. In other words, publics challenge the existing order because it cannot offer the proper handling of events. Anyone involved in current politics is aware of this, but appreciates it mostly negatively, labelling it as a displacement of politics with democratic deficits as a result (for example, Marres 2005, Verhoeven 2009). But as Marres (2005) notes, this detour of issues via a public can also be appreciated positively: only displacements of a particular nature show signs of democratic deficits. According to Marres, involving publics is a process of opening up an issue for the public (which I call the identification of an event; the researching public can be both object and subject), then actively shifting the issue away from existing institutions that fail to provide a settlement for them (displacement), so that the public can articulate the issue (researching public as a subject) and find the addressee capable of resolving it. Whether a democratic deficit occurs or not is a matter of good or bad displacement. Bad displacement means privatising or politicising the issue, keeping it away from its public or shifting it to locations that harm the opportunities for the articulation of public affairs or make this impossible. Good displacement means shifting the issue to locations that are hospitable to its articulation and allow for (re)configurations of rules, ideals, routines, actors, claims and definitions (Marres 2005). In other words, it means offering the procedural conditions for a researching public. Although policy-makers can be part of publics, they need to remain in service of the public. In general, paraphrasing American police officers addressing suspects in cars, we need to say to the existing structures: "Step away from the public."

Displacing issues means that politicians or governments do not have a monopoly over democracy. We need to consider democracy as a matter of both politics and publics. This goes against current conceptions of politicians and governments about who decides what the issues are and how they are supposed to be addressed. However, media, sociologists and, in fact, anyone with the capacity to identify patterns and publics, should be supported instead of hindered in their researching publics activities. This entails a difficult but important task for meso-sociology, since it must be susceptible to new patterns and publics and at the same time put these on an official research agenda as results of institutional failure (including possibly its own) to handle events if means are not otherwise generated. It requires a paradoxical attitude: being committed to create productive researching publics, whilst being indifferent to the outcomes. Marres (2005) states that it is inappropriate to uphold a legitimate order as the standard a practice must live up to. This does not mean that democratic procedures, subject definitions and ideals are left out of the process. On the contrary: to open up issues for public involvement requires a healthy dose of disrespect for procedural obligations, but once democratic spaces have been modified so as to facilitate the articulation of a public affair, procedural constraints are among the prime instruments available to prevent the disintegration of such spaces and the disarticulation of the affair in question. In order to evaluate the level of democracy in publics, we need to see it in the light of their practical achievement and we need to take into account how democratic ideals are effectively evoked (Marres 2005).

In the so-called democratic spaces, we do not so much learn the operations of a formal democracy, but we learn to produce knowledge under democratic conditions. Democratic spaces are primarily aimed at articulating the issue well and finding the proper addressee, rather than solving the issue. It is, as I noted earlier, the public that addresses politicians, not the other way around.

8 Relevant Research in a Knowledge Democracy: Citizens' Participation in Defining Research Agendas for Europe

Anders Jacobi, Lars Klüver and Mikko Rask

Abstract

In our rapidly changing societies there is an on-going and increasing demand for research and development of science and technology. Therefore defining of research agendas becomes of great importance for the societal development. In a democratic perspective the process of defining relevant and proactive research agendas could in many respects gain from consultation of citizens. The citizens are the carriers of the concerns and expectations for the future and with the right facilitating methods, such concerns and expectations can be collected and transformed into relevant research agendas. In the case of involving citizens in identifying new and emerging needs for S&T, these added qualities to the analysis are extremely relevant. The need for high political credibility and for counteracting the risk of lobbying taking over the search for new research agendas is prominent. The knowledgebase needs to be widened into social life in order to be able to identify the emerging issues among the public. The new research agendas may very well be found among some of the tensions and frictions in our societies, for example social problems, health challenges and work life balance, and the citizens have special qualifications for identifying those.

Europe has built up a profound experience of citizen consultation on science and technology issues during the last 20 years, mainly through technology assessment activities in the member states, but a few also trans-national experiences[1]. These examples show that lay citizens are fully capable of contributing with strict analysis, unique and original perspectives, and relevant value-based assessments on highly complex and specialised issues.

In this chapter we argue that the creation of European citizen participation processes will allow for analysing different sets of knowledge about everyday reasoning, daily life and locality that contain cultural values and biases within a

---

[1] For example, The Prise project www.prise.oeaw.ac.at, STOA Long Distance Transport project http://www.tekno.dk/subpage.php3?article=1386&survey=15&language=uk. Meeting if Minds www.meetingmindseurope.org

R.J. in 't Veld (ed.), *Knowledge Democracy*, DOI 10.1007/978-3-642-11381-9_8,

societal, social and cultural context, and transform this analysis into relevant research agendas for European research and development. We focus on an on-going action research project, CIVISTI, which aims at identifying emerging issues for European S&T and producing a set of policy options of relevance to future European framework programmes. We present and discuss the ideas behind and the methodology for consulting European citizens. On the basis of the CIVISTI case we argue that involving citizens in defining research agendas will contribute to the democratisation of knowledge and knowledge production. This is in our view a corner stone in a knowledge democracy.

8.1 Introduction: foresight and citizens' participation on a transnational level

The European society today changes and develops rapidly and science and technology have an important role in this development both as knowledge base for decision-making and as an accelerator of innovation and societal development. This means an increasing demand for research in new science and technology to support the societal development and handle societal challenges, and therefore the defining of research agendas becomes increasingly important.

In a society where development is so closely linked to research there is great need for interaction between civil society and the Science and Technology community to narrow the gap between these two realms, which threatens to be distanced from each other due to the specialising and autonomous tendencies of the latter. Therefore, it is currently a commonly shared understanding in several contexts of S&T policy and research that narrowly rationalistic, technology-centred and expert-based decision-making in science and technology is in a state of crisis. The European controversy over biotechnology exemplifies the symptoms of the crisis: the insufficiency of democratic legitimacy and social acceptance, and the difficulty of effective policy-making (see for example, Durant 1998). The introduction of participatory forms of governance has been the generally recommended correction to the assumed problems of technical decision-making (see for example, Frewer 2001). Research fields such as the social study of science and technology (for example, Jasanoff et al. 1995), sociology of public understanding of science (for example, Irwin 1995), risk studies (for example, Jaeger et al. 2001) and studies in technology assessment and fore-sight (for example, Joss 2002) have suggested that S&T decision-making would strongly benefit of increasing participation by citizens, stakeholders and heterogeneous experts external to specific fields of S&T. Recommendations for increasing participation have also been made in various policy contexts. The need for public involvement in the agenda-setting for European policies and priorities has been indicated in documents and activities of the European Union, such as the Lisbon Agenda, the Plan D initiatives, the Aarhus Convention, in the Science and Society Action Plan of FP6 and the Science in Society activities of FP7 (See, EC 2001, 2002).

8.1.1 Foresight in Europe

Foresight praxis in Europe has taken place for many years but it has developed drastically during the last 5–10 years. This development is to a large degree motivated by the activities of the European Commission[2,3]. Foresight activities have mostly taken place on regional and national level, while trans-national foresight – medium- as well as long-term – has been far more limited and has not yet reached a level that comes near to the regional and national activities.

The praxis of foresight is still dominated by expert and stakeholder involvement, and a methodology that allows for relatively low transparency for the surrounding society. Foresight often takes place in closed scientific/political forums. However there is a movement towards the principles of open, transparent and public foresight processes and in the foresight community there is a broad acceptance of this.

8.1.2 Citizen participation in Europe

Europe has built up a profound experience of citizen consultation on science and technology issues during the last 20 years. This experience is mainly based on technology assessment activities in the member states, and again trans-national experiences are very limited. But during the last 5 years, the national experience has been supplemented with a few examples of trans-European activities[4], and also the world's first global citizen consultation[5]. The multitude of activities has made use of a comparable multitude of participatory methods, tailored to specific issues, problem situations and contexts[6].

The experience from the large number of participatory projects conducted for example by The Danish Board of Technology is that if supplied with the necessary information and surrounded by a proper project set-up and proper project management, lay citizens are fully capable of contributing with strict analysis, unique and original perspectives, and relevant value-based assessments to highly complex

---

[2] The European Foresight Sharing Platform has established monitoring, a web-based training and information tool (For-Learn), and has generally promoted foresight in the framework programmes and the EU member states http://cordis.europa.eu/foresight/platform3.htm

[3] The ForSociety ERA-net has established benchmarking and evaluation procedures, methodology assessments, et cetera, and has networked 16 EU member states around the idea of foresight. http://www.tekno.dk/EPTA/projects.php?pid=140

[4] Such as for example the "Meetings of Minds" project under the Science and Society Action Plan of FP6, and the PRISE project of the PASR programme of FP7.

[5] World Wide Views on Global Warming is the first ever global citizen consultation www.wwviews.org

[6] Some of the available and well tested methods are the Consensus Conference; Citizen Summit; Voting Conference; Interview Meetings; Scenario Workshop; Citizen Jury.

and specialised issues. Citizen participation consequently opens up for new roles and functions of policy analysis[7].

Citizen consultation adds to other forms of analysis in several unique ways that can be divided in two overall perspectives; democratic perspectives and perspectives about the societal relevance of the analysis.
Democratic perspectives:

- Citizens carry a democratic credibility into the analysis, which is intuitively acknowledged by political decision-makers.
- Citizens are independent of the direct interests often involved in science and technology issues, which adds to the credibility of the process, and makes a more objective analysis possible.
- Citizens can play a role comparable to the jury in the courtroom – in order to convince them, the actors will have to put forward their arguments, which adds to the transparency of the analytical process.

Perspectives related to the societal relevance of the analysis:

- The knowledgebase becomes more relevant, when the scientific approaches are supplemented with daily life experience and "tacit knowledge".
- Citizen consultation often leads to results, which are recognised as socially robust. The citizen includes the societal "frictions" in their considerations, which makes them relevant in proactive policy-making.
- The complexity of the issue is most often embraced very well through citizen consultation processes, which may be explained by the fact that the citizens tend to look at the issue from the context viewpoint – instead of the other way around.

Citizen participation also has limitations:

- While citizen participation has some obvious democratic advantages in relation to policy analysis and advice, the scientific or professional value of citizen participation has been questioned.
- Some experts and stakeholders have criticised citizen participation for not giving useful input because citizens simply don't have the expert knowledge needed to give meaningful input for political decisions on specific issues.

We believe that the right set-up of participation and expert involvement is the answer to this critic.

---

[7] The EUROPTA project (FP5): Klüver, L. et al. "European participatory technology assessment", at www.tekno.dk/europta. Or, "Participatory technology assessment; European perspectives", ed. Joss & Bellucci, Centre for the study of democracy, London, 2002.

8.1.3 Combining foresight with citizen participation

Characteristic to long-term futures research, both in its traditional and current form, is that visions of future have mostly been build on the basis of the ideas and concerns of futurists, scientific and technical experts, and societal visionaries. This has contributed to a dominance of techno-economic framing of future challenges and in the tendency to seek remedies from experts' visions of techno-science. Such were the findings of a recent report by ForSociety ERA-net project[8] that studied the state-of-the-art of the European foresight: Most foresight projects involve national policy-makers and S&T experts, while they neglect citizen participation in their methodologies. ForSociety also concluded that the issues of European foresights studies focus mainly on R&D development and competitiveness, thus giving a limited picture of broader future issues such as trans-national infrastructures, natural resources and demography.

These limitations can in many ways be dealt with by combining foresight with citizen participation. Combining the two approaches can potentially broaden the picture of the future issues and enhance the relevance of the policy advices produced by foresight. On the other hand citizen participation should be build upon the knowledge of S&T experts to ensure the quality of the results of citizen participation. The involvement of S&T experts and knowledge in building a knowledge base for the participatory process and in analysing the results of the participatory process can comply with some of the critics of citizens' participation for not having scientific value.

So while there is much research and praxis experimentation that currently focuses on both foresight and citizen participation – separately – there is less attention to the combination of the two. We believe that there is a high potential of finding new means to tackle some of the problems of foresight in the intersection of foresight activity and the deliberative participatory approach; the combination of these two could be called Long-term Participatory Foresight.

8.1.4 Defining new research agendas

In the specific case of identifying new and emerging needs for S&T on a European level, the added qualities of citizen participation to the analysis are very relevant. The need for high political credibility and for counteracting the risk of lobbying taking over the search for new research agendas is prominent. The knowledgebase needs to be widened by identifying the emerging issues among the public. The new research agendas may very well be found among some of the tensions and frictions in our societies, for example social problems, health challenges and work life balance, and through their daily life experience the citizens have an-other viewpoint than scientist and thereby special qualifications for identifying those. Instead of analysing the needs for S&T from the viewpoint of the scientific disciplines

[8] See www.eranet-forsociety.net

(inside-out perspective) there is a need to include the opposite perspective – looking at the S&T needs from outside. And finally, for a search of new research agendas to gain legitimacy there has to be a very high standard of transparency in the search process, which a properly designed citizen consultation can supply.

8.2. The CIVISTI case: citizens' visions of European research

For Europe to become the most advanced knowledge society in the world, it is imperative that legitimate societal concerns and needs related to science and technology development are taken on board, entailing an enhanced democratic debate with a more engaged and informed public and better conditions for collective choices on science issues. Knowledge and innovation could very well become the main sources of wealth creation globally, and that societal relevance of science and technology will enhance the European economy in the global competition. EU Seventh Framework programme aims at increasing the societal relevance of research, and thus encourages greater public engagement and promotes the participation of society in research and science policy-making. This change in perspective recognises that research activities are a special type of social activity that is embedded in a wider societal context.

CIVISTI[9] (2008–2011) is medium-scale action research project under the EU Seventh Framework Programme. The project involves seven partner organisations[10] from smaller countries across EU, which are selected to provide a balance of geographical representation from the European area. The participating organisation include public technology assessment institutes, research institutes in the field of consumer, innovation policy and market research, and a governmental S&T advisory body.

The CIVISTI project is based upon the idea that the process of defining relevant and proactive research agendas could in many respects gain from the consultation of citizens (for example independence of direct interests, democratic credibility, wider knowledge and value base etc.). Our societies are changing rapidly as a consequence of globalisation, new technologies, multi-cultural societies, media developments, environmental and climate challenges, new energy futures, increasing welfare and consumption, etc. These are developments, which all involve an interface between science, technology and society and raise issues arise about societal management of the involved needs and uncertainties – for society as well as for the individual.

---

[9] For further information, see http://www.civisti.org/.

[10] **Denmark (1)**: The Danish Board of Technology; **Finland (2)**: National Consumer Research Centre; **Belgium (3)**: IST, Institute Society and Technology; **Malta (4)**: Malta Council for Science and Technology; **Bulgaria (5)**: Applied Research and Communication Fund, ARC; **Hungary (6)**: Medián Opinion and Market Research Institute; **Austria (7)**: Austrian Academy of Sciences, Institute of Technology Assessment, OeAW-ITA.

The purpose of the CIVISTI project is to help European decision-makers in the process of defining relevant and proactive research agendas. This will be based upon a novel process of citizen participation in seven member states, supported by the analytical capacity of experts and stakeholders. CIVISTI will produce a list of new and emerging issues for European S&T. This list will be direct input for the design of the future EU research policy and more specifically CIVISTI will produce a set of policy options of relevance to future European framework programmes (FP8).

8.2.1 Methodological considerations

CIVISTI is designed to specifically meet the objectives of the Blue Sky Re-search call[11]. This has been facilitated by an adaptive methodological approach from technology assessment of analysing the "problem situation" and designing the process to the specific needs (Decker and Ladakis 2004).

This approach has led to a logical set of considerations on the methodological design:

1. The call for directly applicable policy-relevance points at a methodology with a maximised political credibility and a direct link to the societal context for S&T, which again points at a method, which includes citizens as assessors and priority-setters;
2. The need for European applicability of the results points at a process that includes a wide set of cultures and a balance of geographical representation from the European map;
3. The integration of citizens and the extremely wide range of possible issues to take up in the process involve a problem of ensuring that these participants have a common knowledge on the diversity of developments that, so to say, can lead to the future. This point at defining certain questions that prompts the citizens to think of some important perspectives on the future. It also points at the inclusion of a common information-base for the involved citizens, to ensure that they have a ground level of knowledge about future thinking;
4. The need for identifying emerging issues makes it necessary to incorporate a structured approach to the search for "weak signals" and emerging trends, as well as for describing the desired futures, which could lead to new policy developments. Thus, the design must include the development of an analytical model, which facilitates the identification of the new and emerging issues that may affect European S&T;
5. There is a need for mirroring of the results into existing research activities (in search of the "new"), which demands the use of the knowledge and analytical

[11] The European Commission has published a Call for Proposals exclusively dedicated to Foresight research under the heading "Blue Sky Research on Emerging Issues affecting European S&T". This Call is funded out of the Seventh Framework Programme (FP7) in the form of collaborative research projects.

capabilities of experts and stakeholders in identifying, sorting and characterising the S&T component from the "emerging issues";

6. The need for integration of experts and stakeholders in an important phase of the process points at the installation of some mechanisms that can assure the authenticity of the results made by the citizens. This could be a surveillance mechanism or – as we have chosen – the citizens could be involved in the last phases to re-examine the results and state their priorities.

8.2.2 CIVISTI methodology

These considerations have resulted in a methodology that consists of three major steps. First citizens around Europe are asked about their visions for the future. Second experts and stakeholders analyse the citizens' visions and transform them into research agendas and policy options for European research. Thirdly the citizens are consulted again to validate and prioritise the new S&T agendas and policy options.

Step 1: asking European citizens about future visions

The first part of CIVSITI is the establishment of seven national Citizen Panels; one in each of the partner countries. The national Citizen Panels consist of approximately 25 citizens, which are selected from random (or quasi random) samples of citizens that are collected through different media, for example, from person registers or through newspaper announcements, from which target individuals are selected according to particular social criteria: sex, age, education, occupation and residence. The intent is to provide highly heterogeneous panels that to a large extent correspond with national population structures.

Each Citizen Panel makes a long-term view into the needs, wishes, concerns and challenges to the future through a process of deliberation, informed by introduction material and expert and stakeholder input. The information material is very important in creating the common knowledge base for the citizens. To make sure the information material is understandable and attractive to the citizens it is tested nationally on a small group of citizens and then improved and adjusted in relation to their comments.[12] Deliberations will be organised around a set of questions structured by two equally important perspectives:

1. What kind of challenges do citizens expect from the future, and what kind of research is needed to meet those challenges?
2. What kind of visions and wishes for the future should guide the European research agenda (normative perspective)?

[12] Find the information material at the Civisti website http://civisti.org/publications/information_material

The result is 70 visions for the future, 10 from each national Citizen Panel. These visions are created during 7 national two-day Citizen Consultations (carried out in May–June 2009).

Before the Citizen Consultations the citizens receive information material (in the form of a CIVISTI Magazine called "Eyes on Tomorrow") that will prompt them in a structured way to consider different aspects of the future in a 30–40 years perspective. The information material is designed to be inspiring more than limiting. The magazine describes different ways of thinking about the future and give examples of future visions. The citizens are also prompted during the Citizen Consultation – by the process itself and by a set of questions in a questions catalogue that is the same in all countries – to encourage views on both the past and the future, which are new or "below the radar" and not necessarily generally recognised as policy issues. The questions put to the panels in the first round of citizen consultation is broadly phrased in order to allow for original input and ideas from the citizens, but the replies given are as concrete as possible. This concreteness in the answers is reached through facilitation.

The 70 visions will in themselves be a result, since they will represent trends of relevance to S&T in the future.

Step 2: experts and stakeholders transforming citizens' visions into research agendas

In order to transform the insights of the citizens into operational recommendations for S&T policies and agendas, a filtering mechanism is developed, which can extract the S&T "component" from the 70 visions. The filter is an analytical model, which will first guide a clustering of the visions for overview and further analysing. The clustering includes characterising the profile of a typical vision by describing (quantitatively) the number of topics it includes and (qualitatively) in which ways it presents future issues[13].

The actual transforming of the citizens' visions, wishes and concerns into future research agendas will be made in a two-day expert- and stakeholder workshop in April 2010. The framework for speculation of new S&T policy options emerging from citizen visions practically builds on Kingdon's (1995) streams model (of policy agenda-setting), which is a widely applied approach in policy analysis (see Pralle 2006, Kingdon 1995). The model assumes that a successful design of policies relates to the bringing together of three kinds of elements: problems, solutions and political contexts. The streams model, translated into the vocabulary of the CIVISTI, proposes that policy design should consider how the new visions and proposals, as well as risk concerns raised by citizens, can be transferred to relevant

[13] It was the original intention to characterise the visions by distinguishing between single vs. multi thematic and abstract vs. concrete visions. The data only allowed, however, to count the average number of topics where as the level of abstraction (vs. concreteness) proved to he too difficult to judge, since most visions contain both abstract ideas and concrete examples.

policy contexts and dealt with in a productive way. Experts and stakeholders with insight into research policy and relevant research fields and is-sues will be responsible for making the citizens' input operative. The S&T issues will relate to scientific disciplines and technological development, and/or complex trans-disciplinary challenges. This will result in an overview of potential new areas for S&T, including an overview of policy options.

In other words there will be two overall results of the expert- and stakeholder workshop. The first is a list of research agendas derived from the citizens' visions. The second is a set of policy options related to these research agendas or to other aspects from the citizens' visions. These are the results that are given back to the citizens in the third step of the process.

Step 3: citizens validating and prioritising research agendas and policy opations

The third step is a quality and authenticity assurance and priority setting by the citizens. In terms of citizen participation philosophy, the involvement of experts and stakeholders in step 2 will represent a delegation of power over the results made by the citizens, and thus it will potentially degrade the authenticity of these results. Further, the new level of concreteness, which the experts and stakeholders will add to the issues of the citizens, will imply a risk of losing the visionary scope of these issues. To ensure that the S&T issues that come out of the valorisation process still attach to the real priorities of the citizens, a second round of citizen participation is made. The Citizen Panels will gather again for a one-day meeting in October 2010. The objectives of this meeting are the final priority decisions, including the quality and authenticity assurance by the citizens. The citizens′ will evaluate the way the experts and stakeholders have transformed their visions and the results of this work. The citizens′ will then state whether they are satisfied and if they can recognise their visions in the suggested research agendas and policy options. Further the seven Citizen Panels will prioritise the research agendas and policy options thereby giving their final recommendation to the European politicians about future research in Science and Technology.

8.2.3 Results of CIVISTI

The results of CIVISTI will be recommendations for future research agendas and policy options, which the citizens find most important for their future. The design of the results ensures that they can be fed directly into the processes of defining FP8. Experts and stakeholders in the S&T field will base these recommendations on 70 visions produced by European citizens with diversity in their cultural backgrounds and analysis. CIVISTI will look for similarities in as well as differences between the results of the national citizen consultations. Comparisons will be made after both phases of citizen consultation in order to be able to identify broader trends as well as weak signals.

8.2.4 Long-term Participatory Foresight

The CIVISTI project takes an original approach to identifying new and emerging issues for S&T activities still building upon the praxis that has been developed during the last four decades. This approach we have called Long-term Participatory Foresight. By that CIVISTI will contribute to the State-of-the-art in foresight. The methodological and experience-based additions from CIVISTI are very much coupled to the aspect of citizen consultation:

- A prominent product of Future Studies is trend-analysis, often presented as wide societal scenarios. CIVISTI will add to this tradition by inviting European citizens to describe their ideas of the developments of their societies. These visions will specifically be used in an analysis of their meaning for European S&T activities in the future.
- Horizon Scanning has during the last 10 years been developed into an important tool for Science, Technology and Innovation planning. The products often consist of a broad catalogue of signals and ideas, and a list of high priority themes. The methodology is diverse, and often includes face-to-face brainstorm sessions with experts/stakeholders/policy-makers, Delphi studies, open web-based templates for adding issues to the scanning, and different forms of interview techniques. Citizens have in some projects[14] had the possibility of inserting ideas through a website template. The approach of CIVISTI will add to the praxis of horizon scanning by delivering a methodology, which potentially can be used for structured regional/national/trans-national citizen contributions to horizon scanning, which could possibly increase the political relevance of the outcomes of the scanning.
- Foresight praxis in Europe has developed drastically during the last 5–10 years. The praxis of foresight, though, is still dominated by expert and stakeholder involvement, and a methodology that allows for relatively low transparency for the surrounding society. CIVISTI especially adds to the praxis of foresight by supplying means for long-term view on emerging issues for S&T planning that is based on a combination of citizen consultation and expert/stakeholder support.
- Trans-national foresight. The state-of-the-art for trans-national foresight – medium- as well as long-term – has not yet reached a level that comes near to the regional and national activities. CIVISTI will in many ways imply an important progress in this area by (a) concretely produce policy-relevant input to the European FP8 by making use of a trans-national setup; (b) increase the attention to the need for trans-national policy analysis in Europe; (c) add an important public participation element to the established procedures of defining the framework programmes;

[14] Examples are the UK Horizon Scan, and the Danish Horizon Scan.

(d) establish a method for trans-national public participation of high discourse ethical standard (authentic, transparent and fair).

8.3 Conclusion: the CIVISTI concept in relation to knowledge democracy

The CIVISTI case is an example of how citizens can be involved in defining research agendas. Below we will conclude on how CIVISTI gives an original contribution to long-term foresight by combining foresight with citizen participation and thereby connecting research and development of science and technology closer to civil society.

The increasing demand for science and technology in today's society underline the importance of how research agendas are defined. We believe that in a knowledge democracy where development is so closely linked to research there is great need for interaction between civil society and the Science and Technology community. Therefore in a democratic perspective the process of defining relevant and proactive research agendas could in many respects gain from consultation of citizens. Citizen participation in defining research agendas will contribute to the democratisation of knowledge and knowledge production. This is in our view a corner stone in a knowledge democracy.

Involving citizens in defining the long-term visions for the development of our society has the capability of meeting some of the challenges related to increasing political populism and short-term political decision-making affected by the ambition of being re-elected. Citizens can give independent input and offer new modes of insight and reflection in the knowledge production. Involving citizens the way it is done in the CIVISTI project also increases transparency, secure the relevance of future research and allow "below the radar" issues and "unwelcome knowledge" to come to light. In that way the CIVSTI methodology support pluralism in research.

In relation to knowledge democracy we believe that involving citizens in the defining of research agendas the way it is done in CIVISTI will contribute to the value of research and development of science and technology with:

- Democratic credibility;
- A wider knowledge- and value-base;
- Independence of direct interests;
- More socially robust research agendas;
- A new complexity – a view from the outside in on S&T needs.

In a knowledge democracy the dispersal of knowledge must flow freely. But also the production of knowledge should be based on democratic principles meaning that knowledge production must be open to input from all levels of society. This is what CIVISTI is trying to improve.

9 Why more knowledge could thwart democracy: configurations and fixations in the Dutch mega-stables debate

Katrien Termeer, Gerard Breeman, Maartje van Lieshout and Wieke Pot

Abstract

This chapter focuses on how governments can deal with knowledge-intensive issues. Especially it seeks to understand why information and knowledge could thwart democracy. Using the public debate about a mega-stable in a small town in the Netherlands, we demonstrate the role of communication and research in establishing and losing trust. In this town, citizens protested against the arrival of a mega-stable in their backyard, while politicians and researchers strongly supported the concept because of its alleged sustainable character. The more information and knowledge by means of research reports and information exchange evenings became available, the more people began to distrust their administrators and vice versa. Configuration theory, a social-cognitive approach to change, provided the theoretical basis to analyse this paradoxical situation. A configuration is characterised by a group of people with an intensive interaction pattern, agreed upon interaction rules and shared meanings. By being aware of the different configurations in which stakeholders operate, and using arguments which relate to these configurations, one might escape fixations in the decision-making process and the negative spiral of losing trust.

9.1 Introduction

In her 2002 Reith lectures, the British philosopher Onora O'Neill posed a puzzling question about why the increasing amount of information in our era of information technology does not coincide with rising levels of social trust. She wonders why we believe that more information, more knowledge and more transparency would increase trust in society and adds to the improvement of democracy. She states that "if making more information about more public policies, institutions and professionals more widely and freely available is the key to building trust, we must be well on the high road towards an ever more trusting society" (O'Neill 2002). Since this is not the case, as many public opinion polls show us time and again, we should look for alternative understandings of the relation between information and

R.J. in 't Veld (ed.), *Knowledge Democracy*, DOI 10.1007/978-3-642-11381-9_9,

knowledge on the one hand and trust and democracy on the other. In her mind, more information spreads suspicion more easily, causing distrust rather than trust.

In this chapter we describe a case study where the provision of more information about a wicked policy problem had some unexpected consequences. The more information was given and the more research was conducted, the worse the decision process proceeded. Our case study is about a decision-making process concerning the arrival of a "mega-stable" in a small municipality in the Netherlands.

A mega-stable combines scaling-up with the latest insights in the fields of sustainability, animal-welfare, animal-health, and landscaping. The concept of a mega-stable is developed by researchers, who are passionately engaged in so-called "mode-2 science" (Gibbons 1999). This means that the format of the stable is elaborated in transdisciplinary cooperation between researchers and private partners, and that they focus on people, planet, and profit, get civil society involved, and organise participatory workshops (Smeets 2009). Several research programmes have demonstrated the sustainability of mega-stables in the Netherlands. But this has appeared to be insufficient to raise public support.

On 11 February 2008, a town council in the South of the Netherlands agreed on the plans of the construction of a mega-stable, officially named as a "New Mixed Company" (NMC). This company would accommodate 3,700 sows, 9,700 pigs, 19,700 hogs, 1,200,000 chicks, and 74,000 chickens and would have its own fermentation installation, hatchery, and abattoir (Termeer et al. 2009). Supporters pose that this NMC is innovative, environmentally friendly, energy-sustainable, animal friendly, and fits very well in the landscape. However, the town council's approval triggered a lot of media attention. The policy-makers were overwhelmed with fierce protests and emotional reactions of the local citizens. Besides environmental and animal-related concerns, a local Medical Doctor emphasised the potential health risks of the mega-stable. The city council conducted additional research to take away the concerns. Consequently, the outcomes were interpreted very differently by advocates and opponents of the mega-stable. The enormous information overload caused citizens to distrust their administrators, rather than that it won their support for the NMC. The more information and knowledge by means of research reports and information became available, the more citizens began to distrust their administrators and vice versa. More information and more knowledge thwart democracy.

In the following we analyse this paradoxical situation, but we also provide ideas about how (local) governments could deal with sensitive and knowledge-intensive issues that trigger a lot of resistance and increase the levels of distrust. We use notions of the configuration theory and connect these with concepts from the trust literature. In the next section we first introduce our theoretical framework. We then argue that the combination of fixed beliefs in different groups and the misfit between knowledge-based argumentations and citizens' concerns, has caused a spiral of distrust. We finally discuss some possibilities policy-makers and process managers have to prevent and solve these kinds of negative spirals.

9.2 Theoretical framework

9.2.1 Configuration theory

Actors are continuously involved in sense-making processes in which they make their world logical and meaningful through talking and acting (Weick 1979, 1995). During these social-cognitive processes actors develop shared understandings, meanings, and rules of interaction (Weick 1995). The concept of configurations is used to describe the patterns that emerge from these sense-making processes. Configurations are social relationships between people who determine the meaning of what they do together. They can be characterised as a connection between a social structure, that consists of a stable pattern of interactions ("who"), agreed-upon rules of interaction ("how"), and a cognitive structure of shared meanings ("what"). Configurations usually do not coincide within existing arrangements like organisations or departments.

Configurations arise because people not only develop shared meanings in interactions but also often lean towards people with similar backgrounds, assumptions and beliefs (Van Dongen et al. 1996). Value judgements, rules of construction and routines are nested in the configurations. They structure the sub-sequent interactions, without fully determining them (cf. Giddens 1994). A dynamic process begins however when a configuration is confronted with other realities, people or interaction rules (Termeer and Kessener 2007). At the same time, this dynamic process has the tendency to stagnate immediately, because configurations tend to exclude other worldviews and thus become increasingly closed. "Through a process of interaction, members of a community come to use the same or similar cognitive mechanisms, engage in the same or similar acts and use the same or similar language to talk about thought and action. Group processes reinforce these, often promoting internal cohesion as an identity marker with respect to other communities" (Yanow 2003: 237). When actors become included in configurations, they run the risk of only confirming their own perspectives and stop being open to actors with different meanings or to different routines (Termeer 2009).

If meanings and rules of conduct become so self-evident that people are no longer capable to reflect on them, we speak of fixations (Van Dongen et al. 1996). In our case study, the relevant groups of actors were indeed no longer open to appreciate variety. Some of them had very clear ideas about the NMC, which did not change even when new reports with new information were released. Symptoms of fixations are taboos, repetition of moves, vicious circles or argumentation, exasperating delays or an escalated conflict. We assume that these fixations cause many barriers to effective decision-making processes. Breaking through these barriers requires critical investigations of these fixations and the mechanisms producing and perpetuating them (Termeer 2009).

Most people are often unaware of the fixed pattern which they have fallen into. Once fixations block further developments, intervention strategies are needed. Interventions are aimed at loosening up fixations and breaking through barriers to "revitalise" learning processes. Many scholars stress the difficulty of loosening up fixated patterns (Argyris 1990, Schön and Rein 1994, Van Eeten 1999b). In some situations, actors are no longer able to reflect and to change their behaviour. Following the social-cognitive approaches to change, we put forward that it is only possible to break through such fixations by changing the context (Termeer and Kessener 2007, Voogt 1991).

9.2.2 Dynamics of processes of trust

Trust is essential for making successful public policies (Breeman 2006). If the general public does not trust a policy plan in advance, it will be difficult to establish trust during implementation. Therefore, knowledge about the way in which trust is won and lost during the decision-making process is essential. Building trust is more than only communicating properly; knowledge about the background of the stakeholders, the configuration they are interacting in, and the social context in which the policy problem arises is essential for establishing and losing trust.

Trust is defined as "an intentional status of favourable expectations" (Castaldo 2002, Holton 1994). The basic idea is that humans continually interpret the behaviour of other people, the qualities of objects, and the features of events. They are constantly developing all kinds of intentional states through their interpretative activities. Following Searle (1983, 1996), we assume that intentional states only function "in relation to numerous other intentional states". Arriving at an intentional state of trusting happens through interpretative activities, which are structured by all kinds of other intentional states. This means that building trust is a rather subjective activity, although it takes place in interactions with other persons. Note however, that the reasons to justify one's trust do not depend on the consent of others. Trust does not need others to agree with the reasons provided. It is also not necessary that one's reasoning is based on rational argumentation (although this could be the case). Initially, only the person involved believes that he has good reasons to trust (Möllering 2001). Moreover, trust and distrust are always projected (O'Neill 2002). Usually, trust is assumed to be projected on other persons, but it can also be projected on something abstract such as democracy, or (the plans of) the municipality.

But beside good reasons for trusting, Möllering argues that people only come to a state of trust if they suspend uncertainties, ignorance, and risks. Trust involves situations in which persons are not entirely certain, but act as if they are certain. "Suspension, then, can be defined as the mechanism that brackets out uncertainty and ignorance, thus making interpretative knowledge momentarily "certain" and enabling the leap to favourable (or unfavourable) expectations" (cf. Giddens, 1991: 3, 244). Figure 9.1 summarises this process.

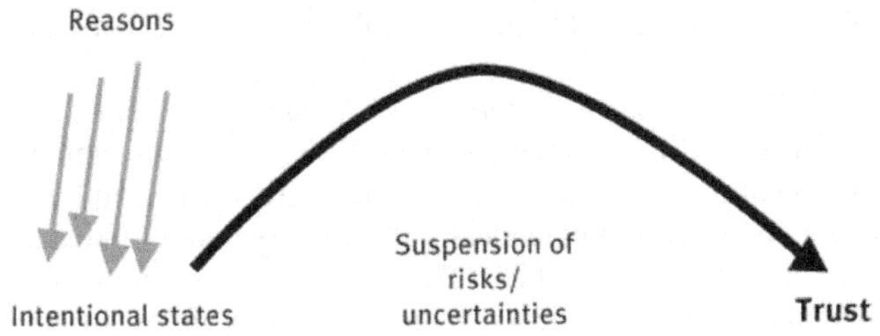

Fig. 9.1 Leap of trust.

Hence, through interpretation, a trustee gathers reasons for trusting. A precondition for these reasons is that they should relate fruitfully to the many other intentional states a trustee already possesses; they have to fall on fertile grounds. In addition, the trustee also needs encouragements to suspend uncertainties and risks to finally take the leap into trust. This is especially relevant when it concerns complex questions with high levels of uncertainty. This means that if someone wants to win the trust of another person, he must use argumentations and actions which relate to the experiences or intentional states of the other. Insight in the configurations in which people operate is therefore important.

9.3 Methods

To assess the issue, we held 17 semi-structured interviews. The themes we discussed were the decision-making process, the concept of the NMC, the interactions they were involved in, and the influence they (think they) have had. We also held several short interviews with local citizens at the supermarket on the basis of a couple of concrete questions. All these interviews were audio-taped and typed out verbatim. Subsequently, they were read repeatedly and analysed using the theoretical framework as discussed above. Additionally, we used websites, weblogs, and files of the municipality, province, the Ministry of Agriculture, Nature and Food Quality (ANF), and the local protest group to analyse our case. These files were mainly used as background information.

9.4 Results

9.4.1 Five configurations

We were able to distinguish the five following configurations: "1. NMC as mega-sustainable", "2. Mega-stable as mega-wrong", "3. An innovative, sustain-able company in our area", "4. No mega-stable in this area", and "5. Following procedures":

1. The configuration "NMC as mega-sustainable". Actors in this configuration have positive ideas about the NMC. In their minds, a NMC is a sustainable combination of livestock breeding, crop cultivation, manure processing, and energy production. The concept comes close to the ideas of "cradle to cradle" and is much more sustainable than "just any mega-stable". They argue that as long as people want to eat meat, sustainable meat production by means of a NMC is the way to do it. This configuration is not bound to the region. The actors involved helped to develop and promote the NMC concept on a national and international level for a longer period of time. These actors include researchers, scholars, initiating entrepreneurs, and some governmental officials.

2. The configuration "Mega-stable as mega-wrong". Actors within this configuration are against the development of mega-stables, which they downgrade to "pig flats". They find it unethical to keep so many animals on such a small area. Furthermore, they argue that the expansion of the intensive livestock sector brings along unjustified and unknown health risks. Actors involved in this configuration are nationally operating political parties, animal activists, and environmental groups. But also public officials from within the agricultural sector are part of this configuration. They believe that mega-stables are a threat to the small family farms and to the reputation of the entire sector.

3. The configuration "An innovative, sustainable company in our area". Actors in this configuration consider the innovative, sustainable mega-company to be a welcome development. Such an innovative concept has not been built anywhere else, and, in their minds, it would be great if they would have the first. It also fits with their regional ambitions of sustainable and innovative agribusiness. Furthermore, they argue that if the NMC will not be built in this area, it is likely that other, less sustainable, mega-companies will be build there anyway. This configuration is regionally embedded, with the municipality and province as important actors.

4. The configuration "No mega-stable in this area". This configuration is against the building of a mega-stable in this particular area. It displays typical NIMBY-behaviour. Not the mega-stable itself, but the choice for this specific location is perceived as the problem. The countryside should remain open. Also, the consequences for public health are too uncertain. The actors in this configuration highlight that the NMC is not the only problem, but that their village is also being enclosed by a sand-processing installation in the adjacent river and the large scale development of an intensive glasshouse area. The NMC is seen as the straw that broke the camel's back. Representatives of this configuration are the village council, the local protest group and a large part of the village's citizens.

5. The configuration "Following procedures". In this configuration, procedural rationality takes the lead. As long as the NMC fits existing rules and legislation, a mega-stable is no problem. People in this configuration argue that they implement national programmes that fit with EU programmes. But they also argue that the municipality remains responsible for consequences of the NMC even though the

NMC has consequences across the borders of the municipality. Public officials from local, regional and national government are part of this configuration.

9.4.2 Tensions between configurations and a spiral of distrust

Configurations can be dynamic. However, in this case all configurations have fixed beliefs and convictions, deeply rooted in value systems and grounded in identity. All of them are relatively closed and mainly focused on confirming their own beliefs and excluding other opinions and arguments. Thus, when people of different configurations tried to communicate with each other, tensions were the result (see Figure 9.2).

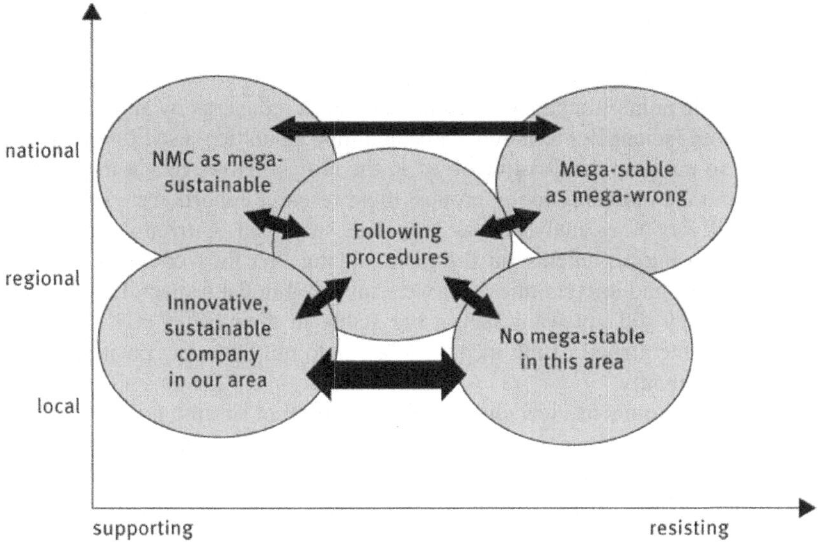

Fig. 9.2. Tensions between configurations.

In general terms, these tensions grow bigger if there are more interactions and if the differences in opinions are bigger. Thus, in our case, the tensions were especially strong between the actors of the locally embedded configurations "Innovative, sustainable company in our area" (the local advocates) and those from the configuration "No mega-stable in this area" (the local opponents). They were constantly confronted with each other in the decision-making process, because they were dependent of each other. They both got the feeling they were not heard nor properly understood by one another, which is typical for a confrontation of two groups with fixed beliefs. The actors from the configuration "Following procedures" were especially employed to avoid intervention and legitimise aloofness.

The tensions between these local configurations became evident rather late in the decision-making process. The citizens' involvement and protest began only after the building plans had become concrete. Citizens were invited earlier to information gatherings and workshops, but at that time the plans were rather vague and only a few very well-informed citizens showed up.

The city council was already convinced early on of the benefits of the NMC. It had put the risks and uncertainties between "imaginative brackets" and gave its full support to the plans of the NMC. The arguments of the entrepreneurs and scholars about mega-stables being very sustainable and innovative fitted very well with the entire set of mental states of the members of the city council. Especially the accountable alderman was pleased with the plan because he used to be an entrepreneur with an agricultural background himself. Somewhat to the surprise of the city council, it noticed that not all stakeholders shared this positive attitude towards the NMC. However, the council tried to win trust for this plan with the same arguments that were convincing to them. It communicated that the project was sustainable, would deliver employment, would improve animal welfare, and finally would be very innovative. All these arguments fitted within their set of mental states and hence, within their configuration.

As a reflex the policy-makers reacted to all citizens' concerns by announcing or conducting more (scientific) research. Time and time again they used research outcomes to try to mitigate the risks involved in the project. However, in the eyes of the citizens and the opposing lobby groups, these research reports were only more of the same. Every new analysis was met with suspicion. Citizens and protest groups put opposing arguments on the table, saying that they could not simply leap over the risks and uncertainties that were involved in the project. Beside their argument that they did not want such a big stable in their backyards, they also pointed out that the arrival of the mega-stable would not have any positive effect on the local community.

These different points of view characterise the different starting positions of the two configurations: the city council reasoning from a broader regional perspective, in which innovation, sustainability and entrepreneurship are important, and the local citizens and lobby groups reasoning from a local perspective, highlighting the absence of positive effects of the project for the local community. Strong fixations without any space for reflection emerged within these configurations. Their fixations also included images of each other. Actors from the configuration "Innovative, sustainable company in our area" were called too eager, and those from the configuration "No mega-stable in this area" too worried. Due to a lack of actual dialogue, the interaction between these two groups had the character of a recurrence of moves. In the end, the distrust shifted from the mega-stable concept onto the actors involved. Citizens blamed the alderman accountable for the project for being prejudiced. The supporters of the NMC on the other hand blamed the protest group's spokesman of creating and abusing people's fear. This turned out to be a bad situation for both the city council and citizens, because the council had to execute plans that were not supported by the general public, whereas citizens had the feeling they were not being heard or taken seriously.

The consequence of this situation was that every argument given by both parties was interpreted from a different perspective. The result was a spiral of distrust. This spiral started with annoyances. Actors first blamed each other for not listening or not wanting to understand one's position. Typical action-reaction patterns evolved, resulting in "dialogues of the deaf" (van Eeten 1999a) and a continuation of distrust. Every given argument became a reason to highlight the risks and uncertainties of the NMC. In this situation, we observed two processes which could follow each other in time, but could also occur at the same moment (Table 9.1). In the first phase, the configuration of regional advocates wanted to win trust by providing more information and discussing the risks and uncertainties involved through information exchange gatherings. These exchanges of information and debates however, only resulted in rising levels of distrust. During the second phase, key actors started blaming each other for all kinds of different things.

Table 9.1. Spiral of distrust

Process 1: Providing information, debating	Process 2: Blaming and perseverance of points of view
Effects:	Effects:
More information also leads to more counter-argumentations	Arousing a negative mood
More information reveals more risks and uncertainties	A negative interpretation of all information
More debates → more people get involved	Perseverance becomes a goal in itself
Simplification of the problem	Conspiracy theories
Final result: growing distrust	Final result: continuation of distrust

Process 1: More information and more debates aimed at building trust, lead to distrust

- Through the continuous debates and meetings about the NMC and the area around it, many citizens learned that the NMC was just one of the many projects that are on the roll in the area.
- Transparency and complete openness of information could result in selective shopping and the production of misinformation and suspicion (O'Neill 2002). Every new research and every new bit of information was used to sharpen the uncertainties.
- The numerous debates attracted many more parties than the city council had foreseen. National lobby groups who were against mega-stables in general affected the local debates.

- More debates and information resulted in simplified definitions of the problem. Political one-liners and emotional statements had a serious constraining effect on the processes.

Process 2: Blaming and perseverance of points of view

- With rising levels of distrust, the mood changed from discussing to blaming. Opponents started to exaggerate the risks by erecting billboards along the highway with families wearing gasmasks.
- Every piece of information was interpreted negatively. All new suggestions or plans from the city council were met with suspicion.
- The perseverance of their own position became a goal in itself. Giving in would mean losing out.
- The perseverance of positions resulted in conspiracy theories. The alderman was a Christian-Democrat and would have defended the agricultural interests against all prices, whereas the opponents would have conspired with the left-wing parties and environmental groups.

9.5 Strategies for reflection

What strategies are available to a local council in order to prevent the spread of suspicion and distrust, if not by providing more information or the conduction of more research? We answer this question by evaluating our case study, based on the notions presented in our theoretical framework. In general however, the best strategy is to prevent the growth of fixed beliefs that causes dialogues of the deaf and spirals of distrust. Once a decision-making process escalates and distrust rises it usually is very difficult to revitalise the process and regain trust. Trust comes on feet, but leaves on horseback.

9.5.1 Strategies to prevent fixations and negative spirals of distrust

Our case study shows that it is important to use arguments which relate to the configurations involved and the existent intentional states of people. So a first strategy governments could use would be to identify different configurations surrounding the sensitive policy issue. Yet this can be hard because configurations manifest themselves only if issues become concrete. In our case, we saw that citizens and their concerns and objections became only evident when the decision-making process was already in an advanced stage.

Second, governments could try to analyse its own configuration and identify possible blind spots. They could appoint a "devil's advocate" who criticises the council's argumentations and tries to identify other perspectives. In interactions between people there is a significant chance that a dominant discourse will arise quite quickly. The devil's advocate can continually try to find out what is being excluded, either consciously or subconsciously. Signals for such a "risk of a dominant discourse" are a big support or a large consensus. Usually this means that things are too good to be true. Processes of consensus seeking or political strategy are susceptible for exclusion, too.

A possible third strategy is to organise one's own reflection. Inevitably, case studies always provide backward glances. In retrospect it is easy to pinpoint the moments of lack of openness or to observe the weak signals of protests. However, during the heat of the policy processes most people are not able to reflect on what is going on. To paraphrase Mead: "we are conscious always of what we have done, never of doing it" (Mead 1934: 136). Scheduling fixed moments of reflection during intensive decision-making processes can help to anticipate and counter this mechanism of blindness.

Fourth, an essential strategy is to develop an advanced communication arrangement. Communicating uncertainties can help to establish trust. On the other hand, we saw that distributing information randomly can have severe consequences for democracy. More information is not always good (O'Neill 2002). The work in organisational studies shows that more information is not what people need when they are overwhelmed by equivocality (Weick 1995: 27). Weick proposes an alternative communication arrangement that focuses on values, priorities, and clarity about preferences to help people to be clear about what really matters to them (Weick 1995: 27). First of all, governments should stop their reflex of organising information exchange evenings when dealing with sensitive issues. These gatherings are usually seen as a one-way communication lane from government to citizen, adding only to the spread of suspicion and distrust.

9.5.2 Strategies to loosen up fixations and revitalise stagnated policy processes

In our case prevention strategies came too late. Fixations and distrust were already a fact. The decision-making process can be very costly, especially with regard to trust and democracy, if the process is continued in this context. Reflection is needed to loosen up fixations, break through barriers, and to revitalise learning processes. A first strategy can be to make fixations and the mechanisms underlying them explicit. We presented our own analysis to the members of the town and city council for instance. They recognised our findings and this helped them to become aware of the fixed pattern they had fallen into. In the case of new sensitive issues they would surely take advantage of these insights.

Initially, the town council did not allow us to discuss the ongoing decision-making process concerning the NMC. This fits with the theory that when fixations occur, people are no longer able or willing to reflect and to change their behaviour within the existing context. Trying harder does not suffice (Termeer and Kessener 2007). For instance, we organised a meeting of reflection with the town council, but this did not help because they reproduced their fixated patterns. According to the configuration theory it is only possible to break through fixations by organising context variation (Van Dongen et al. 1996, Voogt 1991). As an intervention we organised a new context: a role play. We first asked the administrators and the politicians of the municipality to imagine themselves as being part of a different configuration so that they would see other possible perspectives and feel different emotions. Then we asked them to use arguments which relate to these configurations to discuss different scenarios regarding the mega-stables. This exercise resulted in strong statements. However, when we reflected on the consequence of these insights for the ongoing mega-stable process, they got stuck in their fixation, positing that the point of no return has already been passed. We cannot expect the loosening up of fixations to occur overnight. An important conclusion from these kinds of interventions is that change comes step by step: "small wins can churn old routines into new learning" (Weick and Westley 1996: 454).

9.6 Discussion

In this chapter we addressed the question of how local governments can maintain or regain trust amongst citizens when dealing with sensitive knowledge-intensive issues that could trigger resistance and distrust. Based on our findings, we now want to highlight why information and knowledge could thwart democracy.

We identified five configurations, of which the regionally embedded configurations "Innovative sustainable company in our area" (the local advocates) and "No mega-stable in this area" (the local opponents) were of particular influence for the local decision-making process. Beside their argument that they did not want such a big stable in their backyards, the local opponents also pointed out that the arrival of the mega-stable would not have any positive effect on the local community. On the other hand, politicians strongly supported the concept because of its alleged sustainable and innovative character. Because of this divide between configurations, every given argument is interpreted from a different perspective and actors are inclined to confirm their own perspectives while disqualifying others, thereby making a real dialogue extremely difficult. Consequently, each configuration does not feel acknowledged in its opinion. In our case this resulted in a spiral of distrust in which perseverance became a goal in itself, conspiracy theories grew, and all information was interpreted negatively. More research and the use of technical frames did not help to shift the focus of attention away from the mega-stables nor limit the scope of participation surrounding the issue. Instead, it turned out to be useful for the opposition, because the act of scientific research became connected to the configurations which were positive about mega-stables. This way, more knowledge became disadvantageous for local democracy by bringing up more counter-argumentations, uncertainties, and debates.

Governments who deal with sensitive issues might escape the negative spiral of trust and the stagnation of the decision-making process by being aware of the different configurations in which stakeholders operate, and using arguments which relate to these configurations. Strategies they can apply are: identifying configurations, appointing a devil's advocate, scheduling fixed moments of reflection, and developing an advanced communication arrangement. Trust is crucial for creating public support for a certain policy; but regaining trust is extremely difficult. Once the decision-making process escalates, a continuation of the decision process can be very costly. In these cases, reflection is needed. In our case we have seen that a reflective conversation can help people to become aware of the fixed pattern they have fallen into. However, it proved difficult to loosen up fixations and to revitalise learning processes.

In general, the best strategy is to prevent the development of fixed beliefs, causing dialogues of the deaf and spirals of distrust. Preventing these pathways does not necessarily mean that one should increase transparency and produce more knowledge and more information. A first step to avoid the circles of distrust is at least to establish the awareness among policy-makers and process managers that information and knowledge could have these perverted effects: effects which are usually not expected by them.

Acknowledgements

We would like to thank the brave city council of the little village in our case that requested us to evaluate the decision-making process around the establishment of a mega-stable in its municipality in order to learn from it. This chapter was written in the context of the IP/OP "Scaling and Governance" Research Programme, which has been spearheaded by Wageningen University and Research Centre (Wageningen UR), as part of its mission to contribute to solutions for the most pressing global environmental problems.

10 Media, Democracy and Governance

Miguel Goede

Abstract

The purpose of this chapter is to present a conceptual framework for the functioning of the media, democracy and governance. Politics function like a television reality show in which the media frame the debate. Mediacracy has its own language and rules; it simplifies content. Cyber democracy has increased the participation of the creative user, who co-creates the content. These developments create the conditions for the reality show. This chapter contributes to an understanding of the media, democracy and governance. It contains both hope and a wish – the hope for more democracy, but also a wish to improve this institution.

10.1 Introduction

In the novel "1984" written by George Orwell in 1949, he presents his vision of the future and introduces the concept of "Big Brother". Two aspects of his vision are relevant for this chapter. First of all, in his book, there are cameras everywhere and people are monitored 24 h a day, 7 days a week (24/7). Secondly, he writes about the Ministry of Truth of the imaginary inter-continental super-state, Oceania, undertaking content management while the content is altered all the time. Our current society reminds us of Orwell's vision. Our wireless Internet society connects everybody, with a wide range of gadgets including smart phones and small digital cameras, and with applications and platforms like Google, Google Earth, YouTube, I-reports, Facebook, MySpace and Twitter. Cities like London and Johannesburg are protected by surveillance cameras. But that is not all. Global Positioning Systems (GPS) make it possible to locate people and objects anytime and anywhere. Next to this, there are many databases containing personal information, including financial records, consumer preferences, behaviour on the Internet and even medical records. Some of these databases can be connected. Society has indeed become a society in which Big Brother might be watching us.

Big Brother is also the name of a successful franchised television reality show. Reality television uses ordinary people in unscripted situations. The participant co-creates (Tapscott and Williams 2008) the content. This is a relatively inexpensive concept, which makes it attractive for today's commercial television. The "Big Brother Show" was first aired in 1999 in the Netherlands. The concept is as follows: 12 persons are placed in a house together, without contact with the

R.J. in 't Veld (ed.), *Knowledge Democracy*, DOI 10.1007/978-3-642-11381-9_10,

outside world, for a 100 days. This group can be observed 24/7 via the Internet, and the highlights are displayed on television daily or weekly. Once a week, some inhabitants of the Big Brother house are nominated to leave the house and go home. The viewers get involved by voting for the nominees on the Internet or by text messaging (SMS). The last remaining candidate wins a sum of money.

The question addressed in this chapter is whether the concept of the reality show has become a metaphor for today's political system. Politics have become a 24/7 activity that is permanently monitored by citizens via the media. Political decision-making is framed by the media. Election campaigns and elections increasingly look like a casting for the reality show of politics. The polls fulfil the function of providing voting opportunities for the public in order to choose who leaves the reality show, and talk shows and call-in programmes are a chance for the public to get involved during the reality show. By examining this extended metaphor of the reality television show, this chapter will examine the governance of the media, identify the role and evolution of the media and its contribution to democracy.

Some use the term "perpetual campaign" to indicate that politics have become a reality show. But the model of the reality show is not limited to the world of politics. The reality show model is also applicable to media coverage of the world of sports and entertainment, war and natural disasters (Klein 2007), to name just a few areas. The so-called Balloon Boy incident in Colorado in the United States of America is good example of the reality show model. On 15 October 2009, the father of a six-year old boy reported that his son had taken off in a homemade helium balloon. All resources were mobilised to rescue the boy and the events were covered live by the traditional corporate media, the new media and social networks for hours. After several hours, to the relief of everybody the boy turned out to be at home and not in the balloon. The family ended up on the "Larry King Live" show that evening. During that interview the six-year old answered a question of the host Wolf Blitzer, stating he did this for the media show. Soon it became clear that the whole thing was a hoax (Reuters 2009). Andy Warhol's prediction, "In the future everyone will be world-famous for 15 minutes", is more true now than ever.

10.2 Framework

The reality of the interplay between media, democracy and governance is complex and dynamic. To study this reality, the development of a conceptual framework is needed to structure this complexity. A conceptual framework is used in research to outline possible courses of action or to present a preferred approach to an idea or thought.[1] A conceptual framework is an intermediate theory that connects aspects of the research and so it provides logic, order and consistency between the different elements. The framework to understand the media, democracy and governance

[1] http://en.wikipedia.org/wiki/Conceptual_framework. Accessed on 13 November 2009.

starts with the normative frameworks of De Tocqueville and Habermas and develops via different stages into a model for cyber democracy and networks.

In 1830s, Alex de Tocqueville was one of the first to identify the importance of the free media (press) as a powerful force for the promotion of democracy (Graber 2003). Habermas (1962) formulated the concept of the *public sphere* between family life, business life and the state: a sphere where citizens could engage in rational dialogue, free from power, shaping their lives. He states that the proliferation of commercial media has destroyed this public sphere. Some argue that the new media will rescue the public sphere (Bardoel 2003).

The media are defined as "communication channels through which news, entertainment, education, data, or promotional messages are disseminated". The media include every broadcasting and narrowcasting medium such as newspapers, magazines, TV, radio, billboards, direct mail, telephone, fax, and Internet.[2] In today's world media corporations combine traditional platforms like radio and TV with the Internet, using websites and social networks like Facebook and Twitter.

The media have evolved from the marketplace to newspapers and magazines, the radio, television and the Web, versions 1.0 to 3.0. Every time a new medium emerged, some people claimed that the new developments will kill the existing media. But to date, we have seen that the emergence of new media transforms the other media and the media landscape, rather than destroying anything.

According to the literature and the definition given above, the media have several functions:

- To inform the citizens;
- To criticise situations in society;
- To express opinions and let others express their opinions on issues;
- To entertain;
- To educate citizens;
- To promote commerce: the media are just a business (Reinders 1996, Maduro 2004, Goede 2006, Graber 2003).

Some of the functions of the media might conflict with each other, for example the entertainment and the information functions (Prior 2007). That is why in the past, the media differentiated themselves according to their core function and in their programming. Today it is more difficult to distinguish between the different functions. Politicians appear in entertainment programmes. Who does not remember presidential candidate Obama's dance moves in the "Ellen DeGeneres Show" on 30 October 2007?

Many consider that the media play an important role as a watchdog and as a part of the system of checks and balances in a political system (Gerstl-Pepin 2007). Castells (1996) elaborates on the relationship between politics and the media in his trilogy on the network society. The network society is an Anglo-Saxon

---

2 http://www.businessdictionary.com/definition/media.html

worldview (Meuleman 2008). The media are the main source of information. Citizens base their actions on this information, but they do not do this blindly, because despite concentration, the media are still too diverse for that. Citizens do not receive the information passively; they actively process the information from their own perspectives. Communication is a complex process and those who try to influence public opinion via the media are always confronted with unforeseen effects. The media frames the political debate and thus influences it.

10.2.1 Mediacracy

In 1975 Kevin Philips, in his book *Mediacracy: American Parties and Politics in the Communications Age*, introduced the concept of mediacracy, arguing that in a democratic society those who rule the media (indirectly) rule society, and also suggesting that the media, as a collective actor, rule the country. In this system politicians stop thinking and listen exclusively to the media to identify issues. Since the media are in the hands of corporations, or are financed by corporations, the corporations rule.

Mediacracy has its own language and rules; it simplifies the content, it is about image building, about the personification of politics, about the spreading of rumours, and about character assassination of political rivals and public figures. It is in this light that scandals should be evaluated. Mediacracy is expensive and this fact makes politics dependent upon financial contributors and lobbyists. Castells states that in the United States this interdependency is partially responsible for the fact that there is insufficient regulation of party funding.

Because of the media, citizens are more involved, but nevertheless their trust in politics has been diminishing. Citizens express their concerns through mechanisms that are outside the system of parliamentary elections, or vote for alternative parties and candidates. In this context the Internet, or new media in general, play an important role. It provides platforms for citizens to contact each other and creates alternative ways for funding politics (Hertz 2003, Castells 2009).

The relationship between government, society, citizens and organisations and the role of political parties and the media are illustrated in Figure 10.1. This model is based on the System Analysis Model of David Easton (1965). It is a greatly simplified model of reality, as it is limited to the national level and does not include multinational media corporations and the Internet.

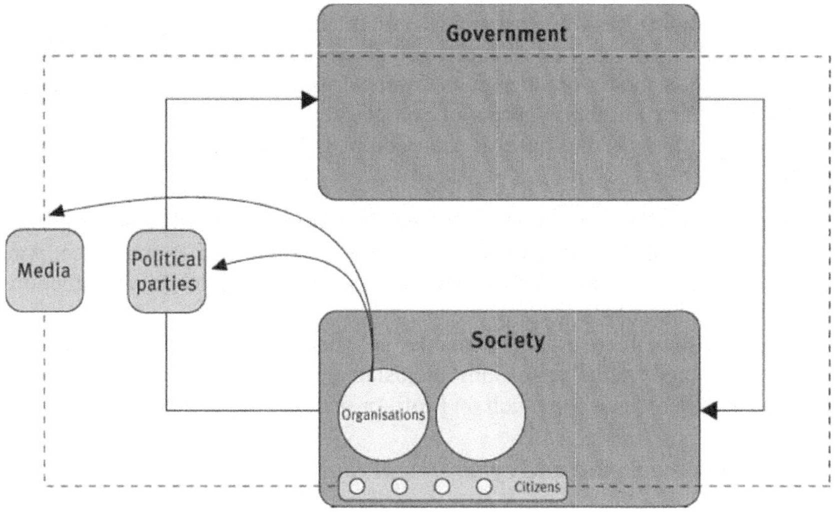

Fig. 10.1 The framing of politics by the media.

The model illustrates the functions of the media. They inform the citizens and so frame the discourse in society. They criticise situations in society and give opportunities to citizens to express themselves and so act as the gatekeepers of the political agenda. But the media also educate and entertain the citizens. This is only possible if the media generate a healthy profit or are subsidised (Bardoel 2003).

Some observers argue that politicians are more and more inclined to listen to business groups, organised interest groups and the media. The voice of the people is lost, even if they are shouting in the many daily talk shows on the multitude of radio and television stations and web logs. Genuine dialogue is not possible; the media are just a billboard of opposing views. It is in this context that the media present themselves as the voice of the people, keeping the politicians honest. But is this really true? The question is: who controls the media? (Scheuer 2007). The media are funded by the same interest groups that fund the political parties (Castells 2009). But other observers argue that journalists are leftist liberals and thus anti-corporate (Gerstl-Pepin 2007).

The citizen cannot break the triangular relationship between politics, business and the media, just as he or she cannot break the triangular relationship between politics, business and the unions (NRC 9 July 2004):

> The public is clearly dissatisfied with the current political media offerings. While many Americans consider themselves to be "news junkies" and express a strong need to keep informed, they don't trust many news sources. A majority of citizens believe that the news is unduly influenced by powerful business and political interests who play into the media's own desire to make profits. Further, they consider the news to be too sensational and scandal-ridden. The public feels that the press is intrusive, and goes too

> far in invading people's personal lives in the interest of getting a story. Audience members are concerned about the accuracy of reporting, especially as media organisations compete to be the first with a breaking story. In fact, journalist norms of sourcing and fact-checking largely have become a thing of the past, as the pace of news reporting has accelerated (Owen 1999).

Graber (2003) warns against stereotyping the (American) media. She argues that, although many of the criticisms on the media are legitimate, "on balance, American democracy has managed to sustain its chief goals despite the imperfections of its tools" (Graber 2003).

In conclusion: there is an imbalance between the values People, Planet and Profit as dictated by the philosophy of sustainable development when it comes to the media. The focus is too much on Profit or market (Bardoel 2003).

10.2.2 The new media and cyber democracy

A specific topic that is widely discussed is the penetration of the new media. *Time* magazine, in December 2006, declared "You" as person of the year. This you highlights the emergence of Web 2.0 (Grossman 2006). As a consequence of the new media, young people read less and watch less television (Broertjes 2006, Scheuer 2007, Gaber 2007, Bardoel 2003). In July 2009 a 15-year old intern at Morgan Stanley presented a research note on how teenagers consume the media. The report shook the City of London and beyond. In his report he states, among others things, that teenagers do not read newspapers on a regular basis and that they do not listen to the radio very often. On the other hand, almost all teenagers have a PC with access to the Internet and a mobile phone, but they do not use the Internet on the mobile phone because this service is too expensive. Teenagers watch television very selectively (guardian.co.uk 2009). Many people think that the new media will change everything when it comes to the power of media corporations and thus democracy. This development is illustrated in Figure 10.2. The share of the old media has been reduced to less than 30% in 10 years.

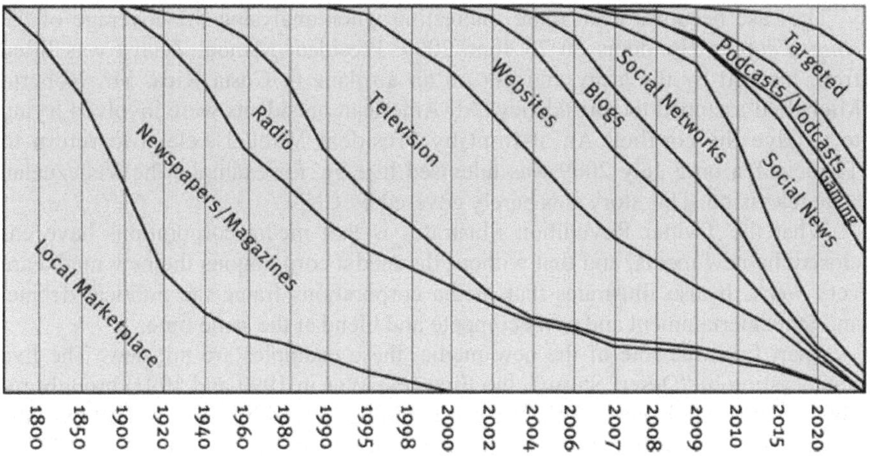

Fig. 10.2. The development of the media through time (Baekdal 2009).

> … today, the new Internet is completely dominating our world. The newspapers are dead in the water, and people are watching less TV than ever. The new king of information is everyone, using social networking tools to connect and communicate. Even the traditional website is dying from the relentless force of the constant stream of rich information from the social networks (Baekdal 2009).

At this stage some believe that the new media have fundamentally changed the model of mediacracy (Baekel 2009, Friedman 2005, Tapscott and Williams 2008, Anderson 2009). Gaynor uses the term *Cyberdemocracy*. Others use the term digital democracy. Some *cyberutopians* (Gaynor 1996) point to examples like the so-called Iranian Twitter Revolution to make their case. He states that the new media, especially the social networks, played an important role during the presidential election campaign in Iran. When the outcome of the election was published on 13 June 2009, hundreds of thousands protesters who voted for reformist presidential candidate Mir-Hossein Mousavi took to the streets denouncing fraud by President Mahmoud Ahmadinejad. The regime tried to shut down the protests by closing down the media. The people had to bring their story to the world using social networks like Twitter. Twitter had to postpone their maintenance to support the movement. CNN installed an Iranian desk to bring these images to the mainstream media (Schectman 2009). But this desk disappeared into the background on 25 June 2009 when www.tmz.com announced the death of Michael Jackson on their website and the mainstream media took over the story. The Michael Jackson story dominated the media for months. The latest event is this saga is the release of the movie "This is it" in October 2009, based on recordings of his last rehearsals. In November the Iran desk appeared again.

The case becomes even more interesting when analysing the coverage of the *coup d'état* in Honduras on 28 June 2009. President Manuel Zelaya was lifted from his bed by the army and put on an airplane to Costa Rica. Mr. Roberto Micheletti assumed the presidency. All American presidents were involved trying to resolve the conflict. An attempt by President Manuel Zelaya to return to Tegucigalpa on 5 July 2009 was televised live by, for example, the Venezuelan state television. This story was barely covered by CNN.

What the Twitter Revolution illustrates is that media corporations have enclosed the new media, and that without the media corporations the new media are very weak. It also illustrates that media corporations frame the political debate, and that entertainment and news compete and blend at the same time.

Apart from the role of the new media, these examples are not new. The live broadcasting of "Desert Storm", the First Iraq War in 1990 and 1991, brought reality TV to a whole new level. The war could be viewed live on CNN all over the world. The Second Iraq War was a direct consequence of the attacks of 9/11 on the Twin Towers in New York: the impact of the second airplane into the tower was broadcasted live on television. The "War on Terror" was started based on misleading information on weapons of mass destruction. The media framed the story creating and maintaining public support for the war (Bennett et al. 2007). The new media were not able to reframe the war. On the contrary, corporate media used the new media to frame the story. New media were used by embedded mainstream reporters.

10.2.3 Adjusting the framework

Prior (2007) presents, in his book *Post-Broadcast Democracy*, a Conditional Political Learning model (CPL) that describes the tendency for popular acquisition of political information to be dependent on the availability of television programmes. Simplifying reality, the model states that people have stable, competing preferences for news or information and entertainment. The increased availability of entertainment leads to a decrease in the number of people following the news. The fragmentation of audiences due to the proliferation of media, especially television, leads to polarised elections because news junkies attend to political news while less interested citizens flock to entertainment (Prior 2007).

The CPL is a simple model, just like the models of Philips and Easton. A more complex model is presented by Castells. In his book *Communication Power* (2009), Castells argues that communication is the central power in today's society. This confirms Philips' account of mediacracy.

The model that Castells (2009) offers to describe governance in today's global network society consists of four forms of power:

- Networking power: The power of actors and organisations included in the networks. It is about inclusion and exclusion.
- Network power: The social coordination between multiple networked actors. It is about imposing a protocol in a network.

- Networked power: Who has power in the dominant networks? This is not a simple question. Many have power; it is not in the hands of any specific person.
- Network-making power: The most crucial form of power is the competence of Programmers and Switchers. The Programmers state the agenda of the network and the Switchers connect separate networks.

Switching (connecting) different networks requires the ability to construct a cultural and organisational interface, a common language, a common medium, a support of universally accepted values: exchange value. The all-purpose form of exchange value is money. Programming is the ability to generate, diffuse and affect the discourse that frames the human action. Discourse shapes the public mind via communication networks that organise socialised communication. Programming and communication networks are the decisive source of cultural materials that feed the programme goals of any network. Alternative discourse has to go through the same programming and communication networks. "Power in the network society is communication power" (Castells 2009: 53). In other words the networks of communication, finance and politics are interlinked. Together they create a climate for mediacracy and mediocracy in which populism rises. The creative audience tries to reprogramme the networks but has to go through the same communication networks.

Global social networks and social networks of social networks enabled by global digital communication are the fundamental source of power and counter-power in present-day society. There is a contradiction between multinational corporate media networks and the creative audience, framing and counter-framing the news. The corporate media try to commodify the Internet and the creative audience tries to establish a degree of citizen communication power. Power is differentiated in the network society. Power is not fully determined by one group or one kind of power structure, but whoever has enough money, including political leaders, will have a better chance of exerting power. An example of this is Mayor Michael Bloomberg whose election campaign for a third term as mayor of New York cost $64,756,118.47 (Lisberg 2009). Another example is Prime Minister of Italy, Mr. Berlusconi. It is said that he maintains his political position thanks to his economic power and the power of the media in Italy. President Obama also won the election thanks to the huge budget at the disposal of his campaign. Some state that his story is different because a significant part of the budget was from small donors who donated via the Internet (Castells 2009). Some believe that the Obama campaign is an illustration that the new media can lead to more democracy. But the fact is that candidate Obama needed money to ensure access to corporate media.

Singapore is also an interesting case for analysis in terms of the media, democracy and governance. Singapore developed from a third world county to a first world country in one generation. The PAP political party has been in power since the 1960s. This has been possible because it restricts the media. The question is: why did the new media not change this? Could the answer be that in Singapore hierarchical structures are still in place? (Kuan Yew 2000).

The question is whether mass self communication – Web 2.0 and Web 3.0 – will shift the balance of power between multinational corporations and the creative audience. According to Fuchs (2009) there is no empirical evidence that Web 2.0 is autonomous from the power of capital. The trends towards increased economic concentration, diversification of platforms, customisation and segmentation of audiences, and economies of synergy continue. But there is also potential for counter-power within Web 2.0. Mass self-communication allows citizens to watch the powerful. But the powerful have made it their main concern to enclose these alternative platforms. The competition is unequal, but there are examples of successful counter power ventures. In fact, there is a stratified online economy devoted to managing attention, in which the trademarks of the established media play an important role in attracting attention. The creative audience remains fragmented. The power relationship between the corporate media and the creative user is asymmetrical, to the advantage of the corporations. In other words, the world is not flat (Friedman 2005) but it is potentially flat.

The model developed by Castells models today's globalised network society, powered by the Internet, where there are basically no frontiers for actors. The role of the state has therefore diminished.

10.2.4 Reality show

Power in media politics is exerted by triggering emotions. This is done by the mainstream media via sensationalism, theatrical politics, personification, dramatisation, the fragmentation of information and audiences, negative stereotyping, attack politics, and the creation of scandals. A blend of the traditional media and the Internet is a new phenomenon: co-creation. Stories enter the traditional media almost as they happen via the Internet, filtered by the corporate media. This creates reality media. The same mechanisms that can be seen in a reality show apply to media politics.

> For Castells, there are the following new aspects of media politics: the use of the Internet in political campaign (p. 230), the multiplication of entry points of political reports, on which an interaction between mainstream media and the Internet is based (p. 234), an unprecedented prevalence and significance of scandal politics (p. 246), the easy and immediate diffusion of scandal politics over the Internet by everyone (pp. 247f), an increase of publicity and perception of corruption and the impact on public trust (p. 289). The result would be a worldwide crisis of political legitimacy, a decline in public trust, and a crisis of democracy. These crises could possibly, but not automatically result in depolitisation, and would in many cases also create a desire for insurgent politics, social movements and new political space (Fuchs 2009: 98).

The Clinton Lewinsky scandal in 1998 is an illustration of scandal politics. This happened in an era when Internet proliferation was relatively low. It led to the second attempt to impeach a president of the United States. In retrospect it is unclear what it was all about. It started with the investigation of the Whitewater deal in 1970s and 1980s. The scandal affected the election campaign of Al Gore, who lost the election against president George W. Bush.

Within the format of the reality show, created by the blending of traditional corporate media and new media, there is the possibility for hypes and hoax. Hype is extreme publicity resulting in tumult. Hoax is an act intended to mislead or scam. The death of Michael Jackson is an example of hype, and the Balloon Boy is an illustration of a hoax. Other hypes are the millennium bug or Y2K bug in the late 1990s; SARS in 2002; and H1N1 in 2009. Through the media global panic is created for unclear reasons. Some state that it is done to serve the interests of specific industries.

A recent example of reality show politics is the bankruptcy of the DSB Bank, a small bank in the Netherlands in October 2009. The DSB went bankrupt when a financial expert, Peter Lakerman, stated in a talk show that the bank was exploiting mortgage costumers. He advised the clients to take their money out of the bank. This started a run on the bank, leading to its bankruptcy.

The meltdown of the financial markets in the last quarter of 2008 had several noticeable media events that illustrate this theme. The first was when the former chairman of the Federal Reserve Bank confessed to the Senate that he was wrong in his belief in deregulation and self-regulation of the financial market. Another moment was when the CEOs of the automobile corporations of Detroit flew to Washington in their corporate jets to ask for a bailout.

The consequences of reality show politics are that the political campaign has become permanent, undermining representative democracy and creating the illusion of direct democracy. The campaign is not about issues and content, but about emotions. Campaigning is about packaging, branding and marketing. There is no room for long-term objectives and ideology. Political parties have become marketing machines, financed by stakeholders, catering to the needs of voters. The electorate has become extremely volatile. This creates the conditions for a radical shift in the electoral outcome, meaning that politics as a rational means of sustainable governance is further away than ever, despite the potential of the new media. The ability of politicians to lead has decreased. The (new) media have weakened representative democracy. The possibility of knowing the likely public reaction to possible policy has led to a twisted direct democracy. The new media have led to permanent elections. Political effects of proposed policy are constantly measured. This leads to pressure, even within parties, who aim to improve their ratings. In other words, there is a climate for populism (Pehe 2009, Gaber 2007).

10.3 Conclusions

The media have changed over time and so have the frameworks to apprehend them, from the models based on checks-and-balances of representative democracy of De Tocqueville and Habermas, to the mediacracy of Easton and Philips, to cyber democracy. To cope with the proliferation of media, especially television and radio, the Conditional Political Learning model was presented. Castells' network society provides a framework to fit new media into the way the media are understood.

The United States and other western countries are concerned about the concentration of the media as a consequence of liberalisation of media regulation and the operation of the market (Jackson and Stanfield 2004). This applies to some other countries as well (Trakhtenberg 2005). According to Champlin and Knoedler (2006), the media should educate and inform, and so strengthen democracy. Because of the pressure of the market, the media have become primarily focused on generating revenues, and the audience is primarily interested in entertainment. But increasing competition is not an automatic cure for the present imbalance between the three Ps (Planet, People and Profit).

One consequence of the oversupply of (new) media is that the media are very accessible. This leads to the paradox that democracy diminishes because the media corporations became dependent upon the advertising revenues from the business community. New media look like an alternative but they are enclosed by corporate media. Some commentators argue that the Internet has democratised information, while others argue that the Internet has merely created information overload (Gaber 2007).

The fact remains that the media play an important role in disclosing cases of bad governance. However, the media do not stick to the role of presenting the news, but in many cases make the news, and in some cases the media have become the news. The emergence of the new media has not changed this pattern. In fact the media have transformed society into a reality show, with their many talk shows and call-in programmes. The question is: who watches over the watchdog? The media are no longer the watchdog of society but are a part of the whole system of checks and balances in the fragile democracy. The question is whether citizens will use the new media as a part of the system of checks and balances on the media.

After observing global trends one might conclude that the convergence of politics and the media towards a reality show is now universal. The words "reality show" and "mediacracy" have a negative connotation to them. But this is not totally correct, because although they have drawbacks, they also hold the promise of a direct or participative democracy in which the people play an active role in their own governance (Coleman 1999, Cover 2004). This all might bring us closer to President Lincoln's "government of the people, by the people, for the people", a goal that will be advanced by the further development of ICT and with it e-elections. But there still is a long way to go.

11 How can transdisciplinary research contribute to knowledge democracy?

Joske F.G. Bunders, Jacqueline E.W. Broerse, Florian Keil, Christian Pohl, Roland W. Scholz and Marjolein B.M. Zweekhorst

Abstract

In any society, a wide diversity of actors has relevant knowledge concerning important societal problems. In a knowledge democracy both dominant and non-dominant actors have equal access and ability to put this knowledge forward in the process of solving societal problems. In order to enable these actors to contribute meaningfully to decision-making around public policy and research agendas, we argue that a transdisciplinary research process is needed. In this chapter we critically reflect on the principles, concepts and core methods of transdisciplinary research. We first look at the national historical roots of transdisciplinary research, specifically focussing on two countries – Switzerland and The Netherlands. Next we develop a typology of transdisciplinary research. From the perspective of knowledge democracy, we can distinguish two important dimensions in research approaches: the degree of *knowledge input* of lay groups that is included in a specific transdisciplinary project and the degree in which non-dominant actors are explicitly *involved in the decision-making* of the development process of policies or research agendas. This results in two different styles of transdisciplinary research. We discuss the similarities and differences of these different styles and approaches. We close this chapter with a discussion on transdisciplinary research styles in relation to forms of democracy – on the one hand basic and representative democracy and on the other hand deliberative democracy.

11.1 Introduction

Knowledge democracy connotes a society in which a wide diversity of actors hold relevant knowledge to address important societal problems (In 't Veld 2009). In such an ideal democracy dominant and non-dominant actors have equal access and ability to bring this knowledge forward in order to contribute to solutions for societal problems. Such a knowledge democracy has no bias regarding access of knowledge, ways of knowledge sharing and the role of

R.J. in 't Veld (ed.), *Knowledge Democracy*, DOI 10.1007/978-3-642-11381-9_11,

knowledge on decision-making. Clearly we are then discussing an ideal, a normative statement which has led to various reactions in favour and against such a perspective. In this chapter, we will not contribute to this debate. Instead we will follow Kant (1781) with his statement "ought implies can".

If we say that we ought to give actors, who have relevant knowledge for addressing societal problems, the possibility to influence decision-making for public policy and research agendas, we need to know how to do that. What are the mechanisms that have proven to be helpful? This question points in the direction of specification of methodologies and processes. Processes in which the knowledge of different actors are brought together and that are designed to realise a decision-making process which explicitly takes a variety of inputs into account. There are different names for these processes, such as transdisciplinary research (Thompson Klein et al. 2001), knowledge co-creation (Regeer and Bunders 2009), multi-stakeholder interaction (Sheppard and Meitner 2004) and interactive policy-making (Driessen et al. 2001).

Nowadays, it is standard to ask for societal relevance, transdisciplinary research and multi-stakeholder involvement in research proposals. This practice seems to suggest that we have a good methodology for organising the required processes. But is that the case? In our view it is time to assess these approaches and to learn from best practices in order to find out under which conditions they can be applied, and what they mean in the context of knowledge democracy. There is an increasing urgency to get a better grip on the possibilities and limitations, as well as to reflect critically on the principles, concepts and core methods of transdisciplinary research. This is particularly warranted since transdisciplinary research appears to be a very demanding and challenging endeavour in many cases.

What is currently labelled as "transdisciplinary research" grew and flourished in the rich soil of the debates on knowledge democratisation in the last decades of the twentieth century. The pioneers analysed science and society relationships and experimented with interventions known under various labels, such as Constructive Technology Assessment (Rip et al. 1995), Participative Action Research (for example, Kemmis and McTaggert 1988, Reason and Bradbury 1990), Post-normal Science (Funtowicz and Ravetz 1993) and Mode1/Mode2 knowledge production (Gibbons et al. 1994). Nowadays in various countries, research groups and special institutes have been established that label their work as transdisciplinary research. These groups interact closely in a global context. If we compare the different research groups, we can see similarities, for example in some of the tools they use, but also differences in the way transdisciplinary research is conceptualised and the products created in the context of knowledge democratisation.

To begin to understand these differences, we first look at the national historical roots in Switzerland and the Netherlands (Sect. 11.2) and then develop a typology of transdisciplinary research processes in the context of knowledge democratisation (Sect. 11.3). In Sects. 11.4 and 11.5 we focus on three transdisciplinary approaches, the Transdisciplinary Case Study (TCS) approach, the Institute for Social-Ecological Research (ISOE) model and the Interactive Learning and Action (ILA) approach. Section 6 deals with various requirements for mainstreaming transdisciplinary research and the development of a transdisciplinary research tradition. We close with a discussion on transdisciplinary approaches in relation to forms of governance and knowledge democracy (Sect. 11.7).

11.2 Historical roots of transdisciplinary research

Transdisciplinary research developed during the 1980s and early 1990s of the past century. Multidisciplinary and interdisciplinary research can be placed in a continuum between monodisciplinary research and transdisciplinary research. Thompson Klein (2001: 7) defines transdisciplinarity as:

> A new form of learning and problem-solving involving co-operation between different parts of society and science in order to meet complex challenges of society. Transdisciplinary research starts from tangible, real-world problems. Solutions are devised in collaboration with multiple stakeholders.

Transdisciplinary research is embedded in local scientific, cultural and political practices that differ for each country. The fundamental embedding of transdisciplinary research in society leads to different routes, in which windows of opportunity and challenges in development are taken into account. Although we distinguish common characteristics of transdisciplinary research as it is practised now in various countries, there are also still many differences. In order to shed light on the process of development of transdisciplinary research, we will in this section describe some important events in two countries – Switzerland and the Netherlands. This is not intended as a comparative or comprehensive analysis, rather it provides an illustration of how paths to transdisciplinary research can be shaped in different ways. Scientists and policy-makers in certain countries that want to develop and institutionalise transdisciplinary research in their institutions might benefit from these descriptions (as a naturalistic generalisation).

11.2.1 The emergence and institutionalisation of transdisciplinary research in Switzerland

In Switzerland the term "transdisciplinarity" gained momentum during the early 1990s and is still the topic of lively discussion. During this period the meaning of the term shifted. The shifting can be tracked if the concept of transdisciplinarity is seen as a group of features that differ in significance over time. An analysis of current definitions of transdisciplinarity identified four such features (Pohl and Hirsch Hadorn 2007: 70):

- (a) The transcendence and integration of disciplinary paradigms;
- (b) Participatory research;
- (c) The focus on real-world problems;
- (d) The search for unity of knowledge beyond disciplines.

The meaning of transdisciplinarity shifts with the relative weight that is given to each of the features. For example, the understanding as promoted by Basarb Nicolescu (1996) mainly emphasises feature (d), the search for unity of knowledge beyond disciplines. Most definitions combine several of the features.

In the early 1990s two initiatives of environmental research promoted transdisciplinarity in Switzerland: the scientific journal "GAIA – Ecological Perspectives for Science and Society" (launched in 1991), and the research programme "Swiss Priority Programme Environment" (SPPE). GAIA was an academic initiative of scientists of the "Zentrum Philosophie und Wissenschaftstheorie" (University of Konstanz), the Institute for Economy and the Environment (University of St. Gallen) and the Department of Environmental Sciences (ETH Zurich). Writing the editorial of the fifth issue of GAIA, the philosopher Jürgen Mittelstraß claimed that environmental sciences are on track to transdisciplinarity. To him:

> [T]ransdisciplinarity refers to knowledge or research that frees itself of its specialised or disciplinary boundaries, that defines and solves its problems independently of disciplines, relating these problems to extra-scientific developments (Mittelstraß 1992: 250, translated).

Such transdisciplinarity accentuates features (a), the transcendence and integration of disciplinary paradigms and (c), the focus on real-world problems. This is in line with Erich Jantsch's original definition of transdisciplinarity as a complex systems theory approach. For Jantsch transdisciplinarity meant the integration and reorientation of the whole education and innovation system with the purpose of addressing real-world problems (Jantsch 1972). Transdisciplinarity is a recurring issue in GAIA, be it in the kind of research projects that present their results, or the discussions of transdisciplinarity as a mode of research. The focus on (a) and (c) pertains as can be seen in GAIA's statement that "environmental problems cannot be solved by one academic discipline. The complex natures of these problems require cooperation across disciplinary boundaries."[1]

Within the second initiative, the SPPE (1992-2000), transdisciplinarity was taken care of mainly by the management of SPPE, especially by Rudolf Häberli and Walter Grossenbacher-Mansuy. SPPE was the main national source of funding for problem-driven environmental research, disposing of a total of 100 Mio CHF (~ 66 Mio €). SPPE was expected to help solve environmental problems through the programme's research projects. The management of SPEE considered the transdisciplinary mode of research instrumental for that purpose and furthermore as a core innovation of SPPE (Häberli and Grossenbacher-Mansuy 1998). Initiated by the Swiss Academic Society of Environmental Research and Ecology – a promoter of problem-driven research – SPPE created a forum on transdisciplinary research in 1997. The forum was managed by two philosophers, Philipp Balsiger and Rudolf Kötter, primarily interested in the epistemology of transdisciplinarity. The forum was created as a platform to discuss and promote transdisciplinary

---

1 http://www.oekom.de/etc/gaia.html, October 23rd 2009.

research processes and continued until the end of SPPE in 2000. In 1998 the steering committee of SPPE mandated two researchers from the University of Berne (Antonietta di Giulio and Rico Defila), both interested in the management of inter- and transdisciplinary processes, to elaborate on criteria to evaluate inter- and transdisciplinary research. The criteria were published in a special issue of SPPE's Newsletter (Defila and Di Giulio 1999). Compared to GAIA's definition given by Mittelstraß, the discussion within SPPE expanded the understanding of transdisciplinarity based on features (a) and (c) by emphasising feature (b), participatory research. An important reason for that shift was that the SPPE considered the inclusion of the users in the research as a key element for effecting social change. However, within SPPE different positions existed regarding the overall significance of feature (c). In the work on evaluation criteria it was even said to be *the* distinguishing feature of transdisciplinarity:

> Transdisciplinary research [...] denotes interdisciplinary cooperation, involving not only scientists but also practitioners from beyond the realm of science (for example the users) in the research work (Defila and Di Giulio 1999: 13)

In 1998 the management of SPPE started to plan implementation and synthesis of SPPE. One of the central actions was an international conference on transdisciplinarity, which took place in 2000 at ETH Zurich under the title "Transdisciplinarity: Joint Problem Solving among Science, Technology and Society". The conference was co-organised by the management of SPPE and Roland W. Scholz from ETH Zurich who by that time had implemented six so-called transdisciplinary case studies in Switzerland (see below). Furthermore, leading expert in inter- and transdisciplinarity Julie Thompson Klein was included in the planning of the conference (Thompson Klein et al. 2001). Scholz, based on his case study research emphasised the aspect of close collaboration and mutual learning with stakeholders. Thompson Klein had recently published a book on inter- and transdisciplinarity, in which she introduced the perspective of the social studies of science, namely of boundary work and boundary crossing (Thompson Klein 1996), and of disciplines struggling for "cognitive authority" (Gieryn 1995: 405). The conference also brought transdisciplinarity together with knowledge production in Mode 2. As keynote speakers, Michael Gibbons and Helga Nowotny presented the concept of knowledge production in the context of application that provided "socially robust knowledge". In their thinking transdisciplinarity was one of the features of Mode 2 (Gibbons et al. 1994, Thompson Klein et al. 2001). The Mode 2 discussion might have accentuated the understanding of transdisciplinarity as mainly standing for (b), participatory research and (c), the focus on real-world problems. At the time of the conference, transdisciplinarity was strongly based on features (b) and (c): not only in Switzerland, but also in research programmes in neighbouring countries – like the Austrian Landscape Research (KLF, since 1995) and the Austrian research programme "Transdisziplinäre Forschung" (TRAFO 2004–2007). In addition, the German research programme Social-Ecological Research (SÖF, since 1999), also focuses on (a) by underlining that transdisciplinarity means "that the research process exceeds the boundaries of individual academic disciplines and indeed of the academic system as a whole" (PT-DLR 2008).

In the years after 2000, researchers at several Swiss universities practiced or analysed transdisciplinarity, such as in Geneva (Lawrence and Després 2004), Sion (Perrig-Chiello and Darbellay 2002), Berne (Defila et al. 2006), Basel (Burger and Kamber 2003, Maasen and Lieven 2006) and Zurich (Hirsch Hadorn 2002, Scholz and Tietje 2002). Furthermore, participatory and action-driven research were developed in a large national research initiative, the National Competence Centre in North-South Research. With the end of SPPE however, the integrating networking structure for transdisciplinarity vanished. The Swiss Academic Society of Environmental Research and Ecology (SAGUF) took the initiative to preserve and further develop the experiences gained in SPPE. SAGUF assumed SPPE's web address (www.transdisciplinarity.ch) and launched the SAGUF-net for exchanging experiences and learning between scholars of transdisciplinarity. In 2003 the network was renamed transdisciplinarity-net (td-net) and taken over by the Swiss Academy of Sciences. The td-net for transdisciplinary research has been part of the Swiss Academies of Arts and Sciences since 2008. The way in which the work of td-net once again shifted the meaning of transdisciplinarity was twofold. Firstly, because of the inter-academic affiliation of td-net, the network connected researchers of various fields engaged in transdisciplinarity – for example public health, migration, north-south partnerships, technology assessment, urban studies or environmental studies – in order to enable cross-field learning and community building beyond environmental research. Secondly, td-net focused on how to practice transdisciplinary research rather than on how to define transdisciplinarity. Accordingly, the understanding of transdisciplinary research is based on the purpose of addressing real-world issues:

1. To grasp the complexity of an issue;
2. To take into account the diverse perspectives on the issue;
3. To link abstract and case-specific knowledge;
4. To develop knowledge and practices that promote what is perceived to be the common good.

The features (a), the transcending and integrating of disciplinary paradigms and (b), participatory research of transdisciplinarity in that reading become means to reach those purposes (Pohl and Hirsch Hadorn 2007, Hirsch Hadorn et al. 2008b).

11.2.2 The development of transdisciplinary research in the Netherlands

In the development of transdisciplinary research in the Netherlands, we can distinguish an academic-theoretical line, a governmental policy line and an academic-empirical line, which are elaborated on below.

In the Netherlands the *academic-theoretical framing* was developed by Arie Rip (see for example Rip et al. 1995) and was named "Constructive Technology Assessment" (CTA). CTA includes the following features: firstly, CTA stimulates the creation of an infrastructure through which users and producers, and others who will be affected by the technology, can interact with each other and exchange information on a regular basis (Smits and Leyten 1991). Secondly, learning processes between various actors in research, diffusion and application are enhanced to create a more sophisticated understanding of the problems and of possible (technological) options (Schot and Rip 1997). Thirdly, reflexivity is fostered to avoid falling back on old positions and preconceived opinions. At the end of the day, this results in a societal agenda for technology R&D. Important tools include interviews, focus groups, dialogue workshops and consensus conferences. A CTA activity is conducted by a CTA "agent", who acts as a facilitator, intermediary and change agent at the same time. A CTA agent is, thus, an actor him- or herself. However, Bijker (1995), Fischer (1991) and Schot and Rip (1997) concluded that, although there are theoretically a multitude of opportunities for steering, hardly any social steering experiments had been performed and published halfway through the 1980s.

From the *governmental policy side*, there was one leading and inspiring policy memorandum of the Ministry of Education and Science (1984) entitled "Integration of Science and Technology in Society". This document stated explicitly that, in order to realise a proper embedding of the findings of science and technology in society, it is necessary that more actors and more aspects are integrated into the decision-making process on knowledge development for science and technology. Over the past ten years, it has been specifically the RMNO (Netherlands Advisory Council for Research on Spatial Planning, Nature and the Environment) that has taken the responsibility of focusing on the interface between science and society and the development of transdisciplinary agenda-setting and approaches (see for example, RMNO publications: In 't Veld 2000, 2001, Regeer and Bunders 2009, De Cock Buning et al. 2008). In "The rehabilitation of Cassandra" (In 't Veld 2001) a plea is held to include "future research" into transdisciplinary research. This insight has also found resonance in the academic empirical line.

With respect to the *academic empirical line*, the start of transdisciplinary research in the Netherlands was not within the health and natural sciences, but within agricultural and environmental sciences (as was also the case in other countries). Most notably at Wageningen University there were various groups – often working with groups in developing countries – that experimented with new research approaches like Participatory Rural Appraisal. From here we will follow one well-documented transdisciplinary research programme to highlight the succession of the different stages through which a specific approach to transdisciplinary research was developed and institutionalised.

In 1985 the Department of Biology and Society (now the Athena Institute) at the VU University Amsterdam, started a research programme on biotechnology and resource-poor farmers in developing countries, which is still active today.

Throughout the period the programme has been executed with many colleagues[2]. After an initial period of study and analysis of the development of research agendas on biotechnology for university-industry collaborations financed by the government, the possibilities of a transdisciplinary research programme on biotechnology for research-poor farmers was explored and modelled in the same way as the analysed university-industry-government programmes. From the outset, the programme was also embedded in the teaching programme of the Biology and Society department.

In 1985–1986, the Netherlands Ministry of Education and Science (see De Bruin and Bunders 1987) commissioned the department to conduct a study that started with the idea that biotechnology could contribute to the needs and interests of societal groups other than industry. It assessed if and how an effective interaction process between dominant and non-dominant actors could be created so that more aspects and more actors could be included in the decision-making process on agricultural biotechnology. Dominant actors in the decision-making process included biotechnologists, while non-dominant actors included farmers, environmental groups and development assistance groups. One of the results of this study was that differences in perceptions existed between biotechnologists and non-dominant actors concerning certain aspects of the impact of agricultural biotechnology that could negatively influence communication between biotechnologists and non-dominant actors.

Based on the results of this and other studies, researchers from the Department concluded that it was important as well as feasible to influence the biotechnological innovation process. The basic structure for the later optimised Interactive Learning and Action (ILA)[3] approach was designed to influence decision-making on biotechnology R&D in universities and institutes through facilitating communication and cooperation between biotechnologists and other societal actors, particularly non-dominant actors. Within the field of biotechnology for resource-poor farmers the following transdisciplinary ILA programmes were executed (amongst others):

- Development of biotechnology research agendas in Zimbabwe, Pakistan and Bolivia. This programme resulted in detailed research reports, a book, and scientific articles.
- Development of a national policy advice on biotechnology and developing countries. In this programme a public debate was organised between (for that time) an extraordinary variety of actors. This programme resulted in a special feature in the journal "Trends in Biotechnology" in

[2] These include colleagues from the Communication and Innovation Studies Group of the Wageningen University, biotechnologists of many Dutch universities and research groups, NGOs and governments in developing countries, and after 1989 with the Netherlands Ministry for Development Cooperation.

[3] At that time the working title of the methodology was "Interactive Bottom-up" (IBU) approach.

which not only research results were described (an approach to the development of appropriate biotechnology and examples showing how the approach could be used in practice), but an article was written by the Minister for Development Cooperation (Bukman) in which he presented his plans to implement a coherent programme on biotechnology and developing countries, which was to be executed in four counties: Zimbabwe, Kenya, India and Colombia.

- Development of a model for institutionalising a transdisciplinary approach in an NGO (Grameen Krishi Foundation). This project was executed because evaluation studies had shown that after the end of a project period, the contributing institutions continued with "business as usual" with no institutionalisation of the new way of working (that is systemically including non-dominant actors in the innovation process). This programme resulted in changed working procedures towards the ILA approach in GKF, as well as a PhD thesis (Zweekhorst 2004).
- Development of a model for tailor-made biotechnologies for resource-poor people in India (based on the ILA approach) through a consortium of Indian PhD students and Indian and Dutch experts (in the field of preventive medicine). This programme has just started.

To indicate the appreciation of programmes using the ILA approach in developing countries, at a World Bank conference on Science, Technology and Innovation for Development in February 2007 (attended by, amongst others, ministers from developing countries) eight showcases were selected as "best practices". Two of the eight cases were in the field of agricultural biotechnology for resource-poor farmers (the Indian and Colombian case) and used the ILA approach.

11.3 Different transdisciplinary approaches

Based on the wide diversity of transdisciplinary research we can ask the following questions: What similarities and differences of these programmes are relevant from the perspective of knowledge democracy? Which specific characteristics need to be analysed if we want to understand how transdisciplinary research can contribute to the process of knowledge democratisation?

An initial look reveals a difference in time scales. We have examples of transdisciplinary research processes that take only a few months (for example, some consultation exercises), while there are also programmes that take over 10 years, and all options in between. The methods and tools used also appear to be quite diverse. Regarding involvement of non-scientific actors for example, they range from interviews to group sessions in all kinds of designs (focus groups, expert meeting, dialogues, citizen juries et cetera).

Notwithstanding these differences, we observe that in scholarly literature the core of transdisciplinary research is most often presented as a shared set of principles (see Box 11.1 for an example). Principles differ from theories, methods, tools and conditions because they refer to the researcher; the researcher is said to perform genuine transdisciplinary research as long as he or she acknowledges and acts in accordance with the intention of these principles. As such, a set of principles describes the intentions that guide the researcher in choices he or she has to make for the design of the project or programme, that is the choice of methods, tools and the sequence of these. In other words, "the approach" is the manner in which the issue at stake is approached. This is in line with the wide-spread convention of labelling specific realisations of transdisciplinary research as "approaches" (see for example Sects. 11.4 and 11.5).

Box 11.1 Shared principles of transdisciplinary approaches

- *Joint process* initiated by non-academia (government, industry, public, NGOs) or scientists on an "ill-defined", societally relevant, real-world problem;
- *Joint problem definition* (including system boundaries);
- A *method-based* analysis of the complexity of the system (actor analysis, causal analysis, system analysis);
- *Mutual learning* enhanced in focus groups, round tables, expert sessions, stakeholder dialogues, etc.);
- The construction of "robust orientations" for the development of the case as outcome.

If the type of approach is more important for the variations in transdisciplinary research than the choices of tools, it is relevant to analyse the variety of approaches within transdisciplinary research in more detail. From the perspective of knowledge democracy, we can distinguish two important dimensions in approaches: the degree of *knowledge input* of lay groups that is included in a specific transdisciplinary project and the degree in which non-dominant actors are explicitly *involved in the decision-making* of the development process of policies or research agendas. Four research styles based on these two dimensions are distinguished in Table 11.1. With these two dimensions we can develop a typology of research relevant from the perspective of knowledge democracy.

The *self-referential knowledge production style* (mono-, multi- and interdisciplinary academic research) might take into account questionnaires and polls from the stakeholder groups related to the issue. These research projects certainly enrich the academic expert's view on the issue. However there is little active engagement of the stakeholder groups in the research, nor is the intention to transmit or share academic knowledge with the non-academic lay groups. For this style of knowledge production, knowledge democracy goes hand in hand with accountability and transparency. Society has the right to know what is done in the ivory tower of research and researchers have a duty to make information transparent. Democratic societies are interested in what experiments are done, whether the costs are justified, and whether there might be some unexpected side effects. Inappropriate use therefore means lack of transparency and accountability.

Table 11.1. Four research styles with respect to two dimensions: the relationship between the degree of input of lay knowledge and the degree of focus on non-dominant actors

Degree of of focus on involvement non-dominant actors: / Degree of lay knowledge input:	Low	High
Low	Self-referential knowledge production	Knowledge dissemination (transmission)
	Mono-, inter- and multi-disciplinary research	Creating access to knowledge
High	Mutual learning for knowledge production between scientists and societal actors	Knowledge co-creation between scientists and societal actors, with specific focus on involvement of non-dominant actors

The *knowledge dissemination style* can be described as a process in which knowledge, which is developed largely without the input of lay knowledge, is transferred to the wider public. Knowledge dissemination can be found for example in relation to health promotion and disease prevention activities by encouraging improvements in life-style and behaviour. This dissemination style implies a one-way interaction between scientists and non-scientists and does not have the characteristics of mutual learning and a joint problem definition. In this type of knowledge production, knowledge democracy means the responsibility for balanced information. The responsibility is with those who disseminate knowledge. They have to make sure that they are not blindly advertising views of specific pressure groups, like those who uncritically promote biotechnology, nanotechnology or enhancement medicine as panacea. Dissemination in knowledge democracy means providing society with state of the art information on pros, cons and uncertainties of new technologies in order to enable society to come up with a well-informed decision. Inappropriate use would imply the provision of biased information, manipulation and coercion of societal actors.

The *mutual learning for knowledge production between scientists and societal actors style* is well described in the Transdisciplinary Case Study (TCS) approach by Scholz and co-workers, and comprises multi-phase projects (2–4 years) to support societal decision-makers and the public in a joint analysis with academic researchers to tackle complex multi-stakeholder problems at the regional level. The transdisciplinary process usually starts with a collaboration between a legitimised decision-maker (for example the community mayor, the owners of a brownfield, the head of a local environmental agency). The involvement of members of relevant stakeholder groups is an essential part of the case studies. Mutual learning among various actors involved is the key objective, but actors have different societal roles in the process. Thus for example, the TCS approach is conceived as preparation not a replacement for a (subsequent) democratic decision process where all members of the society should have a say about the concrete actions to be taken. This is an appropriate approach if relevant information on the issue is available among participating actors and can be utilised in the transdisciplinary process, and if the decision-makers involved continue to stay in power. The approach faces challenges if non-dominant actors posses important information, which could not be included in the transdisciplinary process for instance because of a lack of time, if they have not been identified or if the subsequent decision process is not organised in an inclusive way by decision-makers. In that situation fierce resistance during implementation phases may be expected.

The *knowledge co-creation between scientists and societal actors, with specific focus on non-dominant actors style* is captured in the Interactive Learning and Action (ILA) approach that contains cyclic multi-phase programmes stretching over a longer time period. Here dominant and non-dominant actors are supported by the transdisciplinary researchers to engage in a joint exploration and analysis of the social problem they choose to solve. Co-creation of insights and solutions in the midst of academic and non-academic expertise is facilitated by various tools and aims at becoming a part of the competences learned in the process. This style of knowledge production is most appropriate if the decision-making process and its implementation depend on a number of different actors within academia, civil society, governmental agencies and the private sector, and if the knowledge needed to address the issue is distributed among these actors. Here the challenge for knowledge democracy is to find the balance between the knowledge of those who are in power and the knowledge of those who are marginalised, as most existing mechanisms would lean towards the exclusion of non-dominant actors. The worst case scenario in this case is a democratic, open and creative process which is followed by a final decision made on the basis of new criteria by a dominant actor.

In the next sections we focus on the last two styles and (three) transdisciplinary research approaches within these styles. We look at their specific sets of principles, and discuss how they structure the design and scope of the projects and/or programmes and the implications within the context of knowledge democratisation.

11.4 Mutual learning for knowledge production between scientists and societal actors style

Within the mutual learning for knowledge production between scientists and societal actors style, two approaches, the Transdisciplinary Case Study Approach and the Institute for Social-Ecological Research (ISOE) model, are described below.

11.4.1 Transdisciplinary case study approach

Starting in 1993 Roland Scholz and co-workers developed the Transdisciplinary Case Study (TCS) approach (Scholz et al. 1995), which was applied in more than 20 studies in Switzerland, Sweden, Austria and Germany (Scholz et al. 2006, Stauffacher et al. 2008). The approach was developed as part of a teaching course at the ETH Zurich (Stauffacher et al. 2006) and is still conceptualised as a (societal) learning process towards sustainable development among the involved actors (capacity building). The six key steps are (Scholz and Stauffacher 2007, Scholz et al. 2006, Walter et al. 2007):

1. Defining a guiding question to be agreed upon and owned by both researchers and stakeholders; this step also includes the crucial phase of framing the problem which should integrate different perspectives in society;
2. Sub-dividing the problem in a limited, but functionally sufficient, number of sub-questions and/or projects;
3. Problem representation by a system model that describes and analyses the functional components and their mutual impacts;
4. Creating scenarios (different windows of the future) on the basis of the variables of step 3 and detailed knowledge acquired therein;
5. Conducting a Multi-attribute Utility Analysis (multi-criteria assessment) based on both scientific evaluation as well as stakeholder preferences;
6. Developing robust orientations for future development based on negotiations between science experts and stakeholders.

Several principles, presented in Box 11.2, are specifically relevant in regards to this transdisciplinary research approach.

Box 11.2 Principles of transdisciplinary case study approach

- Complement (inter)disciplinary scientific activities with knowledge and values from various societal actors (*industry, policy-makers, public at large*);
- Contribute to sustainable development;
- Organise *mutual learning* among university and actors from outside academia;
- Organise knowledge integration;

- Reflect on *risks and benefits* of possible interventions;
- Understand *roles and responsibilities* of different actors;
- Identify needs for knowledge;
- *Joint leadership* of university and actors from outside academia on equal footing for the process and/or project;
- *Joint responsibility* for the process but taking different or complementary roles in line with functional differentiation in societies.

The participants in the TCS approach are scientific and technical experts and decision-makers from relevant stakeholder organisations, such as CEOs of companies, government officials and academic experts. The public at large is involved whenever considered necessary and useful (functional involvement) (Stauffacher et al. 2008). During the project,

> ... stakeholders are actively and continuously involved in the production of scientific knowledge through mutual learning among researchers and themselves (Walter et al. 2007: 326).

The last step (6) is done collaboratively, but the subsequent implementation of necessary democratic decision processes is regarded to be the sole responsibility of the decision-makers involved in the process. Researchers take a modest advisory role. This is in line with a clear distinction of roles between transdisciplinary researchers, scientific experts and stakeholders:

> … in our view both stakeholders and researchers have their own goals and interests and profit in different ways from the cooperation. They are separate entities with different characteristics and must be treated as such (Walter et al. 2007: 326).

The different gains include new scientific insights into for example urban development, transport behaviour, clustering of industries, risk perception and sustainability assessment. While societal gains include changes in the knowledge, the decision-making capacity and at times consensus-building or negotiation among different interests of different actors involved (Scholz 2010). This hybrid approach addressing both practical problems, but at the same time furthering scientific knowledge, is in line with the classical action-research paradigm developed by Kurt Lewin (1946).

Scholz identifies complementary roles for scientists and non-scientists as a key element of his approach. This is in line with functional differentiation in present societies and negotiated throughout the process as a form of boundary work (Gieryn 1995). Scholz distinguishes clearly between different ongoing processes: the scientific research process, the political decision process and the related public discourse (Scholz 2010). The transdisciplinary process is placed at the interface of these three, but the process has a temporary nature and primarily serves as preparation for subsequent democratic decision-making processes involving the public at large. In the transdisciplinary process, non-academia take responsibility for decisions jointly made in the process and provide scientists with unbiased insight into the complexity of real-world problems. Science takes the responsibility for the academic quality of products and provides assurance that scientific knowledge can be used in an unbiased manner to accomplish a multi-disciplinary (environmental sciences, economics, legal sciences) analysis of the case that belongs to the real-world complexity (CEOs, officials from municipalities and Cantons). For this purpose non-academia and scientists join in a transdisciplinary taskforce and together define the knowledge gaps that have to be investigated. Knowledge and values from relevant actors are collected in a transparent and method-driven manner and integrated analytically (Stauffacher et al. 2008). Care is taken that knowledge of those who have relevant expertise is integrated, be they from academia or not.

As Scholz emphasises, this approach certainly needs a new type of researcher who is open to complex real-world challenges with economic and political dimensions. His system analysis, scenarios and multi-criteria assessment (Steps 3, 4 and 5) are important methods in constructing new ways for the participants to analyse and to reflect on the complexity of the problem at hand from a bird's eye position. As such, it is a transdisciplinary process organised and framed by knowledge integration methods (for example scenario analysis, area development negotiation, life cycle analysis, integrated risk management, see Scholz and Tietje 2002). It gives the actors involved the possibility to learn more about the (decision) problem in a structured and transparent way.

As said above, the TCS approach has been implemented not only in Switzerland (16 case studies, published yearly as case study books for the general public, see for example Scholz et al. 2007 and as research articles, see for example Scholz and Stauffacher 2007, Stauffacher et al. 2008), but also in Sweden (eight case studies at Gothenburg University/Chalmers), Austria (four case studies at Graz University and BoKu Vienna) and Germany[4].

11.4.2 The German ISOE Model of Transdisciplinary Research

Transdisciplinary research has been the focus of different groups in Germany. Well-known is the Institute for Social-Ecological Research (ISOE), which has developed the ISOE model of transdisciplinary research. The principles of the model are described in Box 11.3. Below, we briefly summarise the ISOE model that comprises three phases (Jahn and Keil 2006, Jahn 2008).

[4] These universities and further interested scholars have founded in 2002 the International Transdisciplinarity Network for Case Studies in Sustainable Development (http://www.uns.ethz.ch/translab/itdnet) which meets annually and has published for example a special issue of the "International Journal of Sustainability in Higher Education". In this network, experiences in transdisciplinarity are exchange and respective knowledge and expertise is further developed.

Box 11.3 Principles of the ISOE model of transdisciplinary research

- Enhance the societal *and* scientific capacity to deal with complex problems of *sustainable development*;
- Enable *joint problem formulation* between scientific and societal actors;
- Relate societal problems to problems of (scientific) knowledge;
- Produce scientifically certified and action-oriented knowledge;
- Organise methodologically reliable *mutual learning processes* involving both scientific and societal actors;
- Contribute to *changing problem perceptions* of societal actors by organising feedback processes;
- Enhance the societal capacity to deal with complexity, uncertainty, ignorance, and contested knowledge;
- Integrate *different types of knowledge* (disciplinary scientific as well as non-scientific knowledge);
- Contribute to the differentiation and integration of the claims, wishes and expectations of individuals, institutions and groups concerning possible solutions to problems;
- Anticipate and reflect the impacts of solutions on the original societal and scientific problems.

At the beginning of the transdisciplinary research process (phase 1) a common research object is constituted and an appropriate research team is assembled. This phase is normally marked by a high degree of tension caused by a mix of different interests, individual and institutional goals, disciplinary backgrounds, and claims and norms concerning what is good science. The extent to which the research team succeeds in balancing all of these conflicting pressures and makes use of them productively will be decisive for the output of the research project. The constitution of a common research object, the so-called problem framing, is of particular importance right from the outset. What happens here is that problem descriptions, whether formulated in everyday language or in the language of a discipline, are reworked into an "epistemic object", that is, into a scientific object that we can investigate and understand in a discipline-spanning manner.

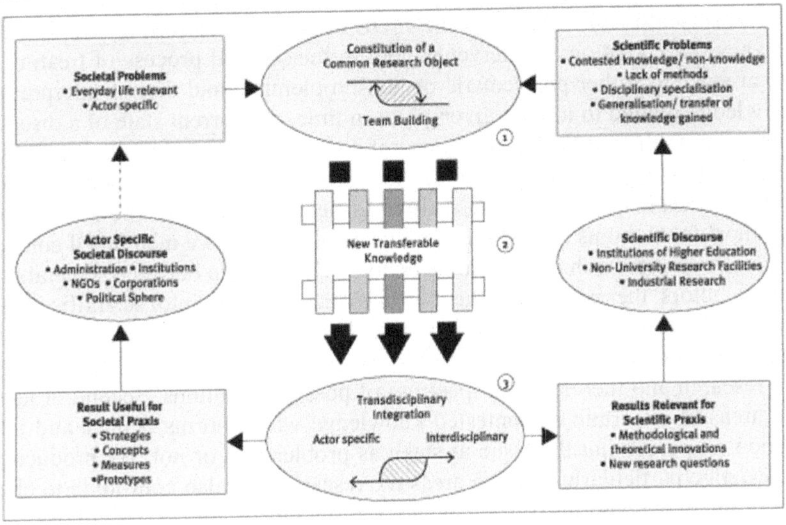

Fig. 11.1 The ISOE model of the transdisciplinary research process (Jahn and Keil 2006: 321; modified).

In a second phase, in which new (disciplinary) knowledge is to be generated, the emphasis is on interdisciplinary integration. Here it is a question of assuring the transferability of the new disciplinary knowledge within the overall process and of working on a common "object of knowledge" (models, theoretical concepts, et cetera). In this phase there is a particular need to avoid the dangers of turf-building based on individual interests and the problem of language differences, particularly between disciplines. It is important, therefore, to foresee the need for early integration measures (for example, interface workshops, facilitated discussions in working groups or cross-disciplinary projects), as symbolised in Figure 11.1 by the cross bars to the "disciplinary" or sub-project columns, and to plan for these.

In the last phase, there are two methodologically linked integration steps. First, the results of the previous phases are summarised in an initial version of the project's results. After this the validity and relevance of the results (new scientific/theoretical knowledge or practical knowledge useful for solving problems) are assessed and evaluated in terms of their range of efficacy and their appropriateness for the scientific or practical problem selected at the outset. This may lead to the results of the first integration step being subjected to a (partial) "de-integration", followed by their reintegration in a new, second consolidation of problem components and their possible solutions, bringing about a stronger integration of the overall results in the end. From the model it is clear how important the integration work (represented by the middle column in Figure 11.1) is: the specific scientific challenges are here. How well one responds to these – for example by developing new methods for knowledge integration – will determine the quality of the research results for both the societal and scientific praxis, as each follows its own epistemic path.

Transdisciplinary research in the ISOE model is conceived as a 2-fold critical discourse intervention: it intervenes both in the societal process of treating an issue at stake as either problematic or non-problematic and that of interpreting the knowledge related to it. At a given point in time, the current state of a discourse is mapped onto the controlled conditions of a structured research process. “Mapped” here implies a participatory approach; stakeholders become involved into a research process that models the real-world decision-making. The most important and most momentous part of this involvement is the above mentioned constitution of a common research object. In the course of a dialogue between societal and scientific actors the issue at stake becomes transformed into scientific questions thereby determining the corridor in which new scientific knowledge can arise. This transformation is so important for two reasons. First, it determines the goal of the research and therefore the spectrum of possible solutions. Second, it identifies the areas of uncertain or contested knowledge where norms, values and interests decide on perceiving the issue at stake as problematic or not. By producing new knowledge particularly in these areas the research can also contribute to changing the problem perceptions of the stakeholders (and the scientists!) involved.

At the end of a transdisciplinary research process this discourse intervention manifests itself in concrete results, like innovative concepts, strategies or prototypes, which are delivered to the realm of true decision-making. Beyond that it is the potential of transdisciplinary research to more directly influence decision-making by changing the problem perceptions of stakeholders, which creates an “added value” compared to conventional forms of research. It is by organising such learning processes between and within society and science where transdisciplinary research can effectively generate real-world impacts in a representative democracy.

11.5 Knowledge co-creation between scientists and societal actors, with specific focus on non-dominant actors

A good example of this research style is the Interactive Learning and Action (ILA) approach. In the Netherlands, starting in 1985, Joske Bunders and co-workers developed the ILA approach which was applied in over 20 projects in various domains, including agriculture, health, environment and water management. The ILA approach consists of the following four phases (Broerse and Bunders 2000, Bunders and Broerse 1991):

Phase 1. Initiation and preparation: The objectives of this phase are to establish and train an interdisciplinary team of intermediaries, and to become familiar with the setting and the local community. A scientific state of the art analysis is performed as well as a stakeholder and value analysis to identify the actors that need to be involved in the process. In this phase the focus is on realising a wide scan.

Phase 2. In-depth study of needs and visions: Through various data collection methods, such as interviews and focus groups, the needs and visions[5] of different stakeholders in science and society are identified. The different actors tend to frame the issue at hand differently, and may have (negative) presumptions about other parties in the innovation process, which might hamper a constructive, meaningful dialogue (Schon and Rein 1994). In the ILA approach the premise is that interaction between dominant and non-dominant actors is much more effective if the different "frames of reference"[6] are studied and made explicit before heterogeneous dialogues are organised.

Phase 3. Integration: Heterogeneous dialogue meetings (carefully structured and facilitated workshops) are organised in order to exchange information and stimulate mutual learning between different stakeholders. Apart from discussing findings of the previous phase, this phase aims to identify shared future visions, quick wins (concrete applications that can be realised in a relatively short time frame) and contested visions (where stakeholders disagree).

Phase 4. Public priority setting and planning: Although actors may decide to test relevant options at any stage of the process, it is advisable at some time to organise and hold a priority setting and planning workshop that brings all actors together. The objectives of such a workshop are: (1) to allow review and criticism of the team's findings by a wide audience, (2) to legitimise the findings, (3) to allow room for new contributions, (4) to enhance the visibility of the needs of non-dominant actors, and (5) to establish a plan of action. Discussions at the workshop should lead to shared decisions on the most important topics for research and on other relevant matters (links between research at different levels, changes in policy, etc.). Thereafter, the results of the information analysis and integration exercise can be published, together with (or separately from) the workshop proceedings.

Phase 5. Project formulation and implementation: The plan of action which resulted from the previous phase forms the input for the specific projects that are formulated and implemented. These projects are or should be a direct response to the needs of users and other stakeholders. Activities could include: experiments at local level, institution-based R&D, changes to the policy environment, training in the ILA approach at institutional level, and improvements to the approach followed. Implementation takes place through reflexive learning cycles of planning, action, observation, reflection and re-planning.

These phases can be broadly distinguished on the basis of their chronology, the outcome of the previous phase being the input for the next. Yet the phases overlap, as each consists of activities which may be undertaken several times in a different order throughout the process. In this way an interactive and iterative process evolves, instead of a linear one. The different principles of the ILA approach are given in Box 11.4.

---

[5] Visions can be described as mental images of attainable futures that are considered desirable and shared by a collection of actors.

[6] A "frame of reference" can be viewed as a combined set of knowledge, norms and values and (societal) background by which people weigh, value and interpret new information.

Box 11.4 Principles of interactive learning and action approach

- Establish *trust* relationships;
- Engage *(end) users* (and those affected by the changes);
- Identify a shared vision;
- Enhance coalition building;
- Facilitate knowledge integration;
- Guide and/or coach intermediaries and/or teams.

The ILA approach applies tools in which contributions from one actor in the process are visualised in connection with contributions from other actors, such as actor network analysis (actor charts) and causal analysis (argumentation trees). However, the differentiated roles of the players/actors seem to be a major difference with the TCS approach. The ILA approach distinguishes between "academic experts" and "non-academic experts", "dominant actors" and "non-dominant actors" (that is patients, farmers, citizens/consumers), and the Transdisciplinary knowledge brokers (or Transdisciplinary researchers). Experts, non-academics and patients/small-scale farmers/citizens/consumers should be understood and approached in accordance with their specific interest in order to accomplish an open dialogue for the learning processes. The non-dominant actors are specifically relevant from the perspective of knowledge democracy.

Another aspect of ILA approach is the development of new, interactive research methods. Although more conventional methods such as interviews and focus groups are also often used, there was a need for new methods such as the argumentation tree or the dynamic learning agenda. Table 11.2 gives an illustrative, non-exhaustive overview of different research methods in the ILA approach.

Examples of ILA applications in the field of biotechnology for resource-poor farmers in developing countries were given in Sect. 11.2. Many of the results and recommendations of the projects have been implemented (research agendas, policy development and implementation, institutionalisation in institutions). This therefore raises the question of how the impact of this approach can be explained. Here we look at that question from the perspective of the ILA methodology as described.

Focus on implementation in all phases: An issue usually addressed at the later stages of a policy or research cycle is the implementation of decisions. In the ILA approach there is a preoccupation with anticipating implementation problems in all phases of the process. The fact that the inclusion of non-dominant actors in the decision-making process is a focus in the ILA approach is probably the cause of this concern. It is extremely easy *not* to implement a decision or policy when the decision affects mainly non-dominant actors and when the recommendation does not fit with the existing "routines" of organisations, such as academia, government agencies, industry and NGOs. Thus the difficulty of focusing on the needs of those with less power creates a focus on anticipating implementation problems as a condition sine qua non. The trusted coalition partners are crucial in providing knowledge on how to phrase and embed the recommendations to facilitate implementation. Appreciative inquiry is a crucial element in this delicate process (Regeer and

Bunders 2009). Also the research spiral leads to an increasing understanding of how to improve the link between goals and practical reality.

Table 11.2 Different research methods (non-exhaustive) used in the ILA approach

Research methods	Tool description	Role of the tool in project context
Report analysis	Report collection, analysis and systematisation	Clarification at the start of the project
Questionnaire	Poll, systematically gathering information	Insight into plurality and distribution views experts
Semi-structured interview	One-on-one sessions investigating contextual aspects and deeper motives	Investigate implicit arguments and positions, evaluate results quantitative polls
Citizen panel	Panels that obtain deliberated positions of citizens on a social issue (inventory opinions and arguments)	Explore different structures of meaning and the way of sense-making of citizens
Focus group	Applied to a topic to shift focus from vague to clear, converge from general to particular and detect the essential notion	Overview of diversity of perceptions
Socratic dialogue	Intensive joint group investigation that aims to make a systematic analysis of a concrete case focusing on a "why"-question	Describe variety of interests and opinions, investigate the conceptual and philosophical foundation of a single concept
Argumentation tree	Visualisation of interrelations of sets of arguments	Show argumentation relations between separate arguments used in meetings as citizen panel, focus group or Socratic dialogue
Expert meeting	Synthesis of expert knowledge) (knowledge convergence?)	Discussion of results of other tools, looking for falsification, and bring results a step further
Linking interactive priority setting to research activities	Confront the needs of knowledge with supply of knowledge necessary for agenda-setting	Tool is a link between the outcomes of interactive process and (research) activities taking place in society. Show added value of interactive priority-setting

Policy advice	Selection and prioritisation of options for policy action	Indicate how analysis of interested, non-involved citizen differs from policymakers, politicians, key figures and stakeholders. Tool presents policy options
Reflection session / eye-opener workshop	Structured process that makes learning experiences explicit and available to outsiders	Generalisation can make learning experiences in a project more superficial or obvious. An eye-opener workshop aims for in-depth sharing of project insights with outsiders
Audiovisual learning history	An accessible way to capture learning experiences of different participants using video clips to enhance reflection also of other actors	Participants tell their own story on film, which provides perspectives from different team members about their own challenges and struggles during the process
Dynamic learning agenda	Change agenda which enables the discussion about (long term) challenges in system innovation projects	Identifies long-term challenges and helps with concretisation and action for different participants. The agenda is a short list and during the process challenges appear and disappear. The dynamic learning agenda captures learning experiences

Knowledge integration and depth of analysis (increase complexity first, then converge): The issues addressed by the ILA approach are extremely complex and cannot be framed into simple problem definitions. Due to the wide variety of actors and frames, many possible problem definitions and solutions become available. With respect to knowledge integration the following aspects are considered (see for example, Thompson Klein et al. 2001: 239, Van Mansfeld 2003: 37):

- The type of knowledge that all participating actors possess;
- The type of knowledge that is gained in the process;
- The foundations, validity and limits of data and statements;
- The optimisation of the use of all these forms of knowledge in the process of problem solving;
- Thorough consideration of which set of methods to apply in order to integrate the different types of knowledge;
- The justifiability and objectiveness of knowledge;

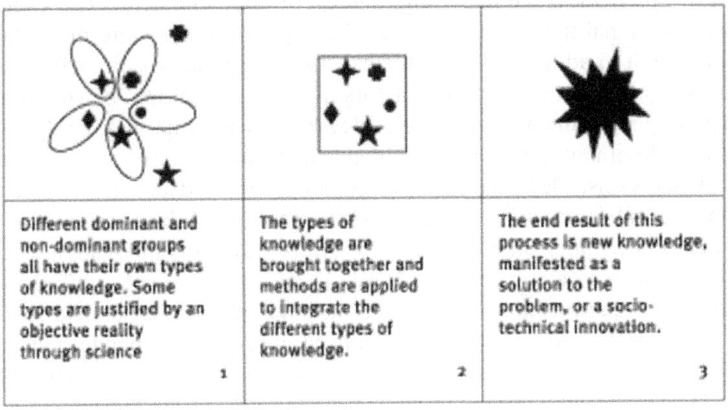

Fig. 11.2 The process of knowledge integration.

In general, scholars of transdisciplinary research pay much attention to the methodology of knowledge integration (see Figure 11.2: 2). Various inventories and checklists have been developed, enabling transdisciplinary researchers to choose from a range of instruments the one most appropriate tool for the phase their project is in (see for example, Dammers et al. 2002). The way in which knowledge integration is facilitated in the ILA approach creates a deep understanding of the various issues through the process of appreciative inquiry (both in interviews and focus groups). Not by going for consensus, conflict or negotiation, but primarily through a shared and deep understanding of the various positions, new suggestions for inclusive solutions emerge. Of course it is necessary that such solutions can later be validated by the knowledge produced throughout the process.

Work on enabling conditions during the process: It is common practice for intervention approaches to formulate a set of conditions under which the intervention process can be successful. The ILA approach does not apply such a list, because conditions conducive to including non-dominant actors in decision-making usually do not exist; belonging to a non-dominant or marginalised group means that a range of favourable conditions, like validated expert knowledge and financial resources, are lacking. The crux is that the process is designed in such a way that these conditions are developed *during* the process. This often implies a long time scale. The creation of such conditions through a mutual learning process in which all partners acquire additional relevant knowledge (about content and strategy) becomes the starting point of a new knowledge infrastructure for knowledge democratisation.

Unexpected results, popularity of ILA among dominant actors: An unexpected result of this work is the increasing interest of dominant actors (for example, ministries, municipalities, industry) in the ILA approach. They are interested in using this approach to address their problems. How can an approach, deliberately developed for including non-dominant actors in decision-making, be so interesting and attractive for dominant actors themselves? Two reasons may apply. Firstly, not only non-dominant actors face problems with decision-making and implementation of decisions. Dominant actors have to face and deal with a wide variety of routines of other organisations in order to implement their results too. This may considerably hamper their ambitions to realise (system) innovation. Secondly the ILA approach has developed through an analysis of university/industry/government relationships that focused on innovative policies. The ILA approach can therefore be seen as a professionalised approach to change which dominant actors have already been using for a long time in a less informed and sophisticated way.

11.6 Mainstreaming transdisciplinary research

At the RMNO conference on Knowledge Democracy in Leiden 2009 many transdisciplinary researchers discussed the challenges they faced in working in this field – they were remarkably similar. From these discussions we derived various requirements important for mainstreaming transdisciplinary research and for stimulating a process that supports the development of a transdisciplinary research tradition: the need for action by academia, and evaluation and quality control. Each is discussed below.

11.6.1 The need for action by academia

Transdisciplinary research is conceived as a mode of research that promises to produce knowledge of immediate relevance for solving complex societal problems. However, academia as the place where knowledge production still mainly takes place does neither encourage nor reward transdisciplinary research nor appreciates the added value it can bring for enhancing the problem-solving capacity of societies. University curricula and careers still mostly proceed along lines of disciplinary specialisation. Transdisciplinarity is often seen as blocking the way to scientific excellence rather than paving it. Behind this lies the debate regarding the relationship between the absolute truth and the contextual, practical relevance of scientific knowledge. Visioning knowledge democracy requires balancing this relationship in favour of the latter. The following adjustments in today's higher education and training are considered important in promoting these changes:

– Transdisciplinarity in fact needs disciplinary knowledge that can be related in novel ways in order to produce integrated knowledge about complex problems. The ability to relate disciplinary knowledge to the other types of knowledge requires reflecting upon ones own boundaries. Thus an important element of higher education in knowledge democracy would be conveying to students the limits of knowledge of their respective disciplines and the methods necessary to explore beyond.

- Institutions of higher education should increasingly offer inter- and transdisciplinary curricula. There are already a number of highly successful examples at established universities across Europe and elsewhere, which demonstrate that scientific excellence and a transdisciplinary profile are not at odds with each other. These courses, however, should not be a mere addition of existing disciplinary teaching. Instead they have to offer the opportunity to acquire individual skills which are generally not part of disciplinary curricula.
- One of the core capacities of a professional transdisciplinary researcher is the ability to integrate. Integration has four levels: (1) integration of (different forms of) knowledge, (2) social and organisational integration, (3) communicative integration, and (4) technical integration. This requires a mindset that is able to explicate and recognise differences with the aim of identifying novel relations. Developing such a mindset has to be supported by allowing for practical inter- and transdisciplinary research experiences early on in higher education.
- Above all, integration in the transdisciplinary context requires a methodology and a validated use of tools. This toolbox of methods should be shared and discussed in relation to good and bad practices, and taught in dedicated courses.
- The institutions of higher education should provide equal opportunities for young researchers who decide for an inter- or transdisciplinary career. In particular, professorships or lecturer posts with a pronounced inter- or transdisciplinary profile should be established.
- The aforementioned adjustments of the current system of knowledge production, however, will probably not be enough for realising the full potential of transdisciplinary research. Instead new institutions may be necessary. They may be realised as individual institutes or as networks and should be embedded in the existing structures. In knowledge democracy these "transdisciplinary academies" are the places where a new relationship between science and society materialises. It is here where more societal participation in setting research agendas is realised and where different forms of scientific and non-scientific knowledge are systematically related to each other.

11.6.2 Quality criteria and evaluation methods

No scientific community, or even a given research joint venture, will be able to canonise one particular understanding of transdisciplinarity. On the contrary, such a result will only be reached through a long process of creating a common understanding – a process that will require building a tradition of transdisciplinary research and establishing better institutionalisation (for example with a firm place in higher education or dedicated journals, see above). This process cannot be steered; it is evolutionary and requires time. Nevertheless the necessary precondition for – or at the same time the result of – this "community building" is the development of quality criteria and evaluation methods for transdisciplinary research. The following aspects should be considered in this endeavour:

- The composition of the research team should be well-targeted and appropriate in terms of personnel, scientific fields, and practice orientation. Accounting for this composition in design and evaluation is essential because of its influence on problem formulation and thus on the possible outcomes of a project. Specific transdisciplinary quality criteria, which are tailored to this requirement and the associated integration tasks, are needed.
- The variety of research approaches in transdisciplinary projects needs to be acknowledged and mirrored in the evaluation process. A peer review in the conventional sense – that is, an evaluation by colleagues within the scientific field – is thus hardly conceivable. Instead project evaluations need to be conceived as an expert review in which the group of evaluators is composed of (a) specialists who can judge the object of investigation from an individual disciplinary perspective and/or from a perspective of integrated fields, and (b) scientists who have experience in carrying out transdisciplinary research.
- Conventional scientific evaluation is not sufficient for appreciating the entirety of a transdisciplinary research project. For this, discursive evaluations are required where the evaluators and the evaluated jointly conduct an analytical discourse on the backgrounds of the successes and failures of the research project in question. Only in direct discussion will it be possible to gain a deeper understanding of the complicated processes, steps toward integration, revisions of plan, etc. Discursive evaluations do not have the character of a purely summarising inventory of project results. Such "formative evaluations" should rather emphasise the goal of learning (either for a still continuing project or for the design and processing of new transdisciplinary projects).
- The evaluation needs to be based on a clear understanding of transdisciplinarity, in the sense that the evaluators and the evaluated have clarity about the chosen approach, for example, the conceptual interpretation of transdisciplinarity.

11.7 Concluding remarks

In the introduction we stated that if we say: "We ought to give actors, who have the relevant knowledge for addressing societal problems, the opportunity to influence decision-making around public policy and research agendas", we need to know how to do that. What are the mechanisms that have proven to be helpful? We discussed the notion of transdisciplinarity and distinguished two different styles of transdisciplinary research and their similarities and differences in terms of principles, concepts and core methods.

In order to understand how transdisciplinary research can contribute to knowledge democracy, it is helpful to distinguish between different forms of democracy in which transdisciplinary research can play a role: basic and representative democracy on the one hand and deliberative democracy on the other hand. For these forms of democracy, transdisciplinary research can rely on interactions between actors of the establishment. From the perspective of knowledge democracy, it is however also important to have a specific focus on involving non-dominant actors in the transdisciplinary research process as well. That implies that both within the context of a basic and representative democracy and in the context of a deliberative democracy, enriching the transdisciplinary research process with the involvement of non-dominant actors is relevant. However the inclusion of non-dominant actors is more likely to be effective in a deliberative democracy (Hajer 2003).

In the *mutual learning for knowledge production between scientists and societal actors style* (of which the TCS approach and ISOE model are examples), the transdisciplinary research process is specifically tailored to enrich the decision-making process which is regarded as the sole responsibility of the decision-makers involved in the process. It is here that the public at large can exercise its democratic rights. Thus, the TCS approach and ISOE model are conceived as preparation and input, not a replacement, for (subsequent) democratic decision-making processes where all members of society should have a say. Transdisciplinary research is then exercised within the boundaries of a basic or representative democracy.

In the *knowledge co-creation between scientists, dominant and non-dominant societal actors style* (of which ILA approach is an example), the transdisciplinary research process can in principle support decision-making in both a basic or representative democracy and a deliberative democracy. Governance in a deliberative democracy is the cooperation of government, civil society, the private sector and NGOs to solve complex problems in the public domain. Policy-makers with mandates that concern only one specific sector find complex problems, in which different sectors are involved, difficult to deal with. If governments cannot deal with complex problems that do not fit into their structures and cultures, they can participate in and facilitate governance arrangements with other actors who introduce different (types of) knowledge and other resources. The increased occurrence and recognition of complex (wicked) problems propel the rise of deliberative governance. The governance structures contain often partners from the establishment: industry, government, universities. Other, non-dominant, actors like resource-poor farmers or patients in those cases are not necessarily included in the knowledge sharing and production in this form of governance.

The inclusion of non-dominant actors and their knowledge and interests in the transdisciplinary research process was the main drive for development of the ILA approach. It is, however, in the rise of deliberative governance structures that the use of the ILA approach is strongly enabled, since for every complex problem a new level playing field for actors has to be established, allowing for non-dominant actors to realise their involvement (a window of opportunity is created).

So the TCS, ISOE and ILA approaches are driven by different concerns and opportunities. According to Meuleman (2009a, b), national traditions and cultures may influence which approach emerges and is most applicable. This might explain why the ILA approach emerged in the Netherlands, a country with a long history of consensus democracy and network governance.

The two transdisciplinary research styles might also enrich each other, especially if experts who are trained in different approaches become available. It is likely that TCS, ISOE and ILA approaches are increasingly used and will become more developed. For this to happen, it is important that further mainstreaming of transdisciplinary research takes place.

Mainstreaming of transdisciplinary research is likely to stimulate a climate for innovation (see also Chap. 22). This is also suggested by the finding that the processes of including non-dominant actors into decision-making are now seen as attractive by many dominant actors. This would imply that a focus on knowledge democratisation may indeed lead to a change of knowledge infrastructure in a way that is appreciated by the establishment. This will certainly support the further development of transdisciplinary research practices as useful strategies to create conditions for sustainable innovation and change, as well as knowledge democratisation.

Acknowledgements

We specifically like to thank Tjard de Cock Buning for taking the first steps in realizing this collaborative partnership. In addition, Mariëtte van Amstel's intellectual support in the writing of this chapter is warmly acknowledged. Also we would like to thank the anonymous reviewer who made some highly valuable comments on an earlier draft of the chapter.

12 Knowledge synchronisation: interactive knowledge production between experts, bureaucrats and stakeholders

Jurian Edelenbos, Arwin van Buuren and Nienke van Schie

Abstract

In this chapter we analyse the process of knowledge production between experts, bureaucrats and stakeholders. From our two in-depth Dutch case studies we conclude that the interplay between experts and bureaucrats is not very problematic in knowledge production, because of discipline congruence and institutionalised relations between the two in the field of water management. The interplay between stakeholder knowledge on the one hand and expert and bureaucratic knowledge on the other is more problematic and leads to problems of legitimate knowledge production and decision-making.

12.1 Introduction

Citizen involvement is increasingly implemented in complex water management projects in the Netherlands (Edelenbos et al. 2009), but also abroad (Rinaudo and Garin 2005, Petts and Brooks 2006). Through the active involvement of citizens and other stakeholders, new insights, information and knowledge is brought into the assessment and decision-making processes. The field of water management is traditionally dominated by water professionals (Lintsen 2002). A strongly closed and interconnected organisation of water management authorities and public and private knowledge institutes has developed (Petts and Brooks 2006). Through the introduction of stakeholder involvement this traditional emphasis on expert knowledge gets competition from the local knowledge of citizens. In this new situation, clashes between expert knowledge and stakeholder knowledge can easily take place (McClean and Shaw 2005).

In this chapter we are interested in the relationship between experts and stakeholders in the process of knowledge production for assessment and decision-making. However, we want to further elaborate the much used division between expert and stakeholder knowledge (Rinaudo and Garin 2005, Petts and Brooks 2006) by introducing a third form of knowledge: bureaucratic knowledge (McClean and Shaw 2005), that is the knowledge held by bureaucratic officials (civil servants) that is necessary to guide knowledge through governmental and

R.J. in 't Veld (ed.), *Knowledge Democracy*, DOI 10.1007/978-3-642-11381-9_12,

political institutions to be used in formal political assessments and decision-making. The worlds of experts, bureaucrats and stakeholders are rather different (Hunt and Shackley 1999) and these differences may hinder the knowledge co-production process between these three domains.

The goal of this chapter is to describe and analyse the knowledge production process in terms of this threefold division. We are specifically interested in the level of interplay between the three knowledge domains. Therefore, we start this chapter from the following research question: what is the level of interplay between experts, bureaucrats and stakeholders in the production of knowledge for water related spatial decision-making?

To answer this question we conducted comparative case study research on two water cases in the Netherlands: around Arnemuiden and Gouwe Wiericke. In both cases water was an important issue in decision-making. Moreover, in both cases it was attempted, in different ways, to relate or integrate stakeholder, bureaucratic and expert knowledge. We conducted research through a number of methods: document analysis, interviews and participatory observation (that is through action research).

In Sect. 12.2 we present our theoretical focus and analytical framework. In Sect. 12.3 we subsequently give two case descriptions, Gouwe Wiericke and around Arnemuiden. In Sect. 12.4 we analyse the two cases comparatively on the level of interplay between the three knowledge domains. Section 12.5 provides conclusions and discussion.

12.2 Knowledge in complex decision-making

Knowledge in complex decision-making is often disputed (Van Buuren and Edelenbos 2004). Nowadays network societies' decision-making has become a social issue, and the mobilisation of different sources of knowledge as input for this decision-making has increased tremendously (Pielke 2007). The provision of knowledge is no longer the sole province of society's elites. The vocal, self-assured, highly-educated, and well-read citizen of today has obtained much more insight into the nature of scientific knowledge (Nowotny et al. 2002) meaning knowledge has become public property (Bernstein 1991).

As a result, the relationship between scientific advice and the policy process has changed (Pielke 2007). Scientists have been knocked off their pedestal and have lost their "a-priori authority".

> The deficiencies of science-based appraisal, particularly in complex and uncertain decision contexts, are not only evident to the public but are also increasingly questioned by experts who are challenged by counterclaims (Petts and Brooks, 2006: 1046).

A "knowledge market" has emerged with many suppliers (and customers), competing in their attempt to prove the significance of their knowledge (Edelenbos, 2005).

12.2.1 Expert, bureaucratic and stakeholder knowledge

In complex decision-making, actors produce and rely on knowledge that differs in both their content and orientation (Eshuis and Stuiver 2005). It also emerges within different institutional and social contexts (Hajer and Wagenaar 2003). In general, three types of knowledge can be distinguished within the context of decision-making processes (Rinaudo and Garin 2005, Hunt and Shackley 1999):

- scientific (or expert) knowledge;
- bureaucratic (or administrative) knowledge; and
- stakeholder (lay, practical, non-scientific or professional) knowledge.

Scientific knowledge is mainly developed by experts outside the government (Van Buuren and Edelenbos 2004). The validity of this type of knowledge is based on scientific models and methods, and on the rigorous quality checks of peer review (Irwin et al. 1999). Of course, there are differences between natural and social sciences in using different premises, methodologies, norms, and values (Nowotny et al. 2002). In this chapter we focus on mainly technical expertise, due to our focus on water management.

Bureaucratic knowledge is heavily intertwined with administrative and governmental practices. They stress the political and strategic use of knowledge, and less the substance or intrinsic value of knowledge (Kingdon 1984). However, bureaucratic knowledge also has a professional and scientific grounding, but a less strict checks and balance system than scientific peer review (Lintsen 2002).

Table 12.1 Overview of the differences between expert, bureaucratic and stakeholder knowledge.

	Expert knowledge	Bureaucratic knowledge	Stakeholder knowledge
Norm for knowledge production	Scientific validity	Policy usefulness	Social validity
Warrant for useful knowledge	Positive peer review and publication prospects	Appropriateness with regard to standards and warrants of bureaucracy, and political use	Fitness with the own business, local experiences, and interests
Core business	Scientific research: systematic and objectified observations	Rule-following behaviour: bureaucratic practices	Daily-life, private business, defending certain societal interests
Criteria for success	Validating scientific hypotheses; expanding the knowledge domain	Political-administrative support for proposals	Support for the own interests and agenda

Stakeholder knowledge is often grounded in experience or is context or location related (Eshuis and Stuiver 2005). Expert and stakeholder knowledge are still approached differently.

> Expert-knowledge generation is institutionalised and exclusive and shared through peer-reviewed processes, whereas lay knowledge is embedded in the world around and directly impacting on individuals (...) (Petts and Brooks 2006: 1046).

Moreover, whereas technical experts are often striving for universal prescriptions (depending on the specific discipline), stakeholder knowledge is contextual and local (Petts and Brooks 2006, Wynne 1991, Irwin et al. 1999).

Foremost, the three types of knowledge are essentially part of different practices. These practices can be characterised by their different languages, their different norms and values, their different systems of warrants and their own rules of the game, procedures and criteria (see Table 12.1).

12.2.2 Negotiated knowledge: where experts, bureaucrats and stakeholders meet

Many scholars, mainly in social sciences, stress that knowledge production is a process of social construction (Latour 1999, Knorr-Cetina 1999). In this social construction of knowledge production, the worlds of experts, bureaucrats and stakeholders are combined and interconnected (Woolgar 2000). The way in which this connection is organised explains the legitimacy of the knowledge used in making policy decisions. The proper organisation of this connection is stressed in, for example, literature on joint fact finding (Ehrmann and Stinson 1999), participatory policy analysis (Hoppe 1999), collaborative dialogues (Innes and Booher 1999), collaborative analysis (Busenberg 1999), interactive social science (Caswill and Shove 2000), interactive knowledge (Lindblom and Cohen 1979), co-generation of knowledge (Petts and Brooks 2006), and civic science (Backstrand 2003). Knowledge in these approaches becomes a "serviceable truth":

> a state of knowledge that satisfies tests of scientific acceptability and supports reasoned decision-making, but also assures those exposed to risk that their interests have not been sacrificed on the altar of an impossible scientific certainty (Jasanoff 1990: 250).

Some authors emphasise that both expert and lay knowledge should be used in the production of knowledge (Petts and Brooks 2006, Rinaudo and Garin 2005, Yearley 2000, Petts 1997). Backstrand (2003) identifies experts, policy-makers, and citizens as relevant knowledge providers. In such an approach, there is explicit recognition among traditional decision-makers that others can fruitfully contribute to the identification and solution of problems, especially when decision stakes or uncertainty about information is high (Gallopín et al. 2001, Ravetz 1999). This requires a more open approach to what constitutes legitimate knowledge and expertise compared to the technocratic approach. Hence an important question is: how to balance the different sources of knowledge (Backstrand 2003: 25).

In the interaction between experts, bureaucrats and stakeholders knowledge is made that can not only withstand scientific standards (scientific validity), but also fit into the system of the bureaucracy (policy relevance) and has societal relevance or is supported by stakeholders (social robustness (Edelenbos et al. 2009)). When knowledge is scientifically valid, socially robust, and useful for policy-making it can be coined as "negotiated knowledge". Knowledge that lacks scientific validity turns out to become "negotiated nonsense", knowledge that lacks input from stakeholder knowledge becomes "superfluous knowledge" (De Bruijn and Ten Heuvelhof 1999); knowledge that lacks policy relevance will end up unused because it is politically and administratively inappropriate.

12.2.3 Analytical framework

In this chapter we are interested in gaining insight into processes of negotiated knowledge production in complex water related decision-making (Figure 12.1). We study what the role and contribution of expert (1), civil servant/bureaucrat (2) and stakeholder (3) knowledge is in this process, and at what moments, and how (methods, process, instruments) inclusive knowledge between these three domains is developed.

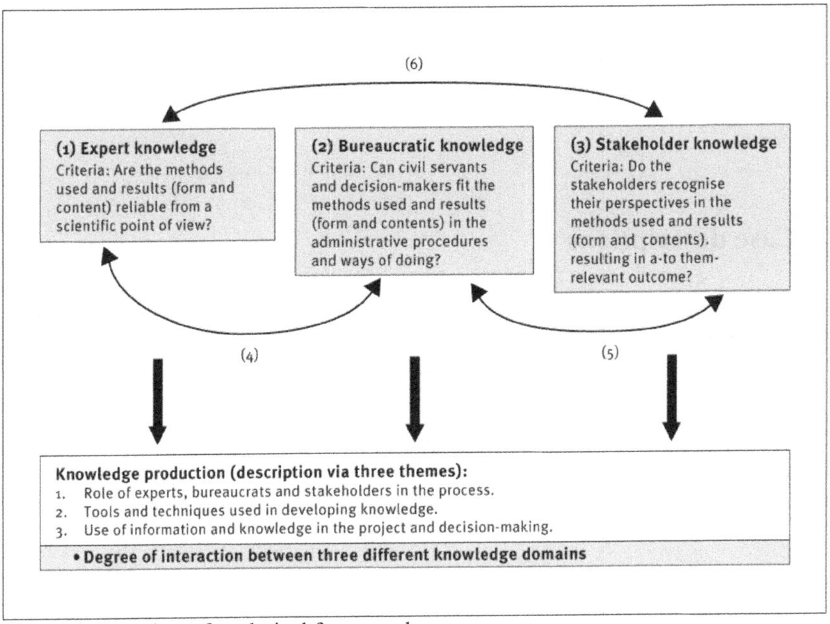

Fig. 12.1 Overview of analytical framework.

We examine to what extent there is interplay between expert, bureaucrats, and stakeholder knowledge (4, 5, 6, Figure 12.1). In addition we study the nature of this interplay if present and the arrangements (models, instruments, etc.), which are used to arrange this interplay. Finally we look at to what extent the three knowledge domains contributed to the process of decision-making.

With interplay we mean the interaction or collaborative process between the three different forms of knowledge. We use a three-point scale to measure the degree of interaction:

– Major: joint activities are truly developed to prepare or to actually develop a common knowledge base. We speak of a major degree of interaction when stakeholders, experts and bureaucrats show an open attitude and active role in expressing their information and knowledge to each other, are receptive for other insights and sources of knowledge, and regularly meet from start until implementation.
– Medium: joint activities are developed strategically or symbolically with no real intention to create a common knowledge base. We speak of a medium degree of interaction when stakeholders, experts and bureaucrats do meet each other, but show no real open attitude and active role in expressing their own information and knowledge. Moreover, they are not receptive for other sources of knowledge and do not succeed in creating a common knowledge base.
– Minor or absent: no real joint knowledge production activities are developed, with no explicit intention to create a common knowledge base. We speak of a minor or even absent degree of interaction when knowledge is developed solitarily. No common and supported knowledge base is created for decision-making, and if so it is between experts and bureaucrats only.

12.3 Case descriptions

In this section we describe the two cases on the integration of stakeholder, bureaucrat, and expert knowledge, Gouwe Wiericke and around Arnemuiden. Both case descriptions start with a brief introduction. Subsequently, three themes are discussed:

1. the role of stakeholders, bureaucrats, and experts;
2. the models and instruments to generate information and knowledge; and
3. the use of information in the project and decision-making stages.

12.3.1 Case 1: Gouwe Wiericke, introduction and general process description

The Dutch peat soil meadow areas do have remarkable problems with their water management. Due to a decline in the soil surface water management is a difficult and expensive job and low ground water levels (necessary to enable agriculture in these areas) are difficult to realise. The reason for this is that low water levels fasten soil drop and threaten the overall water quality, because of the intrusion of salt water.

These problems gave rise to the development of far-reaching proposals on behalf of the Water Board Rijnland. This water management authority conducted research on the feasibility of water retention areas in the deep polders of Gouwe Wiericke West to solve a couple of water problems. These studies by some renowned consultancy bureaux showed that water retention in this polder would be a "one catch all solution" for the problems with regard to water quality and quantity.

These studies formed the starting point for a short but intensive decision-making process with the Province of South Holland and the Water Board as initiators. An Environmental Impact Assessment (EIA) was the first step of the formal planning process to realise these retention areas. When the EIA was launched, fierce resistance from the inhabitants of the polder became public. The authorities felt that neglecting them would seriously complicate future discussions and the implementation of their ideas and decided to form a Working Group out of the angriest inhabitants.

In its first months the Working Group could not do very much because the researchers that had to conduct the EIA were working on their own research, which was clearly demarcated by principals from governmental bodies. Stakeholders were not allowed to change the research focus of the EIA. Ultimately, the EIA was not finalised at all. During the research it became undoubtedly clear that retention areas would be too expensive and would also generate too many technical risks. The Working Group gained the possibility to deliver an alternative proposal with more room for agriculture.

The Working Group eagerly accepted this opportunity and within a few months they produced a first rough sketch of the physical nature of the area. This sketch was the basis for more thorough analyses of the problems and potencies of the area, and the optimal mix of functions. Experts and stakeholders worked together in the development of the Working Group proposal, in joint field excursions and joint design sessions.

The Working Group proposal was enthusiastically presented to the various authorities involved. However, the proposal could not convince the responsible officials and governors. They were unwilling to agree on this proposal because in their eyes it contributed too little to the realisation of their ambitions. The Water Board and Province decided to implement some small elements of the proposal and postponed the ultimate decision to a new policy initiative: a Peat Meadow Contract for Gouwe Wiericke.

Role of stakeholders, bureaucrats and experts in the process

We see an interesting alteration of roles in the process as described above. In the first round, experts dominated the policy process and expert knowledge was the main building stone for policy decisions of the Water Board Rijnland and the Province.

Stakeholder knowledge was for a long time neglected. However, after the disappointing results of the EIA, stakeholders were given a much more central role in the process and were put in the position of developing their own proposal. Experts acquired the role of critical reviewer and provider of supplementary data.

The bureaucrats in this process seem to have, in both rounds, a more subordinate role. Their knowledge about the ambitions of their administrators, the procedures that their organisations follow and the conditions put forward by other policy departments was used to fine-tune the proposal, but – as we can conclude afterwards – it was not sufficient to prevent the debacle that happened.

Models and instruments to generate information and knowledge

In the first round of policy-making the mathematical and technical methods of the experts dominated the knowledge production. After the installation of the Core Group these models were supplemented with field visits and lay knowledge of the farmers from the polder. However, the stakeholders remained disappointed with the way in which they could recognise their input in the ultimate EIA report.

In the second round a multi-criteria analysis (MCA) was used to judge the proposal of the Core Group and to compare it to two other scenarios. The MCA – without many limitations with regard to form and content – was able to bring together expert, bureaucratic and stakeholder knowledge. The resulting comparative and quantitative table was seen by all and involved actors as a good instrument to communicate the proposal of the Core Group.

Use of information in the project and decision-making stages

Although the added value of these retention areas was demonstrated convincingly (at least in the eyes of the authorities), its feasibility was not studied at all. The outcomes of the EIA, led to the decision to cancel the retention areas and to start an alternative exploration. The proposal of the Core Group brought together a variety of facts and insights, but was not able to convince the authorities of its added value and its long-term sustainability.

In the second round we see that only a limited range of bureaucrats and their knowledge was involved. They strategically stayed at a distance. This is an important explanation as to why the proposal of the Core Group was not approved by the political decision-makers. In general, we see that expert knowledge is more valued by the authorities, compared to stakeholder knowledge. They approach expert knowledge as more legitimate and trustworthy.

12.3.2 Case 2: around Arnemuiden, introduction and process description

Located in the Zeeland delta in the Southwest of the Netherlands, the redevelopment of a rural area near the city of Middelburg caused severe resistance from the local public, because of the sensitivity of the issue due to the flooding in 1953 where many people were killed. From the 1990s onwards, the governmental planning process concerning this area shows a turbulent history of plans proposed and obstructed successively. Governmental parties aimed at a revival of water recreational functions and a large scale housing project in the area with these plans, while the local stakeholders – mostly inhabitants of a small neighbouring village called Arnemuiden – preferred to maintain the area in its current rural state. As both actors hardened their positions this ended up in a deadlock situation.

In order to mediate between these opposing positions, at the beginning of 2006 an interactive process was set up, aiming at a joint vision on the area.[1] The aim of this process was a plan for the reorganisation of the respective area in a participatory process, involving relevant (governmental and non-governmental) parties and organisations as well as local actors, stakeholders and non-governmental organisations (NGO) bearing a stake in the issue. The (non-binding) plan was presented to the city council of Middelburg at the end of 2007. Currently the city council is pondering the plan for the area.

The process started at the beginning of 2006. Stakeholders were gathered in a "planning group". Their task was to develop scenarios for reorganising the area. Experts on a variety of subjects and from differing backgrounds were gathered in an "expert group". Experts were positioned in a supportive role in the process, supporting the stakeholders in the development of feasible scenarios, answering their questions, and providing them with advice.

In a series of workshops and meetings, scenarios for the redevelopment of the area were formulated. Based on initial interviews and policy analysis, the stakeholders developed four "dream" scenarios, representing the ideal futures of the area irrespective of formal or technical constraints. The group of experts reacted to these scenarios after which the stakeholders adjusted them accordingly. The stakeholders then valued the scenarios, revealing the highly valued elements which were then gathered in two new scenarios. Stakeholders further specified these new scenarios and experts again discussed the results. Based on the expert comments the stakeholders again adjusted and developed the scenarios into the eventual plan, proposing to develop the region in an integral fashion following either of the two scenarios developed.

Role of stakeholders, bureaucrats and experts in the process

Bureaucrats set the project's aims and limitations. Apart from existing policy documents and prior (local) agreements, the project and its outcomes were kept as open as possible. Stakeholders were actively involved in the process from the very start. Their perspectives were central to scenario development. Experts and bureaucrats were gathered in an expert group. This group was involved in the process at a later stage, only after the stakeholders had formulated their first ideas. They had a merely reactive role.

The communication between stakeholders and bureaucrats/experts was mediated through the process team. Former governmental plans for the area under consideration were dominated by bureaucratic and expert views on the area and were not recognised by the stakeholders. The process team hoped that a distance between

---

[1] This project was funded by "Living with Water", a Dutch knowledge impulse programme aimed at the study and implementation of changes in water management.

the experts/bureaucrats and the stakeholders in the project would create more room for the development of stakeholder views and knowledge in the scenario development and would prevent further domination by expert views.

Models and instruments to generate information and knowledge

To identify and use stakeholder values (knowledge) for scenario development, an approach of "covaluation" (collaborative valuation) was developed during the process (Van Schie and Bouma 2008). In interviews, stakeholder values and perspectives on the respective area were identified and based on this information scenario development began. The stakeholder perspectives were characterised by statements on what was "important" to them, usually expressed in qualitative terms. Experts (both external and governmental) were also interviewed, revealing their main points of concern for redevelopment of the area. Generally, technical and financial aspects characterised these concerns.

In order to integrate the perspectives the process aimed to develop a broad analysis combining the financial measures and perspectives provided by the experts as well as the non-financial perspectives and values provided by the stakeholders. This proved difficult as the stakeholders preferred to involve no financial information in such analysis, while the bureaucrats pressed the need for financial information only.

Use of information in the project and decision-making stages

The project aimed at a plan that was supported by stakeholders as well as bureaucrats and experts. The project took the perspectives of stakeholders as a starting point: the end result was predominantly a product of the stakeholders involved. Still, the bureaucrats and experts actively supported the stakeholders. The stakeholders implemented most of the changes proposed by the bureaucrats and experts and generally respected their expertise on professional subjects. The bureaucrats and experts themselves, however, saw no use in the inputs of the stakeholders in the process, because in their view they lacked sufficient scientific and expert ground.

The decision-makers and politicians approached the eventual plan with reservation and a severe dose of scepticism. The municipality was used to base decisions on short-term financial effects and knowledge provided by (bureaucratic) experts only, hence bureaucrats felt adequate information for decision-making was missing. Experts felt they had not been able to contribute their specialised knowledge. Being unable to handle the results of the interactive process within the existing procedures of decision-making, politicians and municipal civil servants postponed the decision on the plan.

12.4 Case comparison and analysis

In this section we compare and analyse the two cases on the way knowledge is produced and implemented in the process. Firstly we present an overview table for the two cases. Secondly we discuss the two cases in more detail and distinguish between the main differences and similarities.

12.4.1 Overall picture of knowledge production in the two cases

Based on the analytical framework presented in Sect. 12.2, Table 12.2 provides an overview of the knowledge production processes in the two cases discussed.

Table 12.2 Overview of knowledge production in the two cases.

Theme	Case 1: Gouwe Wiericke	Case 2: Around Arnemuiden
Role of stakeholders, bureaucrats and experts	Stakeholders are first neglected but after fierce resistance they are involved Experts are first dominant. Later they functioned to fine-tune the stakeholder proposal Bureaucrats have a subordinate role in the whole process	Stakeholders had a prominent position Experts had a more reactive role Bureaucrats were involved from the start of the process, in the set up of the process and in monitoring the course of the process
The use of instruments and models in generating knowledge	The EIA was opened up for stakeholders: they could bring in knowledge, but the scope could not be altered. This was followed by more participative methods	Both stakeholders and experts were interviewed. Stakeholders developed scenarios in workshops A broad analysis is carried out, in which both qualitative information, and quantitative information is involved
Use of knowledge in project and decision-making	Stakeholder knowledge is used for the development of the alternative plan. Expert knowledge was the basis for authorities to abandon the alternative of retention areas. Although, this plan was approved, decision-makers, they appreciate more the expert knowledge in the process	Stakeholder knowledge is the base for developing the plans. Expert and stakeholder knowledge is used to make the plans more feasible. Bureaucratic knowledge stresses short term financial feasibility. Decision-makers more appreciate expert and bureaucratic knowledge in the process

12.4.2 Interplay between stakeholder, expert and bureaucratic knowledge

In both cases experts, as well as civil servants and stakeholders, provided knowledge relevant to the decision-making process. The relationship and interplay between these different sources of knowledge differed and was problematic for a number of reasons. Below we will discuss these in detail. Table 12.3 provides a classification of the level of interplay between the different sources of knowledge following our analytical framework.

Table 12.3 Assessment of the interplay between different sources of knowledge in the two cases.

Interplay between... Cases	(1) Experts and civil servants	(2) Experts and stake-holders	(3) Civil servants and stakeholders
Case Gouwe Wiericke	Medium (+/–)	Medium (+/–)	Minor (–)
Case around Arnemuiden	Medium (+/–)	Minor (–)	Minor (–)

Interplay between experts and bureaucrats

This kind of interplay is well established in existing institutions and working procedures of knowledge generation and decision-making. The cases showed that experts tend to listen to their principals from within the government. They want boundaries and conditions for the knowledge they must produce. Moreover, experts focused on issues lying within their field of expertise and therefore did not easily transcend their own field of expertise (case around Arnemuiden).

In the case of Gouwe Wiericke, in later phases of the project, civil servants stay at a distance from the experts to prevent commitment to the process and outcomes. In the case of around Arnemuiden we see a similar attitude from civil servants, they are reluctant to start interacting with the experts in the expert group. The experts regarded their role in the interactive process as very different compared to their common tasks in the internal organisation. As a reaction, the civil servants started their own internal working routines and developed project groups inside the municipal bureaucracy, far away from the project.

Interplay between experts and stakeholders

This kind of interplay is problematic in both cases. Stakeholders are involved too late in the process of water management (case first phase of Gouwe Wiericke). While working on the EIA, experts had a predefined research question. Classical instruments were used to facilitate the interaction between experts and stakeholders: experts presented their research approach and stakeholders could reflect upon this. However, after the cancellation of the EIA and the retention-alternative the level of interaction between experts and stakeholders drastically changed. Stakeholders and experts worked together to maximise the quality of the proposal. In the design of the interactive stakeholder approach in the case around Arnemuiden, no direct interaction was arranged between experts and stakeholders because of the fear from the process facilitators that the experts would dominate such processes through difficult technocratic speech. The experts also had the opportunity to reflect critically on the drafts of the scenarios. They were more at ease with questioning the scenarios than providing concrete suggestions for improvement. Even though this prevented a clash between different knowledge bases, the experts did not perceive the stakeholder inputs as very useful to the planning process.

The tools, instruments and methods for knowledge generation commonly used by experts and decision-makers can hinder the process of joint fact finding (both cases). A model or instrument can be strongly expert driven. Application of these methods is often very rigid, as is shown by the fruitless attempts in the around Arnemuiden case to combine stakeholder information and bureaucratically required financial information. Also the procedure of EIA in the Gouwe Wiericke case could not easily be adjusted to the wishes, questions and input of the stakeholders. Such procedures thus reinforce the distance between expert and stakeholder knowledge. Moreover, the use of different methods to involve interests and knowledge did not stimulate the interplay between both stakeholder and expert inputs (case around Arnemuiden). The different background and orientations of both experts and stakeholders were not reconciled in the project.

Interplay between civil servants and stakeholders

This kind of interplay was troublesome due to the rigidly existing (technocratic) ways of knowledge generation and decision-making, which exclude stakeholders from the process.

In both cases, civil servants are not receptive or responsive to the knowledge provided by stakeholders. They show an attitude similar to that of the experts in both cases. This can be explained by the fact that the civil servants in the field of water management and urban and regional development are often experts in these domains themselves, at least in The Netherlands.

Besides, newly developed models or approaches (case around Arnemuiden) based on "negotiated knowledge" between experts and stakeholders may not be accepted by civil servants and policy-makers, because they do not fit with the regular working methods and procedures within bureaucracy. Institutionalised procedures and methods that focus on expert knowledge (perspectives and values) complicate the development, implementation and legitimisation of new working methods in which stakeholder knowledge is integrated. Approaching the decision-making stage, it turned out that decision-makers and politicians were unable to incorporate the results of the interactive process in the existing institutions and decision-making procedures (case around Arnemuiden).

12.5 Conclusion and discussion

In this chapter we reported our research of two cases in order to gain an understanding of the relationship and interplay between experts, bureaucrats and stakeholders in the production of knowledge for water related decision-making. The comparative case study research showed that this threefold interplay is problematic.

The two cases showed that, in general, both experts and bureaucrats are not willing to acknowledge that stakeholder knowledge has the potential to improve the identification of problems and the search for feasible solutions that meet the circumstances of the direct environment. Stakeholders, on the other hand, do not have much eye for the scientific soundness of knowledge development and the political and strategic relevance of knowledge. They only look at what is relevant or appropriate for them. They often, beforehand, undervalue and distrust the input of bureaucrats and experts. In both cases we saw that stakeholders questioned the expert input and did not take their input for granted.

The interplay between experts and civil servants is – compared to the other two forms of interplay – better developed. The reason for this is that experts often get research assignments from civil servants. Moreover, in the field of water management and urban and regional development, civil servants often have similar backgrounds as the (external) experts, which make it easier to communicate and to interact. However, when experts are more in touch with stakeholders, as in the Gouwe Wiericke case, we see that civil servants strategically move away to keep room to manoeuvre and prevent commitment.

Our research provides a strong indication that knowledge is not value free. The fragmentation of perspectives and values between experts, civil servants and stakeholders is a strong force and incentive for a modular and fragmented knowledge process. Visions and viewpoints of experts, civil servants and stakeholders reflect their deeply rooted ambitions and interests (cf. Rinaudo and Garin 2005: 287). All actors involved (experts, stakeholders, civil servants, but also decision-makers) have different perspectives on relevant issues, and different and opposing knowledge and values were involved. It is difficult to achieve a body of information that is legitimate and useful to all parties involved to apply in such situations. In both cases we saw that experts, bureaucrats and stakeholders use different norms and criteria for knowledge production ranging from scientific validity (experts), policy usefulness (bureaucrats) and social validity (stakeholders). These different orientations lead to different valuations of the relevance of knowledge to be used for assessment and decision-making.

The synchronisation of expert, bureaucratic and stakeholder knowledge will not take place automatically. Even when the three forms of knowledge are brought together deliberately, through process facilitation (in the case of around Arnemuiden) and by deliberately putting external experts and stakeholders in a Working Group (in the case of Gouwe Wiericke), interplay between the three knowledge domains does not develop. The cases presented in this chapter reveal some indications for such arrangements. Values, facts, and ambitions need to be related constantly to each other in a process of joint fact finding in order to produce knowledge that is meaningful for stakeholders, experts and decision-makers (cf. Van Buuren 2006). With respect to the organisation of the knowledge production process, it is important that stakeholders, as well as experts and civil servants, are involved at an early stage and that their inputs are jointly combined in assessment methods, models or instruments. These measurements should be anchored to the actual decision-making procedures, in order to be approached as legitimate by decision-makers. Only when knowledge of bureaucrats, experts and stakeholders are properly synchronised, will this lead to scientific valid, policy-relevant, and socially robust knowledge.

13 From "knowledge use" towards "boundary work": sketch of an emerging new agenda for inquiry into science-policy interaction

Robert Hoppe

Abstract

This chapter is about a new agenda for inquiry into the relationships between science and public policy. So far, most research has conceptualised this relationship in terms of knowledge utilisation and downstream impact on the policy process. However, this leads to over-instrumentalisation and serious attenuation of expert advice. Therefore, I propose a new perspective: interaction through boundary work, a concept expressing how expert advice simultaneously demarcates and coordinates science and public policy. Research shows that there are many different types of boundary work depending on various types of policy problems. This chapter concludes with a proposal for a multilevel model, which enables us to understand the variety in types of boundary work, and discriminate conditions of success and failure of boundary arrangements and boundary work practices on several levels of analysis.

13.1 Introduction

The history of government, administration and policy-making and its scientific study are replete with paradoxes and irony. During the years that public administration scholars and policy scientists themselves were keen on knowing more about, and tried to measure the impact of (social) scientific ideas on administration and policy implementation, practitioners were hardly interested. At present, scientific advisors are judged by those very practitioners according to norms and criteria shown by previous research to be neither tenable nor desirable. During the 1970s and 1980s, students of public administration and policy sciences wanted to know themselves to which degree scientific advice had real downstream impact on policy processes. Their most important research finding (for an overview see Weiss 1991, Landry et al. 2003) was that the high expectations of direct, instrumental use of knowledge – a policy-relevant study today, a science-based decision tomorrow – had to be considerably toned down. Direct links between a scientific report and subsequent policy decisions were rare. However, on the positive side, it appeared that science and research usually generated conceptual knowledge or

R.J. in 't Veld (ed.), *Knowledge Democracy*, DOI 10.1007/978-3-642-11381-9_13,

new concepts, ideas and theories that enabled policy-makers to gradually revise their framings and definitions of the policy problem.

In the beginning, administrators and policy-makers themselves were strong believers in the usability of scientific policy advice; and thus hardly interested in a serious evaluation of its real use and subsequent impact on the policy process. This radically changed during the 1990s and the first decade of this century. Influenced by the ideas of New Public Management and its key notion that policy "products" should be judged in terms of quantifiable and measurable results, even scientific policy advice itself did not escape the drive for quantitative accountability. In the mid-1990s, in the Netherlands the so-called "desert"-law slashed the number of official advisory bodies to a little over a dozen. About a decade later, policy-makers set out to evaluate the effectiveness and efficiency of this much leaner advisory infrastructure. Trusting incomplete and questionable scientific models of knowledge utilisation, auditors started to "measure" the degree to which policy advice led to knowledge use ("uptake") and "downstream" impact on policy adoption and implementation. These attempts once more demonstrated that the measurability of direct instrumental knowledge use was difficult and at best incomplete, if not impossible (Bekkers et al. 2005: 4, Putters et al. 2004: 4). Nevertheless, the results of these imperfect attempts did lead to proposals for a second round of considerable reduction in the infrastructure for science-based advice on the national level (Hoppe 2008a, b). In the Netherlands, these proposals were officially announced in the new Cabinet's government agreement, based upon a short "analysis" of the situation in 2006 by the permanent secretaries of the Dutch ministries. The official objective was to reduce the number of advisory bodies from fifteen to about five, one in each major policy domain. Moreover, a reduction of the number of the prestigious "planning" agencies to three was recommended – one agency for each of the Ps in the "holy trinity" of sustainable development thinking: Planet, People, and Profit; and this has indeed been implemented during the last years. Thus, the lack of irrefutable evidence on the use and impact of scientific advice did not hamper politicians and top civil servants to continue the policy, launched in the 1990s, that for a leaner and meaner civil service a much slimmer state-supported advisory infrastructure would suffice.

The rest of this contribution explores the scientific ramifications of this irony by posing the question: "What to do next, after impact?" (cf. Halffman and Bal 2008) After all, if conceptualising the problem as uptake of advice, knowledge use, knowledge transfer, knowledge impact, or knowledge dissemination inexorably criticises, attenuates and over-instrumentalises expert advice, is there an alternative way to argue and empirically study the relevance of science-based advice to politics and administration? Perhaps the scientific study of the governance of expertise itself is in need of conceptual overhaul and reframing?

In the next section, I therefore analyse the practical impacts of studying knowledge uptake and use: Why is it that conceptualising the problem as unidirectional transfer of knowledge leads to "anorexia consulta", that is less and less, attenuated, over-instrumentalised expert advice? The third section introduces an alternative perspective: interaction through boundary work. The fourth section shows that boundary work, in fact, occurs in many different shapes. The fifth section links variations in boundary work to different types of policy problems. The sixth section sketches the contours of a new research agenda, which promises to be more empirically and normatively productive than the old impact thinking.

13.2 The impact of impact

The question of what it means for expert advice to be successful seems simple but creates lots of intellectual quandaries. If we define “success” as immediately effective use of new knowledge and advise in the policy process, then considerable disappointment is to be expected, both among advisors and the advised parties (for instance Korteland 2004: 86–87). This is the case because, first and foremost, knowledge use as immediate uptake and implementation of advice tacitly

> rely on one-directional movement of advice. A report or piece of research is produced, after which the completed product has “effect” on the policy maker. This is the case most strongly in the impact metaphor, where research is launched and then “crashes into” policy, but it is also present in the consumerist connotations of the utilisation metaphor (Halffman and Bal 2008: 17).

Second, the model of direct, instrumental use rests on untested stereotypes of the division of labour between policy-makers and experts. The impact model deflects attention from ongoing interaction and negotiation, and focuses on common-sense notions like “research is about facts and truths” and “policy-making and politics are about values and power”.

Third, not all possible impact is desirable per se. Certainly not if the quality and credibility of expert advise are contested. Sometimes, uptake of advice amounts to selective shopping by policy-makers or even biased representation of the contents of advice. In the case of the American “intelligence” that led to the war in Iraq, uptake meant a spectacular media campaign about the presence of weapons of mass destruction based on poor research. Fourth, there are considerable problems in the operationalisation of the concept of “use” or “uptake”. Bekkers and others (2005: 58–60) convincingly show that the shapes, times, loci, institutional contexts and target groups of knowledge use are so multidimensional and multifaceted that the set of indicators is just a garbage can of heterogeneous indices. Even if all these problems could be solved, they lead to a trans-scientific problem (Weinberg 1972): in practice, sound research into the full scope of uptake and impact of expert advice will be so costly and time consuming, and will have to search for so many different sorts of “impacts” on so many different social locations, which also may be very hard to causally attribute to expert advice, that nobody will be prepared to pay for it. Moreover, if executed, this type of research might well be a very costly method of drawing marginal lessons for improvement. After all, from the research to date we have learned that there are numerous necessary, but hardly necessary *and* sufficient conditions for success.

Fifth, operating a restricted but "doable" set of indicators will produce the now well-known dangers of ritual conformance and perverse conduct. This observation also applies to systems of self-evaluation by advisory bodies as experimentally practiced and proposed by Bekkers et al. (2005: 69–70). In addition, a restricted set of indicators will not work because the quality of advice is always judged differently by different actors or stakeholders. After all, policy-makers or administrators who commissioned or triggered uninvited advice, are not the only relevant addressees of an advice. A favourable advice for a ministry is not by definition applauded by all involved interests and actors in the policy domain as a whole. They certainly also involve members of parliament, sub-national governments and non-governmental organisations in the relevant issue or policy network, and the (sometimes) dissident experts related to these other stakeholders.

Like all forms of policy evaluation, the evaluation of knowledge use, uptake of expert advice and its downstream impacts on the policy process, is a political act and therefore likely to be politically contestable. As a matter of fact, research on the uptake and impact of expert advice answers the political question, "Who evaluates what for whom?" by saying: "Disregarding their own discretion and influence, politicians and policy-makers evaluate the degree of instrumental impact on their own work". Although all these nuances and qualifications are mentioned in the scientific literature, practical recommendations all too frequently focus only on this one aspect of knowledge use and impact (for example Bekkers et al. 2005: 66ff; and Putters et al. 2004: 28, 59). This leads to serious shortcomings and biases in the evaluation of expert advice.

Therefore, we badly need a closer look at the nature of advisory work. We need to include the perspectives of the experts and their professional-scientific networks, other policy actors in the policy domain; and, foremost, we need an "up-close and personal" look at the interaction between experts and policy-makers. Interaction and boundary work may well offer us better handles in judging the success or failure of advice.

13.3 Beyond the clichés: boundary work

Under the label of *Rethinking Political Judgement and Science-Based Expertise,* the University of Twente has coordinated a coherent set of interdisciplinary and inter-university projects aiming to improve our insight and understanding of the knowledge- and advisory infrastructure for Dutch public authorities. The research concerned, the manner in which the Centre for Economic Policy Analysis (CPB), the Scientific Council for Government Policy (WRR), Alterra (part of Wageningen University/Research), the Environmental Assessment Agency (MNP), and the public health branch of the National Institute for Public Health and Environment (RIVM) deliver knowledge to and produce advice for Dutch ministries. In addition, to compare Dutch advisory practice to foreign experiences, research projects involved the production of nature balances in Flanders and Denmark, and research and advice on fisheries policies in Norway and the European Union. Although this research has not been completed yet, parts have been and continue to be published (Hoppe 2002, Hoppe and Huijs 2003, Hoppe 2003, Halffman and Hoppe 2005, Hoppe 2005, Scholten 2008, Halffman 2008, De Vries, A. 2008, Hoppe 2008, Halffman 2009, Hoppe 2010). It is possible to present some of the main findings in relation to and against the background of this and other research in the Netherlands (Bekkers et al. 2005, Putters 2004) to date.

The first main finding is that the clichés about the relationships between science and policy-making are obsolete. Following Winston Churchill, policy-makers and politicians like to suggest, that they are "on top", and call on the services of scientists and experts that supposedly are just "on tap". On the other hand, scientists continue to tell their heroic tales about the powerless but neutral, objective, independent smart guys who, in Aaron Wildavsky's metaphor for the art and craft of policy analysis, "speak truth to power". The truly peculiar bias in knowledge utilisation research so far is that hardly any serious attention is paid to the tasks that experts do in fact fulfil. It is uncritically accepted that the experts should and will adapt their own tasks to the needs of policy-makers and administrators. This fails to appreciate that expert advisors place themselves in between policy-making and administration on the one hand, and science on the other; and therefore have to adapt their activities on both fronts. The final section revisits this crucial fact.

Of course, the media and the public at large do not uncritically accept these self justifications. Frequently, they hold the cynical but not unrealistic view that scientists are paid for the production of scientific evidence and argumentation; that they deliver the argumentative "ammunition" or are the "hired guns" for political points of view that were already formulated irrespective of scientific argument and evidence, or for established interests of corporate networks, for instance in the pharmaceutical or food producing sectors.

However, none of these clichés can be upheld after a closer look by advanced research. The game between the commissioners or principals of knowledge/advice production and the scientific knowledge deliverers or advisors is far more complex and varied. Processes for the production of knowledge, expert advice and policy design just can not be described in terms of crystal clear, sharp boundaries. The zones of engagement are fluid and vague by nature. The need for participation of persons with different knowledge and skills inherent in different institutional spheres calls for some division of labour. However, such a division of labour is not easily decided upon.

It is a myth, for example, that politics would only be concerned with values and interests, and scientists or expert advisors would only occupy themselves with facts and causality. In addition, it is incorrect to think that knowledge is transferred unilaterally from scientists and advisors to policy-makers, ministers and politicians. When the latter formulate a question that requires knowledge production or advice giving, they are involved in steering scientific work. As a matter of fact, what happens is that both parties are continuously bargaining with each other about how the exact boundary line between science and politics should be drawn – sometimes even on a case-by-case basis. Such boundary negotiations may concern the exact relations between an advisory body and a government department;

or the formulation of the question or remit for advice; or the way in which a scientific model is to be built, and subsequently used; or about the use (and non-use) of information sources; or about dealing with normative issues; or about managing uncertainties; or, finally, conflicts between scientific domains, or between scientific knowledge and other types of knowledge such as experience-based knowledge or citizen knowledge (Woodhouse and Nieusma 2001).

In advisory relations like for example in the International Panel on Climate Change, experts and policy-makers are at work together. Detailed empirical studies have shown that expertise that is mailed to the policy-maker in reports, articles or books rarely leads to any kind of policy uptake (Nutley et al. 2003). Experts may be ever so sensitive to immediate demands of policy; effective use of new scientific information relies on mutual face-to-face interaction, on working together. From a macro-perspective, science/politics interactions are ongoing dialogues between the scientisation of society and politics, and the politicisation of science. Of course, at micro-level, this does not mean a complete blurring of the boundaries between science and politics as in a seamless web. Rather, it should be conceptualised as *boundary work.*

Work implies meaningful and purposeful activity, directed at the creation of a collective product. Experts do not work on policy reports by blindly and thoughtlessly following scientific algorithms, but through an understanding of the problem at hand, a meaningful comprehension of the knowledge available, the context in which this knowledge is to be used, as well as what kinds of statements are tenable, given professional standards and values and the targeted audience (Wenger 1998). Working *together* means policy-makers and experts have to negotiate tensions and disconnects between their academic-professional and political-administrative worlds. Their concerns and projects never quite coincide, no matter how policy-oriented the expert or how evidence-oriented the policy-maker. Working together implies negotiation of work across boundaries and mutual adjustment between social worlds, and dealing with new, unknown problems as they emerge. Experts that advise policy are engaged in complex, professional work, where not all eventualities have been resolved and all role conflicts have been settled. Inversely, policy-making civil servants negotiate complex streams of puzzling and powering, in which expert advice is but one parameter in a fuzzy set of undefined equations.

Because this work occurs across the boundaries of policy and expert worlds, it is called *boundary work*. Boundary work can more formally be understood as the attempts by actors to define practices in contrast to each other through demarcation, as well as their attempts to find productive cooperation across these boundaries through a division of labour that is more or less accepted by relevant actors (Star and Griesemer 1989, Gieryn 1995, Halffman 2003, Hoppe 2005). One part of boundary work is to continuously draw and guard demarcations in order to guarantee the quality of one's own work. Policy workers do not wish scientists to infringe on their political and policy-making activities; scientists want to guard their domain against policy-makers, but for example also against journalists. Another part of boundary work is to coordinate the separate activities. Demarcation and coordination are two sides of the same coin. Keeping your distance, while simultaneously staying close enough to be effective is the enduring dilemma for scientific advisors in their relationship with policy-makers. Concern for high-quality performance makes expert advisors and policy-makers mutually dependent; yet, they have to guard their separate identities and formal independence. Therefore, boundary work is full of paradoxes and dilemmas; the relationship will never be smooth and easy; it will never come to rest and will always be contested.

13.4 Variation in boundary work

Boundary traffic between scientists (in knowledge institutes), expert advisers (in strategic, technical or temporary advisory bodies) and policy workers (in government agencies) is manifested in very different styles and shapes. Based on an extensive overview of the literature (Hoppe 2005), and using Q-method to empirically assess the range of different types of boundary work occurring in Dutch practice, in the *Rethinking* project seven types of *discourse on boundary work* were identified (Hoppe 2008):

Rational facilitation of political accommodation: boundary workers usually are experienced and prominent members of advisory bodies, or civil servants attending to the knowledge and look-out function in departmental agencies; they strongly believe in the Dutch consensus-type democratic practices of flexibility and compromise; they feed the accommodation process with sound arguments, derived from both sound science and knowledge rooted in stakeholders' knowledge of “best practices”; they facilitate orderly transgressions between politics and science in an atmosphere of mutual trust;

Knowledge brokerage: boundary workers are civil servants or consultants who, in spite of (well-known) cognitive impairments of politics and bureaucracy, and in spite of the inevitable gap between politics and science, under favourable conditions exploit opportunities for instrumental learning;

Mega-policy strategy: boundary workers claim a government-oriented think-tank function; they verify and critically examine long-term strategic policy guidelines and pivotal assumptions in policy beliefs-in-use, in light of most recent sound science and argument;

Policy analysis: boundary workers mostly work in long-standing pragmatic relations and rules of the game of established policy networks for, for example, financial-economic policy; they provide politicians, civil servants, advisors and stakeholder representatives with evidence-based intelligence, that is information based on available and usable sound science;

Policy advice: boundary workers claim to span the boundary between policy analysts and ministers and top civil servants at the apex of bureaucratic agencies; they advise their “princes” about acceptability and feasibility of policy proposals, incorporating usable, best available knowledge on “what works”;

Post-normal science advice: boundary workers operate in (sustainability-related) issue and policy networks where relationships between policy actors are volatile, and anything but settled; they see issues of sustainable development beset by so many uncertainties and conflicts of interest that normal science as "puzzle solving" is obsolete; hence they wish to create and institutionalise more stable role and interaction patterns, so that scientists and policy-makers may engage in productive, open dialogue, and integrated assessment of all advantages, disadvantages and uncertainties surrounding sustainability issues. The aspirations and practices of post-normalists are clearly inspired by ideas about "post-normal science" and "extended peer review" as advocated by Funtowicz and Ravetz (1992), and observed in practice by others (for example Hisschemöller et al. 2001, Anderson, L. 2003);

Deliberative-procedure advice: boundary workers work in advisory bodies, for example as permanent secretaries with civil servant status; they cherish and foster high-quality boundary work; this requires a clear and transparent procedure, and a set of process-criteria which allows robust, but trusting parties, dissidents included, to fully and openly debate, each from their own perspective on the common good, policy proposals and their concomitant uncertainties as well as normative issues.

These findings provoke the question whether the types found are specific only to persons or reflect some kind of "system". The next sections answer this question in favour of the latter option.

13.5 Types of problems, types of expert advice

The variety in typical boundary workers may be linked to the occurrence of different types of problems a political and administrative system has to deal with. I do not mean the common-sense idea that politics and administration usually get organised as "federations" of policy domains, like health policy, youth policy, social security policy; each domain with its own portfolio of more specific policy programmes. Here I refer to the theoretical notion of differently structured problems: domesticated or structured problems, "wicked" or unstructured problems, and in-between types of moderately structured problems. A frequently used typology (WRR 2006) is presented in Figure 13.1.

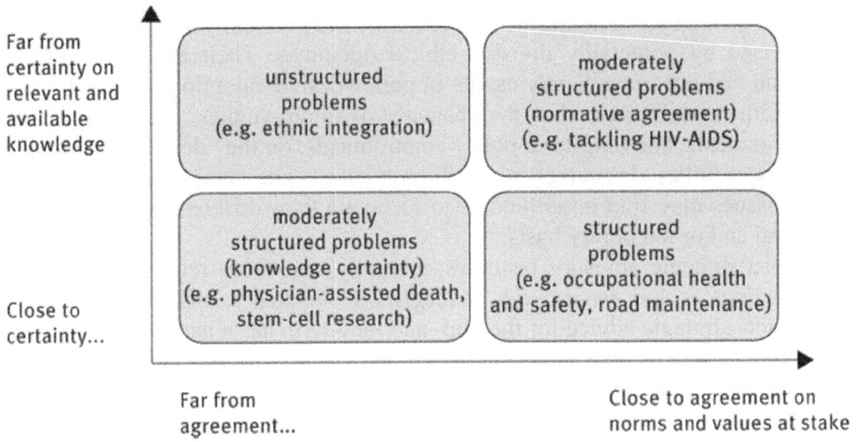

Fig. 13.1 Four types of policy problems.

Students of advisory bodies (for example Putters 2004) routinely distinguish between several types: technical or specialist, strategic, and ad-hoc or temporary. These types by and large fit the problem type they normally deal with. First, consider specialist and strongly technical advisory organisations and knowledge institutes that deliver instrumental, detailed, ready-for-implementation advice on largely domesticated problems. Politicians and policy-makers generally prefer usable or directly instrumental advice. Because political multi-tasking environments easily generate cognitive overload, they put a premium on simplification; and it is easy to delegate or outsource problem-solving to (quasi) autonomous agencies staffed by certified experts. Yet, instrumental advice and delegated technocracy as problem-processing arrangement *only* work well for domesticated problems.

In addition, there are clearly specialist advisory organisations and knowledge institutes of a non-technical nature and broader scope – like the Centre for Economic Policy Analysis (CPB) serving primarily departments like Finance and Economic Affairs, the Justice department's Scientific Research and Documentation Centre (WODC), or the Health Council. Their main business is to keep track of sound science, develop scenarios, and advise on appropriate, effective and efficient means for fairly consensual goals. They are frequently able to also deliver instrumental, immediately usable advice. In the Netherlands, the political consensus on goals is usually documented in a coalition agreement formally adopted by the political parties in office. Hence, instrumental policy advice is welcome during the larger part of a 4-year term of government.

Returning to the types of boundary workers, it appears that many *policy analysts, knowledge brokers* and *policy advisors* are to be located on the right-hand side of the problem typology – that is expert advisors working the boundaries of politics and science on domesticated problems, or on problems concerning appropriate policy instruments, or their zone of overlap.

Next, consider strategic advisory institutes, like, in the Netherlands, the Scientific Council for Government Policy (WRR) as a very clear example. They are concerned with as yet undomesticated problems, and politically sensitive problems characterised by potentially divisive ethical dilemmas. Their advice usually is conceptual and not immediately usable in policy design, adoption and implementation. Rather, such advice has the character of future studies, scenarios, mega-policy arguments, and long-term policy commitments. Or they devise novel policy paradigms or policy discourses in which protagonists and antagonists in ethically divisive issues may find opportunities to reconcile their differences, if only on a procedural and/or temporary basis.

In these strategic advisory institutes, naturally, one finds relatively more *rational facilitators* and *mega-policy strategists*. Compared to instrumental, short-term advice, strategic advice for the mid- and long-term has a narrow "policy window". *Timing* well is both more important, and much more difficult. Just before, during, and in the first year after a change of government appear to be relatively propitious times for strategic advice. However, political developments may well outpace strategic advice. A 2001 WRR study was an intellectually courageous attempt to redefine the policy paradigm for integration and immigration policy in the framework of transnational political trends and economic globalisation. Yet, published and presented briefly after 9/11, the advice had become profoundly unwelcome in a political climate where the political elite overnight converted to nationalistic assimilation (Scholten 2008).

Post-normalists and *deliberative proceduralists* are special types of boundary workers. They are forced to operate across the borderline between domesticated and "wicked" problems – that is, the right- and left-hand side of the problem typology. For example, an expert advisor working for the Rathenau Institute is supposed to inform parliament, but indirectly departments and relevant stakeholder groups too, on technological innovations and their potential ethical, legal and social consequences. This boundary worker needs the skills to "jump", almost literally, between the technical and highly specialist culture of (promises of) nearly domesticated problems, and the culture of social and political debate on fuzzy, "wicked" problems. Boundary workers at the Health Council, too, will be confronted by medical-technological issues with ethically unknown or divisive implications. Hence, trained as medical specialists they also need the skills to give advice that will play an important role in debates on ethical acceptability and goal appropriateness of medical-technological innovation (Hoppe 2008a).

Finally, there is the politically established ad-hoc or temporary advisory committees. To date, this type of politically prestigious "blue ribbon" committee has hardly been seriously researched. This way of organising expert advice appears to be mainly politically inspired. Government and ruling parties create opportunities to refer politically sensitive issues not (yet) dealt with in a coalition agreement, or hard to insert after the fact because they might cause open political conflict, to the relative calm and shelter of "blue ribbon" committees. The hypothesis would be that this concerns problems in the left-hand side of the problem typology, that is unstructured problems and ethically divisive issues. To the extent scientific experts are mobilised (next to experienced high-level administrators and politicians) to serve in these committees, one would expect them to be *rational facilitators, policy strategists* or *post-normalists*.

In conclusion of this section, the links between types of boundary work and types of problems may be approximately conceptualised as in Figure 13.2 (cf. Hisschemöller et al. 2001, Hoppe 2008).

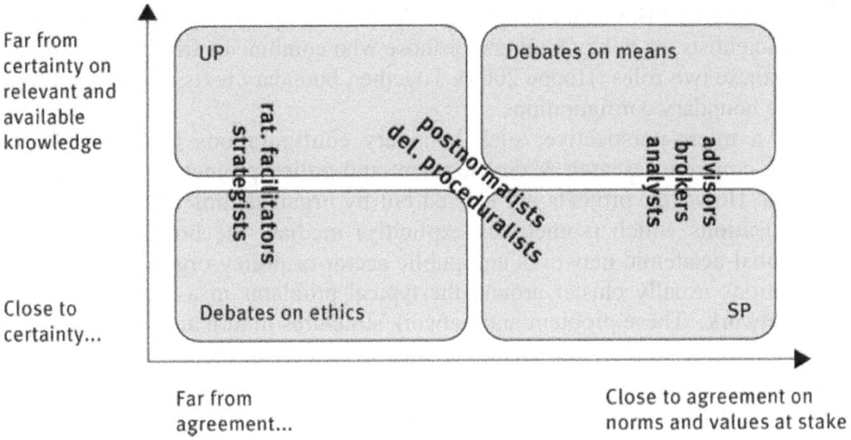

Fig. 13.2 Types of problems and types of boundary work.

13.6 Towards a multilevel conceptual framework for understanding science/policy interactions

If the findings of the Rethinking project and previous research and theory on boundary work are taken seriously, a new research agenda emerges. Its purpose may be described as the discovery of best practices for productive and creative boundary work – not: knowledge use and impact, although they do not vanish from the conceptual map (Guston 2001, Miller 2001, Cash et al. 2002, Hoppe 2002, Hoppe and Huijs 2003, De Wit 2005b). The quintessential insight underlying the quest for best practices in boundary work is an understanding of science/policy interactions as a multilevel system. In the study of the dynamics of policy change and administrative reforms (and technological transitions) there is convergence among researchers and theorists that phenomena have to be approached as embedded in a multilevel system, from macro- to micro perspectives: (inter)national institutional-cultural regime(s) or "landscapes", policy or issue network(s), organisation(s), and project(s). Expert advice is part of such policy and technological change processes; and hence may also be fruitfully studies as a multilevel phenomenon.

The ongoing process of negotiating a division of labour between science and politics can be discerned by looking at texts, objects and people (Halffman 2003).

"Boundary texts" (discourse, language, concepts) are about linguistic repertoires in which both parties speak and define their different roles – the semi-annual reports on the state of the economy by the Centre of Economic Policy Analysis provide a good example (De Vries, A. 2008). "Boundary objects" refer to tangible tools actors use in producing knowledge and advice in policy settings, like testing procedures, standardisation methods, computer models, measurement devices, or indicator systems. "Boundary people" are the different players in boundary arenas – either scientists, or policy workers, or those who combine or frequently oscillate between these two roles (Hoppe 2008). Together, boundary texts, objects and people shape boundary configurations.

From a micro-perspective, such boundary configurations are most clearly visible in concrete research & development-and-policy projects around particular topics. However, projects are carried out by organisations or organisations-of-organisations which (sometimes explicitly) mediate the boundary between professional-academic networks and public sector or policy organisations. Such organisations usually cluster around the typical problems in a specific issue or policy network. These problem-and-network structures in turn are permeated by a political-cultural sphere, the characteristics of which influence science-policy interfaces on all levels. To present a comprehensive picture of the science-policy interface, then, means to understand multilevel science-policy interactions and the ways these levels interact (see Figure 13.3):

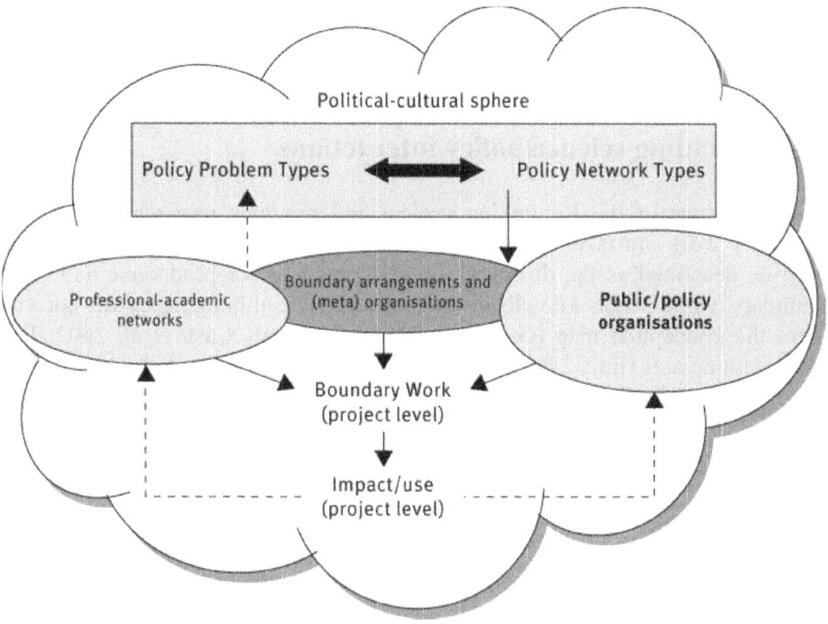

Fig. 13.3 Multilevel conceptual framework for understanding science/policy interactions.

13.6.1 Level 1: boundary work is (trans-) nationally culture-bound

Competing ideas on values and ideals like freedom, democracy, solidarity, fairness, and the trustworthiness of expert or lay knowledge infuse policy debates from the pubs' beer mats to high-level politics and diplomacy. There is overwhelming evidence that public policy gut responses to new policy developments are strongly influenced by *national* political cultures and regulatory styles (Halffman and Hoppe 2005, Jasanoff 2005, Lentsch and Weingart 2009). Hence, it is not surprising that the "same" allegedly scientific, universal knowledge about problems like crime, social security and climate change leads to divergent policy responses in different countries. The credibility and role of scientific knowledge in politics is an integral part of political culture and thus has to be considered as deeply embedded in national institutions. There is also increasing evidence for the emergence of different global or transnational cultures begins to influence national political cultures and policy styles (Jasanoff and Martello 2004, Strassheim 2007). The conversion of European Union directives in national regulation and implementation regimes perhaps is the most illuminating example. Of course, political and academic cultures are hardly manipulable variables in shaping concrete boundary organisations and arrangements, let alone best practices for boundary work at project level. Yet, one should take such overarching variables into account as constraining and enabling factors in more manipulable organisational and project designs.

13.6.2 Level 2: boundary work as policy politics in policy domains

The second level of boundary work is best defined as the *sectoral* or *policy domain* such as emission trade policy, energy transition policy, or biodiversity policy. Above it was argued that a political system at large may be viewed as a "federation of domains" where each domain has a distinct style of *policy politics*. Policy politics is the combination of the types of cognitive processes ("puzzling") and the styles of competitive interaction ("powering") that are characteristic for problem processing in a specific domain (Hoppe 2010). Policy politics describes a particular governance space, which coordinates the production, dissemination and acceptability of knowledges for political decisions. "Knowledges" is used in the plural because normally political decisions have to align different types of knowledge from different actors: citizens, professionals, bureaucrats, experts. The policy politics of a certain domain acquires its special character precisely because it implicitly or explicitly constructs a particular *public epistemology* that is the taken-for-granted expectations about the legitimacy and validity of these knowledges (Jasanoff 2005). Thus, policy politics involves contests about the availability of knowledge, about powers and competencies to frame and define problems, and about the legitimacy of knowledge claims. Policy politics, then, indirectly and tacitly deals with the borders between science and other actors' modes of knowing.

Policy politics strongly affects the boundary arrangements at the next-lower analytic level. Technical-specialist advisory institutes will only flourish in a closed network of professional players dealing with domesticated problems (cf. Hisschemöller and Hoppe 2001). Autonomous but government-supported advisory organs like the Scientific Council for Government Policy will only be successful advice-givers in political task environments of open issue networks around not yet domesticated problems (cf. Hisschemöller and Hoppe 2001). Ethical advisory committees on national level will usually be found in political landscapes defined by deliberately designed and managed discourse coalitions for issues with politically sensitive ethical loadings (cf. Hisschemöller and Hoppe 2001). Planning agencies like the Centre for Economic Policy Analysis or the Environmental Planning Agency may be successful boundary workers in semi-closed or half-pluralistic or neo-corporatist networks dealing with moderately structured problem with a fair amount of value and goal consensus (Hisschemöller and Hoppe 2001, Sabatier 1998). Only in this way their expertise in finding effective, efficient and low-risk policy instruments can be honoured. In terms of the quest for best practices, the policy politics level is hardly a manipulable variable; although there are conditions in which policy and institutional entrepreneurs can nudge a policy network with insufficient problem-processing capacity in the direction of favourable transformation (DiMaggio 1988, Pralle 2003, Garud et al. 2007, Hoppe 2010).

13.6.3 Level 3: Boundary arrangements

The third level in boundary work is a subsidiary part of the policy domain level and focuses on the *boundary arrangements* and *organisations* that institutionally facilitate the science/politics interactions and knowledge/power structures in a given policy domain. The concept of boundary "arrangements" tries to capture the sheer variety of boundary-crossing science/politics hybrids that have proliferated these last decades (Strassheim 2007: 283). In the Netherlands alone, the array of hybrid institutional forms runs from legally established, highly institutionalised, boundary organisations like the CPB (Halffman 2009) or the Scientific WRR (Den Hoed and Keizer 2009), to merged knowledge organisations or organisations-of-organisations like Alterra (for agriculture and environment) and Deltares (for coastal and river management), sectoral advisory councils (like RMNO, for Spatial Planning, Nature and Environment) and research "centres of excellence" (like NICIS, for urban research and policy), all the way to informal hybrid virtual forums where academics, professionals, businessmen and government officials meet around shared problems (like the website of the "coalition" of CO_2-neutral cities). In other words, explicitly established and institutionalised boundary organisations are but one manifestation of a much broader "twilight zone" of hybrid arrangements (Halffman and Hoppe 2005).

In the quest for best practice, for simplicity's sake, five conditions or attributes for successful boundary arrangements can be listed here (see for example Guston 2001, Miller 2001, Cash et al. 2002). Readers should be warned that not all of these occur in each boundary organisation, and that each may be present in stronger or weaker form:

Double participation: People from both the policy/politics and the scientific world are represented and participate in the activities of the boundary organisation or arrangement.

Dual accountability: The leadership or management of boundary organisations and arrangements is accountable to representatives of science and politics, simultaneously. Not surprisingly, this leads to a split between front-office narratives of boundary work for official use in external accountability relations to for example members of parliament and the press, and back-office narratives in internal or insiders' accountability relations, for example between boundary workers of different advisory bodies and departmental policy workers (Bal et al. 2002, De Vries, A. 2008, Hoppe 2008).

Boundary objects: The creation and maintenance of a well-chose set of boundary objects in generating a "world" in which both scientists and policy-makers feel at home and may successfully coordinate their activities. Examples of suitable boundary objects are indicator systems, econometric or climate models, bi-annual audits, report series, etcetera. Textual and graphical boundary objects that immediately support budget decisions appear to be the best guarantee for successful boundary work.

Co-production: Robust knowledge/power structures create social and cognitive order using negotiation, confrontation and mediation. Experience has shown that premature consensus-seeking and compromise-building is a serious threat to successful boundary work. This requires steps that neither politicians nor scientists are necessarily comfortable with: identification of critical scientists, counter-experts, visionaries, and even "dissenters"; in addition, sometimes confrontation is required between decontextualised policy and scientific knowledge and situated, local knowledge, for example through participatory and deliberative policy exercises with stakeholder or citizen representatives.

Metagovernance and capacity building: This is the cross-jurisdictional, cross-level and cross-scale orchestration of distributed knowledge production. This task deserves special attention in order to avoid the pitfalls of incrementalist policy-making: (1) misguided policy trials may produce very costly outcomes, (2) policy moves prematurely declared successful retain too little error-correction flexibility, and (3) learning from error becomes too slow. High-quality metagovernance resists the political "gravity law" of incrementalist policy by careful design of procedures for research, development, deliberation and decision-making, and alert monitoring of progress. Sufficient attention to capacity building in all relevant boundary organisations and projects is important in metagovernance. This is a task in danger of neglect in the age of leaner and meaner government. Former top-level civil servant and minister Jozias van Aartsen opines:

> Where does one still find sound substantive knowledge in contemporary government departments? Civil servants in key positions who are really in-the-know about a particular policy issue are becoming a rare species. All of us are going to suffer for this (Beuvink and Den Hoed 2007: 95; translation RH).

13.6.4 Level 4: Boundary work in projects

Finally, a *micro-level* of boundary work practices in *projects* may be distinguished. This is where the boundary is at its most fuzzy and sometimes even "up for grabs", as it has to be negotiated and renegotiated in the smallest details. For example, in the production of authoritative texts by the International Panel on Climate Change (Petersen 2006), or for semi-annual reports on the state of the economy by the CPB (De Vries, A. 2008), the political and scientific practices of dealing with uncertainty depend on the characteristics of the policy and the knowledge workers involved, as well as on the design of the projects they engage in. Other aspects of good boundary work in projects are rules and habits for dealing with values (is it a political or scientific responsibility, or shared?), dealing with conflicting types of knowledge, the impacts of the project design on the participants' ability and willingness to learn and on the building, maintenance or erosion of mutual trust, and the organisational flexibility of the project itself.

It is at the project level that the considerable body of knowledge of project design ingredients becomes relevant. Research on knowledge about various project designs and their impacts on the quality of boundary work are evolving into an interdisciplinary field of its own. It goes under different labels, from-knowing-to-doing, integrated assessment, participatory and deliberative policy analysis, collaborative knowledge production or joint fact-finding, reflective practitionership, communities of practice, transition management, design rules for inter- and transdisciplinary projects or adaptive management, and many more – almost all featuring in other chapters of this book.

In spite of all these budding communities of learning and practice, the project level of boundary work still hosts many perplexities and dilemmas. All scholars who have reflected on the limitations of the human mind have concluded that boundary work is inevitable in reaching aggregate political decisions for collective action. After all, our inability to know (everything) forces us to at some point stop the cognitive process if we want to make decisions and take actions. Hence, any form of learning in political task fields should not be limited to discursive and scientific analysis-and-instruction; it necessarily takes the shape of pragmatic trial-and-error learning by variation-and-selection in doing. Perhaps, then, the most important question for boundary work at project level is how to arrange projects as field experiments in fast and intelligent trial-and-error learning processes. Important questions to ask are then: How is it possible to specify project arrangements, procedures, and strategies to make errors less damaging and to accelerate learning? Under what conditions do (sets of) politically and scientifically partisan players manage their mutual interactions to deal better than usual with uncertainty, value ambiguities, limited time, and so forth? Under what conditions do they do worse than normal?

We still need much better knowledge about truly intelligent and politically acceptable trial and error learning. In theory, we may formulate key principles for boundary work projects (Woodhouse and Nieusma 2001). They include: early debates involving many divergent perspectives, building flexibility into projects so as to facilitate a change of course in case of negative feedback, taboo- and back-up systems and other precautionary measures to cope with initial, sometimes huge uncertainties and risks, gradual scale-up of activities (again with a view to flexibility), and designed, accelerated feedback through advanced testing and intensive monitoring. Yet we know from experience how difficult it is to design these desirable features into actual projects, and, once designed, to faithfully adhere to them.

13.7 Conclusion

In this chapter, the contours have been outlined of a new, emerging research agenda for inquiry into science-politics interactions. As set out in the first section, this is triggered by the adverse impact of impact models, that is, first, palpable empirical inadequacy of the older models of knowledge use; and, second, the pernicious over-instrumentalisation and attenuation of expertise resulting from the use of such models in the governance of expert advice. In the second section, boundary work was introduced as a more adequate conceptualisation of science-politics interactions. In the third section, the considerable variety in types of boundary work was illustrated on the case of science-policy interactions in the Netherlands. The final two sections hypothetically argued that, underlying the apparent variety, there is more "system" than meets the eye. In Sect. 13.4 it was argued that the seven different types of (discourses on) boundary work, jointly, cover the range of differently structured problems a policy and political system has to deal with (see Figures 13.1 and 13.2). In Sect. 13.5, an effort was made to conceptualise this "system" of types of boundary work in a multilevel model of science-politics interactions (see Figure 13.3).

Awaiting more research and confirmatory evidence for this multilevel model, perhaps the immediate virtue of Figure 13.3 is its exposure of the shortcomings of the knowledge use and impact type of models and research. First, conceptualisation of the problem and empirical research only addressed the micro-levels; in-between and macro-levels were neglected and certainly underexposed. Yet, these higher levels contain important constraining and enabling mechanisms for the (dis-)functioning of boundary arrangements and boundary work projects. Second, attention of both practitioners and scientists was absorbed by the right-hand impact arrow in Figure 13.3. It was not sufficiently realised that, for sound and high-quality science-based policy advice, boundary workers and boundary organisations cannot and may not one-sidedly adapt to the needs of politics and policy-making without gambling away the vital dependence on their nurturing scientific-professional substrate of institutions for knowledge production (including universities and schools for higher professional education) and innovation. This is all the more amazing in an age in which social and economic trends are politically baptised and officially proclaimed as "knowledge economy" or "knowledge society". The prudent governance of expertise starts from as complete a picture of the knowledge system as is possible; not with truncated and therefore short-sighted knowledge impact models.

The aim of the proposed new research agenda is better boundary work in practice. In order to achieve this aim, the institutional domains of science and politics have to be connected where possible and, simultaneously, kept separate where necessary. Not once and for all, but in flexible, renegotiable ways, depending on the changing nature of problem frames and definitions. Ultimately, the idea is to design and construct for the twenty-first century the capacity to maintain and nurture the previously self-evident fruitful mutual dependencies between politics, knowledge, and public policy (Rooney et al. 2003, Anderson, L. 2003, Parsons 2004, De Wit 2005).

14 The public knowledge challenge: where the management of cities and businesses converge towards creativity, innovation and prosperity

Stella van Rijn and René J. Tissen

Abstract

The creative and innovative power of cities and regions is of decisive importance in materialising the knowledge-based economy on such a scale, that it will ultimately have a positive impact on the prosperity of citizens (Grotenhuis 2007, Van Winden et al. 2007, Florida 2005). Similar to what usually confronts businesses, cities and regions are faced with a global competition for talent, as is generally reflected in the form of a race between cities and regions that strive to be as attractive as possible for talented, on average highly educated, and creative workers (Hospers 2003, Florida 2005, Malecki 2002). Knowledge will likely further increase in importance, but it is not yet clear how knowledge can be put to practical use in cities and regions, how it can or should be managed in the context of an appropriate democratic structure and to what extent measurable economic and societal effects occur, especially amidst the clustering of knowledge industries in supra-regional and supra-national economic mega-regions. The knowledge challenge is where cities and businesses converge into a clear, but as yet not explored, shared interest: (creative) businesses locate where (creative) human capital is present (Florida 2005). Participation of creative citizens – both individual as well as company citizens and civil organisations – in the governance of a city is imperative. The concept of the knowledge democracy, and more specifically the way in which the democratic knowledge potential of cities is used through collaborative learning processes, can be further developed by transdisciplinary research into knowledge management policies and practices from business management (Tissen and Van Rijn 2007).

14.1 Knowledge

The influence and importance of knowledge has been broadly discussed over the years in an increasing number of fields, without actually resulting in an established trend to replace industrial-based economic models by knowledge-based ones, other than in theory. Its origins as a practical concept – in addition to the

R.J. in 't Veld (ed.), *Knowledge Democracy*, DOI 10.1007/978-3-642-11381-9_14,

centuries' old epistemological discussion – go back to the second half of the last century when the knowledge-based development of organisations gained a prominent position in business management, once knowledge was linked to organisations as both a competitive resource (Drucker 1995) as well as an asset. In the early sixties of the last century Drucker was one of the first to introduce the term "Knowledge Industries", "Knowledge Work" and "Knowledge Workers". However, decades afterwards (2001) he concluded that with respect to these terms, although broadly defined from the onset:

> … hardly anyone understands their implications for human values and human behaviour, for managing people and making them productive, for economics and for politics. What is already clear, however, is that the emerging knowledge society and knowledge economy will be radically different from the society and economy of the late 20th century (Drucker 2001).

Reflective of this lack of understanding of the knowledge society is the broad range of approaches and definitions of knowledge, and the discussions about the role of knowledge in an increasing number of fields. The influence of knowledge – supported by fast developments in the field of communication technology – is broadly felt in many aspects of our society. Yet, not even in the field of business management where knowledge as a practical concept emerged, has the concept been clearly and unequivocally defined. The role of knowledge in organisations is generally referred to as knowledge management, but a variety of interpretations exists. Boersma (2002) noted that the choice for one of the many descriptions depends on the context in which the concept is being applied. Like Drucker he states that the development of the knowledge society is irreversible, and that knowledge management is a *must* for all organisations. However, in his analysis Boersma categorised no less than 10 different approaches to knowledge management from a variety of contexts, each with its own goals: human resources, intellectual capital, organisational science, learning organisation, networking, innovation, strategic approach, quality management, ICT, and knowledge technology. Peter Senge referred to this phenomenon in his famous work on the learning organisation as the *compartmentalisation* of knowledge. He dismisses such rational subdivisions, and considers this merely *an analytical lens* through which we can look, but not always see. Narrowed views make us believe that problems can be labelled, isolated and thus solved, but according to Senge, the boundaries that separate the compartments are *fundamentally arbitrary*, which makes any solution inherently flawed. Another explanation for the variety of interpretations of the knowledge concept comes from Andriessen (2008), who stresses the influential role of the use of metaphors when discussing knowledge. He refers to their use as *inescapable* because it is the way the human mind works when reasoning about abstract concepts such as knowledge. His research showed no less than 22 metaphors that are commonly used, varying from knowledge as a resource, as an asset, as property or as capital in Western science, to knowledge as thoughts and feelings in Japanese literature. He concluded that:

> The unconscious choice of metaphor has enormous impact on how we reason about knowledge, what is highlighted and what is hidden, what is seen in the organisations as problems and what is understood as solutions (Andriessen 2008: 6).

Considering the variety of approaches, the knowledge concept can be viewed as "work in progress" that is multifaceted, as well as dynamic and fluid.

14.2 Knowledge and democracy

The classical Greek concept of *democracy* has received specific attention in recent decades in the field of social and political sciences with respect to the way in which the voices of minorities and the less educated can be more included in the democratic system through *participative decision-making* (Fung 2004). The research into democratic systems and principles has expanded over time from the representation aspect to the participation aspect of democracy, from government to governance, whereby governance in this context can be defined as the cooperation between governments, citizens, companies, and civil organisations with the aim to solve problems within the public domain (Van der Heijden 2005). The combination of the two concepts knowledge and democracy into the new concept of *knowledge democracy* is very recent, and like the knowledge concept to which it is related, the conceptual boundaries are rather elastic.

The knowledge democracy concept triggers questions about fundamental aspects of our current (Western) society. How will knowledge, which is readily available and can easily be shared thanks to progress in the use of information technology, as well as the trend towards individualisation in the knowledge era, change the way we work, live and organise our society? In 't Veld (2009) noted that the representative, constitutional democracy in recent centuries became *the predominant format of the nation state* and also that it enhanced the notion of state, sovereignty, society and territory, because these notions became *intensely related* with the democratic system. However, these notions appear, according to In 't Veld, to be endangered. Our individual sense of belonging prevails and is no longer related to traditional democratically defined boundaries of a region, a nation or an ideology.

To analyse the concept of knowledge democracy and its impact, we can look at the clear connection that exists with knowledge-based development of cities and regions, which has been studied across a range of different disciplines and fields of research, varying from economics and technology, to geography and urban science (Carillo 2006).

A central aspect across the disciplines in these discussions is formed by the direct link between knowledge and people, who function as knowledge brokers by possessing, sharing, submitting and creating knowledge, also – but not exclusively – referred to as "ideas" or even more widely as "creativity". It was Florida (2002) who stressed that businesses follow knowledge, and thus that cities must not limit themselves to inventing fiscal incentives and creating infrastructural facilities in their strive to attract businesses. Instead they should focus on attracting creative citizens in order to be able to attract knowledge enterprises. Florida (2002) classifies this *creative class* into a *supercreative core* who realise *meaningful new forms of living and working*, consisting of scientists and engineers, university professors, poets and novelists, artists, entertainers, actors, designers and architects, as well as those “brain activists” of modern society who strive to achieve thought leadership: non-fiction writers, editors, cultural figures, think-tank researchers, analysts and other opinion makers. Beyond this core group, Florida also includes *creative professionals* who work in a wide range of knowledge-intensive industries such as high-tech sectors, financial services, the legal and health care professions, and business management. Florida effectively linked creative workers to the “mental capacities” of cities, which becomes visible in the way they profile themselves as cities where people *want* to live. According to Florida, cities and regions that want to gain competitive advantage:

> … need to create mechanisms for harnessing the knowledge and ideas of all citizens at the neighbourhood, local and regional levels for improving their quality of place (Florida 2005: 86).

Malecki (2002) referred to this competitive challenge as a *race* in which the winners will be those cities and regions that succeed in attracting and maintaining the creative resources that offer competitive advantage. The question arises as to how cities achieve this, more specifically as to which knowledge principles, processes and/or mechanisms they need to create and maintain? This is challenging in itself, specifically in relation to an emerging concept such as knowledge democracy. When looked at from a business perspective, some interesting parallels between knowledge cities and knowledge enterprises seem to apply (Tissen and Van Rijn 2007). Comparing these parallels may open the door to a multidisciplinary approach of the concept of knowledge democracy and thus offer opportunities for local and regional governments to advance the notion of knowledge democracy in a less ideological and more practical way.

14.3 Knowledge as a competitive advantage

One of these parallels with respect to knowledge is that cities and regions are confronted with the same challenge as businesses: knowledge and ideas – either in the form of creativity or as such – can constitute a determining competitive advantage (Davenport and Prusak 2000). In the twenty-first century this also applies to cities and regions (Knight 1995, Landry 2000, Florida 2005, Carillo 2006). According to Lever (2002) few studies have been able to empirically connect the creation of new knowledge with innovation and economic growth at the level of cities. Lever applied a multidimensional measure of the *knowledge base* of a city and linked this with the economic performance of 19 European cities. He concluded that good access to the knowledge base on an urban level indeed correlates with positive growth.

Economic growth as such, however, should not be the only aim of knowledge-based development. The competitiveness of cities and regions should contribute to an increased standard of living for its inhabitants (Malecki 2002) and according to Knight (1995) to their sustainable long term development and thus "ingrained" vitality. This links directly to the traditional – sometimes referred to as ritual – discussions in the field of public governance on the extent to which participative processes in representative democratic systems actually result in better "performance", also over time and measured in terms of economic, societal and individual "return on effort".

Just like In 't Veld (2009) remarked that the notion and boundaries of physical states and regions (as defined by our democratic system) no longer fits the overall perception of citizens in the knowledge era, this also applies to the measurement of economic growth. The role of cities as catalytic engines for the knowledge economy is not reflected in their measurement of performance, in policies, nor in laws, which traditionally are focused on indicators and regulations on the national and multinational "space bound" level. This neglects, according to Ohmae (1993), the reality that:

> … regions and cities are more frequently the "motors" of their national economies and less dependent on the national economy than the national economy is on them (Ohmae 1993).

Regional economic activity in the globalised world has little respect for national borders and tends to migrate across politically set boundaries. The newly formed *region states*, as Ohmae refers to these economic concentrations, develop along lines of real economic opportunity caused by "patterns manifest in countless individual decisions" of people and businesses. These region states replace nations as an organising economic unit and each of these region states possesses,

> in one or another combination, the key to ingredients for successful participation in the global economy (Ohmae 1993).

Florida (2008a) takes the regional clustering effect one step further in his latest research and describes that the world economy is organised around a few dozen *mega-regions*, which produce most of the world's economic activity and innovation. He refers to these *mega-regions* as *spikes* in a statistically rather flat landscape of economic activity. Florida argues that:

> Writers like Thomas Friedman have overemphasised the centrifugal forces of globalisation, arguing that the world is flat. In so doing they neglect the powerful centripetal forces that trigger economic concentration (Florida 2008a: 19).

The world is both flat and *spiky*, economic activity is both dispersed and concentrated at the same time, says Florida. While routine economic functions spread geographically, higher level economic activities tend to concentrate in a relatively small number of locations at the same time.

In 't Veld (2009) refers to the "increased predominance of global economic conglomerates" as one of the aspects that may contribute to the democratic decline. Economic activities that surpass democratically set boundaries create tensions with respect to the representation aspects of citizens who cross city or state boundaries in search of connection with their economic and social preferences.

14.4 Knowledge citizens

The fact that the politically set boundaries of democratic entities such as cities and regions no longer coincide with "solidified" economic activity in supra-regional and supra-national clusters, raises questions with respect to how such regions could and should be governed and how the knowledge potential of its citizens can be used optimally. In analysing the needs of citizens that locate in these economic clusters, we find comparative material in the management sciences. The shift from the industrial to the knowledge economy was accompanied by a range of publications concerning the implications of this shift for organisations and their need to refocus their managerial attention in order to benefit from knowledge, among others by taking full account of the needs of knowledge workers as a new specimen of the labour force. Some focused on the need to integrate knowledge management in overall business processes such as strategy, business process redesign, and organisational culture (Davenport and Prusak 2000); others emphasised the need to focus on interpersonal aspects to create a *knowledge-enabling context* in organisations (Von Krogh et al. 2000).

Tissen et al. (2000) foresaw an even more impacting consequence for organisations by sounding the "death bell for the functional organisation", resulting from an intangible process that "blurred the lines between employees and management, between staff and line" (Tissen et al. 2000: 48). In recent research Tissen and Lekanne Deprez (2008) introduced the concept of "space" in organisational design theory, arguing that a spatial approach to organisations allows managers to more flexibly overcome limitations and constraints of traditional organisations and enable them to better face the challenges of dynamic and complex surroundings. The theory describes a threefold approach to space in organisations, consisting of *physical* space, *virtual* space and – more specifically – of *mental* space.

This raises the question whether the development of the knowledge-based city also rings the death bell for the traditional representative democracy in cities and the local government systems, structures and procedures, as demands from knowledge citizens come with new requirements for the governance of cities. Just as companies have to shift away from strictly functional thinking and organising to be able to provide *space* to knowledge workers, city governments have to give *space* to knowledge citizens, as they come with a new set of "place-based characteristics" (Florida 2008) upon which they base their decision to locate in a specific place, looking for a balance between economic opportunity and quality of life.

Fascinated by the role of place in a person's life and how it contributes to overall happiness, Florida expanded his research into creative cities in 2008 in cooperation with the Gallup Organisation with the "Place and Happiness Survey". It was conducted among 28,000 people and concluded:

> … location is as relevant to a person's well-being as are his or her job, finances, and interpersonal relationship (Florida 2008: 13).

According to the survey the places that make people happy have physical and economic security, basic services, leadership, openness, and aesthetics. The list is topped by aesthetics and basic services and Florida calls it "intriguing" that with regard to aesthetics the physical beauty of communities matters most, followed by outdoor parks, playgrounds, and trails.

Earlier research, although less specific, also indicated that the quality of place and the amenities of the urban environment are a key factor to attracting and retaining knowledge workers as citizens (Knight 1995, Van Winden et al. 2007).

14.5 Governance matters to creative citizens

Landry (2000) states that not only "quality of place" (as represented by physical characteristics) influences the location decision of creative citizens, but that the governance structure of a city can be considered a competitive factor too, combined with the role and influence citizens have in the shaping of their city. The attachment to place is seen by knowledge or creative citizens as a *centre of felt value* and brings meaning to life if they can contribute to it. With good governance as a competitive tool in urban affairs, attention is needed for what Landry refers to as the *stakeholder democracy*, which amplifies the basis of power that traditionally consists of elected officials, to groups of committed individuals and organisations that are willing to contribute to enhancing the quality of place. Landry attributes great importance to the organisational capacity of a city and open governance structures; he even goes so far as to consider these aspects *the precondition of all preconditions* for creative cities.

In the field of urban science, political science as well as public management a rich body of research exists into how democratic systems can and should be adjusted to include more participative processes. New governance systems should reflect the *fundamental new sense of individual freedom* of citizens in the knowledge era. Governance can be considered as "participative democracy", but according to Van der Heijden:

> no one yet has the definite answer to the question how participative democracy relates to the representational democracy as we know it (2005: 65).

The tension between the principles of the representative democracy and the participation of non-elected, and often not representative people and organisations in governance processes, was also mentioned in the conclusions of the Demos project (2004), which linked eight city and prefecture governments in seven European countries with research organisations across Europe in innovation on citizen participation in local government. In the Demos project conclusions it was suggested that, where in participatory processes the participants are not representative in a pure democratic sense, as often is the case in participatory processes, it is

> the legitimacy or credibility of community representatives which is important rather than their strict representativeness (Demos 2004: 29).

In 't Veld (2009) considers it a "logical evolution" that citizens prefer partial representation by an NGO per value domain, as they have come to understand the limitations of non-personal representation and/or involvement in decision-making processes which affect their individual lives and futures, both directly as well as indirectly.

14.6 The role of government

The question arises who should initiate, shape and contribute to a knowledge-based governance framework that stimulates creative cities and regions to develop and flourish in the knowledge society? Analysing successful examples is not an option because, according to Hospers (2003), there is no prototype or blueprint for what comprises *the* creative city. He refers to examples of a variety of cities that through the ages can be considered cities where creativity flourished, but where policy-makers have hardly played any contributing role to the degree and level of creativity. Hospers argues that the influence of government on the development of a creative city is limited to offering a *helping hand* to chance. He identifies three factors that can increase the chances of urban creativity development contributing to an urban knowledge economy: concentration, diversity and instability. Hospers views the role of government as facilitating, but not leading, these conditions "to increase the chances that creative powers come into existence (p. 266)." Others consider a more active role of local government of greater possible influence. Van Winden et al. (2007) refer to the quality of urban governance as "organising capacity" which task it is to bring stakeholders together in a lifecycle approach consisting of phases such as the generation of ideas, the development of strategies and policy, implementation and monitoring. This is comparable to the facilitating role for government that Landry (2000) describes in the development of local *partnerships* whose role it is to come up with solutions for identified problems. He attributes great importance to this facilitating role and considers the organisation of local government a key factor for success and competitive advantage for knowledge-based cities:

> Governing, organising and managing better can make the difference between success and failure. They are new sources of competitiveness – good strategic, and effective governance and management arrangements are just as much a competitive tool as is a piece of technology (Landry 2000: 262).

Another aspect to be considered is the question of what comprises an effective use of the local knowledge base in the urban environment. In other words, what are the urban aspects of knowledge-based economic development? For this a framework of analysis was created by Van Winden et al. (2007) for cities in the knowledge economy. Seven structural characteristics were identified which contribute to a city's "ability to acquire, create, disseminate and use (codified and tacit) knowledge" for greater economic and social development:

- the knowledge base of the population, consisting of universities, public and private R&D facilities and the education level;
- the strength of the industrial structure and the degree of specialisation;
- the urban amenities and quality of life as key factors to attract and retain knowledge workers;
- the accessibility of transportation on the (inter-)national and regional level;
- the urban diversity of inhabitants to facilitate interactions between economic players which generates new ideas;
- the geographic and numerical scale of a city, which influences the attractiveness for companies and knowledge workers;
- the degree of social equity to avoid tensions between "haves" and "have nots" and between ethnic groups, to promote a feeling of safety.

These characteristics supersede the abilities and responsibilities of government, and call for a broader governance base and for more inclusive and participatory processes in the knowledge democracy.

Whatever role local government chooses to play as initiator, coordinator or facilitator, Ergazakis et al. (2004: 7) argue that the process of developing a knowledge-based city "is neither quick nor simple". They mention *political will* as the most important factor that should work like a *spark* that ignites action within an *appropriate legislative framework.*

14.7 The knowledge society

In the knowledge society clear parallels between businesses and cities and regions can be drawn with regard to several mutual challenges:

- knowledge or creativity as a decisive competitive factor;
- a relatively high degree of elasticity in setting the conceptual boundaries of knowledge-based development;
- the importance of "place" and the quality of place, both material as well as immaterial;
- the constant need for aligning governance structures and participative processes, to the environment.

Besides these parallels in challenges with regard to knowledge, also shared interests can be identified between businesses and cities in their efforts to further enhance knowledge-based development:

- both need knowledge workers, either as employee or as citizen;
- both derive value from tapping into the knowledge potential of these citizens to enhance the overall quality of a city/region, including its reputation;
- both experience the influence of the geographical clustering effect of talent and economic activity and look for ways to concentrate knowledge intensive activities and people in their region or organisation.

Considering the parallels in challenges and interests, cross-disciplinary or transdisciplinary research seems the logical next step to explore and compare mutual "lessons to be learned", and to share relevant insights.

Currently there is little overflow of practices between business and public sector agencies, concludes Malecki (2002) referring to business practices such as benchmarking and comparative data-gathering as a way to scan the outside environment. He also notices a lack of development of *absorption capacity* in public sector and government agencies, which he describes as "the ability to evaluate potential knowledge, assimilate it and apply it" (2002: 934). While Malecki proposes to use a mix of lessons from the private sector, others warn that business methods cannot be applied as such in the public realm (Landry 2000). A selective choice of instruments is to be preferred, according to Landry, because of the differences between public and private sector in managing risk and working with creativity.

Transdisciplinary research can resolve the applicability issue of methods and instruments by providing a much more inclusive, interactive and process-oriented approach, which is suitable for the kind of unstructured, complex and uncertain problems that cities and regions face in the context of knowledge-based development. Although the present literature on such transdisciplinary research does not propose a coherent theory and methodology (Pohl and Hirsch Hadorn 2008), comparative studies of transdisciplinary processes have developed some useful frameworks and guidelines. Regeer and Bunders (2009) refer to transdisciplinary processes as interactive learning processes, in which integration, participation, innovation and sustainability are key words. The aim is to create and integrate knowledge, based on a commitment of all actors in the problem solving process. One of the challenges in transdisciplinary processes is to deal with the *diversity of perspectives* of the actors involved and have them interact and integrate the different perspectives into solutions that serve the common good (Pohl and Hirsch Hadorn 2008). But, as Roland Scholz of the Swiss Federal Institute of Technology remarked in his keynote address at the conference "Towards a Knowledge Democracy" (2009),

> there are several transdisciplinary processes, but there very few transdisciplinary personalities.

In other words, as Bunders (2009) explained the diversity and integration challenges:

> Routines have to be changed, and changing routines is extremely difficult in institutions and even painful for individuals.

This coincides with one of the lessons learned from management science with respect to knowledge and creativity. Several researchers in this field stress the overarching role of the human aspects of knowledge management as being far more important than for example knowledge management structures, processes and IT systems. (Von Krogh et al. 2000, Davenport and Prusak 2000, Leadbeater and Cottam 2007). They conclude that whatever infrastructure or processes are being put in place, most knowledge sharing and creation – especially of valuable, yet intangible, tacit knowledge – depends on face-to-face socialisation, which can bring certain challenges and tensions in human relations and communication. Tissen and Van Rijn (2007) identified three such human aspects commonly found in knowledge management literature that are essential to knowledge-based processes:

- Genuinely work *with* people;
- A knowledge enabling context;
- A culture of diversity.

Genuinely work *with* people refers to the difference between "giving" people the impression that they are involved ("proclaimed ethics") and actually involving them (real-time participation), which is reflected among other things in the way knowledge-based processes are organised and facilitated, and by the willingness of actors to adapt existing views and plans according to findings from the socialisation processes. The knowledge enabling context refers to the right mindset of (top) management, as well as a knowledge enabling culture, which are considered indispensable for a knowledge-based approach. Von Krogh et al. (2000: 49) refer to this as the "enabling context", which is not necessarily a physical space, but

> …combines aspects of physical space (the design of an office or dispersed business operations), virtual space (e-mail, intranets, teleconferences), and mental space (shared experiences, ideas, emotions). More than anything, it is a network of interactions, determined by the care and trust of participants.

A third aspect involves the importance of being attached to a culture of diversity, in order for organisations and communities to be able to attract and maintain talent. Florida (2005) in his research into creative cities has used specific indices to measure levels of diversity in relation to the presence and growth of high tech industries. Results indicate that

> a connection exists between a metropolitan area's level of tolerance for a range of people, its ethnic and social diversity, and its success in attracting people, including high-technology workers. (2005: 130).

Florida also concluded that the relationship between the *bohemian index* – reflected in the relative presence of people with an artistic profession – and concentrations of high-human-capital individuals and such industry are also significant (2005: 115). In the same context Leadbeater and Cottam (2007) concludes that:

> most innovation comes from combining different ideas and viewpoints to create a new idea. Cities must encourage mixing and mingling. [...] That means creative cities have to be relatively open and cosmopolitan; they have to attract different people, with ambition and talent and then find ways to mix them together. (Leadbeater and Cottam 2007).

14.8 Conclusions

Many economic developments take place at the city and regional level, which are often seen to possess indirect, but genuine catalytic power, particularly in the context of the knowledge-based economy. The need to expand the knowledge base and involve creative citizens in city and regional planning processes requires the involvement and cooperation of both public and private stakeholders in joint exercises (Porter 1998, Knight 1995, Landry 2000). Although these joint exercises take place within the current representative democratic systems, they imply a shift in the current responsibilities because the traditional role-play in city planning needs to change to provide for more influence of citizens and their creativity.

> Residents have had little if any effective voice or influence in the shaping their environment. Elected officials refuse to negotiate their power to decide and architects and engineers refuse to share or question their specialised knowledge. The general public has little choice; either they must accept a deteriorating situation and adapt to what their instincts tell them is an unhealthy, unsafe or unsavoury environment or they can vote with their feet and contribute to the city's decline. (Knight 1995: 250).

Collaborative processes – such as the transdisciplinary research approach towards knowledge management processes and practices – have accumulated valuable and practical insights into knowledge-based development. In a city or regional context collaborative learning processes are beneficial to both private organisations and to city and/or regional governments. Private organisations tend to have the advantage of "outside-in" information on short and long-term developments and trends in relation to the *collective intentions* of the city in which they are located. A city or region in its turn can learn from the experiences of the private sector on how to identify and assess potential knowledge resources (Knight 1995).

However desirable such collaborative learning processes may be from a scientific point of view, empirical evidence in both management science and transdisciplinary research shows that *fresh thinking* is required of all stakeholders involved, as well as acceptance of the blurring of traditional roles (Porter 1998). Here,

Landry (2000) refers to the need for a paradigm shift, as successful cities need "leadership that is widespread, permeating public, private and voluntary sectors."

In 't Veld (2009) even goes so far to call for institutional and functional innovation in light of the knowledge democracy. McCann (2001) more specifically warns that for this a shift is needed in the actual power base in city planning and development. This shift may not be recognised as advantageous by all parties involved, not just because of conflicting interests, but also because of a diffusion of interests, in essence of uncertainty as to who holds the decision-making power. Here McCann rightly states that the location of power ("he who resides in the building") seems to be a neglected, but nonetheless crucial "anchoring" mechanism for the successful execution of collaborative processes, especially in the context of the knowledge democracy.

15 The governance of usable and welcome knowledge, two perspectives

Louis Meuleman and Henk Tromp

Abstract

This chapter concentrates on the use of (scientific) knowledge by policy-makers. The first part of this chapter takes the point of view of policy-makers. There may be many reasons why research is sometimes not welcome, but the most common reason seems to be that the research is not considered as *usable* in a certain situation. The timing may be wrong (too early, too late), or the results does not match with the way the political problem has been framed or reframed. It will be argued that the dominant governance style of the policy-making process may show a preference for certain qualities of the produced research, such as the authority of the researchers, the discourse on the quality of the research, or the price. Policy-makers should therefore be aware that scientists do often not know the *finesses* of political decision-making and its consequences for the usability of knowledge, and should develop a "metagovernance" of usable knowledge. The other way around also applies: it is important that scientists understand the process of political decision-making.

The second part of the chapter illustrates what may happen when researchers produce politically highly *unwelcome* news. There are many examples – starting with Galileo Galilei – of the pressures and sanctions researchers may face when the result of their research is not welcomed. Unwelcome research may be fought, kept quiet, silenced or distorted. It will be argued that scientists should be aware of these mechanisms, and should not give in to such pressures. Students should be trained to deal with this problem, and an award for courageous science should be considered. In a third and closing part both authors share and combine these notions.

R.J. in 't Veld (ed.), *Knowledge Democracy*, DOI 10.1007/978-3-642-11381-9_15,

15.1 Governance and the usability of knowledge for policy-makers

Louis Meuleman

15.1.1 Evident evidence?

To a certain degree political decisions are always influenced by "hard" or "soft" knowledge. However, this knowledge is not always considered to be "sound" by scientists. When policy-makers overlook or have decided to neglect scientifically sound knowledge, the experts who produced the research results may meet silence or may be silenced in one way or another; their *unwelcome* knowledge may even be distorted.

I will discuss why policy-makers and politicians sometimes find knowledge *unusable*. In this part of the chapter, three different perceptions of the use and usability of knowledge for policy-making are discussed, which match with the three basic governance styles hierarchy, network and market. The question is if governance of governance style combinations, or metagovernance, may help to improve the use of knowledge in policy-making, and if this could contribute to developing a knowledge democracy.

One of the reasons why policy-makers do not welcome the results of research is that they prefer a different interpretation of the results, or would have liked to see different results. Even if one believes that there is an objective, sound and undisputed science somewhere out there, it is increasingly accepted that many factors co-determine how the results of research or assessments are interpreted. Some of these factors were revealed through case study research in environmental and health issues (Gee 2009):

- If evidence is evaluated by a committee, factors are: who are the members; what are their interests, preferred paradigms and passions; what is the committee's remit; how are the questions framed?
- Which knowledge is accepted? Only scientific studies or also lay and local knowledge? Knowledge of scientists with minority standpoints?
- Which weights are given to the various items of knowledge? How were biases dealt with? Not only in politics but also in science there are methodological biases and reporting and publication biases, and, conscious (re)framing of results into a desired direction ("spin") can be observed.
- By which rules are, for example, the degree of confidence and understanding of knowledge evaluated?
- By which rules are the strengths of evidence evaluated?

Another factor is that knowledge about complex issues is different from the simple addition of partial knowledge. Moreover, academic knowledge is only valid under certain conditions (like laboratory conditions for physical research and historical/cultural traditions for the social sciences, for example), which are not always met in practice. An additional problem in social sciences is that such research may influence the "research object" (for example in behavioural sciences).

It is therefore safe to conclude that decisions are not taken on the basis of the available knowledge as such, but on the basis of interpretation and selection of knowledge. Interpretations may differ between scientists and policy-makers, but also between individuals inside both groups. Knowledge is disputable and usually will be disputed in the political arena, where clashes of values and interest are part of the game. Such disputes may cause long delays in decision-making, as was shown in five case studies in the Netherlands (In 't Veld 2000).

Scientists are not always aware of such political disputes over knowledge. A brochure for British environmental scientists about how to successfully present research to policy-makers leaves no doubt: research results are objective, sound evidence. However, the authors of the brochure accept that there is competition around knowledge in the political arena and that non-scientific factors play a role. Researchers are encouraged to use the media ("MPs read newspapers and listen to the radio") and build personal contacts with policy-makers ("Policy-makers never have much time so they are likely to just call the scientist they know"). But the underlying assumption is that subjectivity is a characteristic of political life, and not of science. By taking this view, the NERC brochure restricts environmental research to "mode 1 science", a position that is disputable (Bunders and Regeer 2009).

The usability of knowledge for policy-making is therefore not only a matter of objectivity but it is also influenced by values, beliefs, convictions and interests. Such aspects are part of governance practices, and this brings us to the question how different approaches to governance deal with knowledge.

15.1.2 Governance styles and the usability of knowledge

Governance can be defined as *the totality of interactions of governments, other public bodies, the private sector and civil society, aiming to solve societal problems or creating societal opportunities* (Meuleman 2008). In this broad definition, institutions, instruments, processes and the roles of actors are included. Three approaches or governance styles usually form combinations: hierarchical, network and market governance. These combinations may cause mutually undermining effects. The styles differ from and compete with each other in more than 30 characteristics and at the same time have strong internal logics (Meuleman 2008).

One of these characteristics is the role of knowledge. Each governance style has a specific vision of what usable knowledge is. This goes back to the epistemological foundations of the styles: they stem from different cognition theories. It has been argued that they have "incompatible contentions about what is knowable in the social world and what does or can exist – the nature of being – in the social world".[1] Moreover, they "derive their governance 'certainties' from propositions drawn form specific methodological families, which reflect particular configurations of epistemological and ontological perspectives" (Dixon and Dogan 2002: 191). Politicians and public managers who are committed to hierarchical governance see the social world though a naturalist-structuralist lens, those committed to network governance see the social world through a hermeneutic-structuralist lens, and those committed to market governance see the social world through a naturalist-agency lens (Dixon and Dogan 2002: 184–185). These differences will be explained further below and summarised in Table 15.1.

Bevir and Rhodes (2001: 7) argue that network governance often has a "symbiotic relationship" with institutionalism, and market governance with rational choice theory. Rational choice theory views actions of citizens, politicians, and public servants as analogous to the actions of self-interested producers and consumers (Frederickson and Smith 2003: 185). Also hierarchical governance is related to a rational, positivist attitude. The rational public administrator uses a means-end logic: he focuses on (objectively) selecting the best means to an achieve agreed-upon end (Frederickson and Smith 2003: 162). Network governance on the other hand emphasises the boundedness of rationality in public administration, highlights ambiguity rather than rationality, and is related to a more socio-constructivist approach and social configuration theory.

Besides the differences in epistemological background, how people judge or calculate also differs per style. Jessop (2003) distinguishes three "modes of calculation" which may influence the attitude towards science and knowledge. The *homo hierarchicus* judges on the basis of effective goal-attainment and legitimacy. The *homo politicus*, who has a network orientation, uses reflexivity and dialogue in order to achieve an estimation of what would be a wise decision or action. In the term "homo politicus", Jessop uses a classical connotation of politics, which may still be valid for how politicians interact with each other, but is not the first association one would think of in the relation between politicians and citizens: in my opinion, (Western) politicians may *talk* network, but they tend to *think* hierarchical and often *act* conform market mechanisms. Finally, the *homo economicus* calculates primarily with criteria such as efficiency of resource allocation.

The "subjects" of a hierarchical approach have limited access to information. The power of the hierarchical governor is partly based on an exclusive access to certain information. In a network governance setting, information is in principle shared among the partners. However, this information is fragmented: there is no procedure or mechanism that guarantees that *all* relevant information is shared. Market thinking is not free from power games with information, but the main difference with the two other styles is that the price of information is the central issue. If one is prepared to pay that price, the "buyer" may have a total access to information, and may even gain competitive advantage by achieving a monopoly on knowledge.

---

[1] In this citation, 'social world' is meant to be synonymous to the society.

The three basic governance styles all possess typical drawbacks. Hierarchy uses power and imperatives to achieve goals, and its weak spot is the possible *abuse of power*. This can be illustrated by the observation that countries/governments/ cultures with a strongly hierarchical governance style tend to be more susceptible to *nepotism* than for example governance systems with more democratic checks and balances (like those of Scandinavian countries). The drawback of network governance is the opposite of trusted behaviour, namely *manipulation*. Manipulation requires the same insight into interactions between people as trusted behaviour, but it is *abuse of trust*. Market governance also has a "wicked" side, which is the *abuse of the central role of price and individualism*, namely *corruption*: self-organisation leading to self-enrichment.

Table 15.1 summarises the aforementioned knowledge-related differences between hierarchical, network and market governance.

Table 15.1 Different views on the governance of knowledge (adapted from Meuleman 2008).

	Hierarchical governance	Network governance	Market governance
Epistemological lens	Natural-structuralist	Hermeneutic-structuralist	Naturalist-agency
Theoretical background	Rationalism, Positivism	Social constructivism, social configuration theory, contingency theory	Rational choice theory, Public choice, Principal-agent theory
Mode of calculation	Homo hierarchicus	Homo politicus	Homo economicus
Usable knowledge	Authoritative knowledge	Agreed, shared knowledge	Cost-efficient knowledge
Relations	Dependent	Interdependent	Independent
Actors	Subjects	Partners	Clients
Coordination through	Control and authority	Trust and empathy	Price
"Dark side"	Abuse of power Nepotism	Abuse of trust Manipulation	Abuse of price and individualism Corruption

To conclude: the basic governance styles differ strongly in their ideas on/about usable knowledge. In the following sections, the three indicators for usability of knowledge are taken from the overview in Table 15.1, and are elaborated on more extensively: authoritativeness, the degree of agreement, and cost-effectiveness.

Hierarchical governance and authoritativeness

When hierarchy dominates the governance mix of a public-sector organisation, the emphasis is usually put on accepted clear facts and expertise. There is no time (during calamities) or no need (with well-defined, structured problems) to involve many parties in the knowledge basis for decision-making. Knowledge is considered an expert issue, and is used to enhance the effectiveness of top-down control. To a large extent, hierarchical governance builds on a positivistic approach of knowledge.

When the primary orientation of a politician, bureaucrat or a public-sector organisation is hierarchical, *authority* is a key value. In such cases, politicians and civil servants believe that knowledge produced by authoritative experts or institutions is the most usable. Critics will be told that the experts involved have a long-standing reputation in the scientific world, have produced many articles in peer reviewed academic journals, and have been proven "right" in many occasions.

An example may illustrate this. The economic assessment agency of the Netherlands (CPB) has such an outstanding reputation, that it is standard practice for government ministers to comment immediately and publicly on new predictions about future economic growth, although these "predictions" are in fact only scenarios and do not have such a good track record. In September 2008, the CPB predicted a 1.25% economic growth in 2009. Three months later, after the financial crisis which CPB had not expected had begun, the new prediction was a decrease of 0.75%. The next prognosis, on 17 February 2009, depicted a 4.75% decrease.[2] The belief of politicians in the authority of institutions like the CPB is so strong that it becomes immune for simple facts, like that CPB's results are scenarios (describing possible futures) and not predictions. On the day of the –4.75% prediction, the Dutch Minister of Finance commented that "since all *data*[3] are on the table, the cabinet will look at all possibilities with the aim to limit the damage (…)".[4] Of course, the worldwide financial crisis of 2008 was an exceptional event, but that is exactly what the future is about: unexpected things will happen. For this reason, making scenarios for possible futures makes often more sense than producing predictions, especially when the issue is extremely complex, like a nation's economy. Producing predictions involves determining which risks are important and which are not, which is a value-laden type of choice that is typically a task of politics and the media.

From a hierarchical vision, it makes sense that the producer of knowledge should have authority. Hierarchy builds on clear divisions of tasks, and science is responsible for producing evidence. Authoritativeness is the criterion that hierarchical policy-makers use to determine if they have to use knowledge.

Already three decades ago, when hierarchical thinking dominated in governmental organisations in Western Europe, Lindblom and Cohen (1979) analysed why the results of social science were often not considered usable, that is authoritative, in policy preparation. They found five reasons:

- Non-rational responses to what scientists say;
- Science is incompetent on normative issues;

---

[2] Press releases CPB, retrieved on 15th October 2009: http://www.cpb.nl/nl/news/

[3] Sic! (emphasis by author).

[4] Website Ministry of Finance, retrieved on 15th October 2009: http://www.minfin.nl/Onderwerpen/Financi%C3%ABle_markten/Kredietcrisis/NL_Economie

- Divergence: the research leaves more questions than before;
- Definition or constructing problems;
- Obsolescence: behaviour of people changes all the time.

All these reasons still seem valid.

Network governance and shared knowledge

When a *network* approach dominates, criteria like trust, empathy and consensus prevail. Only knowledge commonly agreed upon, produced by trusted experts and lay people, is considered usable. There is an understanding that "fact finding" should be a joint process of governmental actors and non-governmental stakeholders. A report produced by an authoritative institution is not per definition the most valued evidence.
Typical problems with a joint fact finding approach are:

- the knowledge development process may be time consuming (but may also save time in the end), for example because much time may be invested in the prevailing discussions about the research questions to be asked.
- knowledge production may be more expensive, for example when a social cost-benefit analysis is done in a participative way.
- the agreement on evidence may be instable, when it is built on trust: a Dutch saying goes: "Trust arrives by feet, walking, and leaves by horse, running".

If one is convinced that scientific and other knowledge for complex policy is needed and that the decision-making processes should be organised together with relevant participants (In 't Veld 2000, De Wit 2003a), then joint fact finding and transdisciplinary knowledge development are useful approaches. An illustration: The Dutch province of North-Brabant concluded in the early 1990s that a directive approach was not successful in convincing the local authorities that they needed to modernise their land use plans. The province established a team of specialists that acted as a flying brigade to help local authorities with their land use plans on the spot. The specialists did not just bring standard methods and knowledge but took part in a joint process (Meuleman 2003b: 235).

Market governance and value for money

In a policy process in which *market* governance is the dominant approach, efficiency, price and competition are highly valued. When the usability of knowledge is discussed, the cost-benefit ratio will play an important role. Knowledge (producers) may be authoritative or broadly accepted, but if the price is too high, it is not considered to be very usable. This attitude can lead to late and expensive lessons, like in the case of asbestos. The estimated economic cost of the predicted "pipeline" asbestos induced deaths in Europe up to 2035 (since 2000), will be some 400 billion Euros (in costs to society – EU concerns only) (EEA 2001). In this example, a conservative road transport estimate of the value of a statistic life of 1 million Euros per life is used.

Within the market governance approach, knowledge is considered as a good that is available everywhere and that can be bought on a market if one is prepared to pay the price. Knowledge is not a common good, but is owned and is used to enhance competitive advantage, for example by product innovation. Since market governance builds on a rational vision on human actions (like hierarchical governance), a positivist approach of knowledge is predominant. This vision is at odds with the idea of cumulative knowledge production cherished by most universities.

The market governance approach to knowledge may be the proper approach for routine questions and other not politically sensitive issues.

15.1.3 Metagovernance of dealing with knowledge

Since all three approaches of dealing with knowledge have their own failures and drawbacks and usually appear in combinations, the next question is: what works well, and in which situations? The concept of *metagovernance* (Jessop 1997, Meuleman 2008) could be useful here: the design and management of situationally workable combinations of the three governance styles. Because there are many governance dimensions for which such an optimal balance would be preferable, the knowledge dimension is not always given priority. For example, if a problem is extremely urgent (like a large fire, a pandemic, or an economic crisis), it may not be wise to invest much time in stakeholder discussions and joint fact finding, but might it be better to rely on authoritative knowledge producers. However, problems may also have both the characteristics of a disaster and a wicked problem. A pandemic, like the swine flue in 2009, is an extremely urgent problem and a complex and unstructured problem at the same time. The Internet has provided an open platform for those who do not trust the authority of the government and medical science anymore. It seems that even in an issue in which traditionally objective, natural science has been central, the authoritativeness of such knowledge may and will be contested.
If a problem is clearly complex, "wicked" and seemingly unsolvable, there may be a strong case to focus on getting stakeholders to agree on a knowledge base.

Adler (2001: 215) argues that developing a high network governance profile in governance mixtures in knowledge-based organisations and in knowledge-intensive policy issues is a more effective means of dealing with knowledge-based assets, than price (market governance) and authority (hierarchical governance) are. However, if a network focus is chosen, it becomes important to mitigate the typical failures of such an approach. Elsewhere I have proposed that in such a situation the other two styles should be kept "running in the background" and used when necessary (Meuleman 2009b): Hierarchical interventions may strengthen the networked knowledge process by emphasising the need for rules and for securing the results. Market governance mechanisms such as progress reports and some form of budget control, may be helpful to prevent endless talks and exploding costs.

When public managers encounter governance style incompatibilities they apply three metagovernance strategies (Meuleman 2008):

1. *Combining styles and managing linkages* between different governance styles: One style (hierarchy) may be used to solve conflicts and another to develop more solutions (network). Hierarchy can be useful to stimulate the start and to mark the end of a network process. Market techniques like public-relations campaigns may be used to stimulate civil society involvement (network governance).
2. *Switching to another style*, for example from hierarchy to network, or the other way around. Switching takes place within and between process phases or rounds. A change to hierarchy may be necessary when a network process results in "never-ending talks"; a network intervention like a stakeholder dialogue may be used when a hierarchical process does not lead to a broadly accepted problem definition. Being transparent about the style (switch) helps to manage expectations and can be a success factor in this strategy.
3. *Maintenance of governance style mixtures,* a second order strategy that complements the combining and the switching of strategies. One example is style-conflict mitigation by temporarily "closing the doors". Managing dilemmas and paradoxes is also part of the "maintenance" strategy, for example the dilemma of creating strong or weak network ties.

These strategies were observed in cases of environmental policy-making. The next question is whether they also play a role in the metagovernance of knowledge. Firstly however, the relationships between governance styles and models of decision-making will be briefly dealt with.

15.1.4 Governance styles and models of decision-making

There are three popular models with different assumptions on what decision-making is (Teisman 2000): the phase model, the stream model and the rounds model.

The *phase* model is the classical model of decision-making that supposes a commanding focal actor, and a predictable and rational policy environment. This model aligns best with hierarchical governance.

The *stream* model (Kingdon 1984), in which streams of participants, problems and solutions connect, emphasises the contingency of the process environment and the autonomy of actors. It may therefore be loosely linked to the market governance ideal type. Administrative organisations are, maybe even more than business organisations, characterised by complexity and ambiguity. The "garbage can" model (Cohen et al. 1972), which is kind of a predecessor of the streams model, defines an organisation as "a collection of choices looking for problems, issues and feelings looking for decisions and situations in which they might be aired, solutions looking for issues to which they might be the answer and decision-makers looking for work". The garbage can model with its four "streams" (choices, issues, solutions and decision-makers) that are trying to find each other, seems to predict that "pure" hierarchical, network or market governance is not feasible: a fixation on one of the styles would block some of the streams of problems, solutions, choice opportunities and actors.

The third model is the *rounds* model. This model focuses on the interaction between actors, while they introduce combinations of problems and solutions and create progress. This last model is linked to network governance; it supposes some degree of interdependency of actors.

Because the three models of decision-making differ in their usability, a metagovernor would use either one of these models depending on the actual situation. A decision-making process has a start and an end, if alone because of the availability of resources (time, money, people, instruments). The most simplified version of the *phase* model is to distinguish only two phases: divergence (the number of actors, problem definitions and solutions increases) and convergence (the respective numbers are decreasing). The phases of divergence and convergence were even observed in a case in which the public manager acting as metagovernor was not able to directly influence the societal debate on, in this example, land policy in the Netherlands. Nevertheless, during the first half year, stakeholders gathered in working groups and conferences, the media started to write about the issue, and many ideas were born (including stories about who profited from the change from farm land to building land). Gradually, some stories became exposed as myths, and a broad consensus emerged on some of the topics. (Meuleman 2003a: 86).

The *rounds* model reflects the consequences of the fuzziness of boundaries between public-sector organisations and societal groups: there are virtually no decision-making processes in which informal networks do not play some role.

The *stream* model stresses the independency of actors. Therefore this model is useful for understanding some of the market governance mechanisms.

15.1.5 Policy theories, framing and timing

Behind policies, there are policy theories; they are usually implicit. A policy theory is a comprehensive set of ideas about the supposed role of government, about the involved values and objectives, the preferred method of influencing, and the instruments that are supposedly useful (RMNO 2009). Although policy theories, for example the assumption that land use planning should be decentralised and agriculture policy should be centralised, do have a temporal dynamic, they tend to become crystallised or frozen into legal instruments. Policy theories contain assumptions about how the world looks and should look, and about how to change the world. They therefore strongly influence the governance style combination that dominates a specific policy field or public-sector organisation. This explains why knowledge can be considered as "not usable", even when there seems to be a good match between knowledge type and problem type: when research leads to the conclusion that the assumptions on which the ruling policy theory is built are not valid (anymore), this may lead to neglect of the research or even to discrediting the research or the researcher, as Tromp illustrates in Sect. 15.3.

Policy theories are frames. The aforementioned metagovernance strategy of switching plays a role when a political problem is reframed into a different type of problem. This is a very common phenomenon, because all societal problems are socially constructed. Even when a plane crashes, the framing of the accident by politicians or scientists is subjective. It depends for example on the fact whether it is the first time or not, on the damage that was caused, etcetera. Such social constructions are contingent and by definition temporal. Wicked problems may suddenly be reframed into urgent questions, for example when a political window of opportunity finally emerges. Then, a governance style switch from network towards hierarchy may be required. There are many examples of this type of reframing in environmental policy, like acid rain in the 1980s, eutrophication by excessive manuring in the 1990s and climate change in the 2000s.

Addressing problems that are framed as wicked may lead to overlooking rational solutions for sub-problems that can be solved through the application of hierarchical measures or market mechanisms. When after 5 years of a network approach, a conflict between the Netherlands Ministry of Environment and decentralised authorities on soil protection policy escalated, this halted the project. The Ministry restructured the issue as a clear and urgent problem (less complex because it was cut up into sub-problems), which could then be addressed in a primarily hierarchical way (Meuleman 2008: 143).

Sørensen (2006: 101–102) has pointed out the importance of framing in the application of metagovernance. The structure and framing of a problem should first lead to the investigation of the feasibility of the congruent governance style. If the problem is complex, unstructured and value-laden, like the development of sustainable development strategies, network governance will be an important part of the mixture. When a complex problem becomes more urgent, like climate change, and in the Netherlands the protection against rising river and sea water levels, then an increase in the amount of hierarchy in the governance mixture should be considered.

I have argued that market governance is a proper approach for routine issues and for improving efficiency in organisations. However, in many complex societal issues there are so many interests at stake, that elements of network governance will be required. The question of integration of immigrants is such an issue: in the Netherlands, the responsible ministerial unit was moved from the Interior to the Ministry of Justice in 2002, as the result of a political reframing of immigration policy from a complex, unstructured issue (network governance) into a security issue (hierarchical governance). In 2007, when a new government entered office, the unit was moved again, this time to the Housing Department, as a result of a new political framing process: network governance became the imperative again.

How a society at large thinks is the result of framing of the public mind through processes that take place in the media (Castells 2009: 157). The media frame societal problems in their own way, according to their vision, political position, and other factors. They may also be the platform for a competition between different frames. This is especially clear when a disaster takes place and a wicked problem is being reframed into an urgent problem. This central role of the media in the political debate attracts "marketeers" from science and politics. And many politicians try to spin the news in a certain way, in order to influence the public mind.

News frames that journalists use to present contentious policy debates influence and even shape reasoning processes and opinion outcomes. Framing is a cognitive process in which the message affects how individuals weigh existing considerations (that is, political orientations and relevant attitudes/beliefs) to make a judgment. The same issue can easily be presented as a value frame (clash of values and principles) and as a strategy frame (clash of interest and strategies) (Lee et al. 2008).

Governance mixtures applied by a public-sector organisation or an individual public manager may differ over time. Lowndes and Skelcher gave an empirical example of how governance style combinations differ in different phases of a process (1998: 320). They distinguish four phases in the life cycle of public partnerships in the field of urban regeneration: (1) pre-partnership collaboration; (2) partnership creation and consolidation; (3) partnership programme delivery; (4) partnership termination and succession. In the phase of pre-partnership collaboration, networking between individuals and organisations is emphasised. In the phase of partnership creation and consolidation, hierarchy is used to incorporate some organisations and to formalise authority in a partnership board and associated staff. In the phase of partnership programme delivery, market mechanisms of tendering and contractual agreements are applied. Hierarchy is used in taking care of regulation and supervision of contractors, and networking assists in production of bids and management of expenditure programmes. In the last phase, partnership termination and succession, networking between individuals and organisations is used as a means of maintaining agency commitment, community involvement and staff employment.

The temporal dimension of successful governance mixtures is also influenced by other situational factors, such as the type of problems that are addressed. In the Dutch "security regions", a standing co-operation between the police, local authorities, fire brigades and health organisations in case of emergencies and disasters, the style of cooperation follows the type of problems that typically emerge in different phases of a large incident (Meuleman 2008): during a crisis, a hierarchical command and control style should be in place, because time is crucial and quick decisions are needed. After the crisis, efficiency takes over as the main driving force for cooperation: all organisations then rely on their own remits and autonomy in order to "clean up" the remains of the incident quickly and thoroughly. Then an intermediate phase starts: the non-incident phase, in which parties cooperate in the form of a network, and work on the enhancement of mutual trust and understanding, which prepares them for the sudden switch to hierarchy when a new crisis happens.

15.1.6 Discussion: Usable knowledge and knowledge democracy

How may the analysis of the usability of knowledge in different types of governance contribute to a better understanding of knowledge democracy? The latter concept describes relations between "old" and "new" forms of science, politics and media. These arenas are part of the governance system.

Science

Firstly, the emerging knowledge democracy may lead to a new balance between scientific and lay and local knowledge, and may imply a switch from dominance of disciplinary knowledge towards participative, transdisciplinary knowledge. Lindblom and Cohen (1979) and again In 't Veld (2000) have already argued that such a shift is necessary. However, it is still not a mainstream conviction in the scientific arena. The New Public Management movement with its focus on price and efficiency is still very influential in Western bureaucracies, and the rational, positivist pendant in science still consumes most of the research funds.

Politics

Secondly, a new balance may develop between representative (hierarchical) and participative (network) forms of democratic decision-making.

Push and pull factors are at work here. The push away from hierarchy can be observed in the decrease of authoritativeness of classical institutions of the State. Government ministers definitely have less authority than for example 30 years ago. The same applies to national banks for example, after it became clear that they had not been able to control the risky financial products and their producers which caused the global financial crisis of 2008. The pull towards participation is linked with the increased education level and emancipation of citizens and civil society organisations.

This balance will probably lie closer to the end of the participation pole than the representation pole. This would imply that usable knowledge in the future will, more often than nowadays, have the shape of shared knowledge. Joint fact finding and other instruments and values of network governance may become more important.

However , it is quite possible that the rigidness of existing policy theories, for example because they are solidified in rules, regulations, structures and contracts, will slow down the change one might expect from as a result of the emerging knowledge democracy. If this will be the case, more societal tensions are to be expected.

It is also possible that the growing complexity of the knowledge democracy increases the already visible paralysis of key actors. A Dutch journalist and scholar observed that politicians tend to discuss issues until one solution becomes unavoidable, for example because time has run out and a decision has to be taken immediately (Chavannes 2009). Unavoidability also has a positive connotation: The Intergovernmental Panel on Climate Change (IPCC) is one of the best known examples of authoritativeness born out of a very broad consensus which is being prepared via seemingly endless discussions.

Media

Thirdly, the growing importance (and abundance) of informal media brings forth new challenges for the classical media. Will the latter take up more prominent roles in selecting, framing and interpreting knowledge, or will the new, internet-based media play that role (too)? Is the fact that Wikipedia announced in 2009 that it will enforce its editorial control a signal of the inclusion of authoritativeness as quality indicator of new media?

Conclusion

I began by asking why policy-makers find some knowledge usable and other knowledge unusable. We have seen that the three styles of governance which usually appear in dynamic combinations, each have a different idea about what is usable. This leads to the conclusion that what was already claimed for governance styles in general, also seems to apply to the governance of usable knowledge: tensions may be reduced and opportunities may increase when metagovernance is used. It confirms the conclusion of In 't Veld and Verhey (2000: 124), that knowledge production should not take place exclusively within one paradigm (or governance style) that dominates in a specific policy arena, but should take the whole range of paradigms into account.

Although this should be investigated further, it may now also be argued that the metagovernance of (usable) knowledge could contribute to developing a functioning knowledge democracy. Such an approach requires other mechanisms and institutional conditions than mere knowledge "management". Furthermore, metagovernance may help to formulate better research questions which may, in some cases, prevent that scientists experience that their knowledge is unwelcome. However, metagovernance is a public management approach and there are many conditions that limit its application (Meuleman 2008):

- the politico-administrative culture, traditions and history of the administrative and societal system;
- the personal conviction of the responsible politician;
- societal expectations of the role(s) of governmental organisations;
- organisational characteristics (open or closed, professional or task-oriented, for example);
- the type of problem as it is framed (may have little support, which may then also apply to the problem-aligned governance approach). Reframing may be difficult when existing policy theories are strongly embedded.

The rationale of a metagoverning public manager may differ from the political rationale. In the following section, several examples are given in which scientific knowledge provoked strong negative reactions.

15.2 Strengthening awareness about researchers who are bringing unwelcome news

Henk Tromp

15.2.1 Introduction

Galileo Galilei held the view that the earth turned around the sun. But his claim contradicted the teachings of the Catholic Church and in 1633 he had to withdraw his findings in front of the inquisition. If he had not given in to his interrogators he would have been burnt at the stake. This is a moving tale from ancient times, when science had to assert its claims against the doctrines of the church, but it is not something from the past. Nowadays researchers are confronted by powerful institutions that have an interest in research results as well: political organisations, corporate firms and industry. Researchers may become victims if they attempt to present the truth. Ultimately science suffers as well, because the suppression and distortion of the truth may undermine public confidence and lead to cynicism. In this article attention is drawn to the pressures that researchers have to deal with when bringing unwelcome news, and an appeal is made to strengthen awareness for this issue.

In 1999, André J.F. Köbben and myself defined unwelcome news as research which threatens to harm the material or idealistic interests of an organisation or that is politically inopportune, that affects the position or prestige of high placed persons, or that hurts nationalistic, religious or other idealistic feelings. In that case a researcher can come across the following reactions. Those who feel threatened can (1) accept it, (2) fight it rhetorically, (3) keep it quiet, (4) silence it or (5) distort it. Regarding acceptance one can be brief. If the outcome of research is accepted, if a superior or client accepts the outcome of research that contains unwelcome news, then it poses no problem for a scientist. However, it is also possible that the outcome of research and its messenger (the responsible scientist) are attacked rhetorically. It must be noted that rhetoric has a positive and a negative connotation. Positive in the sense that a researcher is presenting his research findings in the form of a convincing and captivating argument and tries to convince others that he is right. The same holds true for those who oppose him and are criticising the outcomes. In this sense every publication contains rhetoric. Negative in the sense of pompous prose, disingenuous or untruthful use of language, aimed at having the last word and destroying the opponent. A researcher who brings unwelcome news will not be attacked with the argument: "We don't like the outcome, therefore your research is defective." It is the other way around. A client or superior will start to discuss the quality of the data, the choice of methods, and the theories used. And if he says that the research is defective, in some way he will always have a point because perfect research does not exist. The criticism may also be formulated as a question: are you absolutely sure that nothing is wrong with your research? Anyone familiar with the nicety of empirical research knows that this touches upon a sensitive issue. Especially if a researcher is trying to explore something new, there will be a gap between theories, experiments and data. Sometimes emotions may run high, and one of the challenges for a researcher is to discern whether his opponent really wants to know the truth or whether he is trying to undermine unwelcome news.

This is a difficult situation for a researcher because many arguments can be used and it takes some experience, perhaps even a special sense, to find out whether a client or superior wants to have a real discussion or not. A familiar argument is the *argument ad nauseam*, in which criticism is sustained by repetition rather than by reasoned proof. The argument may run as follows: "There are 10 studies that entirely subscribe our findings. Your one piece of research is at odds with them, but that makes 10 to one. You have lost." Of course this is not necessarily the case: those 10 studies may have used theories that are false, or their results may be a consequence of distorted experiments. In a sense this argument refers to the important role of consensus in research, but the concept of consensus among scientists has a Janus face. On the one hand it facilitates cooperation among researchers, which is nowadays inevitable in order to make progress; on the other hand it can lead a community of researchers in the wrong direction. Another one is the *argument ad hominem*, to play the man and not the ball. A personal attack on a scientist, one who sticks to the truth such as he has found it, is something that a scientist himself fears. He may be accused of disloyal behaviour. He may therefore fear the Q-word, which means that he is a querulous person, a complainer, a troublemaker. Once expressed, it is a label that may stick on his forehead for a long time.

15.2.2 To keep quiet

To keep quiet about the outcome of commissioned research is not a very spectacular and yet effective way to neutralise unwelcome news. For instance, research findings that support government policies are loudly praised by government officials, but findings that threaten to undermine them are simply laid aside. Sometimes keeping quiet about unwelcome research outcomes can have devastating effects on the health of thousands and thousands of people. An extended case is described by Gerald Markowitz and David Rosner (2003) in *Deceit and denial. The deadly politics of industrial pollution.* They have focused their historical research on the gasoline and paint companies, united under the name National Lead (NL), that used lead in their products. For decades NL promoted and distributed millions of gallons of lead-based paint under its "Dutch Boy" brand name. In their advertisements they were eager to make a strong positive connection between happiness, health and the use of lead-based paints. The aggressive advertising strategy of NL has led to an increase of profits from 80 to 320 million dollars between 1938 and 1948. Nowadays NL is responsible for what is perhaps the most devastating children's health crisis. Lead paint has lead to the death and brain damage of thousands of children. From the 1950s onwards, National Lead could no longer ignore the medical literature describing the fatal impact of lead on children's health. Finally they argued that they had not been aware of the risks when they had waged their advertising campaigns. The research by Markowitz and Rosner (into the archives of companies associated with NL) has shown that alarming reports on the disastrous effects of widespread use of lead in paints had been on the desks of the managers of NL from the 1920s onwards, but that they had chosen to ignore them. Similar examples can be found in the "Late Lessons" report by the European Environment Agency (EEA 2001).

15.2.3 To silence

To silence means, that the commissioner of research or a superior commands a series of negative sanctions to force researchers into willingness to meet his or her demands. The most extreme claim a client may make if the outcome of research threatens to harm his interests is to keep it secret. For instance, an organisation that commissions research may try to demand a right of veto on the publication of research results. But even if the right to publish is recognised by contract a scientist can be silenced. The following case illustrates this (Köbben and Tromp 1999). We interviewed the researchers but were not allowed to give away names and details.

In the Netherlands there is an important state funded organisation, here to be referred to as organisation X. Organisation X receives many millions of Euros each year. How much and for what purposes I cannot tell. Some in the board of directors think that their organisation X is not working efficiently. They ask a team of researchers to start an economical and sociological investigation. This team consists of researchers from a Dutch university, from a commercial research organisation and from a non-profit organisation. They perform the research with money from this university and this important-state funded organisation. After 2 years this team produces its results, which are rather negative and may be harmful for organisation X. They want to publish it in an authoritative scientific journal. Before they will send it to this journal, they send a copy to the board of directors of this state-controlled organisation. But then, to the utter dismay of the researchers, the board of directors decides on a ban on publication. In the memorable words of one of the directors: "Not in the Netherlands, not in the European Union, not in the world, not in the universe." So much did these directors fear for harmful effects for their sector. The researchers have laid aside their research, no reports or articles have been published. A PhD-student has stopped his research, his dissertation was never finished. His professor has accepted something which he regarded as inevitable. We have had the privilege to read the contract that had been signed by organisation X and the research team. It firmly states that the researchers have freedom of publication. Nevertheless the team does not hold to this right. They depend too much on organisation X for research grants and for access to their field of inquiry. The research team does not dare to risk a conflict or a case in court. The morale of this story: it shows with more force how much and how effective researchers may be pressed to keep silent. It also underlines that the institutional arrangement concerning research is not decisive.

15.2.4 To distort

To distort research results rests on a particular attitude. It is aptly described by the English proverb “he who pays the piper, calls the tune” and can be defined in a more abstract way as the attitude of a client or superior that it is his privilege to interfere with the design and execution of a research project, and that he is also authorised to treat the results as he sees fit, aiming to realise an effect that is as favourable as possible for his own interests or for the interests of those he is serving. I want to illustrate this attitude with so-called evaluation research. The government, a ministry, a local authority wants to know whether a particular measure it has taken and that might have cost millions of Euros has produced the desired effects and has commissioning research on it. It is inconvenient if a researcher has to say after several months or years of research: “There have been no effects of this measure” or “The effects of this measure have been counterproductive”.

The Dutch government carries out about 600 evaluation researches every year. The attitude of “he who pays the piper, calls the tune” can be illustrated by the evaluation research on energy-saving as a result of the Law on Investment Account. The aim of this law, introduced in the early 1980s, had been to persuade companies to invest in energy-saving measures. However, the opposition in parliament doubted seriously whether the law would be effective. The Ministry of Economic Affairs therefore ordered the research institute TNO to evaluate the law and the government proudly presented the evaluation to parliament in 1985. There was every reason for satisfaction. According to TNO-research the law had achieved the desired results. Pröpper (1989), a political scientist, has demonstrated that this conclusion is seriously flawed. First of all, he examined the facts in the TNO-report. Taken at face value, they pointed to only one conclusion: the results were rather negative. The facts pointed out that the law had hardly produced any effects. However, the researchers from TNO had formulated the research findings in such a way that the rather negative effects had become fairly positive effects. Then the TNO-research report was sent to the ministry, and a steering committee of public servants at the ministry interpreted the fairly positive results as positive results. Thereafter the Dutch government had sent the TNO-report to parliament, along with the summary and conclusions of the steering-committee. The opposition in parliament proved to be satisfied. A member of parliament commented that the law had “indisputable positive effects”. Pröpper’s book is obsolete according to present scientific standards – it dates back to 1989 – but there is no other book that has tracked all changes a research report has gone through during the policy-making process so meticulously. But he has convincingly demonstrated that power, instead of arguments have tipped the balance. It is not difficult to raise an objection to his research findings. It does not answer the question whether this was an isolated case or a more common phenomenon. You will not find in it a phrase like “in 10% of those 600 evaluation research reports, no faithful picture of reality is presented”. But there are indications that distortion of unwelcome news is not a rare event.

One indication is found in the so called Reports on the Environment (Milieu Effect Rapportages). Dutch law requires that research on the effects of important constructions concerning the infrastructure on the environment is performed. From the 1980s of the last century onwards, hundreds of those research reports have been published. For example on the expansion of Amsterdam Schiphol airport, the bullet train from Amsterdam to Paris or the so-called Betuweroute, a railroad line that links the Rotterdam Harbour with Germany. Winfried de Valk and Michiel de Vries (1994) have gone to the trouble of meticulously reviewing a random sample of 10 out of 450 Reports on the Environment. Very often these reports claim that the plans as intended will not harm the environment. It is disconcerting, but now and then also rather comical to read how hard the writers of these reports have worked towards these reassuring conclusions. For instance on the railroad line of the bullet train from Paris to Schiphol Amsterdam Airport and its impact on the landscape. "This draws", the report says, "a clear line in an at present rather unstructured landscape." The criteria used by the researchers to define whether something is harmful or favourable for the environment vary strongly and they are often chosen in such a way that they produce the results policy-makers wish to read. De Valk and De Vries M.S., also show that there is a considerable difference between the report itself and the summary in tabular form for the benefit of policymakers. Those summaries always produce a more favourable image about the effects on the environment than is actually justified by the facts in the report itself.

15.2.5 Consequences

What consequences might it have for a scientist if he clings to his research outcome and if he tries to defend it against criticism? In short, it can cover a range between severe consequences for his career and hardly any effect for him at all. In the case of contract research at universities or commercial research organisations the consequences can simply consist of withholding further research, or threats to do so. A researcher who is an employee of an organisation can face (1) a withdrawal of privileges, (2) abstention from promotion, (3) a transfer to a less engaging position, (4) a ban on public speaking and writing, (5) suspension, and (6) dismissal, or he can simply be intimidated because he is threatened with one or more of these actions.

In 1999 a film, "The Insider" was released by the Walt Disney Company. telling the story of a tobacco executive, the biochemist dr. Jeffrey Wigand. He was head of the research department of large tobacco firm Brown & Williamson and wanted to disclose the fact that tobacco companies wilfully added ammonia chemistry to allow nicotine to be more rapidly absorbed in the lungs and therefore better affect the brain and central nervous system. Tobacco had been manipulated in order to stimulate addiction and consequently increase profits for the tobacco industry. The movie shows the dire consequences of the choices Wigand had made. He is faced with an opponent with almost limitless political and financial means, and in trying to speak the truth he is putting his career and personal life at a risk. The film has the power to absorb, entertain and create anger. The distressing thing about this movie is that it is true to life. It is based on an existing character named Jeffrey Wigand and on historical facts. He was followed by an ex-FBI agent in the employ of tobacco company Brown & Williamson, received anonymous threats on his life, had to be protected by body guards. Brown & Williamson published a 500-page dossier about everything Wigand had done wrong during his career and in his personal life and took him to court because of a breach of confidentiality. (Brenner 1996)

One might dismiss Wigand's experience as extreme and that this could not happen here in the Netherlands. But take the case of marine biologist Ad Corten. This case, and the following about another Dutch scientist, Veeger, are taken from Köbben and Tromp (1999: 49–72, 119–158). In 1991, Ad Corten works for the Netherlands Institute for Fisheries Research, an organisation funded by the Dutch government. He was a highly respected colleague; everybody recognised that he had expert knowledge on North Sea fishery, especially on herring. He had been mentioned as a possible candidate for the position of director of the Institute. Nevertheless he is permanently at home in 1997, he is no longer the representative of the Institute at conferences and consultative bodies, he is not allowed to enter the buildings of the Institute without prior permission, he is not allowed to do studies on the position of herring and the director wants his dismissal as soon as possible. The background of this reversal of fortune for Corten has to do with his resistance against the susceptibility of his Institute for the political views of the Department of Agriculture and Fisheries. The Ministry, under pressure from interest groups of fishery companies, wanted to replace the fishing quota by a so-called biological fish stock management. In practice it meant that fishers would be allowed to catch fish until a so-called biological minimum had been reached. No one within the Ministry had troubled himself to define this phrase "biological minimum". Corten and his colleagues argued that this new policy was undesirable. It would completely destroy all herring in the North Sea. In vain Corten tried to convince the Ministry, but the Ministry did not accept his criticisms. Then Corten tried to convince his colleagues that the Institute should publish an article and should try to convince politicians in Dutch parliament that a disaster would occur if the policies of the Ministry would be executed. They refused, so he published an article himself. In a letter to the Ministry the director of the Institute immediately distanced himself from the contents of Corten's article. The unpleasant thing is that in private the director did agree with Corten: carrying out the policy of the Ministry would ultimately destroy all herring in the North Sea. But that was in private; in public he supported the Ministry. And then things turned to the worse for Corten. He also got a ban on public speaking and writing. However, in the fall of 1995, after almost 4 years, the facts had proven that Corten was right. The position of fishes in the North Sea had seriously deteriorated, too much fish had been caught and the European countries in Brussels wanted to impose fishing quotas. The situation turned even more sour when the same colleagues who had not supported Corten now claimed that they had argued in advance that the fisheries policy of the Ministry would lead to disaster. It was sour because Corten had lost his job and the judges in the Civil Service Tribunal had put him in the wrong twice.

One might suppose that a scientist who has tenure at a University is safe in controversies like these. The freedom of research is guaranteed by law. And in case of a conflict, the university board will side with his employee. This is not always the case as is shown in the history of the biochemist, professor Cees Veeger from Wageningen University. He happened to be one of the few experts on enzymes in the Netherlands in the 1970s. He had published numerous articles on the subject, often together with Nobel price winners. In 1975 he got a request from a medical specialist to examine so-called enzyme medicines that were produced by the Dutch pharmaceutical company Enzypharm. Professor Veeger discovered that in these so-called enzyme medicines, medicines that cured heart- en vascular diseases, no enzymes were present. So if these medicines cured a patient then it could not be due to the presence of enzymes. Veeger wrote a report and he sent it to the specialist, but also to the Ministry of Health and to Dutch ambassadors in countries that imported these medicines. The consequences of his act were disastrous. Disastrous for himself, because the pharmaceutical company started a lawsuit and claimed damages of 4 million dollars. If a judge had put Enzypharm in the right this would certainly have ruined Veeger for life. The company had stimulated the foundation of a patient's interest group. The patients argued in the media and with politicians that they had benefited from the enzyme medicines. Now this irresponsible professor, as they named him, wanted to steal the one medicine that had cured them. Much pressure was applied to Veeger to recall his research. Veeger and his colleagues were vilified in the media. His employer, the governing body of Wageningen University urged him to recall his research findings. His university detached itself from his actions. Wageningen University feared that in court it – as the employer of professor Veeger – would be held accountable and that it had to pay an enormous fine. Veeger's career was at stake, but his personal life was at stake as well: a fine would ruin him financially. Veeger's lawyer made a smart suggestion to end the controversy. His lawyer succeeded in persuading Enzypharm and Veeger to conduct a joined investigation. However, the researchers of Enzypharm did not show up at the agreed date. Therefore, when the case came to court the judge dismissed Enzypharm's claim.

15.2.6 Compromise, advocacy and cynicism

Sometimes researchers think that they can turn the tide by taking their story to the press. But, in my observation, a journalist is trying to bring news, is hunting for a scoop and will try to persuade an oppressed scientist to make powerful statements. Especially on television there is a tendency to turn things into a 3 min black and white affair. A scientist then may utter statements that may ultimately weaken his case. Sometimes scientists may think that they have to take their case to a member of parliament. But they are not always aware of the fact that the opposition in parliament – if the scientist chooses to contact that side of the parliament – is keen to create trouble for a minister, rather than to unearth the facts. In short, a scientist risks getting into trouble if he brings his case into the open. Therefore he or she is inclined to keep silent or to try and find a compromise. To seek a compromise is a very important subject, but unfortunately so far not much research has been done on it. A compromise is not reprehensible or improper per se. It depends on the contents of the compromise and whether the researcher thinks that he has surrendered truth or not. In a sense it is part of Dutch culture, of our – praised on all sides – "polder model". In a survey by Martinson et al. (2005) of 3,247 early- and mid-career scientists in the United States funded by the National Institutes of Health, scientists were asked to report on their own behaviour. When asked whether they ever change the design, methodology or results of a study in response to pressure from a funding source: 20.5% mid-career scientists and 9.5% early-career scientists answered affirmatively.[7] Unfortunately, this survey did not ask the respondents, most of them with a background in biology, medicine or the social sciences, to make a distinction between an acceptable and unacceptable compromise, but the phrasing suggests that the respondents regarded them unacceptable.

A researcher may become an advocate, which means that he is not so much trying to find or present the truth, but that he gives priority to his own interests or those of his clients or superiors. There is a pretension of disinterestedness, but it is for show. A striking example of this attitude can be found in the book by Van den Anker and Van den Hoogenboom (1997) on laboratories and consultancy firms in the field of the environment. These firms do research on behalf of industry and they have committed acts that can be termed criminal according to the authors. To sum up 3 striking points from their book: (1) an asbestos certificate is supplied in return for cash by a laboratory, but without any research on the spot; (2) samples of polluted areas are taken at a stretch until finally a non-polluted area is found and only these non-polluted samples are reported; (3) a laboratory ascertains cases of severe pollution while there is none – because in that case the waste may be taken to a special dumping site. These facts are shocking. The more so because the advisors and researchers involved had produced their reports without pressure having been exerted on them.

We all know that lawyers or advocates are engaged in a useful profession. In court there is the public prosecutor. He is giving the evidence against the accused and the lawyer is presenting evidence in defence of his client. But there is a third party, a judge who must try and weigh the evidence before reaching a verdict. But this sensible construction does not hold if researchers act as advocates: when they, so to speak, wear the cloak of science to hide their partisan interests. If scientists are no longer inclined to tell the truth or do not dare to tell what their research has pointed out, then science will no longer be an educating or formative force in society. Nowadays an attitude in society towards research can be observed, which boils down to the idea that all results are suspect from the very beginning. Or as someone said on television: "All those research reports on the effects of Amsterdam Airport on the environment and public health. I just take a look who paid for the report and than I know enough." This quote is not meant here as a stand against or in favour of the expansion of Schiphol airport. I have not read the reports either. It only serves to illustrate the point that cynicism with regard to research findings is replacing a healthy amount of scepticism.

A caveat is necessary. Some of the cases presented in this paper belong to the more spectacular derailments of scientific research and it might therefore give a wrong impression. One might think that the world of research is a world of mere misery. But while you read this, many thousands of scientists at universities, commercial companies and the government have been working on their version of the truth – which is what they should do: every scientist gives his observation of the objective studied – and no one has put the slightest obstacle in their way. Not only because they have been conducting research that doesn't contain unwelcome news, but also because they are led by reasonable superiors and commissioners. Scientific research, provided that it has been done by professional and scrupulous researchers is essential for modern society. Nowadays there are more scientists at work than ever before and we have to prevent that big money and other interests will dominate the outcome of their efforts. Our world has to come to terms with important challenges on such diverse terrains as education, security, health, global warming, and cultural heritage. Scientific research, provided it is done by conscientious researchers who can present their findings unhindered, plays a crucial role in that. And that is only possible if we do not resign ourselves to an unfavourable position when pressure is put on researchers to distort or conceal the results of research.

In 2003 the Royal Netherlands Academy of Arts and Sciences (KNAW) has founded a National Organisation for Scientific Integrity (Landelijk Orgaan Wetenschappelijke Integriteit, LOWI). However, so far LOWI has played a moderate role with regard to scientific integrity. This is partly due to the limitations the KNAW has put on LOWI. The scope of LOWI's activities is limited to those researchers who are paid by universities and they can only appeal to LOWI after their case has been dealt with by their university. However, many researchers are in the service of governmental and commercial firms. In the Netherlands there are governmental research institutes like The Netherlands Institute for Social Research (SCP), the Netherlands Institute for Public Health and the Environment (RIVM) and the former Netherlands Institute for Fisheries Research (RIVO). Their researchers can experience the same problems as their colleagues in academia, the more so because their organisations always have been dependent on external funding as well. Furthermore, it has become practice to engage in collaborative research projects between academia and industry. This certainly has positive effects, but can raise issues with regard to scientific independence. If industry wants to enact norms different from those in academia, this might pose problems for researchers. It might be helpful if researchers could rely on LOWI. Among other factors, the limited scope of LOWI may explain why since LOWI has come into existence it has dealt with only a handful of cases, mainly about plagiarism. Another point is that LOWI doesn't pursue an active policy of advancing scientific integrity.[5] This may be due to a lack of resources, yet LOWI could play an important role in establishing cooperation between actors in academia, industry and government on this subject.

I propose the following actions:

1. Raising awareness about bringing unwelcome news. Especially as part of the training of students at universities. Many faculties have made progress in this respect, but it is not a standard item in every discipline. An organisation like could LOWI monitor this and advance cooperation between disciplines for instance by organising conferences, workshops, colloquia and the like. It could record “best practices” in teaching on this subject and make the teaching material available.
2. LOWI should focus more on organising “jurisprudence”, which means systematising and recording the experiences of those who have been engaged in research that has met resistance, research that contains unwelcome news. It would also be interesting to record in which way a compromise is reached.
3. The implementation of a system to report about the experiences of researchers. The internet can play an important role in recording and dispersing the experiences of researchers. One can also think of newsletters, blogs, and conferences. This has to be organised with proper checks and balances to secure the researcher when necessary.
4. The endorsement of those researchers who have withstood the pressure to distort or conceal unwelcome news, for instance by creating an award to be given periodically to the one who has been at the centre of a controversy and who has upheld the norms of science. An award like this has to be a part of ongoing efforts to promote role models of scientific honesty.

15.3 Usable and welcome knowledge?

Louis Meuleman and Henk Tromp

When scientists produce research which is meant to be utilised during the preparation of political decisions, and when policy-makers rely on scientists for such knowledge, much energy and money is wasted if there is a lack of understanding between the two arenas. In this chapter we have sketched the situation on both sides. Scientists from time to time feel that their research is *unwelcome*. We have illustrated that policy-makers have invented a series of “punishments” for the

[5] See Köbben (2003: 60–63).

messengers of unwelcome knowledge. Policy-makers, on the other hand, often find scientific knowledge not *usable*. The timing is not right, or the type of knowledge (process) does not produce the right authoritativeness required for a specific policy process. Another reason why knowledge may not be usable is that it undermines political action already decided upon.

Both sides face a real and important problem. Improvement should be sought in three ways:

1. Scientists should become more knowledgeable about the rationale of policy-makers and politicians; students must be informed about this from the beginning;
2. Policy-makers should understand the constraints of science better, and invest in more specific formulation of the research questions; policy-makers should also be trained in understanding the relation between science and politics; knowledge management should develop into knowledge (meta)governance;
3. Intermediary organisations between science, politics and society play an indispensible role, when they operate as brokers between producers and users of knowledge, develop and apply methodologies for bridging the gap between scientists and policy-makers. The role of independent knowledge brokers like advisory councils may become even more important in the future, because the increasing complexity of the relation between science and politics. In the emerging knowledge democracy disciplinary and transdisciplinary (including citizen's) science compete for funds and attention, and on the side of the decision-makers knowledge governance plays a role in the tensions between representative and participative forms of democracy. The media are on one hand translators of knowledge, but they are also responsible for magnifying conflicts between scientists and policy-makers; conflicts between perceptions of unwelcome and unusable knowledge.

16 Horizon scanning: monitoring plausible and desirable futures

Victor van Rij

Abstract

Horizon scanning is a foresight tool that is created to think, debate and shape the future in the direction of societal desires in a systematic way. Recently three countries (United kingdom, Denmark en the Netherlands) applied this tool on the national level for different purposes, such as the development of more resilient policies and research agenda-setting.

This chapter describes a set of theoretical aspects of horizon scanning that are based on the comparison of these three national scans that took place within the ERA Net For society. It focuses on the way in which issues are selected and prioritised as well as the use of horizon scanning for multiple purposes in a democratic knowledge society and its close relationship with this society.

16.1 Introduction

In December 2004 the Netherlands minister of Education, Culture and Science, Maria van der Hoeven, held a speech at the ERA Net For society,[1] and put forward the rhetorical question: "Is good government simply a matter of foresight?".[2] She referred to the popular saying that foresight and governing somehow are linked but at the same time she showed some scepticism by putting the answer in the hands of the foresight community instead of in the hands of politicians and decision-makers.

Of course it is clear that knowledge about the future is an important aspect of decision-making and comes to us in many forms (Van der Duin et al. 2007). Science as such tries to discover laws to predict how under certain conditions objects move

---

Note: The views expressed in this chapter are those of the author (as coordinator of the Pilot joint horizon scan project) and do not necessarily reflect the views of the Netherlands ministry of Education, Culture and Science, nor those of the other partners involved in the project.

[1] http://www.eranet-forsociety.net/ForSociety/index.html

[2] http://www.cos-toekomstverkenningen.nl/foresightconference/index.html

R.J. in 't Veld (ed.), *Knowledge Democracy*, DOI 10.1007/978-3-642-11381-9_16,

in space and time and allows us to predict the future movement of our planet and other celestial bodies, statistics and modelling of past events allow us to forecast future events within probabilistic ranges. Weather forecasts are used to protect ourselves and our belongings from the consequences of storms and planning agencies deliver yearly data from complex models that are used to guide our economical and financial decisions. All these approaches are used to predict the probability of future events on the basis of known causal relationships and rules. Although they prove to be valid for short term prediction and for longer term predictions in cases where rather simple causal relationships are not disturbed by external factors, they are almost worthless in situations in which complexity reigns and different human actors can disturb predictions by self-denying and -fulfilling prophecies.

For these situations, other tools have been developed to anticipate on uncertain but foreseen major events. Scenarios are used to examine different policy options within an uncertain context and to develop guiding visions (Van Asselt et al. 2005) and Foresight is used to align different stakeholders around shared visions and common activities to shape common desired futures. These tools are not so much about predicting or forecasting but more on the shaping of future to our common desires and needs (In 't Veld R.J. et al. 2007).

Horizon scanning is a special form of foresight that can be characterised by its holistic and systematic approach. It attempts to create a future picture of all policy domains and the future expectations of science and technology in a systematic way, to allow us to zoom in on issues that seem problematic or promising but also to enhance our insight on relationships between events that are taking place in different policy domains and S&T areas.

Horizon scanning is neither about forecasting nor fortune telling. Some issues can be predicted (and will happen, like the orbit of our earth around the suns), others can be foreseen (and may happen), other issues we cannot foresee at all.

The things we foresee that may happen, we can just allow to happen or not to happen (let history take its course) and deal with the consequences, but we might also think of ways (actions, strategies policies) to accelerate things to happen or to slow them down, alter them or to prevent them to happen at all.

Already, by debating things that will happen in combination with things that may happen we may already have changed the way of history, because actors involved in a foresight process will think and probably act differently (than without the foresight). So foresight is about shaping and creating the future more to our will and to activate and align people to coordinate their actions in a shared view (not consensus per se) on possible and desired futures.

Horizon scanning can be considered as a broad scope foresight that usually is used to roughly identify future issues that need our attention in a systemic way to direct the future in a more desirable direction after a participative process of thinking and debating.

16.2 Comparisons of three horizon scans

In 2007 the pilot project joint horizon took place within the ERA NET for society. The pilot joined the data of three national horizon scans that almost simultaneously took place in the United Kingdom, Denmark and the Netherlands. The rationale for the pilot was the expectation that the sum of the scans would reveal issues that have been overlooked in the separate national scans and that the comparison and the exchange of experience and know-how between national scans would be useful in strengthening the design of national scans and would create more insight in its manifold purposes. Last but not least, it was hoped that joint horizon scans might be useful as a common basis for joint foresight or even to identify topics for joint research programmes and common strategies. The result of this project is not only reported within the ERA net but also on the third International Seville Conference on Future-Oriented Technology Analysis (FTA).[3] Therefore we will only highlight some of the outcomes in this chapter.

16.2.1 Definition

Although the national scans were used for different purposes it was not difficult to find a shared definition:

> Horizon scanning is the systematic examination of potential (future) problems, threats, opportunities and likely future developments, including those at the margins of current thinking and planning. Horizon scanning may explore novel and unexpected issues, as well as persistent problems, trends and weak signals. Overall, horizon scanning is intended to improve the robustness of policies and to identify gaps in the knowledge agenda. (derived from UK Foresight Horizon Scanning Centre (HSC) / Horizon scan Netherlands).
>
> Horizon scanning is also: looking ahead, beyond usual timescales (as far as we can see) and across disciplinary and departmental borders[4] seeking out alternative sources of information and challenging implicit assumptions about the future that underlie today's decisions. (UK HSC).

16.2.2 Aims of national horizon scanning

The main aims of the three horizon scans were slightly different, the UK scan was mainly installed to feed the (evidence) base of their policies and to foster the future thinking and culture of policy-makers throughout the whole governmental

---

[3] The results of this comparison have been summarised in the proceedings of the third International Seville Conference on Future-Oriented Technology Analysis (**FTA**) that was held on the 16th to 17th of October 2008.

[4] Crosscutting different policy domains.

system, while the Netherlands were aiming at feeding their foresight agenda and the Danish on direct feeding of their knowledge and research agenda, which was in fact also the indirect aim of the other two scans. In all scans more implicit aims were the development of resilient policies and of sustainable solutions for the societal challenges.

16.2.3 Phases

All three scans were executed in phases. Roughly they all had a first phase of data collection and prioritising, a phase of analysis and synthesis where cross-linkages between issues were examined, an external review phase and a phase in which the results of the scan were used to influence decisions. All scans used literature sources, expert and stakeholder meetings and participatory methods like interactive websites and creative workshops. Underneath in Figure 16.1 a schedule is given of the UK Sigma horizon scan.

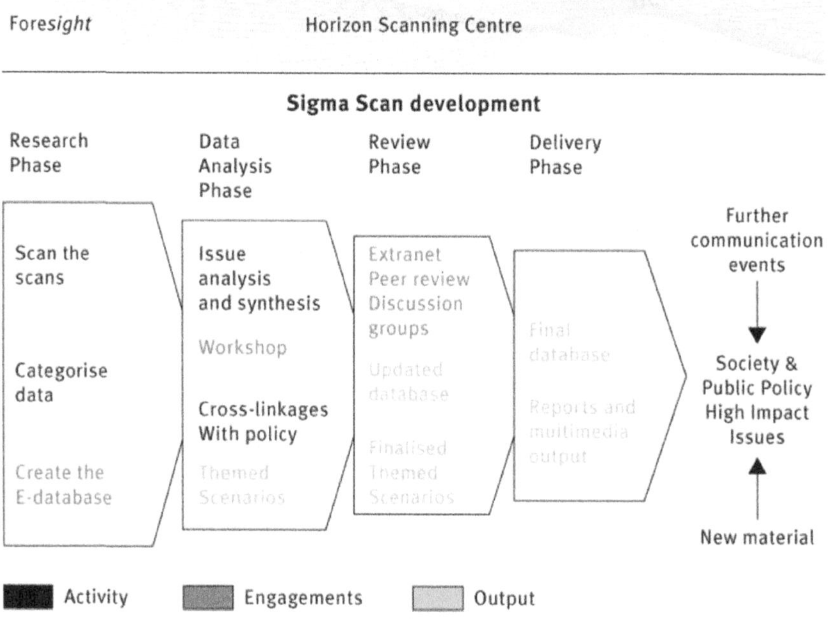

Fig. 16.1 Schedule of the UK Sigma horizon scan.

In each phase, either expert consultation or participative processes were used to enrich and validate the outcomes.

16.2.4 Typical Outcomes

The outcomes of all horizon scans were almost similar: all scans resulted in listings and descriptions of issues with their assessment on different dimensions such as impact and probability – either on websites (UK and the Netherlands) or in published reports (Denmark and the Netherlands). Furthermore analysis of interaction of issues and their combined impact took place by creative clustering processes (NE) or by special workshops devoted to test departmental strategies on resilience in the light of the issues of the scan (UK). All scans claimed process outcomes (learning effects for the participants, raising awareness, cross-cutting scan, way of thinking).

16.2.5 Main conclusions of the comparison

Despite the different aims and the slightly different methods used, the issue lists of the scans were overlapping but also complementary, the comparison shows therefore that HS is a potential multi functional tool which not only can be used for the aims that were envisaged in the three scans but also for additional purposes like alerting for risks-deficits (International Risk Governance Council 2009) and wild cards as the consequences of the subprime loans in the US.

All scans had wide scopes and covered all STEEP areas, although with a different distribution of issues, and offered a source for new ideas on the relations between issues. The scans overlapped for the majority of issues and issue descriptions were roughly on the same level of granulation. Although the importance for public governance was not recognised in all cases, a strong but sometimes silent influence on the agenda-setting of topics could be observed.

Scanning will be most useful when repeated or adjusted on a regular basis. The UK the horizon scanning is embedded in the governmental organisation as twin brother of the thematic foresight function. Originally this was also the idea in the Netherlands but because the revision of the governmental advisory structure the location of the horizon scanning function is still uncertain. In Denmark the scanning process was an experiment which was strongly connected with the research programming cycle.

All scanning teams seem to struggle with similar questions as:

- Who selects and prioritises the issues (who sets the values, criteria)?
- How scientifically or evidence-based should issues be. What about facts, proven facts, imaginative plausible events and desires (scientific quality)?
- How to deal with complexity (non linearity, issue interaction, unknown effects of interference, conflicting values)?
- How to deal with the unknowns, weak signals and the evaluation of the method?
- How to be effective? Client orientation, stakeholder involvement?

In the following chapter a theoretical framework is given to contribute to the answering of these questions in the context of a knowledge democracy.

16.3 Theoretical framework for horizon scanning

16.3.1 Search for Issues within the STEEP domains

The key word in the definition of horizon scanning is the word "issue". Looking at the examples of the three horizon scans we conclude that this word refers to statements about the future, based on outcomes of research, trend analysis, scenario studies, weak or faint signal analysis but also our imagination. Issues are therefore based on a mix of scientific knowledge and tacit knowledge including our imagination.

Issues are researched in future literature (varying form Science Fiction to other horizon scans and foresight reports), websites and weblogs, interviews, brainstorms, expert and stakeholder meetings, and through essays. They were selected with implicit or explicit assumptions on the plausible impact of the issues on our society, which in the Netherlands scan even lead to the description of issues as either Problems, Threats or Opportunities.

To reach a certain degree of completeness categories or domains are used to describe our world. In the three scans that were examined different categories and sub categories were used which could be joined to a slightly altered STEEP domain description. Roughly this domain description is as follows:

Society, human behaviour and interaction (including demography)

Technology and Science plus education, including its governance

Economy and Finance including its services, banks etc

Environment (physical) Earth, Land, Water, Air, Space

Policy, Governance and Law and its services (like health, transport infrastructures, water , energy etc)

These categories (or domains) are not only important to force scanners not to overlook issues but also to facilitate the comparison of horizon scans. Therefore it is advocated to use the STEEP as standard categories in future horizon scanning exercises.

Horizon scanning is different from trend scanning (Rollwagen et al. 2006) in that it does not solely focus on trends, but also on potential breakthroughs, analysis of risks, uncertainties and unexpected events that are considered as potentially disruptive in the future.

16.3.2 Identifying, characterising and filtering issues

Identifying

An intriguing question regards the criteria that are used to prioritise issues but also to point issues as worthy (to be taken up in the scan). In all scans attempts have been made to score the issues on several criteria that somehow were considered to be important indicators for prioritisation. It is logical to assume that the same indicators were implicitly used to select the issues, in the first place because of the enormous amount of data. Usually prioritisation took place through an inter-subjective estimation of the impact of the issue on future society, an estimation on the time frame when the issues would show its effect, the probability or plausibility that the issue would really take its course as described in the issue description and more implicitly its (un-)desirability. In the Netherlands' horizon scan there was an explicit search for (desirable) opportunities and (undesirable) threats and problems. To prevent hidden biases and misinterpretation of the results of scans, it is recommended to make these criteria more explicit beforehand, including the (un) desirability of an issue in respect to explicated value dimensions that were used.

Characterising

As mentioned before, selection of issues is based on assumptions on the impact of the issue on society. Scanning therefore focuses on issues that are expected to have a reasonable or high impact and that are certain to happen or that have a high probability or plausibility to happen but also on issues with lower probability provided that their estimated or assumed impact is high.

After selection, issues were characterised through inter-subjective assessment in different dimensions like their probability (Plausibility or Certainty), their estimated impact and the time in which impact would occur etc. This characterisation lead to the ranking of issues according to estimated impact and plausibility like in the Netherlands horizon scan report. Since it was not the aim to set priorities, the characterisation process was mainly used to select issues for further analysis and clustering.

Characterisation however may be very helpful to use horizon scanning as an alerting tool, but also to assess the development (or the perception of the development) of issues over time through the use of repeated scans. For this, it is important not only to agree on the main dimensions for characterisation, but also to standardise these dimension for future horizon scanning exercises.

The following dimensions to characterise issues are proposed:

1. impact
2. certainty, probability and plausibility
3. changeability
4. desirability
5. time

Impact
As discussed before, issues were identified and taken up in the scans by using implicit assumptions on their impact on future society. The impact usually is described as a positive or negative effect of the issue on the achievement of central values of the welfare state like prosperity, survival, health and so on.

The impact on these values can sometimes be predicted precisely but in most cases the impact could only be estimated roughly or indicated in a (semi-) scientific way. To create comparable issue descriptions it is necessary to explicit the value sets that are used. It is important to recognise that already in the first phase of scanning during the identification of impact rich issues values are involved.

Certainty or plausibility and probability
The probability of an issue (to occur or not) may in some cases be predictable, but for many issues this is impossible. However through our imagination (after debate with experts and democratic representatives) these issues may be considered as more or less plausible to happen.

For instance it seems beyond scientific doubt that the increase of CO_2 in our atmosphere will cause a considerable increase of global temperatures, according to the most pessimistic estimation even with several degrees Celsius over a period of some decades. From the point of view of horizon scanning it is very interesting to see whether this kind of future certainties will sustain and whether policies will be put in place to deal with the expected change of climate.

Changeability
For the analysis of interactions between future issues, but also for the development of strategies, it is very important to know if an issue can be altered in its course. As we know, some issues will follow their course with or without our human interference, examples are known laws of nature like gravity, the course of planets, seasons et cetera, but also commonly known issues like the normal development from childhood to adolescence and aging of people et cetera. On the other hand many issues can be changed by common will and human action, this is the area of self-fulfilling or self-denying prophecies. In this area we will however encounter many disagreements because of the fact that the change of society seems somehow more unchangeable than nature and also than many idealists believe. The possibility and willingness to change an issue or to react upon the supposed impact by deliberate human action should therefore carefully be examined.

Desirability
Almost every issue in an horizon scan is connected to an implicit assessment of its desirability linked to the assumed impact on what we consider to be of value. Issues therefore could be assessed on their desirability by using participative processes. Moreover in our cross-cutting analysis of issues we should especially pay attention to the way interactions are causing more or less desirable outcomes. It is important to notice that this assessment cannot be achieved without explicit values but also mechanisms to resolve or clarify the value conflicts that may lead to

opposite assessments of desirability of an issue. Considerations on these aspects should be made transparent for validation of the outcomes of the scanning process.

The time aspect
In all scans we encounter an estimation of the time in which the maximum impact of the issue will or may be effectuated. It is important to realise that this time aspect may be calculated or estimated in cases where the changeability of the issue is low, but in cases that are changeable we arrive in the domain of self-fulfilling and -denying prophecies, which means that estimations may differ a lot.

Desirable futures the need of explicit values
As discussed before the impact of issues usually is described in the positive or negative consequences for our economy, health, our standard of living, our life expectancy et cetera. To inform decisions on agenda-setting (prioritisation of issues) it is necessary to unravel the impact on the different value sets (or desires) that we foster. In a democratic society we assume that the following value sets are supported by the majority of citizens, but we are aware that the relative weight attributed to the values may differ quite strongly from country to country and individual to individual. Nevertheless, we can identify the issues on their impact on these different value sets.

For governmental horizon scanning in western democracies, the following sets of values seem to apply[5]:

1. Biological values: Quality of life, Ecological Quality (survival, health, longevity of (future) citizens – health of ecosystems);
2. Social: Social Quality (social cohesion in the present and in the future, eliminating poverty, mental health of (future) citizens);
3. Economic financial: Economic Quality (basis for other dimensions but also welfare creation, luxury, leisure, distribution of wealth);
4. Governmental: Juridical and Democratic Quality (rule and policy basis to realise other dimensions, constitutional state, equality of rights, sustain democracy, human rights etc.);
5. Cultural, ethical and intellectual: Cultural, Ethical and Intellectual Quality (stimulate cultural development and cultural expression as long as it does not interfere with other dimensions, increasing the intellectual level in service of the other dimensions);
6. Self-realisation of (future) Citizens (freedom of individuals and of religious and cultural expression);
7. Stability of International Relations (peaceful coexistence with the rest of the world).

---

[5] It should be clear that the pursuit of all these values may create tensions because issues may cause very high positive impact on one or more of these values but at the same time very negative impact on one or more of the others.

16.3.3 Clustering and monitoring issues

Interaction of issues

Issues interact. Sometimes there are clear data available that show the interaction between issues but here we can also use the force of imagination in creative workshops to see what kind of interaction may take place, especially with regards to an increase or decrease of the impact (for example energy).

Clustering of issues, scenarios

Issues were clustered in the scans of the UK and Netherlands. In the Netherlands this was done with the help of creative workshops, to examine impact-rich clusters that are cross-cutting policy areas and scientific disciplines, while in the UK the clustering took place around policy drafts of departments to test their resilience towards issues coming from the scan. It is clear that scan data may be useful for the development of scenarios but also to test the resilience of their outcomes. By clustering issues, strategy options become clear as well as lacks in our knowledge and the need for departmental cooperation as well as trans- and interdisciplinary approaches.

Example of analysis of the joint scan
Aging is considered as a predictable challenge for many European countries because of the expected increase in health care demand and the increase of dependency ratios. Policy-makers tend to stress the financial aspects of this challenge to pressure reform of the Welfare State. Through horizon scanning it becomes clear that there is much more to the aging issue and that the challenge is not only less predictable than assumed because of many wild cards (like epidemics or scientific discoveries that decrease the morbidity period) but also could be used to trigger innovations that lead to increased productivity and to diminished demand for labour.

Next to this, it expands our attention to other aspects of aging as changing markets, accumulation of inherited capital pro capita , educational aspects, regional aspects (depopulated areas) and so on.

Monitoring or continuity

Identification of issues should be done on a regular basis to check new phenomena rising on the horizon. At the same time former selected issues should be newly assessed in the different dimensions to monitor in which direction an issue is moving (to or from our desire) in this way we also could assess the foresight processes that are focused on particular issues.

Figure 16.2 visualises how issues could be placed in a matrix of the dimensions described before, the size of the objects in this representation stands for the estimated impact, the only missing dimension is time. We can, however, imagine a simulation of the outcome of a sequence of horizon scans in which the objects will grow or diminish in size and are moving in the three dimensions depicted. Policies based on the outcome of this scan could be considered to be successful if the majority of objects (issues) are moving to the desirable upper side of the picture, which means that they develop with certainty to our desires. We should take into account that almost all issues are more or less connected or interrelated but also that these interrelation may also vary in time.

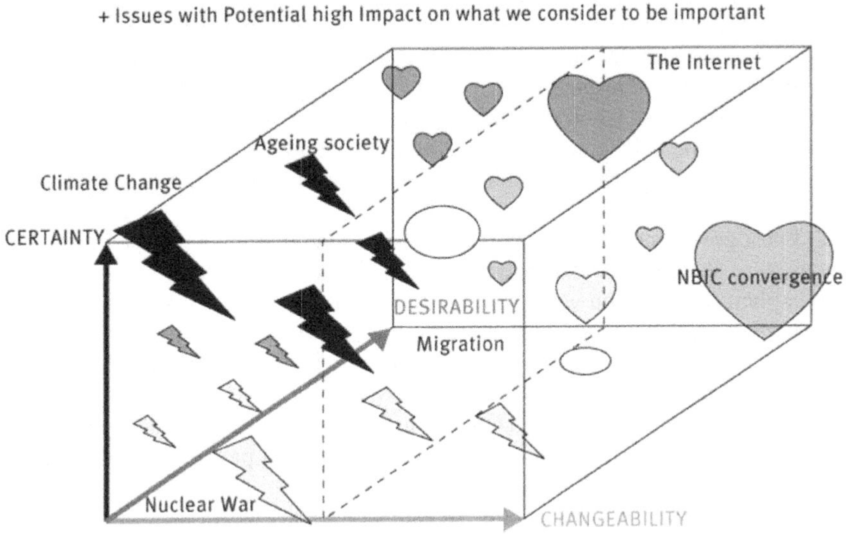

Fig. 16.2 The dimensions to characterise horizon scanning issues in a matrix. The size of the issues reflects the estimated impact.

16.4 The relation of HS with knowledge democracy

Horizon scanning has been developed upon a long standing tradition of foresight. Foresight has evolved from an expert-based process to a more participatory approach during the last decades. Horizon scanning may serve as an important tool to close the widening gap between voters and decision-makers in modern Western democracies but also to empower parliamentarian democracy by linking this to wide knowledge. To understand the meaning of horizon scanning for a knowledge democracy it is important to realise that horizon scanning is a combination of normative and exploratory processes which needs participatory processes on one hand but which also feeds its participants with knowledge and gaps in knowledge that are relevant for optimal decisions (within the value sets that have been agreed upon).

16.4.1 HS as an integrated normative and an exploratory process

In the long history of future research and foresight many attempts have been made to discern between the explorative and normative aspects of these activities. Although this differentiation makes sense in theory, we see that in practice it is almost impossible to separate explorative and normative methods because even the choice of issues in a foresight process already needs a normative consideration, no matter what kind of explorative tools we may use to identify the issue. Therefore we plea not to create artificial fences between explorative and normative foresight approaches but to ascertain that normative aspects within foresight activities are made explicit and that discussions and value-based decisions during the scanning process are made transparent.

The definition of horizon scanning as a wide scope foresight process that is meant to think, debate and shape the future to desires, implies the question whose desires are meant and who should be involved in crucial phases of the horizon scanning process.

For a governmental horizon scan, we conclude that the participation of a wide variety of stakeholders is needed (even before the first phase of horizon scanning) to explicit the common values (and criteria) that will be used to identify the issues that will be taken into the scan. In the following phases, participation is needed to control or even contribute to the issue selection and to discuss and balance countervailing values that turn up during clustering processes.

We can imagine that a horizon scanning process which includes the decision-makers could create a very good knowledge-informed preparation for the real decision-making of elected decision-makers.

It may be extremely useful for decisions on topics where lock-ins are blocking strategies that are outside of the established thinking frame. This statement can be illustrated by the example of the climate change, where for a long time the mitigation debate to reduce greenhouse gases was dominating the adaptation debate on what measures we need to take to make the best of the changes that are unavoidable.

It may be clear that through a horizon scanning process, both strategies could be easily revealed in a balanced way by asking the right questions. See Table 16.1 and Figure 16.3.

Table 16.1 Example: climate change (theory, trends, signals).

Plausibility	High
Estimated impact	High 3 value domains (economic, biological and geo political stability)
Desirability	Low
Issue changeable?	Limited
Impact changeable?	Perhaps

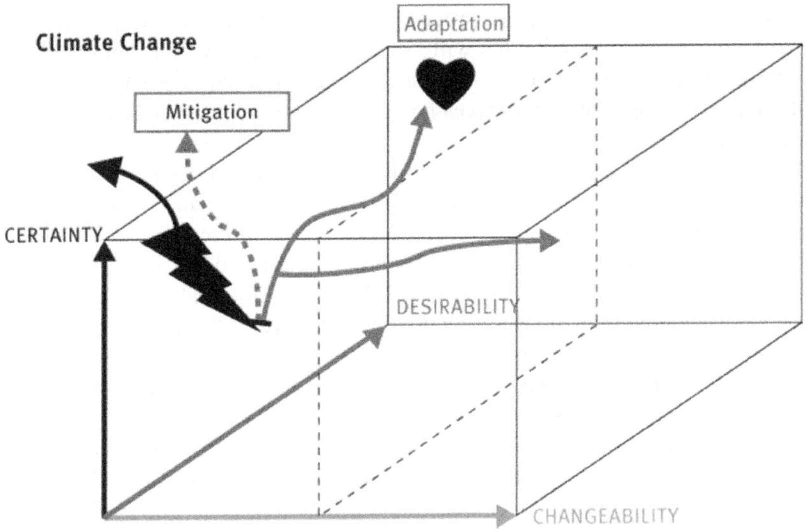

Fig. 16.3 The possible evolution of the issue of climate change in the matrix under the assumption on merely mitigation or adaptation strategy.

16.4.2 The need for participatory processes in HS for other reasons

Participation of a wide variety of experts and stakeholder (including voters) is not only needed because of the normative aspects which are playing a role in every phase of the horizon scanning, but also to establish societal support and to enrich the scanning process by adding different angles and creativity to the process.

16.4.3 The use of HS to inform democratic processes

It is important to see that horizon scanning outcomes can be used by policy- or decision-makers to develop resilient and sustainable policies but also to feed the agenda for research and public debate, or even to alert society and policy-makers about risk-deficits and plausible wild cards.

However it can only do its function well, if enough energy is put in the process by the decision-makers, which unfortunately not always is the case. One of the reasons for this is that decision-makers are overwhelmed by present day priorities. But another reason is that some decision-makers tend to see (future-oriented) knowledge solely as an instrument to support chosen strategies rather than as an instrument to support choices.

Therefore, it is a known fact that one of the greatest challenges for foresight practitioners is to involve high-level stakeholders actively in foresight processes.

To overcome this dilemma, the foresight practitioners try to involve the high-level decision-makers by client-oriented approaches. This means that a client formulates a need for the foresight process. Although this approach leads to greater formal acceptance of results this will not necessarily imply real high-level stakeholder involvement in the process. Moreover in practice this approach contains the risk that the foresight process leaves no space for options that are outside the present scope of the decision-maker.

For this reason I am more inclined to look to the side of decision-makers to resolve the dilemma. Considering the fact that "good governance requires foreseeing" we should review our governmental institutions on their foreseeing capacity. This means that somehow arrangements should be created that deliberately create time for the future in the agendas of high level decision-makers. An example of such an arrangement is "the Committee for the Future of the Finnish Parliament", but we might even think on much stronger arrangements which even uncouple the attention for longer term and short term issues on a constitutional basis by installing separate "chambers for long-term policy".

Next to such an institutional arrangement on the side of the decision-makers, it could be recommended that horizon scanning is embedded and closely related to strategic functions and other forward-looking functions (like in the UK model) in which the horizon scan may be used as an indicator and scoping device for specific strategic forward looking activities (as scenario building, technology assessment and other foresight). By repeating the scanning on a regular basis, more insight can be gained on the impact of these activities since it will give us a picture of what has changed in reality and in our perception of future issues over a period of time.

To prevent lock-in of such an embedded horizon scanning function, it should be given autonomy on its actions and the choice of sources and methods used.

17 Four steps to stimulate meaningful communication on sensitive issues in societal debate: the case of a research agenda for biotechnology and food in the Netherlands

Tjard de Cock Buning

Abstract

The destructive and emotional clashes between stakeholders in innovative fields of technology (nuclear energy, cloning, GMO-crops) have been blamed on the knowledge divide between scientists, politicians and society. Often, a cautious (network) approach to synchronise knowledge levels among all stakeholders is proposed. These proposed solutions are described under various headings such as, "Interactive Science Communication", "Interactive Policy" and "New Modes of Governance". In this chapter a transdisciplinary approach, illustrated by an actual case on around the biotechnology and food debate, is described. Called the "four steps"-approach, it is unique in the sense that it merges classical tools for policy analysis (for example analysis of policy documents, interviews with experts, relational problem analysis) with transdisciplinary tools (for example citizens' panels, focus groups, Socratic dialogues, stakeholder workshops) resulting in what has been termed a "constructed societal agenda". This societal agenda reflects the *interrelated* complexity of the different issues extracted from policy discussions which are expanded, analysed and reflected upon by citizens without a vested interest. At the same time it is a frame of reference to enable communication between citizens and other parties in order to recognise their own position in relation to others in the same comprehensive scheme. In the final steps, common ground might be found to escape from simplistic dead end one-way messages, and to head for meaningful dialogues instead. The thus constructed societal agenda offers in addition a framework for democratic public input at the decision table.

17.1 Introduction

Some scientific innovations, such as nuclear energy and biotechnology, seem to develop a love-hate relationship with society, while other innovations such as ICT are absorbed effortlessly into daily life. Whereas previously the relationship between technology and society was approached from a top-down or technology-push

R.J. in 't Veld (ed.), *Knowledge Democracy*, DOI 10.1007/978-3-642-11381-9_17,

perspective (how can we make an already developed product accepted?), science investigators currently assume a strong exchange and interweaving of technological and societal developments (for example, Nowotny et al. 2001, Jasanoff 2003, Leach et al. 2006, Wilsdon and Willis 2004). For issues relating to the management of knowledge production (and in particular research programming), this perspective is of considerable importance (Caron-Flinterman et al. 2006, Driesen et al. 2001, Wilsdon and Willis 2004). It implies, among other things, that regarding innovation issues the focus of power might shift from an academic/technological elitist mode towards a democratised mode, a shift from elitist steering towards knowledge democratisation. It is no longer about removing society's concerns about technology, but about analysing these concerns and then applying this analysis to the content of research policies (Wynne 2007). In this chapter a four-step approach will be described that makes use of appreciative inquiry in a transdisciplinary research context. More specifically it will introduce the "societal (research) agenda" as a productive instrument to engage the non-dominant citizen in communication about and deliberation around meaningful actions (agenda-setting) in research and politics.

17.2 Agenda-setting in the institutional void

What is the position of societal agenda-setting in present-day decision-making processes? In our Western post-war society, the systems of political decision-making and policy formulation are consolidated within established authorities and institutions. Considerable professionalisation was achieved in the previous century with the segmentation of policy themes between and within departments and the specialisation of policy fields. However, as Hajer (2003) argues, under the influence of globalisation and individualisation, these arrangements do not provide an adequate response to new issues, such as those relating to biotechnology, genetics, food and the environment. According to Hajer, new policy formulations take place *in an institutional void*, when new issues transgress the sovereignty of specific polities. There are no longer generally accepted rules and norms according to which politics is to be conducted and policy measures agreed upon. This void enables a growing role for *civil society* and new forms of public engagement. As an example Hajer cites the "successful" lobby by Greenpeace against the sinking of the Brent Spar.

This growing influence of *civil society* has consequences for the legitimacy and the effectiveness of processes of policy formulation. Whereas in the classical-modern institutions legitimacy could be guaranteed by democratic representation and via formal consultative procedures and professional lobby organisations, in the newly populated political arenas we have to find a new way of legitimising agenda-setting and policy-making processes – all the more so because organisations which are responsible for preparing policies make use of historically developed sets of information channels, that is academic and industry. Ministries frequently negotiate with umbrella organisations (for example the National Farmers'

Association, the Association of Biotech Industry, or the Association of Retailers) which lobby for one or two strategic arrows in their quiver. These priorities are the results of internal debates. In other words, these lobbied "arrows" represent only a selection of a wider and more diverse spectrum of positions among the members of the interest group. The same mechanism of reduction of issues applies for each level of democratic representation (see Figure 17.1): from society at large to interest groups (institutional agendas), from advisory bodies and administrations to ministers (political agenda). Those reductions might in some multi-stakeholder cases such as biotechnology lead to polarised positions that seem to trap the societal and political debate in a deadlock (Gaskell and Bauer 2001, Wynne 2007). In other words, while citizens have been sensitised by environmental groups and are worried about many aspects of biotechnology, but the state seems to lacks proper policy actions: this *institutional void* calls for constructive options to proceed.

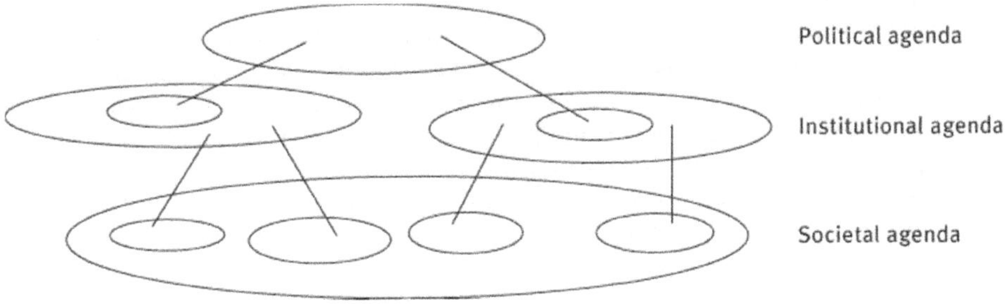

Fig. 17.1 Political, institutional and societal agendas.

The political and institutional agendas are usually explicitly formulated as a small set of priority issues selected from an internal pool of issues. The "societal agenda" is a virtual agenda, without address, but always presupposed in the former two, at least in democratic societies. At the level of the societal agenda the members (citizens) embody the largest pool of issues.

17.2.1 A societal agenda for biotechnology

The developments in the field of biotechnology are a striking example of Hajer's argument that decision-making power in our post-modern society no longer rests with the classical-modern institutions, but that *civil society* is able to organise itself in such transnational way that it has become a significant (f)actor. British opponents of genetically modified food products, for example, were able to reach a broad network of supporters using the media and internet, which led to the collapse of the market for these products. (Wynne 2007). In 2000 in the US, the introduction of genetically modified corn (Starlink) failed after consumers in Japan and Europe refused to accept this technological innovation. The American government, which had approved the product, was unable to resolve the problem (Kettle 2002). This illustrates that in our current political climate, not only is the legitimacy of "traditional" decision-making processes suffering from a loss of power, but its efficacy is in serious doubt (Hagendijk and Kallerud 2005). We see that, although civil society exercises considerable influence on the development and acceptance of, in this case, biotechnology, this is primarily in the form of obstructive actions and *countervailing* power. This has the effect of maintaining or even reinforcing the polarised positions of the established parties (Kettle 2002).

In a comparative EU programme, "Science and Technology and Governance in Europe" (STAGE), which included eight countries and 26 studies, a typology of five forms of governance as an answer to technological debates was formulated. Here the above-mentioned process is referred to as "agonistic governance" by Hagendijk and Kallerud (2005). However, with regard to unstructured issues in particular such as those relating to biotechnology, less obstructive and more deliberative forms of governance are both possible and desirable (Hagendijk and Kallerud 2005).

An important conclusion from studies into deliberative policy-making is that in spite of principles such as equality between participants, some nonetheless have an advantage. "The dice, however, may in many ways be loaded in favour of those with superior resources, including through better access to customised knowledge and rhetorical resources." (Hagendijk and Kallerud 2005: 174).

It is primarily these rhetorical sources which "society at large" lacks because opinions, feelings, knowledge, et cetera about biotechnology are *not articulated* (note that I am not talking about professional cause groups within "society at large" who gather expert knowledge on single issues). In line with Science Technology & Society scholars (Laird 1993, Webler and Tuler 2000) and transdisciplinary researchers (Hirsch Hadorn 2008, Thompson Klein et al. 2001, Pohl and Hirsch Haddorn 2007, Regeer and Bunders 2009) our proposed approach assumes that particularly with unstructured issues, society can play a constructive role in discussion, deliberation and decision on research and policies, provided the working methods facilitate the articulation of opinions which are held but not expressed by non-dominant groups. In research into a public debate on Biotechnology and Food in the United Kingdom, Irwin (2001) observed that there is not a principle deficit from the side of society to participate in a meaningful democratic dialogue:

Public groups expressed well-developed views on these topics (despite their initial unfamiliarity), once they had been given the opportunity to reflect on and discuss them both inside and outside the workshop (Irwin 2001: 12).

17.2.2 From consultation to construction

While the ideas and opinions of the major stakeholders (government, industry, NGOs, the scientific community) have largely been shaped and institutionalised by political history in what Geels (2002) labels socio-techno regimes, the body of ideas held by society is generally under-articulated. So although the institutional agenda includes inputs from society (via their sectoral or cause expertise, but also via their formal and informal relations with ministries) we hypothesised that these may differ from the implicit *societal agenda*. In order to go beyond already well-known political positions and opinions, we excluded professional societal spokespeople from this phase of construction, for example the societal agenda is constructed together with motivated but not professionally involved citizens. Under these constraints the construction of a societal agenda might avoid the pitfall of reproducing the political discourse shaped by those with an interest. Instead, we might encounter new options to overcome the vested polarisation between the institutional agendas. A starting point for elaborating on this issue can be found in the work of Grin and Van de Graaf (1996).

Grin and Van de Graaf indicate that actions of social actors are based on their frames of meaning. This is the set of assumptions held by an actor and which guides his behaviour. It operates at different levels (a multi-layered set of assumptions) ranging from assessing solutions and defining problems, to more fundamental levels of underlying theory and value systems. See Table 17.1.

Table 17.1 Layers within communicative action theory (adapted from Grin and Van de Graaf 1996).

Levels	Notion from communicative action theory	Order
1. Technical	Assess solutions	1st order of argumentation:
2. Situational	Problem definition (policy problems, practical problems)	specific situation
3. System	Background theories (value systems, perceptions)	2nd order of argumentation: value systems and world
4. Societal-rational perspective	Final preferences (for example on the preferred structure of society)	views

Unlike Grin and Van de Graaf, in our approach we treat society not as a singular target group for policy, but focus instead on the multiple patterns of preferences, value systems and problem definitions. The notion of the theory of frames of meaning implies that when engaging in apprehensive enquiry one should not only look at societal assessments of solutions and expressions of concerns (problem definitions), but also examine underlying value systems and world views of the citizens (Chilvers 2008, de Cock Buning et al. 2008b, Regeer and Bunders 2009). We experimented over the last two decades with many designs (for example, Bunders 1994, De Cock Buning et al. 2008a,b, Kupper et al. 2007, Regeer and Bunders 2009, Roelofsen et al. 2008, Zweekhorst 2004) and concluded that the sequence is important to avoid an early closure that might obstruct mutual learning. This learning process starts with second-order arguments, general notions of values that concern participants, and is subsequently guided to the intended focus (that is biotechnology and food). This results in first-order arguments towards jointly formulated solutions to deal with the variety of concerns. The following four principles appear to be important in accomplishing a meaningful learning process (de Cock Buning et al. 2008b, Kupper 2009):

- The starting point is the problems and dilemmas which people themselves experience; not the formal policy agenda
- Relevant issues should be approached integrally fundamentally? (For example, food safety in general rather than specifically the safety of genetically modified food) to avoid closure before communication and learning can start.
- The problem definition is better explored by the participants when intuitive assumptions are made more explicit through appreciative inquiry, for example through the use of "why?"-questions.
- Participants are addressed as persons or citizens rather than as stakeholders.

17.2.3 Focus groups and argumentation trees

The described approach is not aimed at a quantitative distribution of opinions; on the contrary, it is a qualitative exploration of the underlying reasons why people hold a particular perspective. Every effort is made to map a wide spectrum of the lines of argument within the framework under study. One of the methods suitable in assisting people to express concerns, problems and solutions, and which moreover involves the exploration and reflection of underlying values, is the group interview (for example, focus groups, citizen panels and Socratic discussions).

Society in this study

In this approach "society" is questioned about the personal vision(s) held by its members in regard to the challenges and restrictions arising from biological innovations relating to food. Who is this society? And how can one determine the diversity of views relating to biotechnology and food? Because this project is about the *articulation* of the *implicit* societal agenda, a quantitative study of the opinions of a representative selection of all individuals (a large scale enquiry) is not appropriate. A qualitative study was therefore carried out among a diverse group of motivated "citizens" without vested interests in the issue.

In making an inventory of the societal spectrum, participants included were those preferably interested in the subject but not lobbyists for any pressure group; participants motivated to reflect on the subject, but who have not yet adopted any clear position – these participants, as it were, are still trying to make up their minds. Due care was taken not to mix experts (in fields other than biotechnology) and non-experts because of the tendency of experts to lecture other participants and of non-experts to adopt the views expressed by experts. Finally, the decision was taken to keep the groups small and to focus the discussion on the themes emerging from the institutional level (reports, interviews, polls). It was observed that in a public setting, for example a public debate, a farmer will pretend to speak on behalf of all farmers, while the same farmer will take part in a small focus group as an "individual".

These group interviews consist of three stages (Barbour and Kitzinger 1999, de Cock Buning et al. 2008a,b, Greenbaum 1998). (1) In the first instance participants are facilitated through a process where they are able to clarify their views and relate other views to their own, however without coming to a fixed conclusion. Then (2), an inventory of these positions is facilitated by the researcher. Finally (3), the group itself structures the problem. In order to achieve these three objectives in one session of 3 h, a focus group approach was chosen. Starting from a general reflection, the group itself formulates the focal points within a problem via a strictly managed "question and answer"-process (leaving the content to the participants). Using visualisation techniques, the interrelations and priorities of the aspects under discussion are mapped on sheets. A summary and a construction of the discussion, in the form of an argumentation tree (see below), are sent afterwards to the participants for approval and comments.

17.3 Setting the mirror

In his study into the British debate on biotechnology and food, Irwin (2001) describes how the Minister for Science determined the direction of the debate by defining precisely which questions should be discussed. His study showed the significance of *institutional location* and of *pre-framing and pre-defining* the issue (bioscience, biotechnology) for the outcome and the effects of the discussion. The Dutch case on biotechnology and food debate presented below took place in the shadow of the political debate involving mainly interest groups, biotechnology scientists and sectoral advisory bodies. The objective of our approach was to communicate the unarticulated societal agenda. In order to achieve this, articulation at some distance from the institutionalised policy-making bodies was appropriate, especially during the explorative start. Our approach was primarily focused on the *content* of the discussion whereby in the process the emphasis was on uncovering the fundamental reasons behind the concerns, validated in the group process; the "why?" behind the emotions and comments of citizens. The objective was to arrive at well-articulated and meaningful concerns about biotechnology and its causes, rather than a list of separate and unrelated "hot" items. We particularly tried to avoid "hasty" decision-making in our quest to create a space for ongoing communication and mutual understanding.

This interrelated problem field is what we regard to be the structure of the "societal agenda"; a diverse and complex framework that gives meaning to diverse and complex concerns and values in our society. However, although this societal agenda is an important instrument within the four steps, it is not an objective in itself; it gains a critical function within knowledge democratisation when it is placed as a mirror to reflect the current agendas of the established parties. It has the potential to unite the diversity of the public in a schematic problem field that challenges the professional scientists and policy-makers to answer.

In our approach (Figure 17.2), illustrated via the biotechnology and food debate, we start with an analysis of debates at the institutional level (sectoral advisory bodies), and of policy documents and background reports which have already been published.

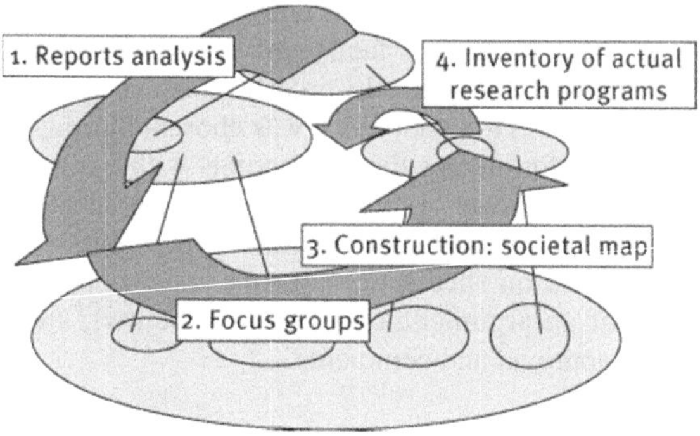

Fig. 17.2 Bringing the political, institutional and societal agenda levels of into cyclic communication.

17.3.1 Step 1 report analysis at the institutional level

Based on an explorative literature survey a selection of advisory bodies on the issue of biotechnology has been made for further inquiry: the secretaries of the advisory boards and relevant scientific members (for example the chairman) engaged in in-depth semi-structured interviews. A first analysis was cross-checked and prioritised by a single Delphi-round with the members of the selected advisory boards. One of those interviewed characterised the current societal debate on biotechnology in the Netherlands as

> a ritual dance which we regularly perform and which only serves to confirm the status quo…. It is communication to the deaf.

In line with the distinction already made between the consolidated institutional arrangements and civil society, the aggregate of the positions, ideas and arguments of the established parties (including the professionalised lobby organisations) will be called the *institutional agenda.*

Since these positions are already relatively well-articulated, an analysis can be made of the relevant lines of argument based on policy documents, Delphi and in-depth interviews. In this form of analysis issues are elaborated on as indicated in Table 17.1. First-order arguments are examined: "what opportunities and threats are mentioned?", as well as second-order arguments: "what are the implicit fundamental values on which these are based?". Our analysis resulted in the identification of some highly controversial areas comprising seven themes. Not surprisingly these sensitive themes appear to have a high "container concept"-characteristic (concepts with a shallow content, or packed with multiple definitions): safety, food quality, consumers' right on freedom of choice, impasse in legislation, roles of government, improved communication and North-South responsibility.

17.3.2 Step 2 focus groups at the societal level

"Society" was explored through focus groups addressing the seven themes that resulted from the analysis in step 1 (above). A focus group is set up when there is a need for focus in relation to a particular issue: What exactly are we talking about? Why is this considered important? First- and second-order arguments are systematically collected *and* analysed by the participants. A meeting consists of a closely guided group discussion, where the participants are invited to voice the relevant aspects of an issue, to relate issues to one another and to establish and argue their relative importance. The discussion is led by a facilitator in line with a plan devised for each specific theme through a set of analytical steps. The facilitator guides the mutual learning process by posing appreciative questions. The participants discuss and decide on the relevance of their own input. One of the tools used in our design of focus groups are argument trees, see Figure 17.3.

An argumentation tree is a diagram with a concrete problem positioned at the top, and increasingly deeper causes for the problem illustrated underneath. By asking in each box the question: "Why is this a problem?", one descends via a line to a lower box which gives the answer to the question. Conversely, if you start underneath, with each upwards line the argument must be that: "If the statement in the lower box is correct, then the effect of this is shown in the higher box." In this way one can move from the top to the bottom of the argumentation tree using "why?"-questions and vice versa by means of steps as "the consequence of this is …". Such trees show the mutual relationships of the various proposed arguments.

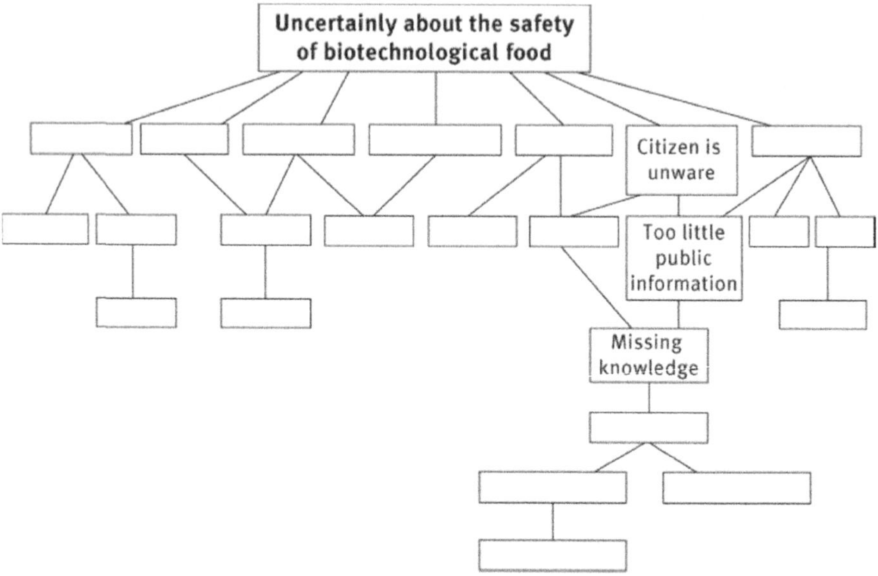

Fig. 17.3 Example of a line of argument within an argumentation tree as a result of an exploratory activity of a focus group aiming to articulate the deeper causes of their insure feelings towards biotech food.

17.3.3 Step 3 construction: societal map

An argumentation tree shows roughly the same structure as the four levels of the theory of communicative action: at the top there are the more concrete and situation-specific questions ("insecure about food safety", "unequal North-South division") while underlying values and dilemmas are at the bottom. These last issues are general in nature, and include for example, "societal security" versus "liberalism" or "sustainability", or "respect for autonomy". These underlying, second-order arguments are generally common to different societal themes (or sub-themes within biotechnology), which means that the argumentation trees of different group meetings overlap at the level of deeper second-order arguments. This gives all seven focus groups the opportunity to connect their argumentation trees (see schematic procedure in Figure 17.4).

The integrated and interconnected argumentation tree therefore provides a reconstruction of the complex interdependencies between arguments relating to the societal aspects of biotechnology. One group of actors may feel their arguments belong mainly (but not exclusively) on the left whilst others feel their perspectives are mostly covered on the right (but again, not exclusively), but both share some deeper positioned second-order arguments, thus enabling options for shared arguments and a fruitful dialogue between people with different views on the matter.

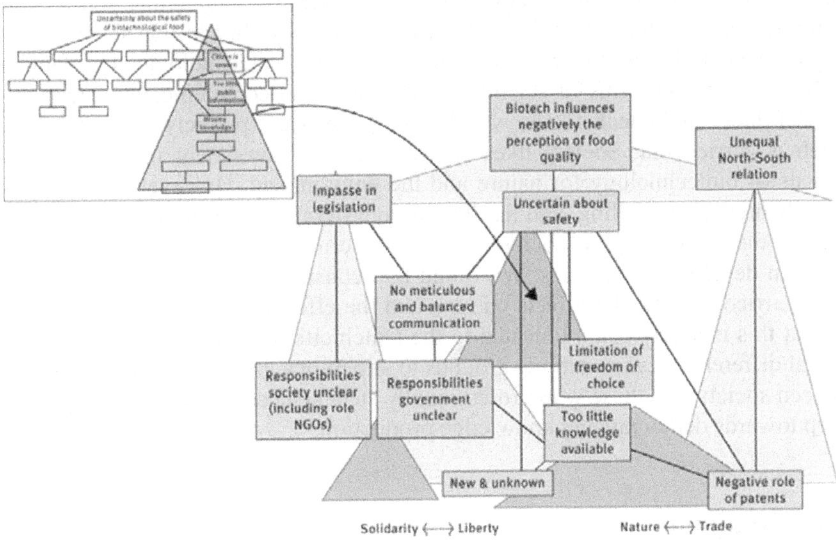

Fig. 17.4 Construction of a societal map.

By connecting boxes with the same content between individual argumentation trees resulting from step 2, a complex interrelationship of articulated worries and their deeper causes emerges in step 3. This scheme shows the relative interconnectivity of the seven themes: safety, food quality, consumers right on freedom of choice, impasse in legislation, roles of government, improved communication and North-South responsibility

17.3.4 Step 4 inventory of actual research programmes

Knowledge deficiencies might be identified in various thematic focus groups (grey boxes in the example of an argumentation tree in Figure 17.4). In step 4, a workshop is organised with citizens. In our case the participants were retired citizens following a course on biotechnology at the university. After explaining and discussing the argumentation tree, they were asked to nominate and then to prioritise research subjects that should be taken up by the government. When these research subjects formulated by non-experts are compared with the current research programmes, which have been determined by diverse national science programme bodies and which reflect the influences of researchers and the priorities set by leading authorities, the result is differences as well as considerable overlap. In a research agenda based on society's requirement for knowledge, important issues are (a) whether the knowledge of risks is available, (b) whether the knowledge is known by citizens/consumers, (c) whether the knowledge comes from a reliable source, or (d) whether the requirement for knowledge is viable for research. Note that these issues show that the citizen took a deliberative democratic perspective aiming to incorporate meaningful knowledge in policies. In addition society likes to have clear information about the added value of biotechnologically changed foods. However, in terms of scientific investment and communication regarding the usefulness of biotech foods, we observed that little (publicly accessible) research is carried out. Society likes to see scientific investment into the consequences of biotechnology for nature and the environment. However, most grants go to theoretical modelling, and hardly any long-term monitoring studies are executed in the fields. Finally, society likes to see critical safety and monitoring research in developing countries. We found that considerable safety research is actually carried out into the effects on man and the effects on developing countries, but that this is barely communicated to the Dutch citizenry. These actual and perceptual differences can constitute grounds to structure a genuine two-way dialogue between society and those who professionally steer science and technology policy, a step towards democratising knowledge production.

17.4 Discussion

This chapter discussed a four-step approach facilitating knowledge democratisation through acknowledging the powerful position of the knowledge elite (academic, industry, advisory bodies), while at the same time offering tools to articulate the need for knowledge of the "non-powerful" (citizens without vested interest) in such a way that it might feed back as an alternative "research agenda" to the institutional and policy decision table. The approach that we described is more than a "consultation". The tool "societal agenda" provides a mirror that evens out knowledge inequalities and invites stakeholders to include reflection on second-order arguments in decision-making.

The four-step approach is based on a methodological and systematic integration of interactive and transdisciplinary research methods. The case of "biotechnology and food" has been chosen as the focus, but the developed approach is applicable to all other areas within biotechnology and genomics, and beyond this, to other complex, unstructured issues relating to the societal connection between scientific and technological innovations. A toolkit manual describing in detail the methodological rationale in designing and using the various methods and how to deal with methodological pitfalls, is published elsewhere (de Cock Buning et al. 2008b).

In addition to the conclusions reached on the specifics of the issues raised in the four-step approach, there is also something to be said about the process-side of the interaction between society and science in the area of biotechnology and food. This is not simply a matter of whether or not knowledge is available, but also relates to the communication processes between the scientific community and society, and the involvement of citizens and consumers in questions regarding the needs and acceptability of biotechnological innovations in food.

By including people from society who do not (yet) have a firm and prejudiced point of view on the development of biotechnological innovations, one can go beyond the polarisation which is typical for the social and political discussion on biotechnology and food. Themes were selected which at institutional level are often indicated as being important but at the same time appear to have little depth and remain rhetorical. Those "high issues" appeared to be fruitful starting points by which to engage the public in a constructive reflective process, leading to concrete and well-argued visions of an alternative research agenda.

By constructing a societal agenda by means of an argumentation tree, participants in the deliberative processes can recognise – and probably also understand – one another's viewpoint and positions. There are also shared lines of argument, which promote open and constructive communication. This means that in follow-up discussions regarding research policy for biotechnology and food that take place beyond this project, stereotypical discussions and meaningless conventions can be reduced by delineating win-win lines of argument shared by most stakeholders but overlooked in the political "black and white"-debates. Acknowledgement of the complexity of the technological and societal issues, allows room for manoeuvre and a difference in the definition of topics. We observed in various projects that a constructive dynamic could be created in which all stakeholders are able to identify themselves through a framework built on issues communicated by the non-professional participants (for example, de Cock Buning et al. 2008a).

The steps followed in this approach lead to an identification of a number of areas where research efforts should be intensified. At the same time, this methodology provides an insight into the process conditions used to address this. And finally, once constructed, it offers a frame of reference to evaluate the effects over years of science policy and communication. It is expected that the application of this methodology to other unstructured issues will give a comparable insight into the cohesion between content and process aspects of science and technology communication in the context of knowledge democratisation.

Acknowledgements

I would like to thank all participants who participated in this exciting project, and especially the members of our research team: Joske Bunders, Bart Gremmen, Josette Jacobs, Frank Kupper, Linda Krijgsman and Anneloes Roelofsen. In addition I would like to thank Barbara Regeer for her contribution to the development of concepts and theoretical framing.

18 Sustainable development and the governance of long-term decisions

Louis Meuleman and Roeland Jaap in 't Veld

Abstract

This chapter outlines an analysis of policy-making about the long-term and affecting the long-term, in particular but not solely in the context of sustainable development, taking a broad "governance" perspective. It provides a framework for looking at different types of future-oriented decisions and the long-term effects of policy decisions (which may be oriented at short-term objectives), and discusses the role of knowledge in each of these cases. It argues that future-oriented knowledge production is scientifically valid and employs specific procedures, but is fundamentally about handling uncertainty. It then assesses how different national policy cultures address futures issues and makes a list of recommendations.[1]

18.1 The problems of long-term decision-making: a first glance

We tend to neglect long-term futures. Human action is often characterised by the ostrich's point of view. Still, politicians develop visions, describing desirable futures. A vision may mobilise voters to support the designer of the vision. However, while developing political *visions* about the future can be attractive for politicians, *concrete* political *decision-making* about the long term is often not popular. The results of such decisions are usually harvested by future politicians but the costs (capacity, money) and other sacrifices have to be made in the present. This is only one of many reasons why long-term decisions tend to be postponed or not taken, even if considerable evidence exists that taking measures *now* prevents enormous costs in the future.

On the political level the realisation of long-term concepts like sustainable development requires an adequate political and societal agenda (*what to do?*) and a well-functioning governance system ("how to act?").

In this chapter we analyse the governance of long-term decision-making, in particular in the context of sustainable development, taking a broad "governance" perspective. We will use the term governance in the meaning of the totality of

---

[1] This chapter is based on the RMNO/EEAC study Sustainable development and the Governance of Long-term Decisions (Meuleman and In 't Veld 2009).

R.J. in 't Veld (ed.), *Knowledge Democracy*, DOI 10.1007/978-3-642-11381-9_18,

interactions of government, other public bodies, private sector and civil society, aiming at solving societal problems or creating societal opportunities. This broad definition of governance is not confined to one style of governing[2] and concerns the design and impacts of, and the interactions between institutions, instruments, processes and actors. It should be noted, however, that our focus on decision-making about the future does not imply that we believe that future problems will always be solved by (rational) decisions of governments. The future is quite unpredictable and uncertain, and apart from this, governments are not the only actors who make decisions with long-term impacts.

18.2 Key problems of long-term decision-making

Firstly, examples are given that illustrate how huge the societal impact of a short term bias in political decision-making can be. Secondly we will argue that the reasons for such myopic behaviour may lie in failures of each of the aspects of the governance system: institutions, instruments, processes and the roles of actors.

18.2.1 Impact of "early warnings, late action"

Reports like EEA's "Late lessons from Early Warnings: the precautionary principle 1896–2000" present powerful examples of the dramatic impact of postponed decisions and non-action in the case of environmental policy-making. Take for example PCBs (polychlorinated biphenyl), the first obvious example of a substance that was not intentionally spread into the environment, but nevertheless became widespread and bio-accumulated to high concentrations. PCBs were used for a range of different purposes in electric equipment, heat exchangers, PVC plastics, paints, adhesives, lubricants, carbonless copy paper, et cetera. This example shows that non-action by regulators had costly and unforeseen consequences for human health and the environment. Early warnings, and even "loud and late" warnings of the emerging problems, were ignored. Mass production of PCBs for commercial use started in 1929. By the late 1930s, evidence already existed, albeit at a low level of proof, that PCBs could poison people. This information was not widely circulated among policy-makers or other stakeholders until 30 years later when there was a higher level of proof that PCBs could cause serious harm to human health and could accumulate in the food chain of seals in the Baltic Sea. It was not until the 1970s, however, that the first regulatory actions were taken by Sweden to ban these chemicals. The EU directive to eliminate PCBs was not implemented until 1996, with a total phase-out planned by 2010 (Gee 2008).

The second example is the case of asbestos. The estimated economic cost to Europe of the predicted "pipeline" asbestos-induced deaths up to 2,035 (since

[2] Unlike other definitions, such as "governance is good governance" or "governance is network governance".

2000), which, using a conservative road transport estimate of the value of a statistic life of 1 million Euros per life, will be some 400 billion Euros (in costs to society – EU concerns only). The Netherlands national government made an estimate of the potential benefits of an earlier ban on asbestos in 1965 (compared to the actual ban in 1993) which would have saved some 34,000 victims (premature deaths) and around 19 billion Euros in building clean-up and compensation costs. This estimate can be compared to the estimated long-term costs of asbestos to Dutch society which they calculated as 56,000 victims and 31 billion Euros over the period 1969–2030 (EEA 2001: 58). The considerable time between the discovery of the effects of asbestos and taking adequate policy measures caused not only societal damage, but was also quite costly.

These examples from the field of environmental policy show that the consequences of inappropriate action, late action or non-action are sometimes huge and in any case concern a broad spectrum: human casualties and suffering, serious damage to people's health and animal welfare, hazard of species' extinction, environmental damage and economic costs. They could be supplemented with examples of social and economic policy-making. The examples have in common that "early warnings" were not listened to, because postponement or the decision to do nothing was considered to be politically more opportune. Problems which are too big, too inconvenient, and for which no solution is emerging, tend to not even reach the policy agenda.

18.2.2 Failures of the governance system

The 2006 EU Sustainable Development Strategy encouraged Member States to develop long-term oriented SD strategies. Increasing political and societal pressure and recent policy failures like the widely-discussed SD impacts of too hastily set targets for biofuels have increased the need for practical governance approaches for long-term decision-making. The problem is that such approaches are not, or only to a certain extent, available. In fact, long-term decision-making is problematic in all four dimensions of the governance system.

The remits of government *institutions* like ministries are usually determined by societal challenges in the past. They often lack the organisational capacity to deal adequately with new and future problems. For example, there are no (national) policy-making bodies with the primary task to deal with climate change, poverty or demographic changes. Another failure is the fact that available data on for example environmental pollution are often not aggregated or otherwise coupled. Since "9/11", in many countries much information is gathered about the behaviour of citizens, which is not accessible, at least not in an integrated way, for environmental policy-making. This may be one of the reasons why the particulate matter problem in Germany and the Netherlands was such a surprise. If new technologies, such as the analysis of exhaust gases via digital pictures had been applied, and other relevant data had been connected, the damage could have been smaller.

Governance *instruments* reflect the "policy theories"[3] of the moment at which they were established. For example, environmental policy instruments made in the 1970s and 1980s were mainly legislative instruments, but since 2000 the general belief of European politicians seems to be that the utilisation of market mechanisms and the application of network concepts (combined in the EU "Open Method of Coordination", for example) are better approaches. Apart from the fact that considering one or two of the three ideal-typical governance styles as a panacea neglects the complexity of societal problems, such approaches also deny policy-makers the use of a rich "toolbox". Furthermore, long-term policy-making requires ex ante assessment methods. The currently available methods, such as cost-benefit analysis, are often disputed: many of them contain concealed normative assumptions.[4] Politicians often do not take the time to make those assumptions explicit and judge upon them timely.

Although the growing attention for the quality of the *processes* of governance allows for more future-oriented thinking,[5] this may make it increasingly difficult to develop and implement unpopular and firm decisions. The longer the impact of a decision, the more uncertainty is involved. This is an often-used argument for postponing decisions. Therefore, also the "governance of non- decision-making" will be discussed in this chapter. In addition, the sheer complexity of the many "wicked" problems on the SD agenda, and disputes about the roles of knowledge (what is "evidence-based" policy?) add to the governance challenge.

Finally, problems also arise on the dimension of *actors* involved in policy-making. Not only can future generations not be asked about their preferences, there are also quite different opinions on who should be involved, when and why. There is a tendency to increase stakeholder participation as well as involving "the public". This has brought about the paradox of: the more support, the less daring the policies. In general, the agenda-setting of long-term problems is difficult. Long-term decisions conflict with the usual 4–5 years political life cycle of a government: the potential successes are not harvested during this period. Therefore, the interests of those who determine the political agenda may be short-term rather than long-term oriented. Unsolved problems and seemingly unreachable results tend not to achieve the status of political priorities. In some cases however the civil society itself becomes long-term oriented. Then politicians have no choice but to follow that point of view and to adapt the long-term problem as an immediate priority. In this manner it can be understood how the issue of climate change finally has become a global political top priority in 2007/2008.

---

[3] A policy theory is the totality of assumptions of an actor regarding a policy (field/issue).

[4] Take for example the discussion on the height of discount rates (Stern Report, 2007; Social Cost Benefit Analysis for Environmental Policy-Making, RMNO 2008). High discount rates make many long-term investments seem unwise in a financial sense.

[5] A process approach is, compared to a project or linear approach, more suitable for dealing with uncertainties. The challenge is always to find a usable balance between these approaches.

18.2.3 Lessons learned?

The accumulated complexity of our societies and of the problems governments and other actors are dealing with, has made the challenge of successful long-term decision-making more important than it already was. The emergence of large scale problems like climate change, energy supply and the global distribution of chemicals in the environment may have raised the political attention for long-term issues. The 2006 EU SD Strategy encouraged Member States to develop long-term oriented SD strategies. A more concrete example of long-term policy-making on the EU level is the "20, 20 by 2020" goal known also as "Europe's climate change opportunity". In March 2007 EU Member States agreed to set a target for mitigating climate change by reduction in carbon greenhouse gases (GHG/CO2) and by increasing renewable energy. The Communication from the Commission of 23 January, 2008 promises a carbon dioxide emission reduction of at least 20% by 2020 (compared to 1990) and an increase of the share of renewable sources (solar and wind power and hydroelectricity) in the energy production by 20% by 2020. Moreover, the EU has set an ambitious goal: a target of 50% cuts in global emissions by 2050.

Why were these policies adopted? The EC believes that climate-friendly policies can be a good driving force for growth and jobs in Europe. This is probably not the only reason for adopting long-term policies. Wind and solar energy had become commercially viable because of new technologies and high oil prices. In addition, public pressure, media attention, the influential Stern Report, Al Gore's crusade against negligence of the consequences of climate change and last but not least the work of the IPCC, have contributed to a context in which long-term policies seem politically less risky than usually. In essence, because the civil society itself has become convinced that the climate problem should be tackled. It therefore seems that "accidental" factors may have quite an impact on the feasibility of long-term decision-making. For the purpose of this report we should look "behind" these contingent factors (without neglecting them) and make an attempt to answer the main question: what are the structural problems with long-term decision-making?

18.3 An analytical framework for long-term decision-making

18.3.1 Typology of long-term decisions

Long-term problems have been defined as "public policy issues that are surrounded by considerable degrees of uncertainty, will persist for at least a generation if the causes operate unabated, the option of 'solving' the issue in one to two legislative periods is either not possible or not politically feasible, and maximum political effort must (at least counterfactually) offer the chance to substantially ameliorate the welfare of all or most entities involved in a specific issue area" (Sprinz 2008).

Different actors typically have different time horizons. Politicians divide their time horizon in short-term (1–5 years), following the political cycle and democratic legitimacy of the current government; medium-term (5–10 years, or the next government); and long-term (more than 10 years, or a generation or more). The time horizons of politicians are partially dependent on the time horizons of citizens. Other actors have different time perspectives. Long-term business innovations usually imply 5 to 10 year time horizons, environmental and SD policies often have a 20 year or more time span. Researchers on climate change or geophysicists can have time horizons ranging from 100 years to millions of years (Goverde 2006: 31).

Long-term decisions are not characterised by the long-lasting character of the effects. Every real-world intervention leads to an infinite series of effects, because of infinite causality. In a certain case the aims and values of decision-makers determine what the *relevant* direct and indirect effects of an intervention are. Tensions between objectives and reality, and between values and status quo, often are described as problems and so become drivers for decision-making. Decisions may be based on lessons from the past, but concern only the present and the future.

Long-term decisions relate to objectives concerning the future that must be reached by taking decisions today. Some of such decisions explicitly aim at achieving results at a certain point in the future, while others have objectives with an indefinite time horizon. The objective may be to have the Olympic Games in the Netherlands in 2028 or to have the Olympic games in the Netherlands sometime in the future, for example. From a politician's viewpoint, a fixed point in the future has the advantage that it may mobilise people to act, but the weakness of deadlines lies in their vulnerability: the distinction between success and failure then is sharp, which brings about a political risk.

When we look at the specific character of long-term decisions, two types must be distinguished (Table 18.1).

Table 18.1 Typology of decisions with a future impact.

	1a. Long-term decisions	1b. Long-term decisions	2. Implementation of short-term decisions	3. Postponed decisions	4. Non-decisions
Objective	Future	Future	Now	Future	No
Action/costs	Now	Series of actions, starting now	Now	Future (postponing)	No
Main impact/ benefits	Future after long lead time	Now – Future	Short term – future	Future	Now – future

The first category concerns cases with a relatively long period between the intervention and the intended effects: a long lead time. Already from a simple economic viewpoint it is clear that the benefits will have to be discounted again and again, while the costs of the intervention have to be made from now on. Climate change mitigation is an example of this category. A too high discount rate in these cases may lead to such a high cost-benefit ratio that the decision tends to be postponed or even turns into a non-decision. A typical complication which this category of problems has to face is the interference between long-term and short-term objectives during policy implementation.

The second category of long-term decisions regards cases in which a continuous series of interventions during a long period is necessary to cause favourable effects. The lead time of each intervention may be short (for example the introduction of some legislation), but the lead time of the total series of actions is long. The "drop in the bucket"-metaphor is adequate here: it may take a long time before effects of measures become visible. Perseverance and consistency are important conditions in such cases. A classical example are the centuries-old Water Boards in the Netherlands, who were only able to do their drop in the bucket work because they had institutional characteristics that ensure independency from short-term (party-)political objectives. Another example is the 2007 sustainable public procurement programme of the Dutch government. This programme is based on a governance philosophy which combines government as launching customer, standards, competition (a score system) and long-term vision. The idea behind the latter is that presenting a "road map" may attract producers and customers to voluntarily "walk" on that road.

Both types have in common that the perspective needed to assess the impacts is long-term, although the impacts may be distributed unevenly across time.

Besides long-term decision-making *pur sang* (1a and 1b in Table 18.1), on which we focus in this chapter, other types of decisions may also have long-term effects:

- Short-term decisions: some decisions are not aimed at the long-term future, but nevertheless may have important long-term consequences. Such decisions should be taken into account when discussing the governance of long-term decision-making.
- Postponed decisions: this category implies that the result of reasoning on a long-term policy objective is to not take a decision *now*. Of course, also in this case consequences of such a decision may have a great influence on the future.
- Non-action: the last category concerns decisions to not deal with a problem politically. The reason may be that the issue is politically too risky, or that there are no solutions to the problem. Several of the retrospective cases presented in this study illustrate that no matter on which grounds non-action was decided, the future impact of such a decision can be substantial. Non-action may be politically difficult, when the pressure to act is high.

18.3.2 Dimensions of long-term decisions

Besides the key dimension of lead time which was dealt with above, other dimensions of long-term decision-making should also be distinguished: The impacts, actions and objectives of decisions are influenced by uncertainty, irreversibility, adaptation, resilience, continuity (effects and conditions), precaution, interest constellations, costs of actions, and the framing of the (long-term) problem.

Long-time decisions may have *irreversible* or almost irreversible impacts, which are not considered when the actual decision is taken. An often mentioned example is the privatisation of US public transport systems in the 1930s, which led to the closing down and destroying of the public transport infrastructure, in favour of automobile infrastructure (Newman and Kenworthy 1999: 30). The same happened in the Caribbean island of Trinidad.

With regard to *uncertainty,* the question arises how much policy-makers should invest in policies to be implemented within an unknown future. Does the wisdom of the decision lie in increasing resilience? Anticipation presupposes that we know something about the future.

Scenarios which picture different possible futures and foresight methods like horizon scanning can be indispensible tools for increasing the potential resilience of long-term policies.

Resilience is the capacity of a system to absorb disturbance and reorganise while undergoing change so as to still retain essentially the same function, structure, identity, and feedbacks (Walker et al. 2004). The concept of resilience addresses both the governance system under consideration and the policy content. How to develop and sufficiently maintain resilient long-term policies is still an important knowledge question. In addition, how to build resilient long-term strategies in the multi-level context of the European Union? Here we not only face the problem that what is resilient on the EU-level may not be resilient on the local level and vice versa, but also the fact that national cultures influence the feasibility of governance approaches. Furthermore, resilience requires "mindfulness" (Weick and Sutcliffe 2001): a critical and reflexive attitude/awareness, both inside and outside organisations, in order to detect and select (weak) signals that may have a large impact.

Resilience and *adaptation* are related concepts: resilience and adaptability relate to the dynamics of a particular system, or a closely related set of systems. Adaptability can be seen as the capacity of actors in a system to influence resilience (Walker et al. 2004). The other way around: increasing the resilience increases the possibility to adapt to new circumstances.

Anticipation and *mitigation are also a* related set of concepts. Anticipation leads to taking measures now as a pro-active reaction to expected future events, and mitigation implies taking measures now in order to decrease or minimise effects now or later (Table 18.2).

Table 18.2 Resilience, adaptation, mitigation and anticipation.

Policy concept	Type of action	Applicability	Result	Example
Resilience	Design	Action now, unexpected future event	Later	Built-in multiple usability of new infrastructure or houses
Adaptation	End-of-pipe; design (of resilience)	Action now, past or current event	Now	Enlarging river beds because of recent increase of maximum water levels
Mitigation	Source	Action now, current or future event	Now, later	Energy neutral building
Anticipation	Source or end-of-pipe	Action now, expected future event	Now	Raising dikes in anticipation of future sea level rise

The concept of *continuity* can prevent a type of behaviour based upon the fatalistic notion of "après nous le déluge". Continuity can make policy-makers and the public aware of irreversible consequences. By continuity of values we mean not the preservation of the same values in the future but the continuity in time: the demand for continuity necessitates putting things in relation to each other now.

18.3.3 Wise decisions?

A normative and therefore contested issue is what "wise" or "good" long-term decisions are. It can be argued that "short-sightedness in purely personal individual decision-making may be merely imprudent; in social decision-making it may also be unethical" (Lagerspetz 1999: 149–150). This ethical dimension can be formulated as follows: "Given our limited knowledge, an 'equal treatment' of future generations means only that we have no right to make decisions which would, according to our present knowledge and values, impose on them such costs and risks as we would not be willing to assume by ourselves. More detailed planning for the future is not possible." (Lagerspetz 1999: 157–158).

Policy-making is per definition normative and there are no scientific algorithms for long-term decision-making. One could say that principles are the politician's algorithms. A wise and broad principle for long-term decision-making refers to Kant's categorical imperative and to the precautionary principle: "We have no right to make decisions which would, according to our present knowledge and values, impose on future generations such costs and risks as we would not be willing to assume by ourselves."

The above also implies that decisions are "wise" from a certain viewpoint. In certain circumstances extensive forms of public participation are necessary, in order to use the "wisdom of crowds", while in others expert knowledge may suffice (Surowiecki 2004); this is the dilemma of collective versus individual wisdom.

The distinction between two categories of long-term decisions is crucial in still another aspect. In the "drop in the bucket"-category, a necessary condition for success is to produce consistency in the drop-wise interventions during a long period of time while the other category demands a once in a life time grand operation. So long-term political stability is necessary in the first case while in the second a forceful momentary coalition suffices.

Conclusion regarding the typology of long-term decisions:
We can define two types of long-term decisions:
1. Cases with a relatively long period between the policy intervention and the intended effects: a long lead time. This type demands firm leadership in order to collect sufficient momentum for the focal decision.
2. Cases that demand a long-lasting series of interventions that as a whole is necessary to cause a favourable effect, following the drop-in-the-bucket metaphor. This type asks for perseverance, consistency, continuity and reflexivity.
As to long-term futures, uncertainty and complexity prevail. In some cases we are able to forecast to a considerable degree, then we may anticipate. In the majority of cases, we have to meet the existing uncertainty by concentrating on the acquirement of resilience.

18.3.4 The governance system and long-term decision-making

The tasks, remits and structures of governmental *institutions* are solidifications and reflections of the past. Institutions are formed and consolidated on the basis of knowledge, gained by lessons from decisions, actions and consequences which manifested in the past. Consequently, institutions usually lack the potential to deal with unforeseen new problems or opportunities. Institutional change is usually slow and incremental. This may also be an advantage: in an ever-changing, dynamic society we need robust structures which can serve as backbones of more dynamic institutions and processes. Slow governmental change accounts for values which are widely appreciated, like accountability and legitimacy.

Governance *instruments* reflect the "policy theories" which dominated when the policies were created. These policy theories contain implicit and/or explicit beliefs, such as a focus on centralised or decentralised government. In addition, decision (support) instruments may also contain concealed normative assumptions.

The "public participation paradox" influences the decision-making *processes*. Participation by private sector and civil society creates more support for a decision, but may because of this also result in less daring policies, as the implications of long-term decisions usually conflict with the political *actors*' 4–5 year lifecycle. Besides this paradox, the decision-making process of course is influenced by the degree of uncertainty. Uncertainty about the processes and outcomes is a well-known argument for governments to postpone decisions. What follows is more research and gaining knowledge, either in an attempt to reduce the uncertainty and complexity of the problem, or in order to "gain time". However, more research often leads to more questions than there were before. This is one of the five reasons Lindblom and Cohen (1979) gave for the failure of authoritativeness of (social) science research, in their seminal work "Usable Knowledge".

The *actor* perspective is essential to look at the actors involved, their roles, and action strategies towards long-term decision-making. Some of the conditions and trade-offs might be more important for one group of actors than for others. The main actors involved in long-term decision-making are governmental actors, business community/private sector, civil society, knowledge and research institutions, the media and intermediary organisations. For a single political actor an attempt to solve a "wicked" problem is often not attractive, because there will be no simple solutions to satisfy the voters. Non-action or postponing the decision may be the consequence. Sometimes complex problems are simply divided into a range of smaller, more "solvable" parts. However, simplifying complex problems may result in a sustained stalemate, as can for instance be observed in the discussion on the future of Schiphol Airport in the Netherlands.

Besides the four dimensions of the governance system (institutions, instruments, processes and actors) two other themes are important determinants of success and failure of long-term decision-making, which we will discuss now. The first is the use of *knowledge*. Different views on governance can result in a dispute on the roles and types of knowledge to be believed necessary for wise decisions (see also Chap. 15, this volume). The second is the role of (national, regional) *cultures*. The success of a governance approach in a specific situation depends also on the culture and history of a nation or region.

18.3.5 Governance approach

Long-term decision-making processes are no exception to the general idea that the governance approach – the combination of elements of different governance styles – should be a situational mixture of network governance (laying the basis of consent and of long-term support), market governance (stimulating entrepreneurship and self-regulatory responsibility of all actors) and hierarchical governance (creating level playing fields, ensuring implementation of decisions, and securing a legal framework with a required level of firmness). However, it should be argued that in such a governance mixture an interactive (network) approach should play a central role, because many long-term problems are complex, "wicked" problems which cannot be solved by one actor, even if this one actor is government (EEAC 2003). However, complexity may provide an excuse for doing nothing. We should acknowledge that not all problems are complex. On the other hand, complexifying an issue can help creating more interesting win-win solutions.

A typical weakness of the network approach is however, that it may result in "never-ending talks". The more an issue is considered urgent, or, at the other end of the spectrum, more a routine issue, the more important the other governance styles (hierarchical and market governance, respectively) may become. One of the most difficult challenges seems to be able to refrain from the dominating governance "fashion". None of the three basic styles is a panacea, and focusing only on "new modes of governance" (like market mechanisms and network management) neglects that experience from the "old" hierarchical governance approach (for example the use of legislation) sometimes is even more accepted, effective and efficient than the newer approaches.

> Conclusion regarding the governance of sustainable long-term decisions:
> The governance of sustainable long-term decision-making requires in most cases some dominance of network governance, with hierarchical and market governance "running in the background". Such a governance mixture presupposes that institutions involved in long-term decision-making are able to act in a resilient way. This implies investing in flexibility and in alertness (creating "watchdog capacity"), without making the institutions unstable and unreliable.

Problems that are too big or too inconvenient tend to be kept away from the political agenda. They are taboos. The asbestos case was an example. Problems which (may) be linked to societal lifestyles, like currently the increase of diabetes, are often politically taboo. The existence of independent bodies (such as advisory councils) which signal such problems can prevent large societal costs. However, politics is no exception to the rule that messengers of bad news tend to be killed, or at least attacked; this is one of the main reasons why advisory councils in many EU countries have to struggle almost permanently for their survival.

When such an issue with possibly long-term impacts finally has arrived on the political agenda, another problem arises. Like all political issues, long-term problems have a political lifecycle which predicts that they will disappear again from the political limelight – and maybe long before all measures have been implemented. This risk seems highest for decisions with a long lead time. The question is how such issues can be kept on the political agenda. Awareness of policy windows and the use of concepts like trajectory management and transition management may be required.

> Conclusion regarding the policy lifecycle:
> It is important to recognise that long-term impacts of decisions may become underestimated, because the problems that led to the decisions have reached the end of their policy life cycle. Long-term decision-making requires policy mechanisms that prolong the policy lifecycle of policy issues.

18.3.6 Policy instruments

Long-term decision-making requires the availability of sophisticated decision support methods. When ethical and political assumptions are used in ex-ante assessment methods, it is important that such assumptions are chosen in the political domain, not in the scientific or technical arena. The main objective of such methods, namely to create a debate in which the "right" (which may mean "inconvenient") questions are asked, may be reached with anything between detailed scenarios and relatively simple questionnaires based on a general horizon scan. The assumptions behind support methods should be transparent for the actors using these methods, and for actors confronted with these methods. Assumptions may limit the use of instruments. For example, cost-benefit analysis is not applicable for very large-scale problems like global climate change, because decisions on such a scale would influence a basic parameter: the future state of the economy and national income. The logic of assumptions generates certain results. Subjective (political, ethical) assumptions used in decision support models belong to the political arena instead of the technical arena in which they often are chosen (RMNO 2008).

Independent bodies such as the IPCC and advisory councils fulfil important roles in facilitating and organising socio-political-scientific discussions. The independency of such institutions which were also established in for example the financial world (European Central Bank) ensures that they are able to take a more long-term perspective and thus create a countervailing power against short-term political thinking.

Conclusion regarding decision support systems:
It is important to be transparent and realistic about the limitations of decision support systems, and to ensure that ethical and political assumptions in decision support systems are chosen in the political arena.

18.4 Knowledge and long-term decisions

18.4.1 Building a joint knowledge base

Policy-making on complex issues like sustainable development is, as is the case with all policy problems, usually a relatively fuzzy process in which many actors in the "policy arena" are involved and influence each other. The production of knowledge to support policy-making is also not a neutral process, but is value–laden and influenced by actors in "knowledge arenas". Therefore, a strict separation between science ("the world of measuring") and the policy arena ("the world of weighing") is not possible.

Knowledge production for complex themes like sustainable development should begin with an open debate about the points of departure that form the basis of knowledge production. Such a debate should lead to a decision by the principal (a cabinet minister, for example), not by the knowledge producer. These are some of the main conclusions of the study "Willingly and Knowingly" which the RMNO published in 2000. In this study, knowledge is considered as *negotiated* knowledge. The assumptions are that knowledge is meaningful information. What is meaningful depends on one's values, and values are often subject of discussion and negotiation (In 't Veld 2000: 127). However, hard facts, symbolised by concrete numbers seem to be extremely attractive for politicians and the media, whereas such facts are often scarce or even absent in dealing with complex societal issues from a long-term viewpoint.

When the decision is made to start a policy-making process with a certain set of goals, policy-makers will start with collecting facts, figures and information from various sources. Together, these will form the preliminary knowledge base. How to do this best depends on the type of policy issue: is it very urgent, or, on the other side of the spectrum, a rather routine issue, then in general there will not be many actors involved in collecting and interpreting the findings. However, for complex and "unstructured" issues, in which many actors have different interests and information, a process of Joint Fact Finding (JFF) is advisable. One reason is that only all actors together can oversee the complexity of the issue. Another reason is that JFF is an approach that helps resolving disputes over the valuation of the collected knowledge. If this is not done in an early phase of policy-making, it will return as a boomerang in a later phase, as the experience with for example the Dutch Betuwelijn railroad has shown (In 't Veld 2000).

The main issue in such a process is not whether the produced knowledge is "true", but if it is *useful* for solving the policy problem. Three types of knowledge questions can be differentiated (Eberhard 1999: 15–18): phenomenal knowledge questions (What is happening? What can we see?), causal knowledge questions (Why is this happening? Why is it the way it is?) and actionable knowledge questions (What should be done? What are the possible actions?). Some actors tend to prefer one type of questions. This causes problems when deciding on the "usefulness" of the gained/negotiated knowledge. NGOs, such as environmental pressure groups, often focus on the first question type: what is happening? Research institutions tend to prefer the second type of question: why is this happening? Politicians seem to prefer the third question type: what actions have to be taken? Therefore, it appears that in (political) processes of gaining (negotiated) knowledge all types of questions have to be covered. Another reason to cover all types of questions is that parties may come up with new questions at an inconvenient moment, such as just before the final conclusion or decision is made, which can cause delay of the process.

18.4.2 The organisation of knowledge production

Although there seems to be a general interest of politicians in "evidence-based" policy-making, there are different traditions in EU countries regarding the institutional conditions for ensuring the use of "best knowledge" in such processes.

The first trade-off here is between knowledge production on arm's length and independent knowledge production. On one end of the spectrum we find ministries which have their own research agencies, and assign research questions to them. The advantage of this system may be that the communication lines are short and that the agencies therefore produce timely answers to their questions. The disadvantage may be that such agencies are only officially independent but in practice may tend to deliver mainly knowledge which fits in the predominant policy theory of the ministries. Moreover it is hard to maintain a high level of quality in this type of research centres. The other end of the spectrum is a situation in which knowledge producers are completely independent. They are embedded in a system of research institutions, for example connected to universities, or they are privatised. The advantage may be independency – although the fact that they need projects in order to survive makes them to a certain extent dependent of the ministries. The disadvantage is that the linkages between policy-makers and researchers are often weaker.

In both systems, intermediary organisations like advisory councils or other boundary workers have been successful to "bridge the gap" between science and policy. This raises the question whether countries that have no tradition of advisory councils, like Italy, are in a worse position than other countries to produce knowledge-based policies.

It is not clear to which extent the *institutional* dimension of knowledge production influences the degree to which "early warnings" are included in policy-making. In the Netherlands the Scientific Council for Government Policies (WRR) has for decades produced future studies of high quality but the degree of utilisation by policy-makers has not been impressive. Horizon scans that collect series of future threats and opportunities until now also lack visible impact, although in the UK there is an institutional responsibility for Horizon Scans with the Chief Science Officer. In the Netherlands, the first Horizon Scan of 2007 (In 't Veld et al. 2007) was developed by a type of knowledge advisory councils ("sector councils") which with the abolishment of RMNO, at the end of 2009, has disappeared.

Another role of advisory councils or commissions is to bring different types of knowledge together into advisory reports. The extensive use of this mechanism by governments can have a positive impact (high quality, independent knowledge) or a negative impact (postponing decisions).

Multi-, inter- en transdisciplinary research, thus using knowledge from many academic fields, as well as creating and using knowledge that is generated by non-scientific actors, are generally considered essential for long-term decision-making, both in the production of shared visions, and in the monitoring and developing of instruments for long-term decision-making. Inter- and transdisciplinary knowledge are especially vital for "unstructured problems", such as sustainable development, which are highly complex constellations of problems with a high degree of uncertainty and high complexity, accompanied by dissent on values and goals.

In a transition process science and daily practice need to be integrated, in order to generate "socially solid knowledge". In this kind of situation the most important goal might be to develop a collective problem definition; thus the *process* of achieving transdisciplinary knowledge might be just as important as the actual *content*. It can be argued that transdisciplinary knowledge-gathering might be one of the methods of dealing with long-term governance issues, since it is a means to create shared knowledge (formal and informal), a shared problem definition, and a way to involve different actors at an early stage. To some degree, knowledge institutes can guide long-term decision-making through the choices they make in their research agendas. Knowledge institutes also gather information about the long-term effects of policies.

Long-term decision support systems are instruments that help in decision-making processes for the long-term, but such instruments are not commonly used, and some instruments are simply not effective in assessing long-term consequences of policy choices. Knowledge institutes have a role in critically reflecting on these decision support systems. Cost-benefit (CBA) as well as cost-effectiveness (CEA) analyses are well-known methodologies.

One example can be the conclusions of the SCBA study of RMNO (2008). In economic models, often political choices are made (on valuation and on the discount rate). Many of the analyses contain more or less concealed normative assumptions.[6] Politicians often do not take the time to make those assumptions explicit and judge upon them timely. As a consequence, the results of the exercise will be under attack from analysts who have other normative assumptions, while the minister involved can hardly defend himself. In order to avoid this situation, politicians should invest in overseeing the process of performing the CBA, but this is rather time-consuming. This implies that a well-executed CBA is costly and time-consuming, which means that not all policy questions can and should be assessed through a CBA.

Other questions related to the knowledge dimension of long-term decision-making that can be asked are the following: which type of research is needed for explaining and developing instruments for long-term decision-making? What are the latest developments in long-term decision support systems, what are the risks and uncertainties linked with different methods, and how do we find a situational optimal instrument mix? Which roles do advisory councils play in influencing the willingness of governments to invest in long-term solutions? How may governments use (sustainable development) advisory councils with civil society and business representatives in order to create more support for long-term decisions?

In order to deal with such questions we will now briefly reflect on the relationship between knowledge and policy. Here we also see a scale that ranges between two poles: from a weak position of knowledge in policy to a strong position of knowledge in policy.

Another mechanism is that systems want to survive, but a system can also become self-destructive, for example because of the quickly rising costs and the decreasing effectiveness of the system. Sectoral interests are often stronger than wise long-term decisions: apparently sectoral systems are very durable. How can such a negative spiral be broken? One possible solution is the development of checks and balances, for example an independent audit institution, which can overrule sectoral interests.

The trade-off between a weak and strong position of knowledge in (long-term) decision-making may also be formulated as balancing between "political" and "evidence-based" decisions. The term "evidence-based" has become quite popular

---

[6] Take for example the discussion on the height of discount rates (Stern Report, 2007; RMNO 2008). High discount rates make many long-term investments seem unwise in a financial sense.

among politicians and administrators. This is an opportunity in the sense that it may increase the attention for knowledge questions, but also a threat: waiting with political decisions until "all the evidence" is collected and interpreted. This "total verification model" may lead to postponing crucial decisions. "Evidence" sometimes is disguised interest:

- The interest of a decision-maker who frames knowledge produced by an authoritative research institution "per definition" evidence;
- The interest of stakeholders, who may call information which is scientifically not (or not yet) verifiable, evidence.

18.4.3 Future-oriented research and future ODR

All of us are informed about future-oriented research like forecasting, extrapolating, building scenarios, simulation exercises, and so on. In these types of research researchers and policy-makers may still operate on their own, separated from each other.

We deal here with a specific type of future-oriented research that may be adequate in particular in relation to long-term decision-making. Our observation is that many problems that demand long-term decisions have a so-called wicked nature. Extreme uncertainty and complexity as well as value disputes underlie wicked problems. "Normal" science or even future-oriented research does not deliver sufficient tools for wise decisions. A more complex methodology is necessary.

Future orientation, design and research, to be called from now on F-ODR[7] is a specific type of research. It is more than gathering information. It contains a creative element. This creativity can originate within a person's brain and/or from a chance encounter. The question is precisely how F-ODR, other future-oriented research and normal research are related to one another. If people regard research from the viewpoint of usefulness, then it can be determined that utilisation of the research is by definition limited to the future, in the same way as policy is by definition future-oriented. All research would then be future research. This can by no means be the intention.

Scientific research is a specific form of research, aimed at the creation or accumulation of scientific knowledge. This knowledge is formalised in a particular way methodologically, for example it is subject to peer review. It is often put into a rule-based form, such as: "A implies B" in a particular set of circumstances, whenever these circumstances occur. Such an assertion is known as a hypothesis. "The more a parent treats a child with respect, the less likely the child is to turn to drugs", is a statement which could originate from empirical research and which

---

[7] After the Dutch-language acronym TO_3: Toekomst -oriëntatie, -ontwerp, -onderzoek. (FODR = Future orientation, design and research).

probably holds true for white families in European cities from 1990 to the present time. But not for rural areas in Colombia. And why should this statement hold true for the future? Scientific knowledge is therefore by definition both fragmented and conditional. Its scientific value is dependent on the correct application of the agreed methodology. Scientific knowledge lays claim to validity and is a protection against criticism. What we are talking about here is what is called "normal research".[8]

It is difficult to integrate different areas of scientific knowledge because scientific knowledge is by its very nature fragmented. And its conditional character means that in order to apply the knowledge in real-world situations, it is necessary to verify whether the conditions set have been complied with. In terms of the future, this question can never be definitively answered. This means that every application of social scientific knowledge for the purpose of policy bears an element of risk.

If a policy-maker in his policies wishes to apply an assertion which is based on a rule, such as "for every X, under condition Y: A implies B", he first has to verify:

- Is the X that I am talking about the same X as in the assumption?
- Are the conditions which I am faced with the same as the Y in the assumption?
- Is there really an A in my situation?
- Will the implication still apply at the time when the policy is implemented?

This implies that applying scientific knowledge in policy does not always follow the accepted route of meeting the methodological requirements which applied when the knowledge in question was developed. The application of scientific knowledge in a political and governmental context is an exercise in uncertainty, partly based on suppositions and it also requires competences other than scientific ones, such as social intelligence and well-developed social intuition. It appears necessary to link scientific knowledge to other types of insights without detracting from its relevance and usefulness. Combining knowledge from different scientific disciplines and mixing it with other insights is an opportunity to try to maintain

---

[8] The term normal research is a free translation of *normal science*. By normal (general) research Kuhn understood: research that is performed by a scientific group within the ground rules of the paradigm applicable within the group. This means precise definition and development of a paradigm and continuing detailed inclusion of reality in that paradigm. Funtowicz and Ravetz (1991) understand by *normal science* the scientific business in which scientific puzzles can be solved along agreed rules and subject to peer review. We recognise that a scientific-philosophical discussion could be held on this subject, where one postulation could be that knowledge from normal research is to a large extent uncertain. In order to clarify what we understand by future research, the assumption is made that normal research produces relatively certain and tenable knowledge.

the relevance and usefulness of such knowledge in the relevant application. Multi-, inter- and transdisciplinary developments in research are in full swing. Anyone who realises this cannot fail to be impressed by the speculative nature of many elements of the methods used. The precision of a great deal of scientific knowledge very soon gets lost in these methods. Robust concepts are often unrefined.

Precise knowledge about natural orders which is gained from normal research is often important for knowledge about the future. This is knowledge which is gained from normal scientific research. It is also possible to make one particular aspect or element of the future the specific object of scientific research, for example the climate in 2100, or the level of the national income in 2010. The issue is then the application of an existing theory which has already been recognised as valid, to future situations. We refer to such research as future-oriented research. This is then a form of normal scientific research.

The nature of our image of the future as related to our own lives is holistic rather than fragmented. We regard our world and the developments therein as a whole and not per element. This does not mean that we can be aware of all the interconnections, but it does mean that anything that affects us now is relevant for the future.

Furthermore, elements of what is as yet unknown will also be important. We recognise that there will be many uncertainties along the way. This awareness creates a thirst for more certainty and probably also more knowledge about this future. Just beyond the borders of what is strictly scientifically possible, and with a renewed striving for integrated images and policy. Striving for certainty about the future is by nature double-edged and relative. On the one hand, it is possible to become aware of threats which we could eliminate by taking sensible actions, and on the other hand there is the possibility to invent windows of opportunity of which we could make use. This knowledge about the future is related to the perspective for (political) action which we adopt. We understand that this knowledge is formulated in uncertainty, but at the same time we know that we have the opportunity to exercise some influence. The link between the type of knowledge and future actions which are tailored to it also has far-reaching consequences for the nature of the relationship between future researchers and other parties involved.

This has given rise to the concept of F-ODR. This is about creating related future images which are based on multi-disciplinary and/or transdisciplinary scientific knowledge, permeated with uncertainty as a result of a high degree of complexity, and which produce the players' perspectives for action. These are the prime characteristics of this type of research.

We also have to recognise the specific characteristics of long-term decisions, in particular those related to environment. It is more than likely that this policy will require particular forms of F-ODR because of its specific nature. In any case, we know that the notion of environment has an anthropocentric character. Unlike in some other cultures, the Western person or citizen does not form part of the environment, but relates to the environment. Physical and social environment are made up of a number of aspects and are complex in nature. Environmental and spatial policy makes use of comprehensive concepts within which there are many interdependencies. The reflexive character of social systems and behaviour prohibits trustworthy forecasting, and creates continuous uncertainty.

Generating knowledge for environmental long-term policy therefore requires many of the obligatory activities described earlier. F-ODR for environmental and spatial policy is therefore twofold complex; it takes place in domains where there is a high degree of uncertainty and probably also engenders considerable dissent. A policy area which is so complex and uncertain demonstrates a high degree of similarity to the field mentioned by Ravetz for post-normal science. Here, too, there are complex problems. The recommendations formulated by Ravetz advocate interaction and ask for intermediaries.

F-ODR is always linked to a principal. This means that the principals determine the function of F-ODR. In order to ensure that the research is not obstructed because the principals decide to shelve it or to suppress it, F-ODR has to be related to the (policy) perspectives for action. But it is the responsibility of the researchers to ensure that they do not indiscriminately implement F-ODR and dance to the tune of the principals. The principals and researchers together have to make sure that the research does not result in undemocratic or useless practices.

We have elected to indicate the route to a methodology for scientific research in two diagrams. These include knowledge requirements and process requirements which have to be met by F-ODR in order to avoid the problems previously described. It is the responsibility of the principals and the researchers to develop their own methodology for F-ODR based on these charts.

The subject of research of normal research, future-oriented research and F-ODR looks as follows (Figure 18.1):

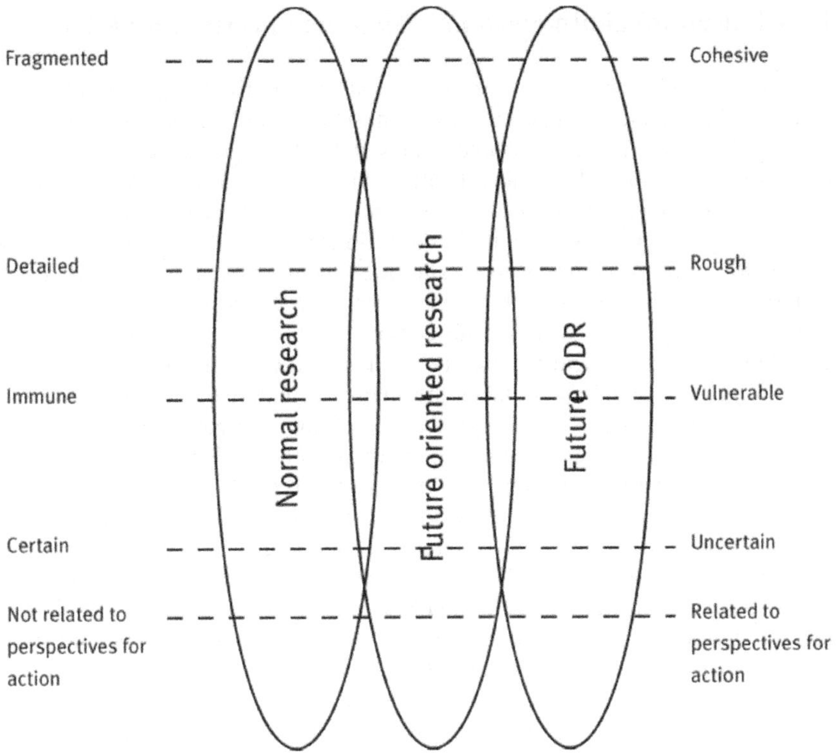

Fig. 18.1 Normal research, future-oriented research and F-ODR (source: In 't Veld 2001).

The discussion on future research leads to two recommendations. The first is more general. The methodology of gathering and interpreting knowledge about the future must reflect the complexity and uncertainty of the future. Generally speaking, it is recommended that scientific and practical knowledge are combined (transdisciplinary research). Such research designs require a certain degree of participation of actors outside the realms of science and politics, and ensure that a rich set of visions, signals and expectations about possible futures develops.

Conclusion about knowledge of long-term decisions:
The knowledge basis for long-term decisions requires a comprehensive approach. Knowledge production for long-term decision-making should be a combination of future orientation, design and research (F-ODR). This demands different process requirements than the requirements for "normal research" and "future-oriented research". Participation of actors is one of the key requirements.

18.5 The cultural dimension of long-term decision-making

Governance styles are, aside from politico-administrative structures, also belief systems. Governance relates to a form of social coordination, and governance *styles* reflect specific sets of shared values and beliefs and certain patterns of interpersonal relations. This makes them cultures, or at least: images of cultures. Culture is an aspect of political and public administration science that was neglected for a long time because it did not fit in the dominant paradigm of the post-war period: rational choice theory. The three main cultures or "ways of life" of cultural theory are similar to the three governance styles. Like the three governance styles, these three ways of life compete with each other, often in a hostile way, but on the other hand require one another, and they therefore continue to co-exist. This co-existence often takes the shape of mixtures: "That what we today define as free societies – those with the rule of law, alternation in office, and the right to criticise – are a product of the interpenetration of hierarchism, individualism, and egalitarianism." (Thompson M. et al. 1990: 50, 257).

The socio-politico-administrative context in a country has an influence on the question which governance style mixtures are feasible. The market culture of Anglo-Saxon countries, the network culture of the Netherlands and Scandinavian countries, and the hierarchical culture of France for example, play a role in the direction and acceptance of public-sector modernisation programmes, and in how policy-making processes are designed (Meuleman 2008).

The influences of historical, socio-political and administrative contexts have consequences for long-term decision-making: some contexts are more conducive for long-term decision-making than others. Hofstede (2001) developed a model that identifies five primary dimensions to assist in differentiating cultures: "power distance, individualism, masculinity, uncertainty avoidance, and long-term orientation". Based on Hofstede's research, we can draw the general conclusion that in comparison to Asian countries, European countries do not have a strong tradition of long-term decision-making and are then rather similar in the fifth dimension, quite different from the variety in the earlier four dimensions.

The dimension of uncertainty avoidance (UA) may be a crucial one with regard to long-term decisions: the future is per definition uncertain. Hofstede found in low UA countries (North-Western European countries) a more open-minded mentality, in searching for information and in accessibility to innovation (Hofstede 2001).

The Netherlands and Scandinavian countries seem to have a more consistent and profound view of the future (especially in comparison to Southern European and Anglo-Saxon countries) together with a lower "uncertainty avoidance index" (on average almost twice lower than in Southern countries). This could mean that, on one hand, peoples in Scandinavian countries do not have to reflect a lot on the future as they think they are able to adjust to changes; on the other hand, due to not having too many uncertainty concerns, they might be more resilient and able to think and make decisions with regard to the future. The cultural orientation of nations and its consolidation in governance structures, instruments and processes, may help to explain why, at least in environmental politics, North-Western European countries have shown to be early movers. This might be related to the fact that they also seem to have a more risk-taking attitude, another characteristic which seems to be beneficial for long-term decision-making. The other way around, risk averseness may be an important factor obstructing long-term policy-making.

Another difference is that Southern European countries are on average more hierarchical (Power Distance Index), which is reflected in for instance the much faster decision-making on long-term investments like (rail) infrastructure (Hofstede 2001).

It is often argued that Asian nations have a strong long-term dimension in their culture. In fact, this was what forced the sociologist Hofstede to add his fifth dimension ("long-term orientation"). However, if Asian governments sometimes seem less reluctant to take long-term decisions, it can be argued that this is also smoothed by the fact that in most Asian countries there is little possibility of participation by civil society and private sector.

When we discuss the cultural dimension the different styles of decision-making, legal families and institutional transplantation should be taken into account. There is a certain path dependency in decision-making, although there is room for carving out new paths. A critical appraisal of the "best" and "worst" examples can be useful, but the influences of the different contexts should not be neglected. Institutional transplantation (learning from distant practices) is not unproblematic, but the "solutions" should be implemented according to the specific contexts in which the solution has to operate.

Cultures and traditions of public and political actors may induce "default" results of trade-offs concerning long-term decisions. Improvement may be sought by "stretching" such results or shifting the results towards the other pole of the trade-off, taking implementation of the decision in the territory into consideration. It is important that all types of actors who have stakes in long-term decision-making on sustainability issues reflect on their specific perspectives and action strategies, regarding trade-offs which have to be made. Long-term decision-making for sustainable development is not only a responsibility of governments. However, governments have a special responsibility for the organisation of the societal discourse regarding the future, and should stimulate consensus on at least the agenda (which trade-offs are to be faced?) for long-term decision-making. Because many actors are involved in long-term decision-making, good governance of long-term decision-making requires clarity about the roles of states, business, civil society, knowledge institutions and intermediary organisations such as advisory councils.

Analysing impacts of cultures on "governance" and "decision-making", one could say that nation states have very different approaches to *long-term decision-making*, roles of stakeholders, established institutions and applicable instruments for long-term decision-making. There is a country-specific understanding and approach to what "governance" and "long-term decision" mean. For instance, "in the UK, Germany and Sweden, long-term targets are considered as useful instrument, which is in line with the attitude towards targets in general" (Niestroy 2005: 31). Meanwhile, the roles of the stakeholders involved in long-term decision-making frequently vary with the three governance styles (hierarchy, network and market). "For example, a strong corporatist tradition might hamper other civil society organisations from getting established and heard; the more civil society is organised, the more governments are open for dialogue" (Niestroy 2005: 37). A comparative research showed that in the UK, the Netherlands and Germany, concerning the same environmental policy problem, first the national "default" governance style was tried, before a specific governance style mixture emerged from the specific conditions of the cases (Meuleman 2008).

The conclusion is that it is plausible that socio-politico-administrative cultures, to a certain extent, induce a specific type of result of some of the trade-offs that have to be made in deciding on future events. Improving long-term decision-making may require changing the "standard" result of these trade-offs; at least, it is advisable to reflect on the question if trade-offs are made along the lines of a (national) culture – and if that is always the best way. Investing in increasing the long-term values of citizens may make long-term decision-making politically more feasible.

> Conclusion about values:
> Invest in increasing the long-term values of citizens: this may make long-term decision-making politically more feasible.

Long-term decisions must be implementable in the specific socio-politico-administrative culture of the territory (for example a country) for which the decisions are meant. Such national cultures and traditions influence to an important extent what works and what does not work. Therefore, it is risky to copy "best practices" from one nation to another. Some principles are recommendable for all countries, but an example from another country cannot be taken as concrete recipe. Learning from each other does not imply that the same approach will work elsewhere.

Therefore, there cannot be a "one size fits all" approach to the governance of long-term decisions. The often-used term "best practice" suggests that copying one approach to a different situation should be successful. However, cultural theory and governance studies show that this is highly implausible. Every case is different by time, country, political reality and many other factors (culture and traditions, level of uncertainty, degree of urgency, available knowledge, accessibility of information etc.). In order to improve the quality of long-term decision-making, specific conditions are required.

> Conclusion about "best practices":
> Instead of copying "best practices", it is better to translate them into a form which works in a specific situation, tradition and culture. The crucial question is: What works where and why?

18.6 Conclusions

We have discussed the complex problems of the governance of long-term decisions, and have argued that it is typically an issue that seems to meet more negative than positive mechanisms. Figure 18.2 shows which issues we have found to be relevant. It is also a field in which more research is required. Nevertheless, several recommendations can be formulated.

Firstly, different types of long-term decisions require different approaches. We should distinguish two types of long-term decisions:

- Cases with a relatively long period between the policy intervention and the intended effects: a long lead time. This type demands firm leadership in order to collect sufficient momentum for the focal decision.
- Cases that demand a long-lasting series of interventions that as a whole is necessary to cause a favourable effect, following the "drop in the bucket"-metaphor. This type asks for perseverance, consistency, continuity and reflexivity.

Regarding long-term futures, uncertainty and complexity prevail. In some cases we are able to forecast to a considerable degree, then we may anticipate. In the majority of cases we have to meet the existing uncertainty by concentrating on the acquirement of resilience.

Secondly, long-term decision-making predominantly requires a network governance approach:

- The governance of sustainable long-term decision-making requires in most cases some dominance of network governance, with hierarchical and market governance "running in the background". Such a governance mixture presupposes that institutions involved in long-term decision-making are able to act in a resilient way. This implies investing in flexibility and in alertness (creating "watchdog capacity"), without making the institutions unstable and unreliable.

Thirdly, it is important to recognise that long-term impacts of decisions may become underestimated, because the problems that led to the decisions have reached the end of their policy life cycle:

- Long-term decision-making requires policy mechanisms that prolong the policy lifecycle of policy issues.

The fourth conclusion concerns decision support systems:

- It is important to be transparent and realistic about the limitations of decision support systems, and to ensure that ethical and political assumptions in decision support systems are chosen in the political arena.

Fifthly, the knowledge basis for long-term decisions requires a comprehensive approach.

- Knowledge production for long-term decision-making should be a combination of future orientation, design and research (F-ODR). This demands different process requirements than the requirements for "normal research" and "future-oriented research". Participation of actors is one of the key requirements.

The sixth conclusion is about values.

- Invest in increasing the long-term values of citizens: this may make long-term decision-making politically more feasible.

Finally, "best practices" may be inspiring, but should not be copied.

- Instead of copying "best practices" is better to translate them into a form which works in a specific situation, tradition and culture. The crucial question is: What works where and why?

Fig. 18.2 Key problems and issues regarding long-term decision-making.

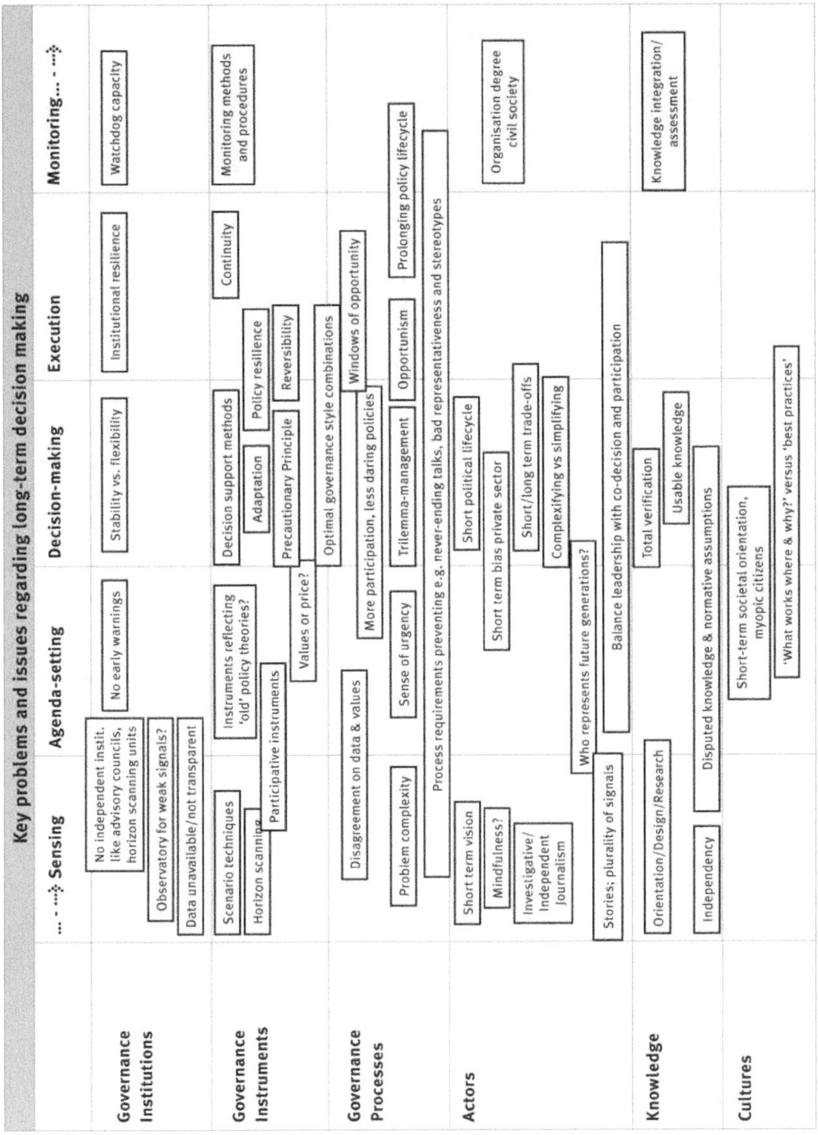

19 Knowledge governance: complementing hierarchies, networks and markets?

Arwin van Buuren and Jasper Eshuis

Abstract

Coordination between actions of individuals can be realised by a specific form of governance: hierarchical governance, network governance or market governance. In current policy processes with regard to climate change, spatial planning and water management, a fourth type of governance emerges which we call knowledge governance. This form of governance is aimed at developing new insights, competencies and ideas via public investments in knowledge development and dissemination, which contribute to the emergence of new pathways for collective action.

In this chapter we answer the question how knowledge governance can contribute to the untangling of collective problems which cannot be solved by hierarchical, network or market governance. We illustrate our argument with an in-depth case study of a Dutch regional planning process. We conclude that knowledge governance is a distinct mode of governance which can contribute to the capacity of actors to coordinate their actions by the development of public ideas, competencies and arguments.

19.1 Introduction

There are enormous differences in how modern societies realise coordination. Characteristic for all societies however, is the plurality of steering principles that is applied to arrive at coordination and order. There is no one way of realising order but there are many. And they are often used in conjunction with each other.

The classical way of realising order is by means of hierarchy. A central Archimedic point is (supposed to be) posited above society and has the ability and power to steer societal developments in such a way that the society evolves towards the situation preferred by this top. This coordination mechanism underlies the rise of modern centralised European countries and is also characteristic for many (post)communist societies.

However, there is more to modern societies and governments. Modern societies are highly complex, possessing powerful self organising capacities and being difficult to understand and steer (Teisman et al. 2009). Governments do not have the

R.J. in 't Veld (ed.), *Knowledge Democracy*, DOI 10.1007/978-3-642-11381-9_19,

necessary resources to steer society in the way they prefer (Koppenjan and Klijn 2004). In many cases of collective action this classical way of coordination is supplemented or even replaced by forms of market governance (Coase 1937, Williamson 1985) and network governance (Kickert et al. 1997, Ouchi 1991, Rhodes 1997) in which either the self-interest of rational actors or the reciprocity of mutually dependent actors explain why coordination and collective action is realised. These two modes of governance make use of the self-organising capacity of the market and society, enabling government to suffice with a much less interventionist strategy.

Within the literature many contributions reflect upon this distinction in forms of governance, their application and their relative merits and disadvantages (Thompson G. et al. 1991, Thompson G. 2003, Considine and Lewis 1999, 2003, Dixon and Dogan 2002, Powell 1990).

In this chapter we argue that there is a fourth form of governance which cannot be reduced to one of the three forms described above; it forms a distinct mode to realise coordination and collective action. We call this form of governance *knowledge governance.*

Knowledge governance is about purposefully organising the development of knowledge in order to deal with societal problems. Knowledge governance is aimed at creating new insights, and innovative solutions which tempt actors to leave traditional insights and practices and get away from inert interaction patterns, stalemate negotiations and interest conflicts. Knowledge governance is also used to raise awareness and deliver suggestions that give actors a perspective on purposeful action.

Knowledge governance has become widely applied in a majority of Western countries, in practices of for example spatial planning, water management and climate adaptation. Oftentimes knowledge governance is institutionalised and implemented via separate knowledge programmes. In the Dutch context these programmes are co-financed by public and private actors. They are aimed at delivering insights in themes as multiple land use, sustainable transport, adaptive water management and climate adaptation. These programmes explicitly aim at delivering new insights, best practices and new competencies meant to creep into existing practices in order to realise new forms of order and coordinated action. Often, these programmes are seen as a useful "mode of governance" because governments do not know what the problem exactly is, and which opportunities and instruments they have to intervene in practice.

In this chapter we answer the question how knowledge governance can contribute to the untangling of collective problems which cannot (or are difficult to) be solved by means of hierarchical, network or market governance. In which situations can knowledge governance be a viable alternative for the traditional forms of governance to realise coordination?

We illustrate the deficiencies of the three traditional forms of governance and the working of knowledge governance with a case study on the reconstruction of a greenhouse area in the Westland area in the Netherlands. With help of the insights from this case study we elaborate on a theory of knowledge governance. We conclude the chapter with insights into the working of knowledge governance and its relation to the other forms of governance.

19.2 Research methods

We conducted the empirical research through a case study (see Stake 1995, Yin 1984). We followed the developments in the case for 8 months, until the final "area-contract" was signed and the implementation of the plans started. We undertook a case study because we wanted to study what actors did in their context, and because we needed an in-depth study to understand the intricacies of the development, application and function of knowledge in realising collective action. Another reason to opt for the in-depth method of a case study was that some of the issues we wanted to address were delicate and complex, such as the struggle that took place around the optimal solution for water-retention. Finally a case study fits best in our ambition to shed light upon a phenomenon which until now is theoretically and empirically poorly understood.

To ensure the validity of our data in the political context where people with particular interests present particular aspects of what is going on, we applied data-triangulation (cf. Yin 1984). We observed various meetings of the project team, and carried out participatory observation in two sessions that we organised with the aim to reflect on the developments with the various participants in the process. We also undertook 15 interviews with 13 respondents, representing all relevant parties. Because of the delicateness and complexity of some of the issues we wanted to address, we carried out in-depth and semi-structured interviews. In addition we analysed the policy documents and scientific documents that were relevant to the project. Thereby we were privileged to get access to the e-mail correspondence of one of the respondents who played a crucial role in the knowledge development process. Thus, we were able to study the communication between the core actors in the process.

The way we present the findings of our case study is meant to facilitate our search towards an answer on the question what constitutes knowledge governance. This is both a theoretical and empirical question and we use bits of our case study as step stones towards a preliminary answer to this question.

19.3 Forms of governance

Governance is about realising coordination between actors with divergent ambitions, perceptions and interests. Without coordination collective action is nearly impossible. To align the actions of actors with different opinions and ambitions and to enable collective action, it is necessary to apply some form of governance: a set of principles, methods and strategies aimed at influencing the strategies of actors who together can realise their individual and collective ambitions.

Many times the form of governance used to realise coordination and mutual adjustment can be best depicted as self-governance: actors make voluntarily agreements. In fact, network governance can be seen as the professionalisation of this form of governance. Based upon mutual dependency and reciprocity actors try to find a common agenda for action. They cooperate to realise an agenda that contains sufficient elements of their own agenda. This form of governance is based upon principles such as solidarity, loyalty and trust (Thompson G. 2003, Entwistle et al. 2007).

Network governance is nowadays seen as a viable alternative for hierarchical governance because of the many shortcomings of the latter (Klijn 2008). Hierarchical governance rests on the assumption that it is possible to realise coordination on the basis of power relations, on ordination and subordination. In essence, hierarchical governance is about top-down steering. The classical bureaucratic organisation is the prototype of hierarchical governance.

This governance approach was useful for realising collective action for a long time. But its application presupposes the availability of enough "capacity" for governments to realise their ambitions without the voluntary cooperation of their subordinates. In the context of current network societies the necessary resources to realise collective action (for example. money, knowledge, organisational capabilities and legitimacy) are dispersed among many actors. Therefore hierarchical governance oftentimes falls short to realise collective action and is regularly replaced or supplemented by network governance (Kettle 2002, Pierre and Peters 2000, Koppenjan and Klijn 2004, Klijn and Skelcher 2007).

Besides these two governance forms which are frequently applied to realise coordination in the public domain, the third coordination mechanism is more often applied in the private domain, but more and more in the public domain due to the raise of New Public Management (Pollitt and Bouckaert 2000). Market governance is based upon the economic principles of the interplay between the demands of consumers and the supply of producers. It coordinates through the invisible hand of the price-based system of exchange between self-interested actors (for example, Williamson 1985). Within the public domain, market principles are used to formulate incentives that safeguard the proper working of imperfect markets. In some cases, governments provide a market for goods with specific merit aspects which are not produced by the common market.

In Table 19.1 we summarise the main differences between the three modes of governance.

In reflections upon the distinction between the three modes of governance, two forms of critique can be observed. A first critique is that the threefold distinction is not refined enough. Some critics have therefore refined the analyses of the network mode of governance by making a distinction between networks and communities or clans (Streeck and Schmitter 1985, Tenbensel 2005). This distinction is made to shed light on the difference between providers of goods and services (which are central in networks) and communities (geographic, ethnic or cultural groups). Others have refined the hierarchical mode of governance. Considine and Lewis (2003) distinguish between:

- procedural governance
- corporate governance
- market governance
- network governance.

Table 19.1 Modes of governance (based upon Meuleman 2008).

	Network	Market	Hierarchy
Basic principle	Reciprocity	Exchange	Power
Coordination principle	Collaboration	Price	Rules
Mode of calculation	Homo politicus	Homo economicus	Homo hierarchicus
Roles of government	Government as partner or network manager	Government as service supplier, contract partner	Government as principal ruler
Key value	Public value	Public choice	Public goods

Procedural governance refers to the following of rules and protocols, high reliance on supervision, and an expectation that tasks and decisions will be well scripted. Corporate governance reflects the application of New Public Management within classical bureaucratic organisations and focuses upon realising coordination in complex public organisations by applying businesslike management tools. However, both procedural and corporate governance can be seen as subcategories of hierarchical governance.

We sustain the threefold distinction between network-, market-, and hierarchical governance as presented above because the fourfold categorisations mentioned above are in essence further refinements of the classical threefold distinction.

A second critique is more fundamental in arguing that the distinction between three (or four) forms of governance is not useful, but rather confusing. This group of critics argues that the distinction neglects the importance of hybrid forms of governance such as public-private partnerships, and other governance practices in which different coordination mechanisms are intermingled (for example, Bradach and Eccles 1989). Economic sociologists, for example (Granovetter 1985), emphasise the idea that markets and economic exchange are embedded in social structures. Reciprocity and other social norms thus play an important role in the market.

In this chapter we do not wish to deny that the threefold distinction could be refined, nor do we deny that different coordination mechanisms are intermingled in practice. However, it is our contention that the analyses of governance practices can be improved by understanding what basic principles underlie these practices. We aim to add to a body of literature in which different forms of governance are distinguished by analysing the basic coordination mechanisms that underlie them (for example, Considine and Lewis 2003, Meuleman 2008, Powell 1990, Thompson G. et al. 1991). Our goal is to add to the analytical toolbox for studying governance processes by distinguishing and analysing a fourth analytical category of governance modes, that is knowledge governance.

19.4 Why these governance approaches do not always suffice

Many problems of collective action can be effectively tackled with a mix of these three forms of governance. Where singular modes of governance do not suffice they can be used in combination with each other. The rich literature on policy instruments sheds light upon the contingency between modes of governance and the context of application.

However, in some situations collective problems cannot be solved by one of these governance mechanisms. Dixon and Dogan (2002) show why the epistemological, ontological and nomological assumptions of the three modes of governance give rise to their own failures. The relative problems of hierarchical governance versus market governance are known: the market is not able to produce collective goods and in several situations the market is not able to realise a macro-efficient allocation, while governments do have the problem of imperfect information, bureaucratic self-interest and imperfect competition (Levacic 1991). Network governance may fail to realise collaboration due to a lack of trust, or is not effective in realising decisive and effective policy choices due to the focus on consensus. The shortcomings of these modes of governance can be illustrated with our case study of the case Waalblok (see Box 19.1).

Box 19.1

In the Dutch polder area Waalblok a large number of greenhouses can be found. It is part of the so called Westland, "the Greenport of the Netherlands". In reaction to trends in the agricultural sector such as scale enlargement and internationalisation many growers develop initiatives to enlarge their business. Therefore spatial restructuring of the whole area is necessary. Such a process can be perfectly done in a private way, by means of market governance. The governmental planning document allows for reconstruction of the greenhouse area.

A complicating factor is that the area of Waalblok is also confronted with more and more water nuisance due to climate change. The increased intensity of rainfall has caused severe problems with drainage in the polder. Therefore the Water Board studied on possibilities to enlarge the retention capacity within the polder. The Water Board did not have the juridical and financial means to realise the necessary retention areas and depends upon the voluntary cooperation of the growers to solve the problem of water nuisance.

However the cleavages between governments on the one hand citizens and entrepreneurs on the other, are too deep to form a fertile ground for fruitful voluntary cooperation between both. In addition the Water Board did not have a tradition of network governance; it relies largely on formal procedures to realise its own organisational goals. The procedures however, are not suitable for realising tailor-made solutions which are needed in the particular situation of the Waalblok area, which is also highly dynamic.

In this case study three forms of government are not sufficient to solve the problems in this area. Hierarchical government does not have the necessary power, competencies (based upon formal legislation) and money to realise its policy goals. At the same time, however, the entrepreneurs are perfectly able to solve their own problem of reconstruction with help of market governance principles. However, the market mechanism does not solve the water problem because of the free rider problem: some parts of the polder do have serious problems with intense rain fall while other parts (higher located) do not have any problem with water nuisance.

Network governance is not easy to apply either, due to the bad relationship between governments and entrepreneurs. Besides, the ambitions of both are complete opposites and will result in a zero-sum game. Water retention requires extra space which can no longer be used by the growers for their business. Actually space is very scarce in the Westland and the spatial use is very intensive. That makes growers unwilling to cooperate voluntarily with governments who want to use agricultural land for water retention.

In this case the three forms of governance do not suffice to overcome the difficulties in realising collective action. Table 19.2 summarises their shortcomings as they are present in our case study.

Table 19.2 The failures of modes of governance.

	Market governance	Hierarchical governance	Network governance
	Retention capacity is a collective good for the growers	The Water Board does not have the juridical means to intervene in the private reconstruction process	The ambitions of the Water Board and growers can be seen as a win-lose game
Why this mode of governance does not suffice	Free rider behaviour prevents realising retention areas solely through the market	The Water Board needs voluntary cooperation of the growers	A history of bad relationships and distrust hinders a cooperative process
		The Water Board did not have the necessary means to realise retention capacity on its own	The Water Board did not have the knowledge and competencies to set up a collaborative process

The market mode is not helpful in overcoming the classical failures of imperfect markets (Bailey 2001). In such a situation governmental intervention seems to be logical to correct market failure. However, in this situation due to private property rights and a diminishing role for government, the authorities do not have the necessary capabilities to realise effective hierarchical interventions. Hierarchical governance presupposes the presence of state capacity but this capacity is no longer unlimitedly available (Kettle 2002).

Departing from such a situation, network governance seems to be the most appropriate answer to government failure. But network governance presupposes both a commonly felt need to align the own intentions and ambitions with those of others, and also a minimum level of mutual trust between interdependent actors. In this case both a shared understanding of mutual dependence and some initial level of trust seemed to be absent. This case thus sheds light on (often unmentioned) preconditions which have to be present to apply a specific form of governance. In Table 19.3 we summarise the main preconditions per governance mode which are oftentimes (implicitly) assumed to be present when the accompanying governance mode is employed.

Table 19.3 Preconditions for hierarchical, market and network governance.

	Hierarchy	Market	Network
Precondition	State capacity: governments do have the necessary financial and juridical means to intervene in societal and private processes	Clearly defined ownership of goods (that is private goods instead of public goods)	Network capital: the necessary relations between mutual dependent actors and the willingness to cooperate

In such a situation it may take years before adequate action is taken. However, from our case study Waalblok we learn that there is another way to realise coordination within a situation wherein three modes of governance are insufficient: knowledge governance.

19.5 Knowledge governance in Waalblok

Waalblok was not the only area within the Westland area with persistent water management problems. Several comparable areas were also characterised by serious water problems which were difficult to solve due to other intense spatial problems, strained relations and conflicting interests between governmental actors and societal stakeholders.

Therefore the various governmental bodies within the City Region of The Hague ("Haaglanden") decided to start an innovation programme "Water Framework Haaglanden". This programme was meant to realise innovative breakthroughs with regard to persistent problems in the spatial planning of the whole area and especially concerning the difficult balance of water management and other spatial functions.

Crucial in the programme was a knowledge programme (financed partly by the central government and partly by the regional and local governments) aimed at developing technical and institutional innovations. The board of the City Region selected six pilot projects – under which was Waalblok – to test a new governance approach aimed at collaboration and bottom-up steering and to develop technological innovations to prevent the zero-sum game between water retention and other spatial claims.

The pilot project Waalblok was started with a subsidy of Haaglanden. Although some attempts were done to find a competent independent process manager, the involved governmental organisation did not succeed in finding a person who fitted their expectations. Therefore they decided to start the pilot project with their own people and work with their own practical knowledge about collaboration and area development.

A new arrangement was developed to organise the cooperation between the various governments (especially the Water Board and the municipality of Westland) and the growers (some individuals, but most of them were united in LTO "Glass Power", an agricultural interest organisation). From Delfland, Westland and the LTO, a representative was appointed to participate in a project team. The various actors received additional means to implement this new way of working.

From the Programme Team of Water Framework Haaglanden much emphasis was given to the development of new and systematic knowledge. They paid for an intensive research process in which more then twenty possible scenarios for the future water management of Waalblok were compared on a number of criteria. They also invested a significant amount of money in the further development of a creative idea of a local consultancy office. This idea is worth to describe in some detail.

AquaTerraNova, a consulting firm specialised in the business of horticulture and floriculture, developed – on demand of a local entrepreneur – an idea to reuse pouring water in greenhouses. By closing the cycle of water use growers were able to solve future problems regarding the dumping of used water in the surface water or in the sewerage system. This idea was enhanced with an idea to realise cellars under the greenhouses to store rain water in times of extreme rain fall in combination with the storage of pouring water.

In fact this idea not only helps to realise a more efficient use of space (by realising water storage in cellars and thus multifunctional land use) but also helps to improve the water management of the polder by closing the cycle of rain water, production water, and sewerage water.

This idea was translated in a subsidy proposal to obtain the necessary financial means to develop this idea further and to realise a pilot project. More then €3 million Euros were placed at the disposal of the municipality of Westland to implement the concept in a pilot project.

Then both projects came together because Westland was already participating in the above mentioned pilot project "area development" in Waalblok. The development of the innovative 4B concept was linked to the pilot project Waalblok. The various governmental actors (municipality and Water Board) and private actors (united in an agricultural interest group) united them in a Project Group. The municipality delivered a project manager. Both the municipality and the Water Board applied a new way of working, called "area-based policy-making" (urged by the Water Framework Haaglanden) in which plans for rearranging areas were accomplished bottom-up with heavily involvement of the direct interested parties.

An intensive period of 2 years started. The Water Board commissioned a research (paid and stimulated by the Water Framework Haaglanden) in which the 4B concept was tested and compared with a couple of other alternatives for the spatial organisation of the polder and the water management. Based upon this research it was concluded that the 4B concept was feasible and robust.

On basis of this conclusion it was decided that the 4B concept could be used to realise a compromise between the desires of the growers and the wishes of the Water Board. A difficult discussion took place between one of the members of the Board of Directors of the Water Board and the involved civil servants. The first had a firm preference for a specific (traditional and thus proven) solution for the water retention challenge and was sceptical about the possibilities of retention cellars. The civil servants however needed the innovation of the 4B concept for realising both the water management ambition and the reconstruction.

It took a long time for the project team to realise consensus among all the actors involved. After 2 years an "area contract" could be signed. Two corner stones for this agreement were delivered as a result of knowledge interventions in the process. The first intervention was the encompassing comparison of the 4B concept with a couple of alternative allocation proposals. The second intervention was formed by a financial analysis – commissioned by the Project Team – in which an independent consultancy firm investigated the costs of the preferred alternative and proposed a specific distribution of the various contributions to these costs.

After all both the representatives of the growers and the municipal and Water Board authorities were satisfied with the ultimate outcome. One individual grower was willing to realise the cellar under his greenhouse and a couple of growers were willing to participate in the collective pouring water plant.

19.6 The role of knowledge governance

The case described in the former section illustrates a situation in which neither of the three modes, nor a combination of them, suffices to realise a sustainable solution for the problems in the polder Waalblok. The development of new knowledge was decisive in realising a solution. This knowledge consists on the one hand in a technical innovation (the 4B concept) and on the other hand a process innovation (the "area development approach").

The technical knowledge was indispensable to overcome the problem of the zero-sum game between the spatial claims of water management and economic development and to find a mutual attractive solution with was both effective and feasible. The process innovation was necessary to overcome the history of strained relationships between the parties and complement the institutional arrangements used by the Water Board.

The Water Framework Haaglanden played an important role in promoting and stimulating the development and application of these innovations. As a governmental organisation they invest intentionally in the application of knowledge governance as a mean to realise coordination. We can distinguish four different elements of their strategy:

- translating policy problems into questions for research and knowledge development;
- mobilising knowledge institutes and consortia to develop innovative ideas and proposals fitting into the problem definitions of the region;
- accompanying the process of fact-finding and facilitating the link between research and policy-making to enable the fit between the coordination problem and the knowledge product;
- stimulating the spread of knowledge between the various pilot projects and throughout the whole programme to enhance the effectiveness of the produced knowledge and its translation into collective action.

In the case Waalblok knowledge governance aimed at stimulating innovation and knowledge development was ultimately helpful in overcoming the conflicts of interest between growers and Water Board. We can distinguish three main contributions of knowledge governance to the realisation of coordination in this case:

- New knowledge inspires actors to leave existing perceptions and insights, and stimulates them to develop new problem definitions. Inhabitants of the polder and representatives from the Water Board get convinced about the possibilities to combine a robust water management system with an economic viable polder and expansion of the greenhouses.
- Innovative knowledge was helpful in bridging existing conflicts of interests by proposing combinatory solutions. Technical innovations can be helpful in proposing solutions that create win-win solutions. Cellars beneath the greenhouses are space-efficient and combine both the need for fresh water and retention capacity.
- New knowledge was used to arrange multi-actor collaboration in more fruitful way. The involved governments were facilitated in starting a pilot project in which they could experiment a new way of working. The programme team tried to facilitate the development of new competencies.

In the case of Waalblok we can identify a couple of elements with regard to knowledge governance that determine its added value in the light of the shortcomings of the other modes of governance. See also Table 19.4.

Table 19.4 The contribution of knowledge governance.

	Shortcoming	Contribution of knowledge governance
Market governance	Market failures (free rider behaviour) with regard to water retention	Idea for the sharing of costs and benefits of the restructuring of the polder Innovation for realising an effective combination of a private good (supply water) and a public good (water retention)
Network governance	Zero-sum game between growers and Water Board	New methods and competences that enable collaboration and trust-building
	Low mutual trust between actors	Insight into possibilities of package deals and win-win solutions
Hierarchical governance	The necessary means (financial, juridical) are lacking The exact allocation of responsibilities and tasks is unclear	Innovation stimulates actors to cooperate voluntarily with the restructuring of the polder: new perspectives stimulating collaboration

19.7 Analysing the characteristics of knowledge governance

In the former section we have analysed the practice of knowledge governance. We are now able to reflect upon the theoretical characteristics of this fourth mode of governance. Table 19.5 gives an overview of modes of governance and their main characteristics, including the fourth mode of knowledge governance.

Table 19.5 Knowledge governance compared to the other three modes of governance.

	Network	Market	Hierarchy	Knowledge
Basic principle	Reciprocity	Exchange	Power	Cognition
Coordination principle	Collaboration	Price	Rules	Learning
Mode of calculation	Homo politicus	Homo economicus	Homo hierarchicus	Homo sapiens
Roles of government	partner or network manager	service supplier, contract partner	principal ruler	knowledge infrastructure developer
Key value	Public value	Public choice	Public goods	Public ideas
Legitimisation	Participation	Fairness	Accountability	Credibility
Resource allocation	Mutual adjustment between mutually dependent actors	Demand and supply between consumer and producer	Political budgeting between politicians and agencies	Creative competition between ideas

Compared to the other three modes of governance, knowledge governance focuses on the coordinative power of shared ideas. Actors who are jointly convinced about the feasibility of solutions and the seriousness of problems are also willing to adjust their strategies and to develop a coherent path of collective action. The role of government is to facilitate the process of knowledge production and its dissemination. In knowledge governance, knowledge is approached as a public good that can be co produced by public, private and societal actors. By facilitating the development of knowledge by and for actors, other ways of thinking, acting and judging are enabled.

Compared to the other three forms of governance knowledge governance can be seen as a way of coordinating action and realising collective action by steering the production of innovative knowledge with is able to overcome technical, organisational and managerial barriers present in collective action settings. Knowledge is a means to provide actors with new insights and ideas which help them to adjust their behaviour in such a way that they are able to realise coordination and collective action.

Of course, knowledge and learning also play a role in the other modes of coordination. Within hierarchies, market and networks knowledge is used to optimise respectively steering interventions, consumer and producer choices and the realisation of package deals. However, in these modes of governance knowledge is always subordinated, and aimed at delivering insights to improve the primary coordination mechanisms of hierarchy, market and network. Within knowledge governance, the mobilisation of knowledge and the development of a knowledge infrastructure is the primary mode of coordination. Actors are provoked to learn, to adjust their behaviour based upon new knowledge and insights.

Knowledge is a multi-faceted phenomenon (Van Buuren 2009). Knowledge governance refers to two forms of knowledge: explicit knowledge in terms of new technological concepts or solutions, impact analyses and benchmarks, and expert knowledge in terms of competencies and new individual or organisational routines (for a further elaboration of this distinction Van Buuren 2006).

New explicit knowledge can be used to overcome value conflicts and lock-in situations for example by developing technical innovations that help to bridge interest conflicts or contradictory perceptions of stakeholders which cannot be overcome by the other modes of governance.

New competencies can help to break through existing routines and ways of doing. Especially when hierarchical ways of governance do not suffice and network approaches are still underdeveloped, new practical knowledge about how to organise collaborative processes can be helpful in stimulating new ways of cooperation and mutual adjustment.

That means that knowledge governance in Waalblok supports other forms of governance, in this case notably network governance. It opens new ways of collaboration and also unthought-of opportunities for package deals and creative combinations which facilitate the dialogue about compromises.

We see many other applications of knowledge governance. A well-known example in the Dutch agricultural domain is the so-called Research – Extension – Education Triangle (in Dutch: OVO Drieluik). This institutional structure was meant to facilitate the realisation of the high agricultural ambitions within the Netherlands in terms innovation, growth of production, and market share. The government did not choose to use hierarchical measures (you cannot enforce farmers to be innovative), but they decided to invest in a knowledge infrastructure aimed at scientific innovation and the application of innovations on farm. Although the system has been criticised for its linear view on knowledge development[1] it did contribute to innovations and higher agricultural productions in a time when there was a broad consensus among scientists and farmers about the main aim of increasing agricultural production (see for example, Rutten and Van Oosten 1999).

The corporatist tradition in the Dutch food sector is a fertile ground for other applications of knowledge governance that are less based on linear views of knowledge production. We can witness so-called "learning tables", subsidised by public authorities and composed of farmers in the peat meadow areas in which they exchange best practices, questions and answers with regard to a climate robust agricultural land use.

Within the climate policy domain there are other examples of knowledge governance, for example the climate impact atlases which are used to communicate the consequences of climate change to local governments and functional authorities within a specific region as an attempt to stimulate them to formulate adaptation measures.

Other examples of knowledge governance can be found in the domain of economic affairs. The Dutch institute SenterNovem executes various programmes to develop knowledge about improving the sustainability of business parks (Boons and Janssen 2004). Consultants are hired to collect and disseminate showcases between private entrepreneurs. Money is invested to develop a knowledge infrastructure to support the development of an "eco-industrial system".

19.8 Conclusion and discussion

This chapter reveals that knowledge governance can contribute to collective action by stimulating coordination of strategies with help of new knowledge. Knowledge governance ultimately is a way of coordinating social life by developing knowledge that facilitates voluntary adjustment of individual strategies. It appeals to the self-organising capacity of actors to adjust their behaviour based upon new insights and ideas. Although we have to be careful in generalising conclusions on basis of one case study, we cautiously conclude that knowledge governance is especially applicable in contexts characterised by:

- uncertainty and ignorance about possibilities and futures;
- a moderate or high degree of consensus about the necessity to solve a specific problem;

---

[1] The OVO system was based on the assumption that knowledge has to be developed by scientists, disseminated by consultants and applied by farmers. The system neglected knowledge development by farmers themselves (see for example, Leeuwis 1993, Roling and Wagemakers 1998).

- problems with regard to the application of other modes of governance;
- actors willing to explore new possibilities and leave existing routines and ideas.

Knowledge governance cannot be reduced to hierarchical governance, networks governance or market governance because at a fundamental level it is based on a different principle. Knowledge governance is based on knowledge, whereas hierarchical governance is based on power, market governance on exchange, and network governance on reciprocity.

Knowledge governance can result in some form of self-organised order and coordinated action. However, knowledge governance does not provide the necessary means to enforce such an emerging equilibrium. It relies on the voluntary dedication of actors to learn and to adjust their behaviour. For enforcing change it relies on the principles of one of the three other modes of governance. In our case, hierarchical means, market principles and network instruments were used to confirm the frame reflection and consensus realised thanks to the knowledge governance.

That points us to an essential difference between knowledge governance and the other modes of governance. Knowledge governance does not provide for the means necessary to warrant (the implementation of) joint action. It helps to realise voluntary self-organisation, but without any obligation. By investing in the development of innovations and competencies, actors within a specific policy domain are enabled to adjust their behaviour by adopting these new insights. This coordination mechanism is based upon the credibility and practical usefulness of the developed knowledge.

In that sense knowledge governance can be seen as facilitative and additional to the other modes of governance. It paves the way for the others by stimulating frame reflection and new ways of thinking and doing. It facilitates the search towards win-win solutions. It rationalises the dialogue between stakeholders with different world views and problem perceptions. It can deliver new methods and approaches for collaboration and dialogue.

20 The positioning of commissions in a knowledge democracy

Martin Schulz and Mark van Twist

Abstract

To deal with a variety of difficult matters, Dutch politics, as well as politics in other countries, makes good use of a well-known and well-tried instrument that is simultaneously highly debated and controversial: the commission or committee. In a knowledge democracy, where the development of knowledge is democratised itself, in which new forms of deliberation and negotiation appear and in which the balance of power between groups is shifting, this classical arrangement of using commissions is given a new interpretation. In current practice we may witness new and innovative forms of commissions that are, by the way, mostly variations of well-known organisational forms, rather than a completely new phenomenon. Be it citizens' assemblies, hubs, or even cascade commissions, these are all new variations on classical commissions with distinctive and characteristic features. This contribution to the book on knowledge democracy discusses societal changes that can be seen in the practices of government, as well as the shift in the use of commissions that occurs as a result of those changes.

20.1 Introduction

To deal with a variety of difficult matters, Dutch politics, as well as politics in other countries, makes good use of a well-known and well-tried instrument that at the same time is highly debated and controversial: the commission or committee. Generally speaking, a commission or committee is a temporary body of people – mostly a mix of former politicians, businesspeople and field experts – from outside government, which is formed on an *ad hoc* basis to perform certain functions in public administration such as: considering a specific problem, or creating an impulse to change the course of certain events (Schulz et al. 2006, 2008). These temporary commissions are being formed on all kinds of topics, for example the political decision-making on the war in Iraq (Davids Commission), the explosion of a fireworks factory in the city of Enschede (Oosting Commission), the growth of national airport Schiphol (In 't Veld Commission), a near-shore wind park (Verbruggen Commission), or the use of Information and Communication Technology by government agencies (Docters van Leeuwen Commission). Various authors

R.J. in 't Veld (ed.), *Knowledge Democracy*, DOI 10.1007/978-3-642-11381-9_20,

have stressed the importance of these commissions in the public sector, towards creating an understanding of the functioning of government (for example, Wheare 1955, Lipsky and Olsen 1977, Popper 1970, Chapman 1973, Cartwright 1975, Roberts 1996, De Bruijn 2006, Howlett and Ramesh 2003, Prahalad and Ramaswamy 2004).

Yet this classical arrangement of governing by commission, in addition to many benefits, has some disadvantages. For example, commissions perform their duties away from, and out of sight of, citizens, corporations and society at large. Society usually considers commissions as a meaningful expression of the political process. The actual size of the gap between commissions and society depends, of course, on the procedure and the formation of the commission, but in general, this is the reality. It is therefore often questionable whether the report of a commission is supported by society at large, or by citizens and companies that are not part of a certain inner circle? The much debated gap between government and society is at the very least not closed by setting up classical commissions to inquire into difficult matters (Ten Heuvelhof and Van Twist 2007). At this moment, a knowledge democracy, in the sense that political positions are supported by a "wisdom of crowds", is not automatically realised.

This raises questions. How should we interpret the role and function of commissions in a changing societal context, where knowledge and expertise continue to broaden and are also becoming democratised? Furthermore, how do commissions fit into questions of boundary work? In this contribution to the book on knowledge democracy we will argue that, increasingly, our society seems to be shifting towards a knowledge democracy as a result of which commissions tend to take different shapes and perform different tasks.

20.2 Definition

Several definitions are in use, which describe what a commission is (Wheare 1955: 4, Brown D.S. 1972: 335). Chapman (1973: 9) chooses this definition: "[...] a commission may be defined as a body set up by government to consider a specific problem or problems." Therefore it seems that commissions are formed to consider matters of some kind. Some scholars avoid definitions, preferring to describe distinctive features of commissions. The fact that commissions are formed by members of government is a characteristic that gives great status to commissions (Cartwright 1975: 1–3, Komarovsky 1975, Flitner 1986). Another characteristic is that commissions are usually made up of people from outside the government (Hoefnagel 1975: 386).

Every country has its own names for and special forms of commissions (and/or committees). In literature, comparisons are often made between the "Presidents Commissions" as they are known in the United States and the "Royal Commissions" as they are known in the United Kingdom and Canada (Hodgetts 1949, Hanson 1969, Chapman 1973, Popper 1970: 8). These commissions are comparable to the ad hoc commissions known to the Dutch public service. The same applies to so-called "inquiries" or "commissions of inquiry" that are set up in, for example, Canada and Australia (compare for example, Salter and Slaco 1981, Wraith and Lamb 1971). In formulating the definition in the next paragraph, we have only looked at literature describing types of commissions that are comparable to Dutch ad hoc commissions.

In our research into the Dutch practices of governing by commission, we have used the following definition of commissions (Schulz et al. 2006: 21): "a (more or less extensive) group of people with origins outside the government, which is set up to consider a matter of some kind within the public service".

This is, by design, a rather broad definition (compare Schulz et al. 2008). The decision to use such a definition was made because not every commission in The Netherlands is using the word "commission" in its name. Special committees, task forces, platforms, working groups, tribunals or steering committees might also be considered a type of commission. In all of these instances, individuals are asked to jointly consider a specific public service matter. Van Poelje (1967: 9) suggests that it is hard to imagine The Netherlands without specialised commissions "regardless of its name or structure" (translation from Dutch, also compare to Van Schendelen 2004, 2005: 58). The phenomenon of a government governing by commissions has not yet met its boundaries in language. The current trend in Dutch public administration seems to be one of verbal renewal (compare Van Twist 1995): fewer "commissions" (at first sight at least) and in their place "task forces", "platforms" or even "hubs" are set up, thus using more appealing names. Still, names are not the only difference between these variations.

20.3 A practice of paradox

The usefulness and the role of commissions are themes both widely discussed in The Netherlands, resulting in diverse opinions.

On the one hand, ad hoc commissions are frequently installed by a member of government to mobilise specific expertise, to guarantee independence of inquiries and to create support. This leads to the result that commissions often mobilise state of the art knowledge available in science or with experts, that commissions try to find solutions for questions that have not been offered by others before them and that commissions strive to reach a consensus among stakeholders. This is usually regarded as a more positive interpretation of the accomplishments of commissions.

On the other hand, the same situation can be explained differently. In debates on the merits of commissions, this is often the case. We frequently hear comments, detailing how the work of commissions offers few new insights, while reducing options for democratic decision-making by taking the edge off the debate. These opposing statements on commissions may be seen as two sides of the same coin. In political and social debate in The Netherlands, most attention is given to the critics. Therefore, the forming and installation of commissions is usually considered a political action and a bad one at that. This is usually regarded as a more negative interpretation of the accomplishments of commissions. In Table 20.1 (based on earlier work by Schulz and Van Twist 2009) we show a comparison of both the positive and negative positions of the same situation.

Table 20.1 Positive and negative interpretations of commissions.

Negative interpretation	Observation	Positive interpretation
Commissions form a shadow power	Commissions and their work are nearly invisible	Commissions facilitate parties feeling each other out in secure surroundings
Commissions are a fridge for hiding problems	The work of commissions takes time to complete	Setting up commissions leads to a (temporary) cooling of political debate
Commissions pre-boil political decision-making	Commissions are influential	Commissions break taboos and create space for decision-making
Commissions never come up with anything new	Commissions also weigh existing knowledge	Commissions reach authoritative conclusions
Commissions and their reports are only used by ministers to hide behind	Ministers make good use of the work of commissions	Commissions succeed in finding useful solutions

The paradox in the Dutch public service is evident in the fact that, in somewhat abstract terms, most people and many officials oppose the forming of commissions, while in practice they make good use of them. Frequently, the same person may oppose the forming of commissions, before installing a couple of them a few days later. As an example we refer to former Minister Pechtold who in 2005 said that the installation of all of these commissions was "driving him crazycrazy". He installed at least two commissions in the period after his speech, which made headlines in several nationwide newspapers.[1]

20.4 Governing by commission in the Netherlands

In this period there has been an increase in the number of commissions formed by different administrations. Table 20.2 below illustrates that the Balkenende administrations have set up many more commissions each year then the Kok administrations that preceded them.

[1] For example, De Volkskrant (10 November 2005: 3).

Table 20.2 Total commissions in The Netherlands between 1995 and 2005, in between brackets the average number of commissions per year.[a]

Ministry	During Kok administration I and II	During Balkenende administration I and II	Total
Education, culture and science	32 (4.6)	23 (5.8)	55
Home affairs and Kingdom relations	15 (2.1)	33 (8.3)	48
Justice	26 (3.7)	20 (5.0)	46
Health and sports	22 (3.1)	12 (3.0)	34
Traffic and water	12 (1.7)	15 (3.8)	27
Economy	9 (1.3)	11 (2.8)	20
Social affairs and work	8 (1.1)	10 (2.5)	18
Finance	7 (1.0)	6 (1.5)	13
Housing, spatial planning and environment	3 (0.4)	6 (1.5)	9
Agriculture, nature and food quality	5 (0.7)	4 (1.0)	9
Foreign affairs	5 (0.7)	1 (0.3)	6
Defence	1 (0.1)	2 (0.5)	3
General affairs	1 (0.1)	1 (0.3)	2
Total	146 (20.9)	144 (36.0)	290

Source: Schulz et al. (2006: 53).

[a] The Kok administrations I and II lasted from 1994 until 2002. The Balkenende administrations I and II lasted from 2002 until 2006.

Balkenende administrations have been in office from 2002 onwards. Table 20.2 therefore clearly shows that the number of commissions set up by government on average is increasing. Of course it is not possible to detect a larger trend from these numbers. Still, it is interesting to see that apparently Balkenende administrations tend to set up more commissions while on the other hand (and maybe because of this) the public and political debate on governing by commission seems to be more present then before. In our opinion the differences between coalition partners in the administrations of Balkenende may be seen as a possible explanation for this development. The setting up of more commissions, in our opinion, shows that not all matters can be resolved easily in policy meaning that other ways of dialogue and impulse are necessary to further policy and society. Before elaborating on these new ways and the new forms of commissions these lead to we will discuss the more classical forms of commissions.

Empirical research shows that the core function of governing by commission is advisory (Schulz and Van Twist 2009). Commissions, in whatever form, always serve the ministers that set them up with recommendations. In practice this function of commissions is combined with other functions, which leads to the existence of different types of commission in public administration. These types of commission function in a more classical way with regard to incorporating outsiders in the work of government, using an *ad hoc* structure. Below we discuss several of these more classical commission types (see Schulz and Van Twist 2009).

20.4.1 Commissions of inquiry

Commissions of inquiry are usually set up to get to the bottom of matters. This generally requires them to reconstruct the facts and organise hearings to interrogate those responsible. The Hermans Commission in The Netherlands, which inquired into the policy process of automatic voting machines, after it became a widely and publicly discussed matter in 2006, is a well-known example. This commission researched recent developments and in doing so also analysed the news brought by the media. There have even been some deliberations with reporters to find out what they knew. All topics were discussed during meetings of the commission. These recent developments have even caused the tasks of the commission to be widened. Not only should it consider the parliamentary elections of November 2006 in its inquiry, it was appointed the task of inquiring into the elections for the democratic bodies of the Dutch Provinces in February 2007. The reconstruction of events, or in this case of the policy process, was discussed by the commission in a report that was presented to the State Secretary for the Ministry of the Interior in the spring of 2007.

20.4.2 Political commissions

Political commissions are often set up to influence the political and public agenda and to deal with crises. They usually have politically tricky matters as a focus of their work. The Wiegel Commission, which considered the refurbishment of national public administration in the early 1990s, may act as an example here (documented at length by Van Twist 1995: 95 and onward). This commission was set up after political and public discussion had erupted about abrogating several ministries from national government. Abrogation, and in some instances combining ministries, was a much debated and politically very problematic subject at that time. Next to other criteria, the political affiliation of the chairman and the members was a well considered factor in the setup of the commission. In the end, the commission was able to put the discussion to rest by inventing the so-called "kerndepartementen" (core ministries), which is an example of the innovation this commission contributed.

20.4.3 Evaluation commissions

Evaluation commissions in practice often have the task to reflect on acting policy, to evaluate and to regularly perform inspections. The Netherlands has known several evaluation commissions over the past years, such as the Leemhuis-Stout Commission, which evaluated the introduction of dualism to local government and the Brinkman Commission, which evaluated and inspected the state's special policy programme for major cities, known by the Dutch name "grotestedenbeleid". The latter also visited and inspected the development of specially assigned areas in the major cities, to observe the effects of the policy first hand.

20.4.4 Task forces

Although they are not called "commissions" directly, task forces often have the job to create an impulse and to act in certain matters, thereby directly making a contribution towards change. A well-known task force is the De Boer Commission, which targeted unemployment among juveniles. The commission was formed following the recognition of the threat that juvenile unemployment would pose. The commission was therefore assigned the task of facilitating the creation of new jobs in cooperation with schools and large employing firms. Thus the commission tried to give an impulse within the boundaries of policy to combat juvenile unemployment. The De Boer Commission has itself undertaken activities among other actors and was made up of individuals with considerable status within the sector. For example, the chairman of the commission is a former chairman of MKB-Nederland (the union for the interests of medium and small companies in The Netherlands).

20.5 Knowledge democracy and democratic knowledge

Regardless of the type of commission, commissions contribute to the policy-making process by developing knowledge. They play a part in the development and utilisation of knowledge in the political democracy (compare to In 't Veld 2009). Nowadays we not only have a political democracy, but we seem to be developing into a knowledge democracy in which, increasingly, democratic knowledge is being developed.

The Netherlands as a state has a tradition of consensual (neo)corporatism. The government has always deliberated and negotiated with interest groups reaching a compromise. This tradition dates back for centuries and characterises both the Dutch state and society. This tradition that incorporates the "pillarisation" and the Dutch "Polder model" has gained the country worldwide fame. Commissions fit into this tradition because they are forums for alignment, deliberation and exchanging interests and knowledge across boundaries of sectors and organisations. Commissions have existed in The Netherlands for a considerable time (Van

Schendelen 2005: 59). Still, for the past decades the societal context has changed, influencing the character of commissions.

In the period following World War II, a rather linear approach of knowledge was used. Measurement meant knowledge and knowledge meant power. Science was on a pedestal and the contributions of experts were rarely contested. Commissions as advisory bodies in their role as suppliers of knowledge had a function on the boundaries of knowledge and policy, which were hardly contested either (for example, Vernon and Mansergh 1940). This changed in the 1960s and 1970s (for example, Havelock 1968, 1971). Knowledge appeared to be controversial and could be explained in several different ways. More and more actors had knowledge that was relevant to the policy process and they often appeared to be better informed than government itself. Moreover, knowledge proved to have an expiration date, because society not only contested governmental knowledge, but also responded and even anticipated it. This made the development of society harder to fathom and the governance more complex. Consequently, in the 1980s and 1990s, the obedience of all sorts of groups in society lessened. Authority and the status of the government were no longer a given. They needed to be earned. Groups emancipated and made good use of their own sources of knowledge to influence policy-making. Following Sabatier (1988), In 't Veld and Verhey (2009) argue the position of value of both groups and individuals in the connection of knowledge and the policy process. Historically known degrees of organisation lessen and tend to become less meaningful. They give way to new (often virtual) networks. Ideas and knowledge of persons and organisations become plural and are dependent on circumstances, situations and roles of actors. The speed of knowledge transfers increases and the involvement of groups becomes more incidental, temporary and fragmented.

As a reaction to the increase of interdependence, in which positions fade and pretentions of control acquire a more relative nature, polarisation occurs. A new trend emerges of calling things by their name, accusing one another and finding exit strategies. Polarisation intensifies conflicts and disagreements that, such is the general understanding, we have to get through in order to continue. New times carry new taboos. For example, it is out of the question to doubt the judgment of the common citizen: "the word on the street". In more recent years this has developed into new concepts of knowledge. Not only are we living in a society that seems to be developing into a knowledge democracy but in this knowledge democracy (part of) the development of knowledge might be democratised. Generally, we use terms such as "the wisdom of crowds" and "crowd sourcing" (for example, Surowiecki 2004).

Not only are there societal changes within the democratisation of knowledge, which influences the future positioning of commissions, but changes are also occurring in our classical governmental culture of deliberation and negotiation. The way in which groups are being involved in the preparation and execution of policy is also changing, as are the way and timing of this involvement. This development is closely related to changes within the ratios of power.

These ratios of power in public administration are also changing. From a more classical point of view, ratios of power are distributed within the "trias politica". Meanwhile, several different powers have been added to the powers of legislation, execution and judgment. Civil servants are often considered to be the fourth power, advisors the fifth power, the media the sixth power and nowadays, organised interest groups are considered to be the seventh power. Power, like knowledge, becomes more divided between different groups. This not only changes the checks and balances in public administration; it also means there is constant movement of power between groups. Who has power and influence is no longer a given.

Based on the above, we may distinguish between three perspectives on the changing role and position of commissions. Firstly, commissions have an almost exclusive role in the development of *knowledge for policy* (until the 1960s). Secondly, they also play a part in processes of *deliberation and negotiation* (since the 1960s and 1970s) in order to also gain position in the struggle for knowledge and advice, while fitting in a third perspective of *power and checks and balances* (from the 1980s and 1990s). Now, at the beginning of a new century, commissions play a part in a society that seems to be changing into a knowledge democracy, based on all of these perspectives.

Of course it is too simple to say that all knowledge has been democratised; scientific knowledge produced by professionals still has a uniquely important place in public administration and indeed its greater use by stakeholders outside government may have strengthened this. However, knowledge, conversely, has become more widely spread across society. Its accessibility to outsiders has increased because of the positions they hold in networks. This, in some way, has emancipated them and because of the different sources of knowledge they can access different actors and parties can themselves become new and enriched sources of knowledge.

Of course it is a mistake to think that governments are at the mercy of the crowd: the manipulation of public opinion by governments and others has always played a role in politics, especially with populist governments. Still, the possibilities government has to use its influence seem to be decreasing since information can be more easily obtained through many different media. People outside the inner circles in general tend to be better informed and educated than was the case in the past. Their influence is growing because of the accessibility of knowledge, making them better equipped to play a role in society and in public processes.

20.6 On fading boundaries and boundary work

For the future positioning of commissions, this context in which, next to knowledge, deliberation and power are also of influence, is important. First of all, these perspectives influence one another and the boundaries between them are not clear cut. To some extent the boundaries are fading. Secondly, the fading of boundaries is a trend which can be witnessed in public administration on a much larger scale.

In order to determine why boundaries and boundary work are of importance to the positioning of commissions, we will first take a look at the larger trends of fading boundaries in society.

Van Montfort (2008) and Van Twist et al. (2008) distinguish between several forms of fading boundaries in public service. However, we will only give four examples here. Firstly, there is a trend of fading boundaries within policy sectors. More and more multifunctional accommodations are being built in which functions are combined, such as sports, theatre, schooling and care. Sometimes these functions are even performed consecutively in the same rooms. Secondly, the boundaries between arenas of decision-making are fading. Ownership of initiatives is equally shared at various levels, such as district, local government, state government and the European Union. Thirdly, the boundaries between public and private domain are fading, for example, identity cards for students or clients, or camera surveillance. It is often hard to determine how responsibilities are divided and where citizens can get justice. Finally, the boundaries between networks and organisations are fading. In practice we can regularly witness organisations becoming assimilated in organisation networks or network organisations.

Especially on the interface of fading boundaries (between government, industry, society and science), we believe that commissions may play an important part (conceptual bases for boundary work with Gieryn 1983, later work by Hoppe 2009). Maybe commissions will not always have their classical shapes, though contested, that we have grown so accustomed to over the past decades. Still, the essential parts of commissions will stay intact when it comes to the involvement of outsiders, on an *ad hoc* basis, to dealing with matters of public administration. Classical boundaries in public administration, between policy sectors, governmental scales and the public and private domain, are fading. This can also be seen in commissions. Here we can witness the distinctions between laymen and experts, between insiders and outsiders, between citizen and official and those between policy-makers and policy performers, to become less important. Through the introduction of citizens' assemblies, conventions, cascade commissions and policy hubs, new forms emerge of the well-known classical commissions, though the advisory core of their work still remains the same and this new repertoire will certainly not replace the old. Instead, it will increase the possibilities.

Of course, commissions will still be useful to politics and public service. However, the question is, in what way? The changes in society, outlined above, do not only influence the way knowledge is produced, and therefore the way a commission is put together and the procedure it uses. The general positioning of commissions is subject to change, as a consequence of fading boundaries.

The future positioning of commissions is determined by all three developments that we have briefly outlined previously. First of all it is a response to the general criticism on commissions and by changing names and functions new possibilities for setting up groups like commissions. Sometimes this is no more than verbal renewal, but in general the function of commissions also changes (although classical types of commissions still exist). Secondly changes in the way knowledge is produced and used has an influence on commissions. Being both developers and users of knowledge these changes also lead to new forms of commissions. Finally we argue that fading boundaries between sectors call for more arrangements between sectors, layers and parties. This also influences not only the number of commissions, but also the way commissions function. They have to incorporate fading boundaries and therefore hybrid forms of policy and other solutions into their procedure.

20.7 Future positioning of commissions

As a result of all of these developments, commissions in their form and function are changing. For example, with regard to the motives ministers have for setting up these bodies and the composition of the commission itself. We have argued in earlier research (Schulz et al. 2006: 41) that expertise and independence are crucial motives for setting up classical commissions. Considering the changes in society it is very likely that the motives such as finding support and creating opportunity for implementation will become more important in the future. In very much the same way we have shown from empirical research that expertise and experience are the most important criteria for selecting members into classical commissions (this is shown in Figure 20.1 below). It is very likely that other criteria will become more important when it comes to selecting members for new forms of commissions. Criteria, like representativeness and authority, may just as well become of greater importance.

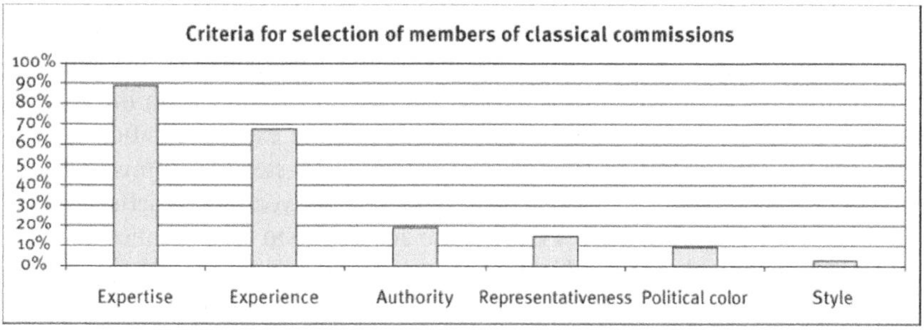

Fig. 20.1 Criteria for selecting members of classical commissions (source: Schulz et al. 2006: 80).

Fitting into the possibility of a future knowledge democracy, we may nowadays witness, in public administration, the existence of new variations of commissions on the interface of government, society, industry and science. Analogical to the abovementioned types of commissions, tasks and procedures of these new commissions are interpreted differently.

The Figure 20.2 below presents an overview of the shift from classical commission types to different and newer variations (derived from Schulz and Van Twist 2009).

Fig. 20.2 Classical and new types of commissions.

20.7.1 Towards conventions and network consultations

In public administration, conventions and network consultation form a variation on the more commonly seen political commissions. Support amongst various groups of experts is becoming more important to the authority of knowledge and information, thereby creating more value to the political policy process. A good example of this is the National Convention in The Netherlands, which advised on several questions on the confidence of citizens in their government. The Convention was made up of a core of members and was surrounded by a larger ring of experts and advisors, who officially had the task of debating with the core members. It is a characteristic of this new variation in the experimentation with commissions that by organising rings of experts around a steady commission core efforts are being made to broaden and bind the network of experts around the commission, by making (more) knowledge accessible to the commission. The debate on the knowledge created in the commission is hereby moved closer in time. Usually the debate takes place once the work of commissions is already finished and positions have been taken. Another characteristic is that, by posting and sharing information through Internet consultations and cooperation, a "living document" is being created, similar to the way a wiki functions, to hold the knowledge acquired by the commission.

20.7.2 Towards citizens' assemblies

Citizens' assemblies are seen as a variation on the well-known commissions of inquiry in public administration. What knowledge is, is no longer based on facts alone or on the more or less authoritative meaning given to knowledge by experts, but on the authoritative meaning given to facts by laymen. A good example of the process is the Citizens' Assembly on the electoral system, though it has, through no fault of its own, had no effect on public administration whatsoever. In this case, 140 citizens, reflecting the current composition of the Dutch population, jointly researched how the Dutch electoral system should function in the future. A characteristic of this new variation in the experimentation with commissions is that it is not made up by expert insiders, but rather by a (preferably large) group of outside ordinary citizens. In the currently accepted procedure of citizens' assemblies like this one, these outsiders are first brought up to speed in their knowledge levels, concerning the theme at hand. They then discuss and advise by covering different angles from their rather unbiased points of view.

20.7.3 Towards policy hubs

Also with regards to more classical evaluation commissions, new variations occur in public administration. In particular the more reflexive components of evaluation commissions may be seen in these new interpretations. Essentially, policy hubs develop knowledge, which is of value to participants from and on the interface of government, industry, society and science. The concept of hubs is derived from "hubs and spokes" theories on networks. Hubs are central nodes in networks. Participants come from all of these and other groups. Hubs, already a well-known phenomenon in trade and industry, will be initiated more often by government in the future. Starting in 2009 on the Amsterdam "Zuidas", a government initiated hub will work on knowledge creation and the introduction of electric transportation in business parks like Amsterdam "Zuidas". Several hubs on water policy and diabetes already exist in The Netherlands. Though government participates in these hubs that were set up on the initiative of the private sector. Hubs are meant to establish connections across organisational boundaries. In this regard it is essential that hubs redefine boundaries, in order to create, for example, smooth transitions between the evaluation, policy preparation and policy execution phases. Also with regard to the boundaries between inside and outside government, some extent of fading can be seen in hubs. The policy hub is in the form of a network, in which selective activation of experts and supporting parties crosses boundaries of governmental and even private organisations.

20.7.4 Towards cascade commissions

Finally we will discuss the so-called cascade commissions as a development of more action-oriented commissions such as task forces. Cascade commissions are commissions that consist of (sub)commissions. In other words, the commission itself forms other commissions or workgroups and develops a network system that reaches into the capillaries of government, society, industry and science, in order to contribute to the implementation of policy in countless organisations. The Innovation Platform, which has been in action for several years in The Netherlands, may serve as an example here. Next to this central platform for innovation, we now know of several secondary platforms, such as the Innovation Platform for the district of Twente and the Health Care Innovation Platform. A characteristic of this variation on commissions in a knowledge democracy is the direct influence these commissions have on policy implementation. Support from all sort of groups and actors, as well as participation in (sub)commissions, enlarges the action orientation of these commissions. Through ongoing development of new working groups, (sub)commissions and think-tanks, in addition to existing instruments, new groups and individuals are given a place and position within the system of the commission. Thus, cascade commissions are able to reach into the capillaries of society. In order to be successful, these cascade commissions generally need to define their approach. Commissions which only develop knowledge or advise government, will have different effects than commissions which are able to influence appropriation of funds.

Of course, the question is whether these new forms add up to something. They can easily be seen as symbolic politics at its most ineffective or as an expression of verbal renewal. Most of the new types of commissions can (and in practice will) be seen as "window dressing politics", as opposed to more classical Dutch councils like the Board of Social Economics (the SER) who still wield the old corporatist power. Comments like these might occur though in our opinion they do not do justice to these new types of commissions. It is very well possible that these new types develop into something more than just interesting experiments of innovative governance. This, of course, is a matter of trial and error to find fitting arrangements. If commissions change in line with societal developments as we suggest and are able to determine from description and analysis of the last several decades, then the emergence of a knowledge democracy can and will not be without consequence for the most classical way of governance in our country: the commission. Then in the future we will see government setting up more task forces, citizens' assemblies, cascade commissions and hubs. Maybe these new forms of commissions will not (immediately) replace the more classical forms of commissions and councils but they will be a serious supplement to these classical forms. Furthermore, with new and further changes in society new forms of commissions will keep emerging although only the future will tell us how far all of these changes will go.

20.8 Conclusion and discussion

Views on commissions are divergent. Positive and negative interpretations can both be true at the same time. Moreover, a rather strange tension exists between principle and practice when it comes to commissions. Or better said, between the general view of commissions and the way we actually use them. Commissions will always be around and the core of their work is clear and does not change. This core deals with advice from small groups, which are gathered on an *ad hoc* basis to achieve a breakthrough. Still on the edge of the more classical commission types is the core of things to come, such as citizens' assemblies, which allow for the participation of outsiders, giving meaning to the wisdom of crowds, or cascade commissions, which not only advise on matters, but also play a part in the enactment of policies.

At the same time, the development of society and public administration is on the one hand marked by fading boundaries, for example between policy sectors and public and private domains, leading to all sorts of temporary alliances and innovations, and on the other hand by intriguing questions when it comes to responsibilities. This can also be seen with commissions. They function on the interface between government, society, industry and science as an institutionalised form, and simultaneously the formation of commissions leads to all sorts of questions regarding political responsibilities.

The development and existence of new variations of commissions builds on more classically known patterns, creating the opportunity to respond to *ad hoc* questions with flexible structures. This flexibility is, at the same time, complicated. At the expense of flexibility, more classical values in public service may not be neglected, such as perseverance, security and trustworthiness. For commissions in a future knowledge democracy, the challenge is to find the balance between opposing values on the interface of organised relationships. In recognising this we may overcome the ambiguity and paradoxical logic, which is still the dominant view of commissions today.

In overseeing the four different future types of commissions it becomes clear that the tradition of neo-corporatism is still very much alive in the Netherlands. Cascade commissions, policy hubs, citizens' assemblies and conventions all share one and the same factor. They all contribute to the policy process by facilitating debate, consensus, compromise and ultimately deliberation. Whereas neo-corporatist views are based on deliberation with a limited selection of recognised interest groups, these new forms of deliberation level the playing field for different organisations and actors to participate, thus opening more arenas for organisations and interest groups of all sorts and sizes to become part of the policy-making process.

21 Knowledge exchange through online political networks

Chris Aalberts and Maurits Kreijveld

Abstract

Web 2.0 offers citizens and politicians new opportunities for exchanging information and knowledge. For citizens it has become much easier to inform politicians about their wishes, questions, complaints and ideas, while it has also become easier for politicians to reach their constituents. Despite these new opportunities, the extent to which Web 2.0 is actually used for knowledge sharing is unclear, as is the question of what kind of knowledge is shared with whom. In this chapter, we look at the contribution of the Dutch online social network Hyves to knowledge exchange. Twelve Hyves profile pages initiated by politicians and nine initiated by citizens were analysed. Our analysis shows that in practice interaction between initiators and members of Hyves pages remains limited and can be characterised as very informal. Although the primary purpose of these networks appears to be to give citizens an opportunity to voice their opinions, in a large majority of the cases analysed there was no interaction, dialogue or knowledge exchange.

21.1 Introduction

Over the past decade, the internet has developed into a social web. Whereas traditional media are characterised by one-way communications between the sender and receiver of information, the social web has made it possible for everyone to send and receive information. Citizens are increasingly using the web to create and exchange knowledge and information. Examples include the online encyclopaedia Wikipedia, to which anyone who wants to can contribute; YouTube, a website where people can upload their own videos; the micro-blogging service Twitter, where people can tell other people what they are doing and discuss topics of interest, and social networks such as MySpace, LinkedIn, Facebook and Hyves, where members can create their own personal pages and fill them with pictures, videos and stories.

Dutch politicians as well as citizens are experimenting more and more with the opportunities that Web 2.0 offers. An independent Member of Parliament wanting

R.J. in 't Veld (ed.), *Knowledge Democracy*, DOI 10.1007/978-3-642-11381-9_21,

to establish her own party asked her supporters to co-write her political manifesto through a wiki, while several political parties have their own channel on YouTube to showcase party events, some politicians, including the Minister of Foreign Affairs, are active on Twitter and many politicians have profile pages on social networking sites. A number of citizens' movements, societal organisations and protest groups have also discovered Web 2.0 and have their own pages on social networks, post videos on YouTube and blog about current affairs. In these ways, Web 2.0 is enabling politicians and citizens to get in touch with each other more easily and exchange knowledge and information. A relevant question, however, is how effective this knowledge exchange is and what the value of these experiments is.

ICT experts such as Frissen (2008) and Harfoush (2009) consider Barack Obama's campaign for the US presidential elections in 2008 to be one of the most successful examples of the use of Web 2.0 in politics. Obama used a combination of Web 2.0 applications, including social networks (Facebook), instant messaging platforms and YouTube, and brought these applications together on his own social network: MyBarackObama.com. Experts claim these applications not only helped Obama to reach his supporters, but also activated those supporters to spread his message and raise new funds. Web 2.0 is said to have mobilised the masses to create an impressive result. In other words, the largest campaign fund raised in history and a landslide victory. In the eyes of these experts, Obama is an inspiring example of how Web 2.0 can engage citizens in politics and lead to greater exchange of knowledge between politicians and citizens. But these positive evaluations also raise important questions. Was Obama's success really dependent on his use of Web 2.0, or were other factors equally important for the outcome of the elections? What effect does knowledge and information exchange through Web 2.0 have on politics? Will it close a gap? What kind of interaction is needed? Is an example such as Obama's relevant to the Dutch situation, with its coalitions and the smaller role played by fundraising? There has so far been little academic research into these questions.

The belief that Web 2.0 will have a major impact seems to contradict the Dutch political reality. According to De Beus (2001) and Aalberts (2006), the Netherlands has developed into an audience democracy, where a majority of citizens are politically inactive and vote only when elections are held. They follow politics through the media and have no direct contact or interaction with their political representatives. This audience democracy makes politics into a profession of a small group of experts. And it seems unlikely that the new technical opportunities created by Web 2.0 will change this. Research also shows that politicians do not currently use the internet as a medium to interact very interactively: most political parties' websites very much resemble printed, offline folders: although they provide citizens with lots of information, they offer very few opportunities for interaction. Most websites provide information that was already available offline. Only a small minority of these websites use the potential of new applications that could result in interaction and encourage knowledge exchange (Gibson et al. 2003, Jackson N. 2007, Jackson N. and Lilleker 2004, Schneider and Foot 2006). There is not much information available from research into websites of protest groups and citizens' movements, and we are not aware of any examples of such groups that have established a prominent role in the political debate through the internet. In general, it seems highly unlikely that Web 2.0 will have any great impact on Dutch politics.

In the exploratory research presented in this chapter, we made an inventory of how Dutch citizens use Web 2.0 at present and whether they use it to exchange knowledge and information with politicians and other citizens. We looked at the Dutch social network Hyves, which is by far the most prominent online social network in the Netherlands. More than half the Dutch population now has a profile on Hyves, which can be seen as the Dutch equivalent of Facebook or MySpace. Many politicians also have a profile on Hyves, as do many protest groups and other citizens' initiatives. Hyves integrates functions: blogging, messaging, uploading movies and pictures. In theory, this kind of social network can create new forms of interaction between politicians and citizens. Politicians are no longer dependent on news media alone to create their supporter base. Instead they can interact with these supporters directly through Hyves, receive direct feedback on their work and get input for new policy measures. Citizens, too, are no longer dependent on the work of journalists: they can spread the word about their cause themselves online, create a group of supporters and catch the attention of politicians. Online social networks have made all these forms of interaction easier than ever. But are these networks really used in these ways? What kind of knowledge exchange takes place on online social networks such as Hyves?

21.2 Method

The research question for this chapter concerned the role that social networks play in the exchange of knowledge between politicians and citizens, and among groups of citizens? This study analysed two types of political Hyves pages, some initiated by citizens and some by politicians.

Nine of these profile pages were started by citizens and focused on a specific political issue. Some concerned topics that were in the news during the research, for example the law requiring secondary school children in the Netherlands to receive at least 1,040 h of education a year. Many young people were against this law because they believed it would have an adverse impact on the quality of their education. Another hyve was about hallucinogenic drugs derived from "magic mushrooms" and was started in response to the Dutch government's plan in 2008 to ban these types of drugs. Other hyves analysed discussed a law designed to reduce global warming, earlier closing hours for cafes, abortion, parents who refused to pay child maintenance, animal testing and a law banning squatters. Some hyves were created by organisations in civil society, such as the climate-hyve initiated by a youth environmental organisation, while another was of a more playful nature: a group of students protesting that they had to send in their photographs several times in order to get a new electronic public transport card.

Twelve Dutch politicians' hyves were analysed: six of leaders of a parliamentary party (Rita Verdonk, Geert Wilders, Mark Rutte, Femke Halsema, Alexander Pechtold and Marianne Thieme), five of Members of Parliament (Boris van der Ham, Tofik Dibi, Mei Li Vos, Fatma Koser-Kaya and Hero Brinkman) and one of a minister (André Rouvoet).

All the citizens' groups and politicians mentioned were asked by e-mail about their reasons for starting their hyves. Six of the nine citizens' groups contacted responded to our e-mail, while the initiators of the hyves on abortion, drugs and 1,040 school hours did not reply. The politicians were contacted by e-mail and telephone. Despite several attempts, five of them (Geert Wilders, André Rouvoet, Femke Halsema, Fatma Koser-Kaya and Tofik Dibi) could not be contacted. On four occasions we had an interview with the politician, while on three occasions it was with one of their employees. The questions asked in all the interviews were why they had started their hyve, what information they put on it and why and whether they thought there was an exchange of knowledge with other relevant people.

The content on all the hyves was analysed, as were the most important applications available: blogging (such as discussions and articles that others can comment on) and the ability to upload pictures and videos. In the case of the citizens' hyves, we also checked whether there was a calendar of events related to the cause, and online polls that would enable members to voice their opinions. In the case of the politicians' hyves, we looked at the advice they gave to their members. To assess the extent of interaction on these hyves, we counted the number of members in May 2009. In the case of the politicians' hyves, we also counted how many messages ("krabbels") were posted on these hyves, how many short funny messages ("tikken") were posted and how many times members reported that they had spotted the politician in real life.

We then contacted the hyves members by sending them a personal message. We kept asking new members until we had eighteen respondents for each hyve. The total response from members of the citizens' hyves was 23%, while the score for the politicians' hyves was 21%. For each hyve, we approached at least five members who were active on the hyve. In other words, members who had posted at least one message. In addition, we tried to reach at least five members who had never posted a message. In this way, we sought to reach a range of active and non-active members. We asked these members why they became a member of the hyve, what they did most frequently on it and what significance it had for them. In this way we gained insight into their reasons for becoming a member and into how Hyves could be relevant for exchanging knowledge with politicians and other citizens.

21.3 Results: citizens' hyves

The contents of the citizens' hyves were analysed on 3 May 2009. We looked at the applications used and the frequency of their use. Table 21.1 shows the amount of content for each application. There are great differences between the hyves in terms of the content offered and the frequency of their use. In some cases, there seems to be a considerable amount of knowledge and information exchange, while in other cases there is almost none.

Table 21.1 Content and members of citizens' hyves.

Hyve	Established	Blogs	Videos	Pictures	Calendar items	Polls	Members
1,040 h	20-11-2007	Unknown	0	87	29	127	55,776
Animal testing	02-03-2006	61	31	266	1	29	13,040
Abortion	23-12-2006	34	18	39	0	11	2,113
Child maintenance	20-03-2008	46	9	16	0	1	1,240
Pictures	22-04-2008	0	4	3	0	3	987
Squatters	29-07-2008	20	4	39	1	8	1,027
Climate	12-12-2007	77	3	62	1	2	616
Drugs	13-10-2007	5	3	4	0	0	387
Cafes	14-12-2007	0	0	0	0	0	103

Our research found that many initiators had been involved in the topic of their hyve for years. They wanted to draw more attention to their cause and had a clear view about how the issue should be approached. Their aim was to voice their opinions and create awareness among citizens. In the case, for example, of the hyve about animal testing, the aim was to make other citizens aware of the initiator's view that animal testing was unethical and a form of animal maltreatment and that measures should be taken. The initiators of the hyve on child maintenance payments sought to draw more attention to the problem caused by some divorced fathers' refusal to pay their ex-wives maintenance for their children. For all these groups, Hyves was a way of getting attention for their goals and arguments.

In most cases the initiators also had a second goal: they wanted to raise more political attention for and discussion about their cause. They believed this would create more support for their cause and so tried to limit the discussion on their hyve: the initiators of the climate change hyve, for example, wanted to discuss what kind of law should be used to protect the climate, not whether such a law was needed at all. Most of the initiators did not have any expectations of what would happen after they started the hyve. Most of them were satisfied because they got more members than expected, had lively discussions or received positive reactions. In general, they got fewer negative reactions than expected. They did not spread the word about their hyve because they were afraid that people would consider it to be spam. They preferred people to invite others to join. In some cases, this did not happen and so the hyve did not attract many members, while in other cases the hyve attracted far more members than the initiator had ever imagined, and this seemed to have happened "automatically".

Table 21.1 also shows the number of members that these hyves have. The hyve on 1,040 h in secondary education and the animal tests-hyve had more members than all the other hyves put together. Just like the initiators, many members had a personal link with the topic of the Hyve, as in the case of the magic mushrooms-hyve, where most members used these drugs themselves. Most members of the abortion-hyve were women with personal experience of abortion. But the degree of engagement was not always strong and personal: some members, for example, did not have personal experience of abortion or child maintenance problems, but knew someone who did. In some cases the engagement was even less strong, for example in the case of the new public transport card. Almost all the members had a certain political interest, but only some were involved in political activities. These members were active in political movements or political parties striving for the same goal as the hyve, although often there was no formal connection between the two.

More than 75% of the members were "sleeping" members and claimed they never visited the hyve. A majority of our respondents had posted no more than one message on the hyve, while a majority of the total population on the hyve had never even posted one message. This meant our respondents were slightly more active than the total population on the hyves, although calling this behaviour "active" would be misleading. The most important "activity" of these members was enrolling as a member, even in the case of those with a strong personal connection to the subject of the hyve, such as women whose former husbands refused to pay maintenance for their children. The limited activity on these hyves was all the more surprising, given that many members said that they used the Hyves medium very often. Most of their activity would appear to be on other hyves. Generally, members discovered the hyve through their other contacts on Hyves. Only a minority explicitly searched for a hyve about the particular topic. For a majority, their interest in the topic was not great enough to take such initiative: it was the cause that interested them, not the hyve about the cause.

Some hyves members had personal reasons for becoming a member. However this was only the case in a few hyves, such as the hyves on maintenance payments and abortion. These hyves had developed into online meeting places where people exchanged their experience and gave each other advice on maintenance payments and abortion. These hyves did not provide much formal information about the topics: our interviews found that traditional media were a more important means of informing members about legislation and other regulations. Nevertheless, the hyves were an important source of information about personal stories and experience that could not be found in the traditional media. Members could speak to fellow-sufferers, exchange experience, give advice and offer support. For these members it was the exchange of experience that was the most important aspect.

The members of the hyves on abortion and child maintenance payments were also seeking to change public policies. This goal was shared by many members of all the hyves in this study. Members who visited the hyve to discuss the particular topic were often disappointed by the quality of the debate, mainly because there was often very little variation in the opinions of the people wanting to discuss these issues: in most cases they simply agreed with each other. This made it difficult to engage in a meaningful debate about the issue because members could not influence each other's views. They became a member to make a political statement and to show others what they thought about the cause. According to many members, Hyves was the only way in which citizens could show other people what they thought about such issues and where they could make themselves heard. Attention from the mass media should lead to a further spreading of the message and thus result in more members of the hyve and more attention for the topic in the political arena. Members were sceptical, however, about whether more people would actually be reached: they thought that people would not become a member of a hyve on a topic in which they had no strong interest and so concluded that the hyve was unlikely to have much effect.

21.4 Results: politicians' hyves

The politicians' hyves were also analysed on 3 May 2009. We analysed which applications these politicians used and how frequently they were used. Table 21.2 gives an overview of the content. All the data are from 3 May, except the blogs. Some politicians have so many blogs on their hyves that only the April 2009 blogs were included.

Table 21.2 Content and interaction on politicians' hyves.

Politician	*Established*	*Blogs*	*Videos*	*Pictures*	*Tips*
Verdonk	08-10-2006	23	10	82	3
Wilders	14-02-2007	4	0	0	0
Halsema	17-10-2006	1	10	6	4
Rutte	02-10-2006	3	13	111	14
Rouvoet	16-10-2006	8	9	9	0
Pechtold	02-04-2006	34	5	18	1
Thieme	13-10-2006	12	2	23	0
Van der Ham	21-02-2006	6	0	290	1
Dibi	15-10-2006	1	0	0	1
Vos	03-02-2005	12	0	7	0
Koser Kaya	22-02-2006	2	3	35	5
Brinkman	25-07-2008	1	2	1	0
Verdonk	68,009	Unknown	2,704	108	Verdonk
Wilders	67,700	Unknown	5,108	126	Wilders
Halsema	16,306	577	427	39	Halsema
Rutte	11,713	58	280	52	Rutte
Rouvoet	8,921	33	Unknown	41	Rouvoet

Politician	*Members*	*Messages*	*Short messages*	*Spotted*
Pechtold	4,971	243	92	6
Thieme	4,448	91	177	9
Van der Ham	4,139	22	51	18
Dibi	2,564	48	138	10
Vos	2,106	37	67	8
Koser Kaya	1,150	15	25	3
Brinkman	465	123	46	1

There were major differences in the information offered on the hyves. Although all the politicians used the blog application, the numbers are sometimes misleading because the interviews revealed that the politicians who seemed to be the most frequent bloggers did not write the blogs themselves and simply posted general news items as blogs. The use of other applications on Hyves was less frequent. Only three politicians posted high numbers of pictures on their profiles, mostly of political meetings where they appeared. Tips and videos were also scarce. Tips often focused on politicians' own books and websites. Blogs would seem to be the most important application: all the politicians used this application and posted new content there on a more or less regular basis.

The interviews showed that politicians made a profile on Hyves because they wanted to bridge the gap between citizens and politics. This was their main and often only motive. They believed that Hyves would enable them to reach target groups other than those who visited the party website or went to political meetings. Hyves is a quick and direct way of communicating with citizens because the medium is easy to use. One politician did not really have much of a choice: all her colleagues had started a profile on Hyves and so she felt obliged to do the same. Another politician already had a profile before she became a Member of Parliament. Although she still saw it as a network of her friends, it now also included people she knew only through Hyves. In some cases, politicians' staff made the updates on Hyves, often because the politician did not have enough time to update it. Citizens sending a message to a politician did not always get an answer. If they simply expressed support, they would not get a reply, whereas citizens asking questions about policy issues or coming up with suggestions did get an answer most of the time. Some of the politicians mentioned that once or twice they had used these suggestions in political debates.

Table 21.2 shows substantial differences in the number of members of these hyves, with well-known, right-wing politicians (Rita Verdonk and Geert Wilders) having the largest number of members. Other prominent politicians' hyves have fewer members. The forms of interaction were counted on 3 May 2009. Because of the large numbers of messages, only the messages sent in April 2009 were included. It appears that the more members politicians' hyves have, the more messages they receive. The number of messages for Femke Halsema, however, is misleading because on 25 April she received 345 messages wishing her a happy birthday.

Many Hyves members analysed were politically active and some even had responsibilities in politics, usually in local politics, while others were planning to become politically active. Although many members sympathised with the politician's party, many of them also sympathised with other parties. The members of a left-wing liberal politician's hyve, for example, also included people with right-wing, Christian Democratic and Social Democratic sympathies. These citizens were often members of more than one politician's hyve, with most of these politicians having similar ideologies. However, there were two hyves whose members were different from this general profile. The members of the hyve created by the leader of the animal rights party did not want to be politically active, but simply wanted to achieve better treatment of animals, while the members of the right-wing Geert Wilders' hyve described themselves as politically inactive.

The members did not remember how they discovered the hyve that they are a member of. Either they did not have a specific reason for joining or they had forgotten it. Some members said that they "just did it" or that it was out of curiosity. Many members never used or visited these hyves. Their limited use of these hyves made it difficult for these members to give an opinion on them. These answers point to a lack of engagement among a majority of the members. According to these members, the hyves did not produce any results, but this was not considered a problem because they did not invest any significant amounts of time in them. They thought it was positive that a politician could be found on Hyves because it showed that the politician was trying to keep in touch with citizens. In addition, the hyves were seen as a good way of attracting young people into politics. The appreciation for the hyves was related to the content found on the page: politicians who did not regularly post new content on their hyve were criticised, while politicians who posted content were appreciated. There seemed to be no other criteria for evaluating their use of Hyves.

The members' reactions showed that there were three reasons for becoming a member. Firstly if you were looking for information about politicians and their views and current activities? Respondents said that they sometimes read the blogs, watched a video or followed the news. In this way, they got an idea of what the politician stood for. Some mentioned that it was an advantage that the information came directly from the politician and not from the media or from journalists. What was more important was what other citizens thought about politics. Members were interested in messages from other citizens because they showed what these citizens thought about political issues. Some members complained that there was not enough information or alternatively too much nonsense information on the hyve. Members said that the hyve did not have an effect on their admiration of the politician: they already admired the politician before they became a member. The only difference was that they now got a more informed image of the politician than before.

A second reason for joining was that members could send messages to their politician. Although a majority of members had never sent a message, a majority of the respondents had. Nevertheless, interaction remained limited. The distinction between "active" and "inactive" members is difficult because more than half had only sent a message once. Around half of the members sent a politician a public message, with only a minority sending a private one. Some of these messages lacked content: citizens wishing politicians a happy birthday or good luck in the elections or something similar. Other messages were about policy issues, asking questions or giving advice. These messages were about issues close to the respondents' everyday life, such as problems in their neighbourhood. These members did not expect a reply. They would prefer interaction, but did not think it was always necessary. They believed that politicians did not have enough time for Hyves and said they understood this. They thought that the politicians read the messages and sometimes acted on them. Only a small group said that if politicians were on an interactive forum, they should also interact with the members. The fact that politicians were on Hyves obliged them to respond to citizens' messages. These members were disappointed when they did not get a message in reply.

A third reason for becoming a member was to show support to others. This was mostly a matter of agreeing with the policies advocated by the politician's political party or with the ideas of the politician as an individual. Sometimes, members agreed only with specific policy issues that the politician had raised in the past. Some opponents of abortion, for example, felt close to the Christian Conservatives, but did not have detailed views on all the policy issues that party advocates. Their virtual membership served as a public display of support, showing that the politician and the politician's ideas had support among citizens. This kind of virtual support is not superficial because members had clear preferences as to which politicians should get their support and which should not.

21.5 Conclusion

Internet has become a social web where citizens can produce their own content and information and exchange it with others, allowing for a two-way exchange of knowledge between citizens and politicians. Barack Obama's campaign showed that using Web 2.0 could be a highly successful way of mobilising citizens into campaigning. These ideas, however, seem to contradict trends in Dutch politics, where citizens are relatively passive and the internet is used more for broadcasting information than for building relationships between citizens and politicians. Politicians are increasingly present on online social networks, and groups of citizens wanting more political attention for their causes have also discovered these social networks. The question arises as to what role social networks play in the exchange of knowledge between politicians and citizens, and among groups of citizens? This question was answered on the basis of an analysis of 21 political hyves: nine initiated by citizens and twelve by politicians.

This exploratory study showed that the initiators of political hyves found the exchange of knowledge and information important. This was particularly true in the case of citizens who initiated a political hyve: their ambition was to make citizens and politicians more aware of their cause and they saw Hyves as a good way of doing this. To them, their hyve was not only about sending out information about the cause, but also about exchanging political views. Politicians had different intentions: they wanted to bridge the gap between politics and citizens, but knowledge and information exchange played a small role on their hyves. These politicians said that – to them – their presence on Hyves was designed to show that they took citizens seriously. However, there were no interactive discussions on their hyves, while the exchange of views was also very limited: citizens sometimes sent messages to politicians, but these messages were mostly personal and informal and not about political content. In some cases citizens did not get an answer. Politicians were not so focused on interaction with citizens as we had expected.

The members of the citizens' hyves considered it important to spread information about and create more awareness of their causes. In this way, their ideas were largely the same as those of the initiators. However, the members played only a limited role; their prime motivation was to show the world around them that they thought the issue to be important. Their role was largely passive and generally involved not much more than adding a hyve to their own profile. The same held true for members of the politicians' hyves: these members added a politician's hyve to their profile in order to make a statement, but this was their only activity. Only in a very few cases did citizens look for information on the hyve, and mainly they looked at content posted by other citizens rather than information posted by the politician. Members did not think that they had a personal role in the discussions on the site and saw little need for discussions as most members shared the same opinions. In some cases there were discussions, but these mostly involved personal advice on specific issues from the everyday life of a member rather than a political discussion about public policy or a different view on the subject. From this it can be concluded that Hyves is not used as a platform for exchanging knowledge.

This study found that citizens and politicians used Hyves largely as a medium for sending messages, not for interaction or knowledge exchange. This is consistent with earlier findings that politicians used their websites purely as a tool for spreading information (Gibson et al. 2003, Jackson N. 2007, Jackson N. and Lilleker 2004, Schneider and Foot 2006). In theory, social networks provide a great platform for knowledge exchange and interaction among citizens and between politicians and citizens, as examples such as Wikipedia and the Obama campaign show. But in practice this does not happen automatically. When it is left to non-professional citizens and individual politicians, the quality of the discussions and interaction is shown to be very limited. These communications can be characterised as informal "small talk". Nevertheless, they seem to meet a need among citizens to feel a link with politicians and to support political causes and the people striving to achieve them. More is needed, however, for a knowledge democracy to become reality. We can see from Obama and other examples that online discussions need active stimulation, focus and moderation. These conditions are not met in the variety of political hyves analysed in this study. This raises the question of whether this lack of knowledge exchange is dependent on the specific platform or the applications used, or whether it is dependent on cultural factors.

22 Designing the conditions for an innovation system for sustainable development in a knowledge democracy

Bert de Wit

Abstract

Sustainable development is a societal goal, requiring innovations in products, services and thinking. What are the requirements for an innovation system that produces more sustainable products and services? What elements should be taken into consideration when analysing a SD innovation system? A combination of elements known to be important for SD research and for innovation at the micro level can serve as an analytical framework. Elements of this framework can also be used for designing the conditions for SD innovation. Analysis of sector innovation systems shows governance aspects are very important too in stimulating or blocking innovation for sustainable development. The institutional embedding of SD research and innovations in the present science system is problematic. From a point of view of knowledge democracy, a lot has to be done to get "people" (one of the three Ps) more into the SD innovation system. So-called "hybrid spaces" (for interaction between scientists, businessmen and other stakeholders) should be an important constituent part of the science and innovation system, allowing more public participation in research into complex societal problems as sustainable development is.

22.1 Introduction

The central question in this chapter is: what is the relation between research for sustainable development and innovations to enable a more sustainable development? (SD). What conditions should be fulfilled to optimise the generation of SD innovations?

To answer these questions, an analysis is needed of innovation processes, research and knowledge use in producing more sustainable solutions.

Some decisions have to be taken regarding the appropriate level of such an analysis and the most appropriate theoretical model:

R.J. in 't Veld (ed.), *Knowledge Democracy*, DOI 10.1007/978-3-642-11381-9_22,

- first: at what level will the analysis be focused. At the micro level of a company or a business line, at the meso level of a region or a sector or the macro level of countries?
- secondly: what kind of "innovation model" is thought to be most appropriate to understand what happens in practice?

22.1.1 What aggregation level seems most appropriate for analysing an SD innovation system?

To decide which level should be taken into consideration, a reflection on the concept of sustainable development can be of help. Some SD scientists think sustainability should be considered as a place-based and time bound quality. As Jäger (2008) puts it, "some of the most important interactions in socio-ecological systems will occur in particular places (or particular enterprises). Science and technology for sustainable development (SD) therefore need be 'place-based', or 'enterprise-based', embedded in the particular characteristics of distinct locations or contexts".

There are several reasons for taking this place- or enterprise-based character of sustainable development serious, not only because several scientists emphasise it, but also because studies of regional so-called "transition processes" (Rathenau-Institute 2009) show these processes may have quite different outcomes, depending on the regional characteristics, the companies and people involved. Even for companies in the same sector the results of innovation for sustainable development may be quite different, depending on the ambition level of the people involved and the context. What should be considered sustainable and what not, is often difficult to determine. Some alternatives may be clearly more sustainable than others, but there is also a large "grey zone". "What people regard as more sustainable, depends on their assumptions and information. One cannot say for example that an electric car in general is more sustainable than a petrol fuelled car. The emissions for driving such a car may be quite different in different places in the world. Values are often not explicitly stated. These can only be revealed by discussions with a lot of stakeholders, including NGOs. Its their opinion we want to hear"[1] The subjective nature of choices and decisions about sustainable alternatives has been emphasised by the Dutch Scientific Council for Government Policy in the Netherlands (WRR 1994). Sustainable development cannot be objectively determined as it includes normative decisions about risks and uncertainties. This idea is in line with an early report of RMNO on sustainable development, analysing the relative and normative character of the concept of sustainable development (RMNO 1990).

That is why it is wise to start from the micro level for an analysis of innovation

[1] BASF spokesman Hanefeld during the EU conference on SD and Research, May 28 2009, Brussels.

for sustainability. An innovation system at this level consists of the companies involved, with their partners, chain dependencies and relations with the outside world.[2]

22.1.2 Why the linear innovation model will not do

The second point is what theoretical model is most appropriate for analysing innovation for sustainable development. The so-called linear innovation model still dominates thinking in policy and science. The basic idea behind this model is that innovation is the result from a linear process. This process starts from the results of fundamental research that, by way of applied research and demonstration projects, are transformed in innovative products and services, ready for market introduction. Supporters of the linear innovation model think more funding of basic research will result in more innovation ("without knowledge no innovation"). Innovation is thought of as a supply driven process, originating from scientific discoveries in universities.

There are several reasons why this model will not do for an analysis of SD innovation systems. First of all, there is overwhelming empirical evidence that the model simply is not in accordance with what innovation researchers find. Time and again experience has shown that where the demand is weak, excellent supply never succeeded in stimulating the demand side. "Basic science" has proven to be insufficient "to deliver the goods", that is to produce innovations (see Boulton and Colin-Lucas 2009). The dominance of the linear innovation model explains why there is a wide spread myth that the primary deficit in innovation is caused by a failing utilisation of research findings and that therefore, universities should become more proactive. This idea still can be found in policy documents, for example documents of the European Commission, stating that innovation will come from universities as the cradle of fundamental research. Generally speaking, Boulton and Colin-Lucas pose that universities are not the places where innovation roots. They emphasise innovation is primarily a process of business engagement with markets, in which universities only play a minor role. Universities can contribute to a good environment for innovations, for example by creating spin-out activities.

A second reason why the linear model is not adequate for analysing SD innovation systems is that one can only decide what alternative is more sustainable than another by integrating knowledge from various sources; knowledge from the social and natural sciences, but also knowledge from stakeholders and local people. Integration of knowledge is something the linear model does not take into account. It is based on the predominant disciplinary division of scientific research. The

[2] WRR (2008) defines an innovation system as: a system of knowledge production and utilisation, entrepreneurship, commercialisation (incl. design), organisation (incl. cooperation), and the distribution of new knowledge and skills.

social embedding of technological research for example is still often thought of as an "add on" and not as a design requirement (Jeeninga 2008).

A third reason for the inadequacy of the linear model is the fact that knowledge in the present era is more and more transgressive (Nowotny et al. 2001), transcending the limits of the domain in which it has been produced. That is why one can expect new kinds of interactions and combinations of knowledge to become more and more important for producing innovations. Quite a lot of innovations have been prompted by people that did not have any sector specific knowledge (Krozer 2008). That is an important point too when considering the concept of knowledge democracy.

So, innovation in reality depends on interaction and collaboration of different actors, not only scientists, but also lay men and people who have a stake in innovation processes. As Ørstavik (2006) states, it is not easy to orchestrate such a co-operation. A well organised communication and comparison of ideas and interests of a group of heterogeneous actors is necessary.

The linear innovation model has also shaped the science-business and science-society interfaces in many countries. That means institutional arrangements to further innovation in many countries are in fact based on an obsolete idea of how knowledge can be put to work to produce innovation. Kuhlmann (2002) states the linear model neglects the complexity and auto dynamics of post-modern innovation processes. Adopting the linear model of innovation will not work in the present society; it will even be counterproductive.

22.2 Renewal of the business model and sustainable development

Which theoretical approach to innovation is most suited for an analysis of SD innovation systems, is a question that is difficult to answer. Starting from the level of companies, the analysis could start with the question how sustainable development influences the renewal of the business model of a company. Renewal of business models is a business administration concept. Renewal of a business model depends on the ambition level of leading persons in the company and their interpretation of developments in its surroundings. Renewal of the business model of a company is in first instance a matter for the company itself. Business people should reflect on future trends in their surroundings, possible new needs and demands and possible renewal of "value chains". Where do they want to position their company in the future? A thorough analysis of value chains is necessary. The next question is how sustainable development can be translated into possible changes in these value chains. Sustainable development brings in ecological and social aspects into the considerations of future possibilities. Often companies have difficulties in making these aspects operational. For example: how can reduction of CO2 emissions be translated in company processes? To answer these questions, but also to get an idea of possible developments in the surrounding business environment, the company also depends on the knowledge from external parties.

Knowledge from clients ("latent needs") but also from societal groups can be very useful to explore possible future orientations of the company. This knowledge can generate selection opportunities that can be taken into consideration in the innovation process.

Experience shows academic knowledge in general is of limited use for companies if this knowledge goes into details and does not produce tailor-made results. Academic studies have limited practical importance for companies if these are not carried out in interaction with the demand side. The same holds for academic literature on innovation, which is thought to be of limited importance for business innovation in practice according to some experts. Nooteboom, B. and Stam point out that regional bottom up initiatives are key for innovation processes (WRR 2008).

Overall, considering both what SD experts and innovation experts say, one may conclude that an analysis of SD innovation systems should start from the micro or regional level.

22.3 A framework for analysing SD innovation systems

As a framework for analysing sustainability innovation systems at the micro level was not available, it has been constructed, combining elements both from micro innovation processes and requirements for SD research.

The requirements for SD research have been defined by ICSU (ICSU 2003, Jäger 2008). SD Research should be salient, credible and legitimate. These criteria can only be met if a researcher knows what stakeholders think, know and value. Interaction with stakeholders and a demand orientation thus can be considered an important characteristic of SD research. It is also an important element for analysing SD innovation systems. Furthermore, a well known fact is that involvement of stakeholders in itself does not produce innovation, and that selection of certain types of stakeholders can be very important (see RMNO 2003), but it certainly is a condition for innovation. Especially, the informal knowledge and values these stakeholders can bring in, is important for the innovation process. Integration of knowledge from various sources is also needed one way or the other.

Other requirements can be derived from recent reports on boosting innovation at the micro level. WRR (2008) mentions several conditions that should be fulfilled. The Council stresses the importance of hybrid spaces for innovation. Stakeholder involvement is also considered to be an important element of a good innovation climate. For innovations to come to maturity, niche markets are often necessary.

For the analysis of an innovation system for sustainable development, the following questions have been drawn up (the preliminary question of course being whether innovations are the main goal):

- To what extent is the interaction with stakeholders an essential part of the innovation process and how does this interaction take place?

- And if research is carried out during this process, is it predominantly demand-oriented or supply-driven?
- Are there any hybrid spaces formed for interaction between scientists, entrepreneurs and societal groups and have private-public-constructions been set up?
- To what extent is there any link between or any coordination of research on the three Ps? To what extent is technological research linked to economic, environmental and sociological research? How are the different types of knowledge integrated?
- Is there a niche for innovative research ?

These questions can be considered as a framework for analysing innovation systems for sustainable development.

22.4 Sector innovation systems analysed for their contribution to sustainability

The framework for analysing SD innovation systems might also be useful for analysing innovation systems in economic sectors such as the food and nutrition sector, the energy sector and the water sector. These sectors are cabinet policy priorities for stimulating sustainable development. That is why they have been chosen as subjects for an analysis using the framework questions.

Of course, knowledge and information from literature regarding these sectors may eventually reveal additional elements that are important for creating the right conditions for innovation for sustainable development.

22.4.1 The food and nutrition innovation system and sustainable development

The food and nutrition sector in the Netherlands is a strong and innovative sector. Its Relative Specialisation Index (RSI) is high (see Faber and Van Welie, 2004). Research in this sector is in part demand-oriented and in part supply driven (especially with regard to new technologies). There are indications that innovative research in the food and nutrition sector is closely linked to chains and vertical cooperation lines. There has to be a stage manager for innovation processes, but this should not be a single dominant player. Innovative research is more often linked to a certain type of entrepreneur who is very strongly market-oriented and has a vision of how to create (new) values. Innovation can be promoted by public-private constructions (for example environment covenants) and specific subsidies (including subsidies for innovative and environmentally friendly product design and research subsidies).

The impression from literature and interviews is that the Dutch food and nutrition sector is innovative. Sustainable development is in some cases an important driver for innovation. But it surely is not always and in every research project the leading principle. Sustainable development is of growing importance for the food and nutrition sector as society asks more and more for sustainable products and services and government has decided to purchase only sustainable products (procurement policy).

Big companies like Unilever at first had problems to get the right knowledge and information for sustainable production from universities, but in cooperation with societal groups and some scientists in particular, the knowledge needed could be generated. Hybrid spaces exist in the form of top institutes on nutrition and food innovation programmes (Food Delta).

22.4.2 The energy innovation system and sustainable development

An analysis of the Dutch energy innovation system (from literature and interviews) points out that energy research is still to a large extent driven by the supply side and predominantly has a technological character. The social embedding is neglected or thought of as an "add on". Integration of the three Ps in research for sustainable development is not consciously planned in general. Interaction with stakeholders (clients, companies, enterprises) is a weak point in the energy innovation system. The present energy innovation system is not oriented to the needs of energy-consuming companies and citizens. Man (the P of People) is under exposed in the sustainability triangle, the focus is on technology and economy.

But there are other elements that are important as conditioning factors in the energy innovation sector.

Arentsen et al. (2007) compared innovation in the telecom and energy sectors in several countries. Their conclusion was that the energy market in these countries is still to a large extent dominated by the energy supply side. In the present situation, government regulations are often the main driver for innovation, contrary to the food and nutrition sector. Jacobsson en Johnson (2000a, b) analysed the energy innovation system in the Netherlands, Germany and Sweden and found a poorly articulated demand and weak networks in The Netherlands, hindering knowledge transfer, or too dominant actors, causing lock-in. They also noted a lack of meeting places and prime movers. Nowadays, meeting places come to existence, like the Cartesius Institute, "Energy Valley" and centres of expertise on sustainable energy for SMEs.

Recent analyses of the driving forces in the energy innovation system, for example by Negro (2007) and Meijer (2008) show that apart from innovation "motors" like a technology that works, a well organised sector and a clear market demand, the predictability and long term consistency of government policy is of prime importance.

It is the lack of a long term vision of Dutch government and a yo-yo policy that have had disastrous effects in the past decade. Often government policy arrangements produced unintended effects. Governments should promote the creation of (niche) markets in a smart way. The German "Electricity Feed-in Law" for sustainable energy is often mentioned as an example ("creating powerful, predictable and persistent economic incentives"). The elimination of barriers (for example, limited grid capacity, spatial planning) is also part of creating good innovation conditions.

Recent reports by the Dutch Energy Council as well as the Energy Innovation Agenda (2008) of the Dutch government emphasise the bottle-necks in the demonstration and market introduction phase. But enquiries among entrepreneurs show the main reason for them for not investing in innovation is the lack of continuity of government policy – a persistent long-term policy perspective – and the lack of corresponding instruments to promote innovation for the long term.

Recently a substantial amount of money has been allocated to energy innovation programmes by the Dutch government (2008). Although the Innovation Agenda pays attention to sustainable development, it does not make clear why particular technological innovation paths are considered to be important and have been selected. In Denmark, the selection of priorities in energy policy has resulted in much more focus for the long term (two priorities: wind energy and energy conservation, selected after a democratic process), whilst the Dutch Energy Innovation Agenda shows at least seven different themes. The obvious explanation is that where a clear future vision (from central government) is lacking, existing dominant interests from the supply side can shape the research agenda, both at the national and the local scale. A study by the Rathenau Institute on local transition processes (2009) shows that local interests shape the regional "transition processes".

From these examples it is clear that our framework for analysing innovation for sustainable development is deficient; it should also take governance aspects into account. Stable long term policy goals and corresponding policy instruments that provide a continuous stimulus for SD innovation are a very important element in economic sectors as the energy sector.

22.4.3 The water innovation system and sustainable development

If one may draw a general conclusion about the water innovation system in the Netherlands it should be that the system seems to be characterised by a fixation of governments, companies and managers on technology and greater efficiency while the institutional and societal context (the P of People, other kinds of stakeholders) receive little attention. Research in the water sector is rather segmented (like the sector itself) and there are too few relations with the external world that give rise to new combinations. This limits the innovative capacity of the sector. For this reason, innovation brokers actively seek possible new links and combinations. Government innovation programmes are exactly focused on these points.

The general impression is that sustainable development is not the driving principle in Dutch research and innovation programmes in the water sector. However, sustainable development pops up here and there in programmes of institutes (KWR, Wetsus) and in the "Living with Water" programme.

This compartmentalised system is considered to be the cause of the underutilisation of knowledge and of the inadequate attention paid to innovative solutions.

Government support is the motor behind the recent Water Innovation Programme. Government and Water Boards are still the dominant agents in the sector (70% of the sector is public). They can by their instructions and commissions stimulate "open innovation" in the sector, or stimulate the development of new technology for the Dutch market.

In practice, government regulation (national but also EU) has proved to be the most powerful innovation incentive in the water sector. There are too few other incentives for innovation. In other countries, especially developing countries, the situation is quite different. Decentralised water production for example is an option for the future that can be expected to become more important. Concepts like water foot print and water self-sufficiency are "new". It is not yet common thinking in the water sector that the sector will not only have to focus on technological innovations, but also on demand-driven process innovations to solve the bottlenecks for sustainable development in the sector.

The *conclusion* from these analyses is that the innovation systems for food and nutrition, energy and water in the Netherlands differ in several aspects. The food and nutrition sector differs from the other ones; it is more consumer-oriented and more innovative. Thinking of value chains and stakeholder involvement in innovation processes is more common. The innovation for sustainable development in the energy and water sectors is to a large extent driven by government demand. Suppliers of new technologies determine the agenda, while the social embedding of research and the role of stakeholders in research is underrated. Man (the P of People) is underexposed in the sustainability triangle (the three Ps).

The impression is that integration of knowledge that is relevant to the three Ps is in general not consciously planned in all three sectors. It is also clear that our framework for analysing innovation for sustainable development is deficient; it should also take governance aspects into account. Stable long term policy goals and corresponding policy instruments that provide a continuous stimulus for SD innovation are a very important element in economic sectors in which government policy for a large part creates the demand for sustainable innovations. Even in the food and nutrition sector, government can create a powerful stimulus for innovation by its procurement policy (buying only sustainable products). From the point of view of knowledge democracy, the conclusion is that a lot has to be done to get "people" in the innovation system.

22.5 Designing the conditions for a sustainable development innovation system and the shortcomings of the present science system in the Netherlands

The conclusion from the previous section is that there are shortcomings in the present SD innovation systems with regard to the involvement of "people" (the third P) and the social embedding of research. Other shortcomings in the past were the lack of clear and consistent long term policy goals.

The question is whether it is now possible to design the conditions for a sustainable development innovation system. What are the ideal conditions for a research and innovation system for sustainable development, what are the demands, especially on the research and innovation system?

22.5.1 Demands on the research and innovation system

Jäger (2008) describes the demands on the research and innovation system from the point of view of boosting sustainable development. He thinks the substantive focus of much of the science needed to promote sustainable development will have to be on the complex dynamic interactions between nature and society ("socio-ecological systems"), rather than on either the social or environmental side. Moreover, some of the most important interactions will occur in particular places, or particular enterprises and at particular times. S&T for SD needs therefore be "place-based", or "enterprise-based", embedded in the particular characteristics of distinct locations or contexts.

The challenge is to help promote the relatively "local" and "regional" dialogues from which meaningful priorities for sustainable development can emerge and to set up local support systems that will allow those priorities to be implemented.

As pointed out before, knowledge for sustainable development should be sufficiently reliable ("credible"), but also relevant to decision-makers ("salient") and democratic in its choice of issues to address, expertise to consider and participants to engage ("legitimate"). These three properties are tightly interdependent. Efforts to maximise one of these attributes (credibility), emphasising the scientific part, may often undermine the other attributes. This interdependency poses substantial challenges to the design of institutions for mobilising R&D, assessment and decision support for sustainable development.

22.5.2 Shortcomings of the present science system

Are there enough possibilities in the present science and technology system in various countries to respond to the challenges that sustainable development poses? Does the present science system enable dialogues with local or regional stakeholders and participation in research? Are scientists sufficiently prepared for a role in such dialogues?

Scientists should be capable of dealing with complex systems, different types of knowledge from various disciplines and also with informal knowledge. They should be able to integrate these types of knowledge to produce a workable perspective. They should have the competences needed for such work, they should be able to understand the different languages.

In most countries, a problem-driven, solution-oriented R&D system with corresponding funding mechanisms for research and technology is lacking or underdeveloped. Hirsch Hadorn et al. (2006) point out that transdisciplinary research is needed to meet the requirements of SD research. The characteristics of transdisciplinary research make it difficult to fit in the existing research institutions. Traditional research organisations are not capable to respond in an adequate manner to the demands of SD research. The reasons can be found within the research system:

- integral approaches are not favoured, as the incentives in the research system are directed to disciplinary excellence; interdisciplinarity is not really favoured as a subject in teaching curricula, let alone as a research requisite;
- interaction with stakeholders is supposed to lead to interference with research objectives, endangering the objectivity of the research; participation of stakeholders is thought of as even worse for scientific independence;
- the dominance of the paradigm of linear innovation, even though there is massive proof against it.

Nooteboom B. and Eshuis (2009) state the academic community at large presently seems preoccupied with its internal competition in terms of published output. It therefore seems less open for new ways of working. It cannot discover what it cannot participate in (transdisciplinary research).

One might expect that influential scientific and research organisations as KNAW (Royal Academy of Sciences) and NWO (Netherlands Organisation for Scientific Research) in the Netherlands have developed ideas about how research may contribute to SD. Although in some reports, the necessity of involving "practice" in research programming is mentioned, the research programming is still "business as usual", that is without real stakeholder participation, without real involvement of the demand side and without integral approaches.

Some scientists do realise the research agenda for sustainability should be set in a different way; not only those scientists and researchers who carry out applied research or work as consultants. A recent report of KNAW (2007) on sustainable energy research states that a system analytical approach would have been the right way to define the research challenges. "That means that in an early stage, 'practitioners' should have been involved in the technology and system development" and: "research should be aimed at the development of a systematic method for the evaluation of new integral concepts. This includes the identification of inefficiencies on an institutional and social-economic level, although until now, this is not the usual way to proceed." Multidisciplinary teams should systematically analyse industry sectors or energy production modes. The KNAW commission concludes that "the call for innovation is loud, but the subsidising programmes are still directed along the worn-trodden paths". The question is: "Why?".

Another example comes from NWO, the Netherlands Organisation for Scientific Research, which is meant to stimulate excellent researchers, but also research for societal purposes. In the past, so called Stimulation Research Programmes have been set up for themes as economy and ecology, biodiversity, system ecology and toxicology. Some observations about the Biodiversity programme have been published (in Dutch) by RMNO (2005). The societal value is a minor selection criterion compared to the rest of the (scientific) criteria. Government officials were a member of a steering committee, but the selection of proposals was eventually carried out by scientists.

The overrating of scientific value of research proposals caused dissatisfaction with policy-makers. After a halfway evaluation of the programme, the programme was set up in a different way, concentrating on agro biodiversity and policy questions that had been articulated on this subject. Thus, the results could be made more relevant for policy-makers. Similar experiences have been gathered for other Stimulation Programmes.

An independent observer may ask why time and again the same mistakes are made. Undoubtedly, the institutional settings create these suboptimal conditions.

Evaluation of the Novel Food Protein Programme (aiming at sustainable food production), learned that institutional barriers also exist within research institutes. Loeber (1997) found that too small a number of actors had been taken into consideration. Dissenting views were not accommodated and discussion on normative issues avoided. Loeber concludes that the institutional embedding strongly influences the methodological elaboration of sustainability research.

The conclusion of this section is that there are quite some institutional hurdles to be taken for the embedding of SD research in The Netherlands. In general, SD research does not fit the institutional settings of the traditional research organisations in the Netherlands. These research organisations could try to adapt and create more space for this type of research, but on the other hand several "hybrid spaces" already exist. As Hjelt et al. (2008) point out, the normal reaction to the shortcomings in the system is to introduce new institutional structures, increasing the need for coordination in the system. Reform of the institutions is a long term goal. The vocation, mission and competences of different institutes are difficult to change (Kuhlmann 2002).

When taking into consideration that knowledge in this society is more and more distributed and that it is not self-evident that the best knowledge is available in universities or in scientific institutes (see Hisschemöller 2008), the conclusion must be that "hybrid places" are more and more necessary. The Cartesius Institute in the Netherlands is an example of such a hybrid space, performing a role in regional energy initiatives (Energy Valley in the northern part of the Netherlands) and there is a similar institute for the water sector called Wetsus. The Dutch Innovation programmes are another example of creating new hybrid spaces.

The logical "place" for transdisciplinary research in the Netherlands until now is in ad hoc and temporary research programmes and institutes, creating bypasses in the existing science system. In countries like Switzerland and Sweden there are more possibilities in the existing science system for transdisciplinary research. Fixed quota can help (Switzerland, Swedish research programmes) as can other mechanisms to strengthen the position of researchers who have experience in inter- and transdisciplinary research.

The conclusion is that there are not enough possibilities for SD research and innovation in the traditional science system and there are quite some institutional barriers too. The need for restructuring the science system is great, because quite a lot of complex, societal problems cannot be adequately addressed by the existing institutional structures.

22.6 Knowledge democracy and innovation for sustainable development

From the point of view of knowledge democracy several challenges and opportunities have been mentioned in the preceding sections.

For example, a lot has to be done to get "people" into the SD innovation system. It is also clear that hybrid spaces are very important to get the knowledge and values of stakeholders and other interest groups in the heart of the deliberations. The contextual embedding of research is important in SD research and innovation. Knowledge integration asks for special competences of researchers. Research should be a co-production (RMNO 2007).

Research for sustainable development does not fit the institutional settings of the traditional research organisations in the Netherlands, making "bypasses" necessary in the form of special research and innovation programmes. Hybrid spaces do exist, but their role as an important constituent part of the science and innovation system is not sufficiently acknowledged by the traditional scientific organisations. This situation is clearly in contrast with trends in society towards more public participation in research when dealing with complex societal problems.

In the coming decades, the role of scientific and other institutions may dramatically change, as more and more it is clear that society transgresses the boundaries that have been put in place between society, science and policy. This has important consequences for the positioning of knowledge producing institutions in society.

Closing chapter

Roeland Jaap in 't Veld

In earlier chapters we have digressed upon the emerging character of the knowledge democracy concept, and summarised the most remarkable contributions to the conference. In this final chapter I formulate my insights concerning the predominant tensions and challenges that have to be envisaged.

We have proposed to replace the concept of knowledge economy by that of knowledge democracy as a focal item of global agendas. The purpose is to illustrate the necessity to respond to the actual evolutionary patterns of advanced societies. These patterns are interwoven technological and social complex transitions in the triangle politics-science-media. Of course the concept has a persuasive nature. We have fabricated the triangle politics-media-science in order to illuminate the connections and tensions between them. The analysis by Turnhout on the character of the concept knowledge democracy, leading to the conclusion that it is potentially both utopian and totalitarian, should be properly interpreted as an early warning signal. Applications of institutional and procedural requirements in knowledge democracies, such as participatory decision-making processes, should continuously be tested in the contingent environments of empirical reality. The danger of totalitarian and technocratic misadventures is always present, but accidents can be avoided if one is prepared to take a careful look into the value patterns of all concerned actors.

The world is changing, it is becoming more and more fragmented and reflexive, and as a consequence all steering relations are complicated. Since the behaviour of a reflexive system can not be forecasted as a matter of principle, illustrated in earlier chapters, the classical ideal of governing a society effectively by regulation, command or subsidies alone, has become obsolete.

Knowledge is fragmented as the organisation of science is based upon specialisation into separate disciplines, each with a specific methodology that serves as a shield against outside criticisms but also as an isolating wall. No societal problem can be dealt with properly by one single scientific discipline. Interdisciplinary cooperation on the other hand may be necessary in order to gain relevance, but will lead to a loss of accuracy, if the methodologies of the interconnected disciplines differ considerably.

The media logic has conquered the political system and media-politics replace the forum-function of parliament and move it to the television studio. Classical top-down media have complex relationships with new bottom-up media.

Public authorities within systems of representative democracy are therefore facing legitimacy and effectiveness problems. Representation in its historical shape has eroded because of structural changes in value patterns, and because of the educational level of the population. Legitimacy and effectiveness of governing and steering in a classical manner are fundamentally undermined.

R.J. in 't Veld (ed.), *Knowledge Democracy*, DOI 10.1007/978-3-642-11381-9,

One of the strategies of these public authorities in order to regain legitimacy is the introduction of citizen participation. Often it remains completely unclear whether this participation should contribute to either the collection of support or to the process of enriching the content of the decision. This is important because the preferable shape of the processes will depend upon the objectives of the participation.

When we think about participatory democracy we usually refer to notions like civil society, stakeholders-citizens, interested parties, etc. In the context of deliberation or participation around a certain issue some public authority usually decides who the desirable partners are. This type of "guided participation" is often tolerated if the boundaries of an invited group are experienced as "logical". However the framing of the problem is decisive for the acceptance of the 'logic'. The inhabitants of a neighbourhood may seem to be a "logical" group if the problematique concerns the roads through the neighbourhood, but in reality the traffic participants crossing the neighbourhood from elsewhere to elsewhere may be as intensely interested. So the answer to the question whether guided participation is acceptable depends on the degree of consensus on the framing of the problem. Therefore in the case of wicked problems where this consensus is absent, open access to participation is recommendable.

As mentioned elsewhere we distinguish "top-down media" and "bottom-up media". Both contribute to the agenda-setting of politics. The top-down media operate in structural interdependency with politics. The expression "media-politics" is devoted to this interdependency. The bottom-up media are to a considerable degree independent from both the top-down media and politics. But bottom-up media often lack the selective function, elsewhere fulfilled by editors. Goede attempts to design a framework for better understanding of the relevant relationships. Participation in decision preparation and -making may be invited by public authorities, but uninvited participation also takes place, in particular with the support of bottom-up media. The theoretical considerations concerning crowds and publics as presented by Kreijveld and Basten relate to phenomena in reality where uninvited groups start to intermingle with public decision-making. On the other hand politicians also utilise bottom-up media in order to communicate, as Aalberts and Kreijveld show us From the viewpoint of checks and balances, and taking into account the fact that we live in a world where frequently too much rather than too little information is available, the key role of the media requires a certain degree of self-reflection regarding the presentation of scientific and other policy-relevant knowledge. The question stays, if both top down and bottom-up media are able to fulfil such a requirement.

The explosion of knowledge and information in this era necessitates attention for the use of knowledge in public decisions more than ever before. Simultaneously the predominant problems on political agendas have developed into wicked problems. The insights in the fragmented character of scientific knowledge, the multiple nature of truth and the importance of other notions of knowledge like citizens' knowledge have led to prescriptive theories on transdisciplinary trajectories, leading to robust, plausible action perspectives with the support of many kinds of knowledge.

The wicked character of the focal problems demands cooperation between scientists, bureaucrats, stakeholders, lay groups and politicians. The more different categories are involved, the more complex the bottlenecks in translation are. As Edelenbos et al. and Bunders et al. have explained, some categories are more related than others. Professional bureaucrats understand scientists reasonably well because scientific products are formulated in the same language as policy theories. But often the devil is in the detail: slight differences in meaning may lead to vast misunderstandings. Boundary functions and/or workers are indispensable as Hoppe argues. Also Schulz and van Twist describe commissions as amongst others boundary organisms. A better understanding of inter- and transdisciplinarity begins with education: universities should ensure that students are familiar with these concepts and have the opportunity to gain experience with these forms of scientific research in their training programmes.

The process of formulating research agendas becomes increasingly important in a knowledge democracy. It cannot any longer be left to scientists alone. Broad participation is desirable. For assessing the need and usefulness of the generation of knowledge by policy oriented research programmes, more reflection in advance is needed. Independent advice (by a system of checks and balances) can further this reflection, as well as a number of process criteria for the assessment. Jacobi et al. and De Cock Buning present suggestions for advanced process formats that may serve to produce optimal research agendas.

The closed character of political processes often prohibits the full utilisation of knowledge. Termeer et al. explain how configurations shape their own specific meaningful worlds and how they become inaccessible for knowledge that that does not fit into their images of reality and truth. Meuleman and Tromp illuminate why available knowledge remains untouched or even is under attack because of different interpretations of what is "usable" knowledge and because of political motives. It is important that policy-makers have mechanisms available to minimise the probability that unwelcome knowledge is ignored

Van Rijn and Tissen illustrate the relationships between knowledge, innovation and creativity in city governance while De Wit combines the challenges of sustainability with designs of innovative democratic approaches.

The need for well-designed decision-making processes becomes even more urgent as the long term character of the decision to be made becomes more predominant. Meuleman and In 't Veld shed a light on these specific design characteristics. Van Rij describes how foresight studies and more in particular horizon scans might contribute to advanced designs.

Knowledge democracy therefore appears to demand at least 2-fold complex participation processes: the transdisciplinary character is necessary to transform scientific insights to robust, plausible action perspectives, and the contribution of stakeholders and citizens is necessary to assure that the decision to be taken will be accepted and effective. Moreover in many cases the specific knowledge of stakeholders and citizens is also necessary to enrich the content of the decisions to be taken sufficiently. All participants have legitimate interests of very different kinds that have to be accommodated. The multi-purpose setup of the processes will vary with the different relative intensities of the objectives: the amalgamation of values, knowledge and interests, the enrichment of content and the gathering of support.

The classical political game will have to change profoundly, and this may be the most important motive for the fierce resistance from many politicians against reform in a participatory direction. Loss of power is the main fear. To accept a role as process architect instead of the position as the final decision-maker is risky because many fear that the voters may not support the architects, but will favour the politicians who present themselves as leaders in substantial solutions.

The quest for acceptable mixed systems of representative and participatory democracy will appear on many agendas in the years to come, and is a focal research question in the knowledge democracy research programme.

Although the most urgent recommendations concern the process aspects of decision-making, one may also wonder if structures should change and institutions should be reformed. New constitutional values as the ecological carbon footprint, presented in the paper by Toepfer and Bachmann could be considered, but also the concept of situational contracting as recommended by Wolfson would certainly contribute to a more adequate pattern of communication between service-rendering public authorities and reflexive citizens. We feel puzzled about the creative suggestion formulated by Van Buuren and Eshuis to introduce knowledge governance as a fourth institutional arrangement after hierarchy, contract and network. It appears to us a more or less elitist assumption that knowledge as a subject matter of coordination would be superior to values and interests.

Observing both the available literature and the emerging practice of knowledge democracy in a number of European nation-states I was struck by the differences between several nation states in the observable tensions between science, politics and media. We therefore make a distinction between quiet and turbulent democracies.

In the quiet democracies the main characteristics to be observed are:

- In important domains there may be conflicts on the preferable substance or content of policies, as based on value differences and variations, but the knowledge base for those policies is not contested; therefore problems do not bear a wicked character. Moreover complicated two-level conflicts, relating both to the substance of policies and the credibility of the different knowledge sources, remain absent or at least an exception;
- The mutual dependence of politics and media is not very strongly developed. Politicians have realised that the locus for political debate should be parliament, and therefore oppose actively to the transfer of political dialogue to mass media orchestrated by journalists; media-politics are not predominant;

- Different types of knowledge – such as scientific knowledge, local knowledge and/or citizens knowledge – are integrated in participatory processes for policy preparation, aiming at socially robust and plausible perspectives for action;
- The societal attention for the maintenance of adequate checks and balances is considerable; not only the respect for the classical Trias Politica is cherished, but also the awareness on the desirability of free basic research and education – free in the meaning of: not influenced by either politics or media – is intense.

In the turbulent democracies we find the following phenomena:

- Many political problems are perceived as wicked: neither on the value aspect nor on the knowledge or information side consensus exists. Many two-level conflicts complicate the political realm. In political environments with a strong meta-value, that leads to a high degree of tolerance and mutual respect: this situation will lead to the development of transdisciplinary trajectories with considerable participation. Populist politics on the contrary will aim at the decrease of this type of complexity by establishing a clear, simple and predominating view both on values and substance;
- The mutual dependence of politics and media is clearly visible: hypes prevail, the political agenda is mainly determined by media utterances, scandals and abuses give rise to political action. In extreme instances (Italy) the reigning political coalition also rules an important proportion of the top-down media. Publics frequently manifest themselves in relation to specific hypes;
- Where media-politics dominate, the space for broad citizens' participation in policy preparation appears to be limited because politicians and media wish to establish a collective monopoly on information-gathering and dissemination; so the stronger the mutual dependence of politics and media manifests itself, the possibilities for unhampered – in the sense of not orchestrated by mass media – influential argumentation and communication seem to be very limited. But on the other hand we observed earlier in this book that the existing technologies enable groups of citizens by internet application as YouTube, MSN Messenger, e-mail and Twitter to create their own mass media, to produce their own expressions of interests and views in a manner that cannot be controlled by commercialised or professionalised media;
- Populist politics disrespect checks and balances: the perceived necessity of transparency of authority demands hierarchy in the political realm; populist politicians will continuously criticise any disagreeable action of uncontrolled professionals, and will try to minimise their influence and to maximise their dependence. Moreover the internal structure of the public sector will be streamlined according to hierarchical principles: as a

> consequence of which the discretion of agencies and other semi-autonomous bodies, but also of inspectorates and supervisors will be diminished.

The foregoing static comparison neglects of course the important and necessary analysis of dynamic developments. Castells in particular words his forecasts in terms of accumulative developments, such as the fatal transition of media-politics to populism, or worse. Our observations on the increasing importance of reflexive mechanisms however hamper us to formulate any deterministic forecasts, laws or regularities as to societal developments. Scenarios, simulations and explorations could serve as catalysers to enlarge our sensitivity for potential developments, but the fundamental character of the existing uncertainty and complexity prohibit us to consider them as building stones for direct action. The indirect use could be that we try to design action perspectives that are robust, for example do not have disastrous consequences in either of the feasible scenarios. It may be clear that the possibilities for such designs are more feasible in quiet than in turbulent democracies.

In addition, the increasing complexity of societal problems should not lead to the prohibition of controversial research; to the contrary: such a pluralist approach of research may open new strategies for problems still unforeseen. In case of doubt as to the scientific integrity of knowledge for policy, it is useful to organise discussions on the desirable research agendas, aiming at wide bandwidths of the opinions, and to seek a common knowledge base, as described by many authors in this book. As a matter of course also oppositional parties in parliaments should be included in these processes. The effectiveness of these such institutional arrangements may differ in different domains, so careful choices should be made.

Finally I will present some observations on the developments in the Netherlands as an illustration. Recently, the attention for the issues that are related to knowledge democracy has increased. But paradoxically, this has not led to innovations in accordance with the theoretical insights of the leading analysts. Boundary functions have disappeared, as the ministries themselves claim to be competent to fulfil these functions themselves. On the national level the degree of participation is rather waining than expanding. This appears to create an unbalance in the relations between science and politics, but the scientific world has remained completely silent. Parliament attempts to decrease its dependence on information from ministries by strengthening its own research activities, but so far the results are of varying quality, to put it mildly. The Netherlands seem to move in the direction of a turbulent democracy as described above with a strong orientation on hypes and some populist characteristics. On the other hand some top civil servants are sincerely involved in efforts to strengthen the knowledge intensity of policy preparation. Disturbing reflexive phenomena complicate the picture further: ministries design strategic research agendas, but actual research activities sometimes move in another direction. The number of public affairs officers and controllers at ministries increases at the cost of cognitive experts. The cleansing operation in order to reduce the number of relatively independent advisory bodies in the public domain as well as the increasing hierarchy of the political realm support the hypothesis that the evolutionary pattern in the Netherlands could be characterised as the gradual decrease of that type of checks and balances that may be defined as shock dampers. Of course reflexivity is also a source of hope and optimism concerning future change.

About the authors

Dr. Chris Aalberts is lecturer and researcher in political communication. He published about political engagement of the young, popularisation of politics and the gap between citizens and the European Union. Currently, he is working on the meaning of Web 2.0 for political engagement of citizens. Chris Aalberts lectures at several universities, among which the master of Media and Journalism of Erasmus University Rotterdam and the master Political Communication of Antwerp University. Contact: info@chrisaalberts.nl.

Dr. Günther Bachmann heads the executive office of the German Council for Sustainable Development. He has been involved in international sustainability issues for many years. Günther chaired a working group for Sustainable Development in the European Environmental and Sustainable Development Advisory Councils network. He was a director and professor with Germany's Federal Environmental Agency. Contact: guenther.bachmann@nachhaltigkeitsrat.de.

Dr. Floor Basten founded her research agency OrléoN with the ambition to help people carry out their own research. Floor is specialised in narrative research. She founded [campus]OrléoN, a full service network for academic research both inside and outside the universities. Floor is also programme leader at the "House for the Democracy". Previously, as a postdoctoral fellow she was engaged in the international EU research project Education and Training for Governance and Active Citizenship in Europe. Contact: floorbasten@orleon.nl.

Dr. Gerard Breeman studied public administration in Rotterdam and got his PhD from Leiden University. He works at the public administration and policy group at Wageningen University. His main research-focus is about how to make policies more trustworthy. He also publishes about agenda-setting, the politics of attention and European Union policies. Since 2009 he has become a research-fellow at the Montesquieu Institute in The Hague. Contact: gerard.breeman@wur.nl.

Dr. Jacqueline Broerse is associate professor of public engagement in health and life sciences and head of the section Science Communication at the Athena Institute, VU University Amsterdam. She holds a master degree in biomedical sciences. In 1998 she obtained her PhD degree on the development of an interactive approach to include small-scale farmers in the biotechnological innovation process. Contact: jacqueline.broerse@falw.vu.nl

Prof. Dr. Joske Bunders is director of the Athena Institute for Research on Innovation and Communication in Health and Life Science at the VU University Amsterdam and responsible for the Master's training Management, Policy Analysis and Entrepreneurship for science students. She worked as an editor at the Great Spectrum Encyclopaedia and rendered education in chemistry and society in Leiden. In 1980 she followed an appointment at the Free University as a teacher in biology and society. Contact: joske.bunders@falw.vu.nl.

Dr. Arwin van Buuren is assistant professor at the Department of Public Administration, Erasmus University Rotterdam. In his work the interaction between knowledge and public decision-making is a major theme. He published in various journals about knowledge production and legitimate and effective policy-making. He is a member of the Scientific Board of the Dutch Advisory Council for Research on Spatial Planning, Nature and the Environment. Contact: vanbuuren@fsw.eur.nl.

Prof. Dr. Tjard de Cock Buning is professor at the Athena Department for research on communication and innovation in the health & life sciences, VU University Amsterdam. His research focuses on methodological and normative questions for a sustainable society. Currently he is internationally engaged on options for tailor made biotechnology in India, translational opportunities in ecogenomics, ethics and new governance in agricultural policy, sustainable transitions in the agriculture (TransForum) and system innovation in health. Contact: tjard.de.cock.buning@falw.vu.nl.

Prof. Dr. Jurian Edelenbos is professor at Erasmus University Rotterdam, Department of Public Administration. He conducts research in the field of complex decision-making, in the field of water management and regional and urban development. He focuses on citizen participation as self-organisation and co-production, multi-actor and multi-level governance, complexity management and leadership, and the role of trust in inter-organisational cooperation. Contact: Edelenbos@fsw.eur.nl

Dr. Jasper Eshuis graduated from Wageningen University, with a major and minor in rural sociology. He then worked at the Agricultural Economics Research Institute LEI. He completed his PhD research on trust and monitoring between the state, farmers and environmental co-operatives in nature conservation policies. In 2006 Jasper became a Post-doc at Erasmus University Rotterdam. He currently conducts research on co-production in policies for spatial development. Contact: eshuis@fsw.eur.nl.

Dr. Miguel Goede is associate professor at the University of the Netherlands Antilles. His area of research is Good Governance for Sustainable Development of Globalising Small Island Developing States in the Caribbean. The government of the Netherlands Antilles frequently solicits his advice. He is currently involved in the ICT Platform of Curacao, updating the government policy to facilitate the knowledge and creative society of Curacao. Contact: mgoede@onenet.an.

Prof. Dr. Robert Hoppe holds a chair in Policy Studies and Knowledge at the University of Twente's Faculty of Management and Governance. In 2005 he joined and helped establish the Department for Science, Technology, and Policy Studies (STəPS). Fields of interest are long term policy dynamics and innovation, especially the role of technology; methodological and institutional implications of deliberative policy analysis; and the governance of expertise. Contact: r.hoppe@utwente.nl.

Prof. Dr. Roeland in 't Veld is chairman of the Advisory Council for Research on Spatial Planning, Nature and the Environment (RMNO). He is professor at the Open University of the Netherlands and professor of Governance at the University of the Netherlands Antilles. He chairs different Supervisory Boards and is a board room consultant. Contact: roelintveld@hotmail.com.

Mr. Anders Jacobi is project manager at the Danish Board of Technology (DBT). He is and has been responsible for numerous projects within various fields such as healthcare, transport, privacy and security, energy etc. Anders Jacobi is currently leading two bigger projects; one advising the Danish parliament about obesity as a societal problem and the other as a coordinator of an EU foresight project about research agendas for FP8. Contact: aj@Tekno.dk.

Dr. Florian Keil is senior scientist and project coordinator at the Institute for Social-Ecological Research (ISOE) in Frankfurt/Main, Germany. His thematic expertise lies in water research (with a focus on water quality and micro-pollutants) and environmental policies. He works both theoretically and methodologically on the concept of transdisciplinarity. Contact: keil@isoe.de.

Dr. Lars Klüver is director at the Danish Board of Technology (DBT). He is responsible for the work programme, methodology, contact to the Danish Parliament and government, and for the administration of the DBT. The DBT has more than 20 years of experience on including participatory processes into technology assessment and policy advice, and Lars Klüver has been central for the development of the methodology behind this praxis. Contact: lk@tekno.dk.

Maurits Kreijveld MSc carries out a foresight study on wisdom of crowds and complex decision-making at STT, the Netherlands Study centre and think tank for Technology Trends. For his project Maurits explores a wide range of applications of "wisdom of crowds", including crowd sourcing and co-creation. In recent years Maurits worked with the Ministry of Economic Affairs on Innovation policy and ICT and new media policy. Contact by e-mail: kreijveld@stt.nl.

Drs. Maartje van Lieshout is PhD candidate in the Public Administration and Policy Group at Wageningen University. She used to work as a researcher in the Communication Strategies Group and the Centre of Methodical Ethics and Technology Assessment in Wageningen University. She graduated at the University of Wageningen in Forestry and Nature Conservation and Communication Science. Contact: Maartje.vanLieshout@wur.nl.

Dr. Louis Meuleman worked as head of unit and project director in the Dutch government, mainly on environmental, spatial planning and sustainable development issues. He was secretary-general of the Advisory Council RMNO, is Chair of the Netherlands Association for Public Management (VOM) and senior lecturer at Nyenrode Business University. He studied environmental biology in

Nijmegen (1980), and concluded a PhD in public administration (1980, Rotterdam) on the metagovernance of hierarchies, networks and markets. Contact: louismeuleman@publicstrategy.nl

Dr. Christian Pohl is co-director of the transdisciplinarity-net of the Swiss academies and senior researcher and lecturer at the Department of Environmental Sciences at ETH Zurich. He was trained in environmental sciences and wrote a doctoral thesis on how to handle uncertainties in environmental assessments by using fuzzy sets. During the last years Christian Pohl's work focused on the methodological particularities of transdisciplinary knowledge production. Contact: pohl@scnat.ch.

Wieke Pot, Msc. studied Public Administration at Leiden University, receiving her MSc-degree in the beginning of 2009 (cum laude). Already during her studies she worked as a research assistant at her department. Since April 2009 Wieke is fulltime employed as a researcher at the Public Administration and Policy Group of Wageningen University. She is involved in several (contract) research projects on adaptation to climate change and sustainable food production. Contact: wieke.pot@wur.nl.

Dr. Mikko Rask (PhD in environmental strategies and technology assessment) is Senior Researcher at the National Consumer Research Centre Finland. He has experience of several national and EU projects on technology assessment, foresight and sustainability policy. He has published for example, in *Science and Technology Policy* and *Technological Forecasting and Social Change*. Contact: Mikko.Rask@ncrc.fi.

Drs. Victor van Rij is senior advisor foresight of the unit of Knowledge connections and Horizon Scanning of the Ministry of Education, Culture and Science in the Netherlands which inherited the horizon scanning task of the former COS. Recently he has been involved in the national horizon scan and lead a pilot project joining the Horizon scans of the UK, Denmark and the Netherlands. Contact: vvanrij@live.nl.

Stella van Rijn MBA is a PhD researcher at Nyenrode Business University. Her research focuses on the context of knowledge cities, in which it is believed to be of key importance for city governments to actively identify, develop and tap into the knowledge potential of urban communities and to systematically promote knowledge creation and sharing. Van Rijn previously had a career in Journalism working for Dutch national media. She also performs non-academic consulting work and is editor-in-chief of the management magazine "Coaching". Contact: s.vrijn@nyenrode.nl.

Drs. Nienke van Schie works on a PhD-research as part of the project "Valuation in Co-production" at Erasmus University Rotterdam, Department of Public

Administration. Her research focuses on the involvement of stakeholder values of water in regional development. Nienke participated in the 2-year interactive decision-making project “Around Arnemuiden”. This project was executed in collaboration with TNO Built Environment and Tauw consultancy. Contact: vanschie@fsw.eur.nl.

Prof. Dr. Roland Scholz holds the Chair of Environmental Sciences: Natural and Social Science Interface at the Swiss Federal Institute of Technology (ETH Zurich, Switzerland). He is adjunct professor of Psychology at the University of Zurich (Privatdozent), and was elected as the fifth holder of the King Carl XVI Gustaf's Professorship 2001/2002 hosted at the Center of Environment and Sustainability of Chalmers University of Technology and Gothenborg University (Sweden). Contact: roland.scholz@env.ethz.ch.

Martin Schulz MA is assistant professor for public administration at Tilburg School for Politics and Public Administration of Tilburg University, The Netherlands. He holds a position as senior management consultant at Berenschot. His research and advisory work focuses on knowledge and advisory infrastructures in the public sector. Recently he evaluated the functioning of several councils and has functioned as a secretary for several ad hoc commissions set up by the central government. Contact: M.Schulz@berenschot.nl.

Prof. Dr. Katrien Termeer is Chair of the Public Administration and Policy Group at Wageningen University. She used to work at the Erasmus University of Rotterdam; Technical University of Delft; the ministry of Agriculture, Nature and Food and at Sioo, a Centre for Organisational Change and Learning. She graduated at the University of Wageningen in Landscape Planning. Contact: katrien.termeer@wur.nl.

Prof. Dr. René Tissen has been Professor of Business Studies at Business University Nyenrode since 1993, and is co-chair of the Nyenrode Research and Innovation Institute. He specialises in economy, management and organisation. Tissen authored various management books and articles, of which translations have appeared in over 15 countries. Next to the university, he has held a number of international board, management and advisory functions for both business and government. Contact: r.tissen@nyenrode.nl.

Prof. Dr. Klaus Töpfer is widely recognised as having spearheaded national and global environmental policy as German Minister of Environment and, later on, when he run the UN Environmental Programme in the position of UN Undersecretary for 8 years until 2006. With his commitment and ground breaking environmental initiatives he actively contributed also to the success of the Earth Summit in Rio de Janeiro in 1992. He was recently assigned Executive Director of the newly established Institute for Advanced Sustainability Studies, IASS, in Potsdam, Germany. Contact: klaus.toepfer@iass-potsdam.de.

Dr. Henk Tromp studied cultural anthropology at the University of Amsterdam. For over 20 years he was research manager for social scientific contract research at Leiden University. In 2006 he published a book on art experts (art historians and chemists) and their struggle with art dealers, collectors, museums and politicians on the authenticity of works by Vincent van Gogh. Contact: tromph@fsw.leidenuniv.nl.

Dr. Esther Turnhout is assistant professor at the Forest and Nature Conservation Policy Group of Wageningen University, the Netherlands. Her research and teaching concerns the relations between science, policy and the public and the dynamics between production and use of scientific knowledge and expertise in the field of nature conservation and environmental governance. Contact: Esther.Turnhout@wur.nl.

Prof. Dr. Mark van Twist is professor of public administration at Erasmus University Rotterdam. He is also dean and member of the board of the Netherlands School of Public Administration, an interuniversity institute in The Hague, that offers study programmes for senior officials in government, and extraordinary member of the board of the Netherlands Court of Audit. Contact: Twist@nsob.nl.

Drs. Bert de Wit is a biologist and a Programme Manager of the Advisory Council for Research on Spatial Planning, Nature and the Environment (RMNO) in the Netherlands. His expertise lies in the field of boundary work between science, policy and society. For the Minister of the Environment RMNO analysed the relations between research on sustainable development and valorisation, innovation, and higher education (2009). Contact: bert.dewit@pbl.nl.

Prof. Dr. Dirk Wolfson is research fellow at the department of public administration of Erasmus University and a member of the Royal Netherlands Academy of Arts and Sciences. During most of his academic life, he served as a member of the Social and Economic Council (SER). He also consulted widely on economic and development policy with the Dutch government, the Foreign Aid department, EU, OECD, World Bank and the UN. Contact: dwolfson@xs4all.nl.

Dr. Marjolein Zweekhorst teaches at the Athena Institute of the VU University Amsterdam. She obtained her PhD degree on institutionalising of participatory approaches. Marjolein is assistant professor at the Athnena Institute for Research on Innovation and Communication in Health and Life science at the VU university and is the mastercoordinator of the master program Management Policy Analysis and entrepreneurhsip in the Health and Life Science at the VU university Amsterdam. Contact: marjolein.zweekhorst@falw.vu.nl.

References

Aalberts, C. (2006). *Aantrekkelijke politiek? Een onderzoek naar jongeren en popularisering van politiek.* Apeldoorn: Spinhuis.

Abbott, A. (1992). From causes to events. Notes on narrative positivism. *Sociological Methods and Research*, 20(4), 428–455.

Achterhuis, H.J. (1998). De erfenis van de utopie, Amsterdam.

Adler, P.S. (2001). Market, hierarchy, and trust: the knowledge economy and the future of capitalism. *Organisation Science*, 2(2), 215–234.

Akerlof, G.A. and Schiller, R.J. (2009). *Animal Spirits.* Princeton, NJ: Princeton University Press.

Anderson, Ch. (2009). *Free: The Future of a Radical Price.* New York: Hyperion.

Anderson, L. (2003). *Pursuing Truth, Exercising Power. Social Science and Public Policy in the 21st Century.* New York: Colombia University Press.

Andriessen, D. (2008). Stuff or Love? How metaphors direct our efforts to manage knowledge in organizations. *Journal for Knowledge Management Research and Practice*, 6, 5–12.

Arentsen, M., Hofman, P. and Stapersma, P. (2007). *Literature Review on Innovation in Telecom, Automotive Industry, Medical Technology, Copiers and Printers.* The Hague: Energy Council.

Argyris, C. (1990). *Overcoming Organizational Defenses.* Needham Heights, MA: Allyn & Bacon.

Arrow, K.J. (1985). The economics of agency. In: Pratt, J.W. and Zeckhauser, R.J. (Eds.), *Principals and Agents: The Structure of Business.* Boston: Harvard Business School Press, 37–51.

Backstrand, K. (2003). Civic science for sustainability: reframing the role of experts, policy-makers and citizens in environmental governance. *Global Environmental Politics*, 3(4), 24–41.

Baekdal, Th. (2009). Where is everyone? http://www.baekdal.com/articles/Management/market-of-information/. Accessed on 18/10/2009.

Bailey, S.J. (2001). *Public Sector Economics: Theory, Policy, Practice.* Basingstoke: Palgrave.

Bal, R., Bijker, W.E. and Hendriks, R. (2002). *Paradox van wetenschappelijk gezag. Over de maatschappelijke invloed van adviezen van de Gezondheidsraad, 1985–2001.* The Hague: Health Council.

Ballard, H.L., Fernandez-Gimenez, M.E. and Sturtevant, V.E. (2008). Integration of local ecological knowledge and conventional science: a study of seven community-based forestry organizations in the USA. *Ecology and Society*, 13, 37, http://www.ecologyandsociety.org/vol13/iss32/art37/

Barbour, R.S. and Kitzinger, J. (1999). *Developing Focus Group Research: Politics, Theory and Practice.* London: Sage.

Bardoel, J. (2003). *Macht zonder verantwoordelijkheid? Media, mediabeleid en kwaliteit van de openbare informatievoorzieningen.* Nijmegen: KU Nijmegen.

Basten, F. (2002). *Discourses of Activism.* Unpublished report for the ETGACE study. http://www.orleon.nl/producten.php. Accessed 2 August 2009.

Basten, F. (2008). Organisaties leren onderzoeken. *Handboek Effectief Opleiden.* Reed Business bv.

Baudrillard, J. (1983). *In the shadow of the silent majorities or, The end of the social and other essays.* Semiotext(e) Foreign Agents Series.

Bekkers, V.J.J.M., Fenger, H.J.M., Homburg, V.M.F. and Putters, K. (2005). Doorwerking van strategische beleidsadvisering. *Bestuurswetenschappen*, 59(5), 431–450.

Bénabou, R. and Tirole, J. (2006). Incentives and prosocial behaviour. *American Economic Review*, 96, 1652–1678.

Benner, J., Leguijt, C., Ganzevles, J. and Van Est, R. (2009). *Energietransitie begint in de regio. Rotterdam, Texel en Energy Valley onder de loep.* The Hague: Rathenau Institute.

Bennett, R., Lawrence, R. and Livingstone, S. (2007). *When the Press Fails: Political Power and the News Media from Iraq to Katrina.* Chicago: University of Chicago Press.

Bernstein, R.J. (1991). *The New Constellation: The Ethical-Political Horizons of Modernity/Postmodernity.* Cambridge (USA): MIT Press.

Beuvink, J. and Den Hoed, P. (2007) *Op de brug tussen politiek en wetenschap.* The Hague: WRR.

Bevir, M. and Rhodes, R.A.W. (2001). *A Decentered Theory of Governance: Rational Choice, Institutionalism, and Interpretation.* Working Paper 2001-10, Institute for Governmental Studies. Berkeley: University of California.

Biesta, G. (2007). Towards the knowledge democracy? Knowledge production and the civic role of the university. *Studies in Philosophy and Education*, 26(5), 467–479.

Bijker, H.G. (1995). Een doelmatige en goed gespreide GGZ dankzij de WZV? *ZM Magazine,* 10.

Boersma, J. (2002). *Management van kennis, een creatieve onderneming.* Assen: Koninklijke Van Gorcum.

Boons, F. and Janssen, M.A. (2004). The myth of Kalundborg. Social dilemmas in stimulating eco-industrial parks. In: Van den Bergh, J.C.J.M. and Janssen, M.A.

(Eds.), *Economics of Industrial Ecology. Materials, Structural Change and Spatial Scales*. Cambridge (USA): MIT Press, 337–356.

Bouleau, G. (2008). The WFD dreams: between ecology and economics. *Water and Environment Journal*, 22, 235–240.

Boulton, G. and Lucas, C. (2008). What are universities for? League of European Research Universities, September 2008.

Bradach, J.L. and Eccles, R.G. (1989). Price, authority, and trust: from ideal types to plural forms. *Annual Review of Sociology*, 15, 97–118.

Bradshaw, G.G. and Borchers, J.G. (2000). Uncertainty as information: narrowing the science-policy gap. *Conservation Ecology*, 4(1), http://www.consecol.org/vol4/iss1/art7/

Breeman, G. (2006). *Cultivating Trust, How Do Public Policies Become Trusted (thesis).* Bleiswijk.

Brenner, M. (1996). The man who knew to much. *Vanity Fair,* May edition, http://www.jeffreywigand.com/. Accessed on 23/11/2009.

Breton, A. (1995). Organizational hierarchies and bureaucracies. *European Journal of Political Economy*, 411–440.

Broerse, J.E.W. (1998). *Towards a New Development Strategy. How to Include Small-Scale Farmers in the Biotechnological Innovation Process.* Delft: Eburon.

Broerse, J.E.W. and Bunders, J.F.G. (2000). Requirements for biotechnology development: the necessity of an interactive and participatory innovation process, *Journal of Biotechnology*, 2(4), 275–296.

Broertjes, P. (2006). *De toekomst van de krant volgens Pieter Broertjes.* Speech at the annual convention of the Netherlands' Society of Editors, Groningen.

Brown, D.S. (1972). The Management of Advisory Committees: an assignment for the 1970s. *Public Administration,* July/August edition, 334–342.

Brown, L.D. (2003). Framing practice-research engagement for democratizing knowledge. *Action Research*, 1(1), 81–102.

Brundtland, G.H. (1987). *WCED 1987: Our Common Future.* Oxford: Oxford University Press.

Buchanan, J. and Congleton, R.D. (1998). *Politics by Principle, Not Interest.* Cambridge: University Press.

Bulkeley, H. and Mol, A.P.J. (2003). Participation and environmental governance: consensus, ambivalence and debate. *Environmental Values*, 12, 143–154.

Bunders, J. (1987). The practical management of scientists' actions: the influence of patterns of knowledge development in biology on cooperations between university biologists and non-scientists. In: Blume, S., Bunders, J., Leydersdorff, L. and Whitley, R. (Eds.), *The Social Direction of the Public Sciences, Sociology of the Sciences Yearbook, Volume XI.* Dordrecht: D. Reidel, 39–72.

Bunders, J. (1994). *Participative Strategies for science-based innovations: the case of biotechnology for small-scale farmers in developing countries.* Amsterdam: VU University Press.

Bunders, J. (Ed.) (1990). *Biotechnology for Small-scale Farmers in Developing Countries: Analysis and Assessment Procedures.* Amsterdam: VU University Press.

Bunders, J.F.G. (2009). Current use of transdisciplinary research: addressing constraints. Presentation at the RMNO conference 'Towards a Knowledge Democracy, consequences for Science, Politics and Media'. http://www.knowledgedemocracy.nl/files_content/2b%20Joske%20Bunders(1).pdf, accessed October 30, 2009.

Bunders, J. and Broerse, J. (Eds.) (1991). *Appropriate Biotechnology in Small-Scale Agriculture: How to Reorient Research and Development.* Wallingford: CAB International.

Bunders J. and Leydersdorff, L. (1987). The causes and consequences of collaborations between scientists and non-scientific groups. In: Blume, S., Bunders, J., Leydersdorff, L. and Whitley, R. (Eds.), *The social direction of the Public Sciences, Sociology of the Sciences Yearbook, Volume XI.* Dordrecht: D. Reidel, 331–347.

Bunders, J. and Regeer, B. (2009). *Knowledge Co-creation: Interaction Between Science and Society.* The Hague: RMNO.

Bunders, J. and Van Eijndhoven, J. (1987). The importance of interactions in broadening the base for decision-making on technology. *Bulletin of Science, Technology and Society*, 7, 687–696.

Bundesregierung (2008). Für ein nachhaltiges Deutschland. Fortschrittsbericht 2008 zur nationalen Nachhaltigkeitsstrategie. Berlin: Bundespresseamt.

Burger, P. and Kamber, R. (2003). Cognitive integration in transdisciplinary science: knowledge as a key notion. *Issues in integrative Studies*, 21, 43–73.

Busenberg, G.J. (1999). Collaborative and adversarial analysis in environmental policy. *Policy Sciences*, 32, 1–11.

Caron-Flinterman, J.F. (2005). *A New Voice in Science. Patient Participation in Decision-Making on Biomedical Research.* Zutphen: Wöhrmann.

Caron-Flinterman, J.F., Broerse, J.E.W., Teerling, J., Van Alst, M.L.Y., Klaasen, S. et al. (2006). Stakeholder participation in health research agenda setting: the case of asthma and COPD research in the Netherlands. *Science and Public Policy*, 33(4), 291–304.

Cartwright, T.J. (1975). *Royal Commissions and Departmental Committees: A Case-Study in Institutional Adaptiveness and Public Participation in Government.* London: Hodder and Stoughton Educational.

Cash, D., Clark, W., Alcock, F., Dickson, N., Eckley, N. et al. (2002). *Salience, Credibility, Legitimacy and Boundaries: Linking Research, Assessment and Decision Making, RWP02-46.* Cambridge (USA): Kennedy School of Government, Harvard University, Faculty Research Working Papers Series.

Cash, D.W., Clark, W.C., Alcock, A., Dickson, N.M., Eckley, N. et al. (2003). Knowledge systems for sustainable development. *Proceedings of the National Academy of Sciences,* 100, 8086–8091.

Cashore, B., Auld, G. and Newson, D. (2004). *Governance Through Markets – Forest Certification and the Emergence of Non-state Authority.* New Haven: Yale University Press.

Castaldo, S. (2002). *Meanings of Trust: A Meta-Analysis of Trust Definitions.* Paper presented at the 2nd Annual Conference on Innovative Research in Management.

Castells, M. (1996). *The Rise of the Network Society, The Information Age: Economy, Society and Culture, Vol. I.* Cambridge (USA): Oxford: Blackwell.

Castells, M. (1996–1998). The Information Age, London.

Castells, M. (2009). *Communication Power.* Oxford: Oxford University Press.

Caswill, C. and Shove, E. (2000). Introducing interactive social science. *Science and Public Policy*, 27(3), 154–157.

Chambers, R. and Ghidyal, B.P. (1985). Agricultural research for resource-poor farmers: the farmer-first-and-last model. *Agricultural Administration and Extension*, 20, 1–30.

Champlin, D. and Knoedler, J. (2006). The media, the news and democracy: revisiting the Dewey-Lippman debate. *Journal of Economic Issues*, 11(1).

Chapman, R.A. (Ed.) (1973). *The Role of Commissions in Policy-Making.* London: Allen and Unwin.

Chavannes, M. (2009). Uitstel als oplossing: interview in *De Standaard* (Belgian Newspaper), 19th October 2009, http://www.standaard.be/Artikel/Detail.aspx?artikelId= LA2GG3JB. Accessed on 19/10/2009.

Chilvers, J. (2008). Deliberating competence: theoretical and practitioner perspectives on effective participatory appraisal practice. *Science Technology Human Values*, 33, 155–185.

Coase, R.H. (1937). The nature of the firm. *Economica*, 4(16), 386–405.

Cohen, F. and Rodgers, J. (1995). *Associations and Democracy.* New York: Verso.

Cohen, M.D., March, J.G. and Olsen, J.P. (1972). A garbage can model of organisational choice. *Administrative Science Quarterly,* 17(1), 1–25.

Cohill, A. (2000). *Networks and the Knowledge Democracy: Nine Challenges for Communities.* Blacksburg: Blacksburg Electronic Village, http://www.bev.net/about/research/ digital_library/ docs/cn_kd.pdf. Accessed on 9/12/2009.

Coleman, S. (1999). Can the new media invigorate democracy? *Political Quarterly*, 70(2), 16–22.

Collingridge, D. (1981). *The Social Control of Technology.* Milton Keynes: Open University Press.

Collins, H. and Pinch, T. (1993). *The Golem: What Everyone Should Know About Science.* Cambridge (UK), New York: Cambridge University Press.

Collins, H.M. and Evans, R. (2002). The third wave of science studies: studies of expertise and experience. *Social Studies of Science*, 32, 235–296.

Commission of the European Communities (2003). *Common Implementation Strategy for the Water Framework Directive (2000/60/EC), Guidance Document No. 8: Public Participation in Relation to the Water Framework Directive.* Luxembourg: Office for Official Publications of the European Communities.

Considine, M. and Lewis, J.M. (1999). Governance at ground level: the frontline bureaucrat in the age of markets and networks. *Public Administration Review*, 59(6), 467–480.

Considine, M. and Lewis, J.M. (2003). Bureaucracy, network, or enterprise: comparing models of governance in Australia, Britain, the Netherlands, and New Zealand. *Public Administration Review*, 63(2), 131–140.

Cooke, B. and Kothari, U. (Eds.) (2001). *Participation: The New Tyranny?* London: Zed Books.

Cover, R. (2004). New media theory: electronic games, democracy and reconfigure the author-audience relationship. *Social Semiotics,* 14(22), 173–191.

Dahrendorf, R. (2002). Die Krisen der Demokratie, Muenchen.

Dammers, E., Klijn, J.A., Kranendonk, R.P., Van der Windt, N.P. and Kroon, H.J.J. (2002). *Innoveren in de groene ruimte: een verkenning van methoden.* Wageningen: Alterra.

Davenport, T.H. and Prusak, L. (2000). *Working Knowledge, How Organizations Manage What They Know.* Boston: Harvard Business School Press (paperback edition).

De Beus, J. (2001). *Een primaat van politiek.* Inaugural lecture at the University of Amsterdam.

De Bruijn, H. (2006). One fight, one team: the 9/11 commission report on intelligence, fragmentation and information. *Public Administration*, 84(2), 267–287.

De Bruijn, J.A. (2007). *Managing Performance in the Public Sector* (2nd edition). London, New York, Melbourne: Routledge.

De Bruin, J. and Bunders, J. (1987). *Evaluatie van de perspectieven voor samenwerking van plantenbiotechnologen en milieu-, Derde Wereld en boerenorganisaties.* Amsterdam: Department of Biology and Society, VU University.

De Bruijn, J.A. and Ten Heuvelhof, E.F. (1999). Scientific expertise in complex decision-making processes. *Science and Public Policy,* 26(3), 179–184.

Decker, M. & Ladakis, M. (Eds.) (2004). *Bridges Between Science, Society and Policy; Technology Assessment – Methods and Impacts.* Berlin: Springer-Verlag.

De Cock Buning, T., Broerse, J. and Bunders, J. (2008a). Public perception of prenatal genetic testing: arguments put forward by the public during an innovative participatory policy project in the Netherlands. *Community Genetics*, 11, 52–62.

De Cock Buning, T., Regeer, B.J. and Bunders, J. (2008b). *Biotechnology and Food – Towards a Societal Agenda in 10 Steps*. The Hague: RMNO.

Defila, R., and Di Guilio, A. (1999). Evaluating trandisciplinary research. *PANORAMA*, 1, 1–28.

Defila, R., Di Giulio, A. and Scheuermann, M. (2006). *Forschungsverbund-management - Handbuch für die Gestaltung inter- und transdisziplinärer Projekte*. Zürich: ETH.

Demos Project. (2004). Citizens Innovation Local Governance; A 21st century approach. Guidelines from the Demos project 2004 presented at the Edinburgh Conference 2004. www.toolkitparticipation.nl/download.php?dir=upload/docs/&file=demos_a4_report_guidelines.pdf Accessed January 3, 2006.

Den Hoed, P. and Keizer, A.G. (2009). The scientific council for government policy: between science, policy, and more. In: Letsch, J. and Weingart, P. (Eds.), *Scientific Advice to Policy Making. International Comparison*. Leverkusen Opladen: Barbara Budrich, 67–82.

Denzin, N.K. and Lincoln, Y. (2005). Introduction. In *The Sage Handbook of Qualitative Research*. Thousand Oaks: Sage Publications, 651–680.

De Valk, Th.W. and De Vries, M.S. (1994). Criteria voor milieu-effectrapporten. *Beleidswetenschap,* 8(3), 274–304.

De Vries, A. (2008). *Towards Doability. Dealing with Uncertainty in the Science-Policy Interface*. Enschede: Dissertation University of Twente.

De Wilde, R. (2000). De voorspellers, een kritiek op de toekomstindustrie. Amsterdam: De Balie.

De Wit, B. (2003a). New governance ideas and their consequences for knowledge management, research and innovation in the European Union. In: Meuleman, L., Niestroy, I. and Hey, C. (Eds.), *Environmental Governance in Europe*. The Hague: Lemma/RMNO/EEAC, 207–218.

De Wit, B. (2003b). *Omgaan met kennis in transities*. The Hague: RMNO.

De Wit, B. (2005a). *De methodologie van grenswerk. Aanzet tot een werkboek*. The Hague: RMNO.

De Wit, B. (2005b). *Interdisciplinarity and Policy Relevance in Research Programmes: A Position Paper*. The Hague: RMNO.

De Wit, H. (Ed.) (2007). *Duurzaamheid duurt het langst. Onderzoeksuitdagingen voor een duurzame energievoorziening*. Amsterdam: KNAW.

De Zeeuw, A., In 't Veld, R., Van Soest, D., Meuleman, L. and Hoogewoning, P. (2008). *Social Cost-Benefit Analyses for Environmental Policy-Making*. The Hague: RMNO.

Diamond, J. (2005). *Collapse: How Societies Choose to Fail or Survive* (German edition). Frankfurt: S. Fischer.

Dijstelbloem, H. (2008). *Politiek vernieuwen. Op zoek naar publiek in de technologische samenleving.* Amsterdam: Van Gennep.

DiMaggio, P. (1988). Interest and agency in institutional theory. In: Zucker, L. (Ed.), *Institutional Patterns and Culture.* Cambridge (USA): Ballinger, 3–21.

Dixon, J. and Dogan, R. (2002). Hierarchies, networks and markets: responses to societal governance failure. *Administrative Theory and Praxis*, 24(1), 175–196.

Dooley, K. (1996). A nominal definition of complex adaptive systems. *The Chaos Network*, 8(1), 2–3.

Driessen, P.P.J., Glasbergen, P. and Verdaas, C. (2001). Interactive policy-making: a model of management for public works. *European Journal of Operational Research*, 128, 322–337.

Drucker, P. (1995). The competitive advantage of the inner city. *Harvard Business Review*, May–June 1995, 55–71.

Drucker, P. (2001). The next society. *The Economist*, November 1, 2001. http://www.economist.com/surveys/displayStory.cfm?story_id=770819 Accessed March 4, 2006.

Duineveld, M., Beunen, R., Van Ark, R., Van Assche, K. and During, R. (2007). *The difference between knowing the path and walking the path. Over het terugkerend maakbaarheidsdenken in beleidsonderzoek.* Wageningen: Wageningen University.

Durant, J., Bauer, M.W. and Gaskell, G. (Eds.) (1998). *Biotechnology in the Public Sphere. A European Sourcebook.* London: Science Museum.

Dworkin, R. (2002). *Sovereign Virtue.* Cambridge: Harvard University Press.

Easton, D. (1965). *A Framework for Political Analysis.* Englewood Cliffs: Prentice Hall.

Eberhard, K. (1999). *Einführung in die Erkenntnis- und Wissenschaftstheorie.* Stuttgart: Kohlhammer Urban.

Edelenbos, J. (2005). Institutional implications of interactive governance: insights from Dutch practice. *Governance*, 18(1), 111–134.

Edelenbos, J., Van Schie, N. and Gerrits, L. (2009). Organizing interfaces in water governance: how to interconnect interactive processes with democratic institutions? *Policy Sciences,* Online First, 05/05/2009 (DOI 10.1007/s11077-009-9086-2).

EC (2001). *European Governance. A White Paper.* Brussels: Commission of the European Communities. 35.

EC (2002). *Thinking, Debating and Shaping the Future: Foresight for Europe.* Final Report of the High Level Expert Group for the European Commission. Brussels: European Commission.

EEA (2001). Late lessons from early warnings: the Precautionary Principle 1896–2000. Environmental issue report No 22. Copenhagen: EEA.

EEAC (2003). European governance for the environment. In: Meuleman, L., Niestroy, I. and Hey, C. (Eds.), *Environmental Governance in Europe*. The Hague: Lemma/RMNO/EEAC, 13–21.

Ehrmann, J.R. and Stinson, B.L. (1999). Joint fact-finding and the use of technical experts. In: Susskind, L., McKearnan, S. and Thomas-Larmer, J. (Eds.), *The Consensus Building Handbook: A Comprehensive Guide to Reaching Agreement*. London: Sage, 375–400.

Ellis, R., Waterton, C. and Wynne, B. (2009). Taxonomy, biodiversity and their publics in twenty-first century DNA barcoding. *Public Understanding of Science*. Online First, DOI: 10.1177/0963662509335413.

Enders, J.C. (2008). *Wissensnetzwerke in der Klimapolitik*. Frankfurt: Peter Lang.

Entwistle, T., Bristow, G., Hines, F., Donaldson, S. and Martin, S. (2007). The dysfunctions of markets, hierarchies and networks in the meta-governance of partnership. *Urban Studies*, 44(1), 63–79.

Ergazakis, K., Metaxiotis, K. and Psarras, J. (2004). Towards knowledge cities: conceptual analysis and success stories. *Journal of Knowledge Management*, 8(5), 5–15.

Eshuis, J. and Stuiver, M. (2005). Learning in context through conflict and alignment: farmers and scientists in search of sustainable agriculture. *Agriculture and Human Values*, 22(2), 137–148.

Etzioni, A. (1993). *The Spirit of Community: The Reinvention of American Society*. New York: Simon and Schuster.

European Union (2007). *Europäische Strategie zur nachhaltigen Entwicklung*. Brussels: European Commission.

Eurostat (2009). http://epp.eurostat.ec.europa.eu/tgm/table.do?tab=table&init .

Euwals, R., De Mooij, R. and Van Vuren, D. (2009). *Rethinking Retirement*. The Hague: CPB.

Faber, A. and Van Welie, W. (2004). *Onderzoek voor duurzame ontwikkeling; research en development voor transities*. The Hague: RMNO.

Fehr, E. and Falk, A. (2002). Psychological foundations of incentives. *European Economic Review*, 46, 687–724.

Fernandez-Gimenez, M.E., Ballard, H.L. and Sturtevant, V.E. (2008). Adaptive management and social learning in collaborative and community-based monitoring: a study of five community-based forestry organizations in the western USA. *Ecology and Society*, 13(2), http://www.ecologyandsociety.org/vol13/iss2/art4/

Fischer, F. (1991). Risk assessment and environmental crisis. *Industrial Crisis Quarterly*, 2(5), 113–132.

Fischer, F. (2003). *Reframing Public Policy*. Oxford: Oxford University Press.

Fischer, P. and Huddart, S. (2008). Optimal contracting with endogenous social norms. *American Economic Review*, 98, 1459–1475.

Flitner, Jr., D. (1986). *The Politics of Presidential Commissions*. New York: Transnational Publishers Inc.

Florida, R. (2002). *The Rise of the Creative Class*. New York: Basic Books.

Florida, R. (2005). *Cities and the Creative Class*. New York, London: Routledge.

Florida, R. (2008). *Who's your City*. New York: Basic Books.

Florida, R. (2008a). Megaregions, the importance of place. *Harvard Business Review*, March 2008, 18–19.

Frederickson, H.G. and Smith, K.B. (2003). *The Administration Theory Primer*. Cambridge (USA): Westview Press.

Frewer, L. et al. (2001). Public participation methods: evolving and operationalising an evaluation framework. Summary Project Report, UK Department of Health: Norwich.

Frey, B.S. and Stutzer, A. (2002). What can economists learn from happiness research? *Journal of Economic Literature*, 40, 402–435.

Frey, B.S. and Jegen, R. (2001). Motivation crowding theory: a survey of empirical evidence. *Journal of Economic Surveys*, 15, 589–611.

Friedman, Th. (2005). *The World is Flat: A Brief History of the Twenty-first Century*. New York: Farrar, Straus and Giroux.

Friedman, T.L. (2008). *Hot, Flat, and Crowded. Why the World Needs a Green Revolution – And How We Can Renew Our Global Future*. London: Penguin.

Frissen, V. (2008). Interview on the television programme "Boeken" (28/12/2008), about the book *De draagbare lichtheid van het bestaan*. Hilversum: VPRO.

Fuchs, Ch. (2009). Some reflections on Manuel Castells' Book "Communication Power". *TripleC*, 7(1), 94–18.

Fung, A. (2004). *Empowered Participation, Reinventing Urban Democracy*. Princeton: Princeton University Press.

Funtowicz, S.O. and Ravetz, J.R. (1991). A new scientific methodology for global environmental issues. In: R. Constanza (Ed.), *Ecological Economics: The Science and Management of Sustainability*, New York: Columbia University Press, 137–152. Cited in Latesteijn, H. van, Land in use, Voorstudie WRR 106, 1999, Den Haag, 41–43.

Funtowicz, S. and Ravetz, J. (1992). Three types of risk assessment and the emergence of post-normal science. In: Krimsky, S. and Golding, D. (Eds.), *Social Theories of Risk*. Westport: Praeger, 211–232.

Funtowicz, S. and Ravetz, J. (1993). Science for the post-normal age. *Futures*, 25, 739–755.

Gaber, I. (2007). Too much of a good thing: the "problem" of political communications in mass media democracy. *Journal of Public Affairs*, 7, 219–234.

Gallopín, G.C., Funtowicz, S., O'Connor, M. and Ravetz, J. (2001). Science for the twenty-first century: from social contract to the scientific core. *International Journal of Social Science,* 168(2), 219–229.

Garud, R., Hardy, C. and Maguire, S. (2007). Institutional entrepreneurship as embedded agency: an introduction to the special issue. *Organisation Studies*, 28(7), 957–969.

Gaskell, G. and Bauer, M.W. (2001). *Biotechnology 1996–1999: The Years of Controversy*. London: Science Museum Publishing.

Gaventa, J. (1991). Toward a knowledge democracy: viewpoints on participatory research in North America. In: Fals-Borda, O. and Rahman, M.A. (Eds.), *Action and Knowledge: Breaking the Monopoly with Participatory Action-Research.* New York: Apex Press, 121–133.

Gaynor, D. (1996). *Democracy in the Age of Information: A Reconception of the Public Sphere,* http://www9.georgetown.edu/faculty/bassr/gaynor/intro.htm. Accessed on 04/11/2009.

Gee, D. (2008). Costs of inaction (or delayed action) to reduce exposures to hazardous agents: some lessons from history. Paper to the SCBA Conference in the Hague, 17/01/2008.

Gee, D. (2009): *Evaluating and Communicating Scientific Evidence on Environment and on Health. Presentation to EEAC,* 12/06/2009, EEA, Copenhagen.

Geels, F.W. (2002). Technological transitions as evolutionary reconfiguration processes: a multi-level perspective and a case-study. *Research Policy,* 31, 1257–1274.

Gerstl-Pepin, C. (2007). Introduction to the special issue on media, democracy, and the politics of education. *Peabody Journal of Education*, 82(2), 1–9.

Gibbons, M. (1999). Science's new social contract with society. *Nature*, 102, 11–18.

Gibbons, M., Limoges, C., Nowotny, H., Schwartzman, S., Scott, P. et al. (1994). *The New Production of Knowledge: The Dynamics of Science and Research in Contemporary Societies.* London, Thousand Oaks, New Delhi: Sage.

Gibson, R.K., Margolis, M., Resnick, D. and Ward, S.J. (2003). Election campaigning on the WWW in the USA and UK: a comparative analysis. *Party Politics,* 9, 47–75.

Giddens, A. (1990). *The Consequences of Modernity*. Cambridge: Polity Press.

Giddens, A. (1991). *Modernity and Self Identity: Self and Society in the Late Modern Age.* Stanford, CA: Stanford University Press.

Giddens, A. (1994). *Beyond Left and Right. The Future of Radical Politics.* Cambridge: Polity Press.

Gieryn, T. (1995). Boundaries of Science. In: Jasanoff, S., Markle, G.E., Petersen, J.C. and Pinch, T. (eds). *Handbook of Science and Technology Studies*. Thousand Oaks, London, New Delhi: Sage, 393–443.

Gieryn, T. (1999). *Cultural Boundaries of Science, Credibility on the Line*. Chicago, London: University of Chicago Press.

Gieryn, T.F. (1983). Boundary work and the demarcation of science from non-science, strains and interests in professional interests of scientists. *American Sociological Review*, 48, 781–795.

Glaser, B. and Strauss, A. (1967). *The Discovery of Grounded Theory: Strategies for Qualitative Research*. New York: Aldine.

Goede, M. (2006). *Media en democatie. UNA 2006 Publicaties*. Willemstad (Netherlands Antilles): University of the Netherlands Antilles.

Goverde, H. (2006). Klimaatverandering en 'politiek klimaat': lange termijn politiek en de intelligentie van democratie. *Topos*, 16(2), 30–33.

Graber, D. (2003). The media and democracy: beyond myths and stereotypes. *Annual Review of Political Science*, 6, 139–160.

Granovetter, M.S. (1985). Economic action and social structure: the problem of embeddedness. *American Journal of Sociology*, 91, 481–510.

Greenbaum, T.L. (1998). *The Handbook for Focus Group Research*. Thousand Oaks: Sage.

Grin, J. (2004). *De politiek van omwenteling met beleid*. Amsterdam: Vossiuspers.

Grin, J. and Van de Graaf, H. (1996). Implementation as communicative action. An interpretive understanding of interactions between policy actors and target groups. *Policy Sciences*, 29, 291–319.

Grin, J. and Van de Graaf, H. (2001). Variëteit in rationaliteit en legitimiteit van beleid. In: Abma, T. and In 't Veld, R. (Eds.), *Handboek Beleidswetenschap*, 208–221. Amsterdam: Boom.

Grin, J., Van de Graaf, H. and Hoppe, R. (1997). *Technology Assessment Through Interaction. A Guide*. The Hague: Rathenau Institute.

Grossman, L. (2006). Time's person of the year: you. *Time*,13/12/2006, http://www.time.com/time/printout/0,8816,1569514,00.html. Accessed on 05/11/2009.

Grotenhuis, F. (2007). *De Toekomst van Creativiteit*. Amsterdam: Dutch University Press.

Guba, E. and Lincoln, Y. (2005). Paradigmatic controversies, contradictions, and emerging confluences. In Denzin, N.K. and Lincoln, Y. (Eds.), *The Sage Handbook of Qualitative Research*. Thousand Oaks: Sage Publications, 191–216.

Guston, D.H. (2001). Boundary organization in environmental policy and science: an introduction. *Science, Technology, and Human Values*, 26(4), 399–408.

Häberli, R. and Grossenbacher-Mansuy, W. (1998). Transdisziplinarität zwischen Förderung und Überforderung. Erkenntnisse aus dem SPP Umwelt. *GAIA*, 7(3), 196–213.

Habermas, J. (1962). *The Structural Transformation of the Public Sphere: An Inquiry into a Category of Bourgeois Society.* Cambridge (UK): Polity Press.

Hagendijk, R. and Irwin, A. (2006). Public deliberation and governance, engaging with science and technology in contemporary Europe. *Minerva*, 44, 167–184.

Hagendijk, R. and Kallerud, E. (2005). *Changing Conceptions and Practices of Governance in Science and Technology in Europe: A Framework for Analysis. Science, Technology and Governance in Europe* (STAGE), 1(2), 155–180, http://www.stage-research.net. Accessed on 25/10/2009.

Hajer, M. (2003). Policy without polity: policy analysis and the institutional void. *Policy Sciences*, 36(2), 175–195.

Hajer, M. (2005). Setting the stage, a dramaturgy of policy deliberation. *Administration and Society*, 36, 624–647.

Hajer, M. and Wagenaar, H. (2003). *Deliberative Policy Analysis: Understanding Governance in the Network Society.* Cambridge (UK): Cambridge University Press.

Halffman, W. (2003). *Boundaries of Regulatory Science.* Amsterdam: Dissertation University of Amsterdam.

Halffman, W. (2008). *States of Nature. Nature and Fish Stock Reports for Policy.* The Hague: RMNO.

Halffman, W. (2009). Measuring the Stakes: The Dutch Planning Bureaus. In: Lentsch, J. and Weingart, P. (Eds.), *Scientific Advice to Policy Making. International Comparison.* Leverkusen Opladen, Farmington Hills: Barbara Budrich, 41–66.

Halffman, W. and Bal, R. (2008). After impact: success of scientific advice to public policy. In: Halffman, W. (Ed.), *States of Nature – Nature and Fish Stock Reports for Policy.* The Hague: RMNO.

Halffman, W. and Hoppe, R. (2005). Science/policy boundaries: a changing division of labour in Dutch scientific policy advice. In Weingart, P. and Maassen, S. (eds). *Democratization of Expertise? Exploring Novel Forms of Scientific Advice in Political Decision-Making, Sociology of Sciences Yearbook XXIV.* Dordrecht: Springer, 135–152.

Halligan, J. (2007). Reintegrating government in third generation reforms of Australia and New Zealand. *Public Policy and Administration,* 22, 217–238.

Hanson, H.R. (1969). Inside royal commissions. *Canadian Public Administration*, XII-3, 356–364.

Harfoush, R. (2009). *Yes We Did: An Inside Look at How Social Media Built the Obama Brand.* Berkeley: New Riders.

Havelock, R.G. (1968). *Knowledge Utilization and Dissemination: A Bibliography.* Ann Arbor: University of Michigan Center for Research on Utilization of Scientific Knowledge (CRUSK).

Havelock, R.G. (1971). *Planning for Innovation: Through Dissemination and Utilization of Knowledge.* Ann Arbor: University of Michigan Center for Research on Utilization of Scientific Knowledge (CRUSK).

Hayek, F.A. (1960). *The Constitution of Liberty.* Chicago: Aldine.

Hennipman, P. (1995). *Welfare Economics and the Theory of Economic Policy.* Aldershot: Elgar.

Hertz, N. (2003). *De stille overname; de globalisering en het einde van de democratie.* Amsterdam: Contact.

Hirsch Hadorn, G. (2002). Unity of knowledge in transdisciplinary research for sustainability. In: UNESCO-EOLSS. *Encyclopedia of Life Support Systems (EOLSS).* Oxford: Eolss Publishers.

Hirsch Hadorn, G., Bradley, D., Pohl, C., Rist, S. and Wiesmann, U. (2006). Implications of transdisciplinarity for sustainability research. *Ecological Economics,* 60(1), 119–128.

Hirsch Hadorn, G., Hoffmann-Riem, H., Biber-Klemm, S. et al. (Eds.) (2008). *Handbook on Transdisciplinary Research.* Dordrecht: Springer.

Hirsch Hadorn, G., Hoffmann-Riem, H., Biber-Klemm, S., Grossenbacher, W., Joye, D. et al. (2008a). The emergence of transdisciplinarity as a form of research. In: Hirsch Hadorn, G., Hoffmann-Riem, H., Biber-Klemm, S., Grossenbacher, W., Joye, D. et al. (Eds.), *Handbook of Transdisciplinary Research.* Dordrecht: Springer, 19–39.

Hirsch Hadorn, G., Hoffmann-Riem, H., Biber-Klemm, S., Grossenbacher, W., Joye, D. et al. (Eds.), (2008b). *Handbook of Transdisciplinary Research.* Dordrecht: Springer.

Hirschleifer, J. (1985). The expanding domain of economics'. *American Economic Review,* 75, 51–68.

Hisschemöller, M. (1993). *De democratie van problemen. De relatie tussen inhoud van beleidsproblemen en methoden van politieke besluitvorming.* Dissertation. Amsterdam: VU University Press.

Hisschemöller, M. (2008). *De lamentabele toestand van het energietransitiebeleid. Observaties en kennisvragen vanuit een interdisciplinair beleidswetenschappelijk perspectief.* Amsterdam: Institute for Environmental Studies, VU University.

Hisschemöller, M., Hoppe, R., Groenewegen, P. and Midden, C.J.H. (2001). Knowledge use and political choice in Dutch environmental policy: a problem structuring perspective on real life experiments in extended peer review. In: Hisschemöller, M., Dunn, W.N., Hoppe, R. and Ravetz, J. (Eds.), *Knowledge, Power and Participation in Environmental Policy Analysis. Policy Studies Review Annual,* 12, 437–470. New Brunswick: Transaction.

Hjelt M., Den Hertog P., Te Velde R., Syrjänen, M. and Ahonen P-P. (2008). *Major Challenges for the Governance of National Research and Innovation Policies in Small European Countries.* Tekes Review 236/2008. Helsinki: Finnish Funding Agency for Technology and Innovation.

Hodgetts, J.E. (1949). Royal commissions of inquiry in Canada. *Public Administration Review*, IX-1, 22–29.

Hoefnagel, F.J. (1975). Inleiding. *Bestuurswetenschappen*, 6, 385–386.

Hofstede, G. (2001). *Culture's Consequences: Comparing Values, Behaviours, Institutions and Organisations Across Nations.* Newbury Park: Sage.

Holland, J.H. (1992). *Adaptation in Natural and Artificial Systems: An Introductory Analysis with Applications to Biology, Control, and Artificial Intelligence.* Cambridge (USA): MIT Press.

Holstein, J.A. and Gubrium, J.F. (2000). *The Self We Live by: Narrative Identity in a Postmodern World.* Oxford: Oxford University Press.

Holton, R. (1994). Deciding to trust, coming to believe. *Australasian Journal of Philosophy,* 72(1), 63–76.

Hoogtanders, K. et al. (2006). Naar een sluitende keten van preventie, verzuim en re-integratie (Linking Prevention, Sick-leave and Reintegration). The Hague, Ministry of Social Affairs and Employment.

Hoppe, R. (1999). Policy analysis, science and politics: from 'speaking truth to power' to 'making sense together'. *Science and public Policy*, 26(3), 201–210.

Hoppe, R. (2002). Van flipperkast naar grensverkeer. Veranderende visies op de relatie tussen wetenschap en beleid. The Hague: AWT.

Hoppe, R. (2003). Werken op de grens tussen wetenschap en politiek: naar een typologie van grensarrangementen. *Beleidswetenschap*, 17(2), 144–170.

Hoppe, R. (2005). Rethinking the science-policy nexus: from knowledge utilization and science technology studies to types of boundary arrangements. *Poièsis and Praxis: International Journal of Technology Assessment and Ethics of Science*, 3(3), 199–215.

Hoppe, R. (2008a). Public policy subsystems dealing with ethically contested medical-technological issues. *Creativity and Innovation Management*, 17(4), 293–303.

Hoppe, R. (2008b). Scientific advice and public policy: expert advisers' and policy-makers' discourses on boundary work. *Poièsis and Praxis: International Journal of Technology Assessment and Ethics of Science*, 6(3–4), 235–263.

Hoppe, R. (2010/in press). *The Governance of Problems. Puzzling, Powering, and Participation.* Bristol: Policy Press.

Hoppe, R. (in press). Lost in translation? A boundary work perspective on making climate change governable. In: Driessen, P., Leroy, P. and Van Viersen, W. (Eds.), *From Climate Change to Social Change: Perspectives on Science-Policy Interactions.* London: Earthscan.

Hoppe, R. and Huijs, S. (2003). *Werk op de grens van wetenschap en beleid: paradoxen en dilemma's.* The Hague: RMNO.

Hospers, G. (2003). Creative cities in Europe, urban competitiveness in the knowledge economy. *Intereconomics*, September/October 2003, 260–269.

Howe, J. (2008). Crowdsourcing: Why the Power of the Crowd is Driving the Future of Business. New York: Random House.

Howlett, M. and Ramesh, M. (2003). *Studying Public Policy: Policy Cycles and Policy Subsystems* (2nd edition). Oxford: Oxford University Press.

Huitema, D. and Turnhout, E. (2009). Working at the science-policy interface: a discursive analysis of boundary work at the Netherlands Environmental Assessment Agency. *Environmental Politics,* 18, 576–594.

Hunt, J. and Shackley, S. (1999). Reconceiving science and policy: academic, fiducial and bureaucratic knowledge. *Minerva*, 37, 141–164.

ICSU (2003). *Science and Technology for Sustainable Development.* Consensus report and background document for Mexico City Synthesis Conference.

In 't Veld, R.J. (2007). *De vloek van het succes. Over de ontwikkeling van democratie.* Hogeschool Inholland.

In 't Veld, R.J. (2009). *Towards Knowledge Democracy. Consequences for Science, Politics and the Media.* Paper for the international conference Towards Knowledge Democracy, 25–27 August, Leiden.

In 't Veld, R.J. (Ed.) (2000/2009). *Willingly and Knowingly. The Roles of Knowledge About Nature and the Environment in Policy Processes.* The Hague: RMNO.

In 't Veld, R.J. (Ed.) (2001/2008). *The Rehabilitation of Cassandra. A methodological Discourse on Future Research for Environmental and Spatial Policy.* The Hague: WRR/RMNO/NRLO (English version available at www.rmno.nl).

In 't Veld, R.J. and Verhey, A.J.M. (2000/2009). Willingly and knowingly: about the relationship between values, knowledge production and use of knowledge in environmental policy. In: In 't Veld, R.J. (Ed.), *Willingly and Knowingly: The Roles of Knowledge About Nature and Environment in Policy Processes.* The Hague: RMNO, 105–145.

In 't Veld, R.J., Maassen van den Brink, H., Morin, P., Van Rij, V., Van der Veen, H. et al. (Eds.) (2007). *Horizon Scan Report 2007. Towards a Future Oriented Policy and Knowledge Agenda.* The Hague: COS, ISBN/EAN: 978-90-72863-24-9. Available from: http://www.horizonscan.nl/uploads/File/COS_binnenwerk%20engels_06(1).pdf, accessed 1 June 2009.

Innes, J.E., and Booher, D.E. (1999). Consensus building and complex adaptive systems: a framework for evaluating collaborative planning. *Journal of the American Planning Association,* 65, 412–423.

International Risk Governance Council. (2009). *Risk Governance Deficits, an Analysis and Illustration of the Most Common Deficits in Risk Governance*. Geneve: IRGC. ISBN 978-2-9700631-9-3. Avaliable from www.irgc.org

IPCC. (2007). Fourth Assessment Report. http://www.ipcc.ch/publications_and_data/publications_ipcc_fourth_assessment_report_synthesis_report.htm

Irwin, A. (1995). *Citizen Science. A Study of People, Expertise and Sustainable Development. Environment and Society*. London and New York: Routledge.

Irwin, A. (2001). Constructing the scientific citizen: science and democracy in the biosciences. *Public Understanding of Science,* 10(1), 1–18.

Irwin, A., Simmons, P. and Walker, G. (1999). Faulty environments and risk reasoning: the local understanding of industrial hazards, *Environment and Planning A*, 31, 1311–1326.

Jackson, N. (2007). Political parties, the internet and the 2005 general election: third time lucky? *Internet Research,* 17(3), 249–271.

Jackson, N. and Lilleker, D.G. (2004). Just public relations or an attempt at interaction? British MPs in the press, on the web and 'in your face'. *European Journal of Communication,* 19(4), 507–533.

Jackson, P.T. and Stanfield, J.R. (2004). The role of the press in democracy: Heterodox economics and the propaganda model. *Journal of Economic Issues*, 38(2).

Jacobsson, S. and Johnson, A. (2000a). The diffusion of renewable energy technology: an analytical framework and key issues for research. *Energy Policy*, 28(9), 625–640.

Jacobsson, S. and Johnson, A. (2000b). *The Emergence of a Growth Industry: A Comparative Analysis of the German, Dutch and Swedish Wind Turbine Industries,* www.druid.dk/conferences/winter2002/gallery/jacobsson

Jaeger, C.C. et al. (Eds.) (2001). *Risk, Uncertainty, and Rational Action*. London and Sterling: Earthscan Publicationds Ltd.

Jäger, J. (2008). Sustainability science. In: Spangenberg, J.H. (Ed.). *Sustainable Development: Past Conflicts and Future Challenges*. Münster: Westfälisches Dampfboot, 166–175.

Jahn, T. (2008). Transdisziplinarität in der Forschungspraxis. In: Bergmann, M. and Schramm, E. (Eds.), *Transdisziplinäre Forschung. Integrative Forschungsprozesse verstehen und bewerten*. Frankfurt, New York: Campus, 21–37. (English version available at www.isoe.de).

Jahn, T. and Keil, F. (2006). Transdisziplinärer Forschungsprozess. In: Becker, E. and Jahn, T. (Eds.), S*oziale Ökologie. Grundzüge einer Wissenschaft von den gesellschaftlichen Naturverhältnissen*. Frankfurt, New York: Campus, 319–329.

Jantsch, E. (Ed.) (1972). Towards Interdisciplinarity and Transdisciplinarity in Education and Innovation, in Problems of Teaching and Research in Universities. Paris: OECD, 97–121.

Jasanoff, S. (1990). *The Fifth Branch: Advisers as Policy Makers.* Cambridge (USA): Harvard University Press.

Jasanoff, S. (2003). Technologies of humility: Citizen participation in governing science. *Minerva,* 41, 223–244.

Jasanoff, S. (Ed.) (2004). *States of Knowledge: The Co-Production of Science and Social Order.* London, New York: Routledge.

Jasanoff, S. (2005). *Designs on Nature. Science and Democracy in in Europe and the United States.* Princeton: Princeton University Press.

Jasanoff, S. and Martello, M.L. (Eds.) (2004). *Earthly Politics. Local and Global in Environmental Governance.* Cambridge (USA), London: MIT Press.

Jasanoff, S. et al. (Eds.) (1995). *Handbook of Science and Technology Studies.* Society for Social Studies of Sciencc. Thousand Oaks, CA: Sage Publications.

Jeeninga, H. (2008). Interview on March 19th 2008.

Jessop, B. (1997). Capitalism and its future: remarks on regulation, government and governance. *Review of International Political Economy*, 4, 561–581.

Jessop, B. (2003). Governance and metagovernance: on reflexivity, requisite variety, and requisite irony. In Bang, H. (Ed.), *Governance as Social and Political Communication.* Manchester: Manchester University Press, 101–116.

Joss, S. and Bellucci, S. (Eds.) (2002). *Participatory Technology Assessment. European Perspective*. London: Centre for Study of Democracy.

Kahneman, D., Wakker, P and Sarin, R. (1997). Back to Bentham? Explorations of experienced utility. *Quarterly Journal of Economics*, 112: 375–405.

Kant, I. (1781–1787). *The Critique of Pure Reason*, 341–363.

Kauffman, S. (1995). *At Home in the Universe: The Search for Laws of Self-organization and Complexity.* New York: Oxford University Press.

Kemmis, S. and McTaggart, R. (1988). *The Action Research Planner* (3rd edition). Geelong: Deakin University.

Kemp, R., Gibson, R. and Parto, S. (2005). Governance for Sustainable Development: Moving from theory to practice. *International Journal of Sustainable Development*, 8(1/2), 13–30.

Kettle, D.F. (2002). *The Transformation of Governance, Public Administration for Twenty-First Century America.* Baltimore, London: John Hopkins University Press.

Kickert, W.J.M., Koppenjan, J.F.M. and Klijn, E.H. (1997). *Managing Complex Networks: Strategies for the Public Sector.* London: Sage.

Kingdon, J.W. (1984). *Agendas, Alternatives and Public Policies.* Boston: Little, Brown and Company.

Kingdon, J.W. (1995). *Agendas, Alternatives, and Public Policies.* Second Edition. New Yrok: Longman.

Klein, N. (2007). *The Shock Doctrine: The Rise of Disaster Capitalism.* New York: Metropolitan Books, Henry Holt.

Klein, E-H. and Snellen, I. (2009). *Complexity Theory and Public Administration. A Critical Appraisal.* In: Teisman, G. et al. (2009), 17–36.

Klijn, E.H. (2008). Governance and governance networks in Europe: an assessment of 10 years of research on the theme. *Public Management Review*, 10(4), 505–525.

Klijn, E.H. and Skelcher, C.K. (2007). Democracy and governance networks: compatible or not? Four conjectures and their implications. *Public Administration*, 85(3), 1–22.

KNAW. (2007). 'Duurzaamheid duurt het langst' Onderzoeksuitdagingen voor een duurzame energievoorziening. (Sustainability takes a long time. Research challenges for a sustainable energy supply).

Knight, R.V. (1995). Knowledge-based development: policy and planning implications for cities. *Urban Studies*, 32(2), 225–260.

Knorr-Cetina, K. (1999). *Epistemic Cultures: How the Sciences Make Knowledge.* Cambridge (USA): Harvard University Press.

Köbben, A.J.F. (2004). *Het gevecht met de engel. Over verheffende en minder verheffende aspecten van het wetenschapsbedrijf.* Amsterdam: Mets and Schilt.

Köbben, A.J.F. and Tromp, H. (1999). *De onwelkome boodschap of hoe de vrijheid van wetenschap bedreigd wordt.* Amsterdam: Mets.

Kok, L. (2006). *Kosten en baten van integratie* (Costs and Benefits of Integration). Amsterdam: SEO.

Kok, L. and Hop, P. (2008). *Langdurig in de WAO* (Duration of Disability Entitlements). The Hague: Ministry of Social Affairs and Employment.

Komarovsky, M. (1975). *Sociology and Public Policy, The Case of Presidential Commissions.* New York: Elsevier.

Koppenjan, J.F.M. and Klijn, E.H. (2004). *Managing Uncertainties in Networks.* London: Routledge.

Korteland, E. (2004). *Doorwerking van strategische beleidsadviezen. Een onderzoek naar de doorwerking van strategische beleidsadviezen van de Raad voor de Volksgezondheid en Zorg.* Rotterdam: Thesis Erasmus University.

Krozer, J. (2008). Interview by RMNO.

Kuan Yew, L. (2000). *From Third World to First World; the Singapore Story: 1965–2000.* New York: HarperCollins.

Kuhlmann, S. (2002). *Governance and Intelligence in Research and Innovation Systems.* Inaugural lecture at the University of Utrecht.

Kupper, J.F.H. (2009). Democratizing animal biotechnology: Inquiry and deliberation inethics and governance. Amsterdam: Thesis VU University.

Kupper, J.F.H., Krijgsman, L., Bout, H.J. and De Cock Buning, J.T. (2007). The value lab: exploring moral frameworks in the deliberation of values in the animal biotechnology debate. *Science and Public Policy*, 34, 657–670.

Kurtz, C.F. and Snowden, D.J. (2003). The new dynamics of strategy: Sense-making in a complex and complicated world. *IBM Systems Journal*, 42(3), 462–483.

Kwa, C. (2006). The programming of interdisciplinary research through informal science-policy interactions. *Science and Public Policy*, 33(6): 457–467.

Laclau, E. (2005). *On Populist Reason.* London, New York: Verso.

Lagerspetz, E. (1999). Rationality and politics in long-term decisions. *Biodiversity and Conservation*, 8(1), 149–164.

Laird, F. N. (1993). Participatory analysis, democracy, and technological decision making. *Science, Technology, and Human Values*, 18(3), 341–361.

Landry, C. (2000). *The Creative City*. London: Earthscan.

Landry, R., Lamari, M. and Amara, N. (2003). The extent and determinants of the utilization of university research in government agencies. *Public Administration Review*, 63(2), 192–203.

Latour, B. (1999). *Pandora's Hope: Essays on the Reality of Science Studies.* Cambridge (USA): Harvard University Press.

Lawrence, R.J. and Despres, C. (2004). Futures of transdisciplinarity. *Futures*, 36, 397–405.

Lawton, J.H. (2007). Ecology, politics and policy. *Journal of Applied Ecology,* 44, 465–474.

Leach, M., Scoones, I. and Wynne, B. (eds) (2006). *Science and Citizens: Globalization and the Challenge of Engagement.* London: Zed.

Lee, N.J., McLeod, D.M. and Shah, D.V. (2008). Framing policy debates. Issue dualism, journalistic frames, and opinions on controversial policy issues. *Communication Research*, 35(5), 695–718.

Leggewie, C. and Welzer, H. (2009). *Das Ende der Welt, wie wir sie kannten. Klima, Zukunft und die Chancen der Demokratie.* Frankfurt: S. Fischer.

Le Grand, J. (2003). *Motivation, Agency and Public Policy.* Oxford: Oxford University Press.

Le Grand, J. (2007). *The Other Invisible Hand. Delivering Public Services through Choice and Competition.* Oxford: Princeton University Press.

Letsch, J. and P. Weingart (Eds.) (2009). *Scientific Advice to Policy Making. International Comparison.* Leverkusen Opladen: Barbara Budrich.

Levacic, R. (1991). Markets and governments: an overview. In: Thompson, G., Frances, J., Levacic, R. and Mitchell, J. (Eds.), *Markets, Hierarchies and Networks: The Coordination of Social Life*. London: Sage, 35–47.

Lever, W.F. (2002). Correlating the Knowledge-base of cities with economic growth. *Urban Studies*, 39(5–6), 859–870.

Lewin, K. (1946). Action research and minority problems. *Journal of Social Issues*, 2, 34–46.

Leydesdorff, L. and Etzkowitz, H. (1996). Emergence of a triple Helix of University-Industry-Governmant relations. *Science and Public Policy*, 23, 279–286.

Liberatore, A. and Funtowicz, S. (2003). 'Democratising' expertise, 'expertising' democracy: what does this mean, and why bother? *Science and Public Policy,* 30, 146–150.

Lidskog, R. and Sundquist, G. (2002). The role of science in environmental regimes: The Case of LRTAP. *European Journal of International Relations,* 8(1), 77–101.

Lindblom, Ch. E. (1977). *Politics and Markets*. New York: Basic Books.

Lindblom, C.E. and Cohen, D.K. (1979). *Usable Knowledge: Social Science and Social Problem Solving*. New Haven: Yale University Press.

Lintsen, H. (2002). Two centuries of central water management in the Netherlands. *Technology and Culture*, 43, 549–568.

Lipsky, M. and Olsen, D. (1977). *Commission Politics: The Processing of Racial Crisis in America.* New Brunswick: Transaction.

Lisberg, A. (2009). Cost of Mayor Bloomberg's campaign? $64,756,118.47. Leading race for City Hall? Priceless! *Daily News New York*, 2/10/2009, http://www.nydailynews.com/news/election_2009/2009/10/02/2009-10-02_cost_of_mayor_bloombergs_campaign_6475611847_leading_race_for_city_hall_priceles.html. Accessed on 05/11/2009.

Loeber, A. (1997). *Evaluatie van het IP-NPF: Gebruikte methoden en behaalde resultaten*. Werkdocument VN23. Delft: Programmabureau DTO.

Loorbach, D.A. (2007). *Transition Management: New Mode of Governance for Sustainable Development*. Utrecht: International Books.

Lopreato, J. and Crippen, T. (1999). *Crisis in Sociology. The Need for Darwin.* New Brunswick: Transaction Publishers.

Lowndes, V. and Skelcher, C. (1998). The dynamics of multi-organisational partnerships: an analysis of changing modes of governance. *Public Administration*, 76, 313–333.

Maasen, S. and Lieven, O. (2006). Socially robust knowledge. Transdisciplinarity: a new mode of governing science? *Science and Public Policy*, 33(6), 399–410.

Maduro, J. (2004). *Radio ambiente op Curaçao.* Willemstad (Netherlands Antilles): University of the Netherlands Antilles.

Maffesoli, M. (1996). *The Time of the Tribes. The Decline of Individualism in Mass Society*. London: Sage Publications.

Markowitz, G. and Rosner, D. (2003). *Deceit and Denial. The Deadly Politics of Industrial Pollution.* Berkeley: University of California Press.

Marres, N. (2005). *No Issue, No Public. Democratic Deficits after the Displacement of Politics.* Amsterdam: Jipskant Printpartners.

Martinson, B.C., Anderson, M.S. and De Vries, R. (2005). Scientists behaving badly. *Nature*, 435, 737–738.

McCann, E.J. (2001). Collaborative visioning or urban planning as therapy? The politics of public-private policy making. *Professional Geographer*, 53(2), 207–218.

McClean, S. and Shaw, A. (2005). From schism to continuum? The problematic relationship between expert and lay knowledge: an exploratory conceptual synthesis of two qualitative studies. *Qualitative Health Research*, 15(6), 729–749.

Mead, G.H. (1934). *Mind, Self and Society.* Chigago: Univesity of Chigago press.

Meffe, G.K. (1998). Conservation scientists and the policy process. *Conservation Biology*, 12, 741–742.

Meijer, I.S.M. (2008). *The Role of Uncertainty in the Development of Emerging Technologies.* Delft: Dissertation Delft University of Technology.

Meuleman, L. (2003a). *The Pegasus Principle. Reinventing a Credible Public Sector.* The Hague: Lemma.

Meuleman, L. (2003b). Flexibly organising governance styles. In: Meuleman, L., Niestroy, I. and Hey, C. (Eds.), *Environmental governance in Europe,* 219–237. The Hague/Utrecht: RMNO/EEAC/Lemma.

Meuleman, L. (2008). *Public Management and the Metagovernance of Hierarchies, Networks and Markets.* Heidelberg: Springer.

Meuleman, L. (2009a). The cultural dimension of metagovernance: why governance doctrines may fail. *Public Organisation Review.* Online first: 12/08/2009 (DOI 10.1007/s11115-009-0088-5).

Meuleman, L. (2009b). *Metagoverning Governance Styles: Increasing the Metagovernors' Toolbox.* Paper presented at the panel 'Metagoverning Interactive Governance and Policymaking', ECPR general conference 10–12 September 2009, Potsdam.

Meuleman, L. and In 't Veld, R.J. (2009). *Sustainable Development and the Governance of Long-Term Decisions.* The Hague: RMNO/EEAC.

Miller, C. (2001). Hybrid management: boundary organizations, science policy, and environmental governance in the climate regime. *Science, Technology and Human Values*, 26(4), 478–500.

Ministry of Education and Science (1984). *Integration of Science and Technology in Society.* The Hague: Staatsuitgeverij.

Mintzberg, H. (1983). *Structure in Fives: Designing Effective Organizations.* Englewood Cliffs: Prentice Hall.

Minx, E. and Preisler, H. (2008). "Die Sonne geht nicht im Osten auf.", Zukunftsfähiges Denken und verantwortliches Handeln. In: Von Mutius, B. (Ed.). *Die andere Intelligenz. Wie wir morgen denken werden.* Stuttgart: Klett-Cotta, 254–269.

Mittelstraß, J. (1992). Auf dem Weg zur Transdisziplinarität. *GAIA,* 1(5), 250.

Möllering, G. (2001). The nature of trust: From Georg Simmel to a theory of expectation, interpretation and suspension. *Sociology*, 35(2), 403–420.

Moore, M. and Hartley, J. (2008). Innovations in governance. *Public Management Review*, 10, 3–20.

Mouffe, C. (2005). *On the Political.* London, New York: Routledge.

Mouffe, C. (2007). Artistic activism and agonistic spaces. *Art & Research. A Journal of Ideas, Contexts and Methods*, 1(2), http://www.artandresearch.org.uk/v1n2/mouffe.html. Accessed 2 August 2009.

Myrdal, G. (1969). *Objectivity in Social Research.* New York: Pantheon Books.

Negro, S. (2007). *Dynamics of Technological Innovation Systems – The Case of Biomass Energy.* Utrecht: Dissertation Utrecht University.

Newman, P. and Kenworthy, J. (1999). *Sustainability and Cities. Overcoming Automobile Dependence.* Washington, DC: Island Press.

Nicolescu, B. (1996). *La transdisciplinarité, manifeste.* Monaco: Le Rocher.

Niestroy, I. (2005). *Sustaining Sustainability: A Benchmark Study on National Strategies Towards Sustainable Development and Impact of Councils in Nine EU Member States.* The Hague: RMNO/EEAC/Lemma.

Nooteboom, B. (2004). Governance and competence: how can the be combined? *Cambridge Journal of Economics,* 28, 505–525.

Nooteboom, B. and Stam, E. (2008). *Micro-Foundations for Innovation Policy.* The Hague, Amsterdam: WRR, Amsterdam University Press.

Nooteboom, S. and Eshuis, J. (2009). *Transitions Through Reflexive Interventions in Governance Networks.* Paper for the international conference Towards Knowledge Democracy, 25–27 August, Leiden.

Nowotny, H., Scott, P. and Gibbons, M. (2001). *Rethinking Science: Knowledge in an Age of Uncertainty.* Cambridge: Polity.

Nowotny, H., Scott, P. and Gibbons, M. (2002). *Re-thinking Science: Knowledge and the Public in an Age of Uncertainty.* Cambridge (UK): Polity Press.

Nussbaum, M.C. (2006). *Frontiers of Justice.* Cambridge: Belknap Press.

Nutley, S., Walter, I. and Davis, H.T.O. (2003). From knowing to doing: a framework for understanding the evidence-into-practice agenda. *Evaluation*, 9(2), 125–148.

Ober, J. (2008). *Democracy and Knowledge: Innovation and Learning in Classical Athens.* Princeton: Princeton University Press.

Ohmae, K. (1993). The rise of the region state. *Foreign Affairs*, Spring, 78–87.

Olesen, O. (2005). Early millennial feminist qualitative research: challenges and outcomes. In Denzin, N.K. and Lincoln, Y. (Eds.), *The Sage Handbook of Qualitative Research*. Thousand Oaks: Sage Publications, 235–278.

O'Neill, O. (2002). *A Question of Trust*. Cambridge: Cambridge University Press.

Ørstavik, F. (2006). *"Nordic Design" in Innovation Policy: Embedding Collaborative Social Relations in Developmental Constellations. Lessons from a Case Study*. Oslo: NIFU STEP.

Orwell, G. (1949). *1984*. New York: Harcourt, Brace and Company.

Ouchi, W.G. (1991). Markets, bureaucracies and clans. In: Thompson, G., Frances, J., Levacic, R. (Eds.), *Markets, Hierarchies and Networks: The Coordination of Social Life*. Newbury Park: Sage, 246–255.

Owen, D. (1999). *Effects of Electronic Media on Democratic Attitudes*. Paper for the international conference Democracy and the Globalization of Politics and the Economy, October 1999, Germany.

Pachauri, R.K. and Reisinger, A. (2007). *IPCC: Fourth Assessment Report*. Geneva: IPCC, http://www.ipcc.ch/publications_and_data/publications_ipcc_fourth_assessment_report_synthesis_report.htm

Parsons, W. (2004). Not just steering but weaving: Relevant knowledge and the craft of building policy capacity and coherence. *Australian Journal of Public Administration*, 63(1), 43–57.

Pehe, J. (2009). *Populism in the Age of Mediocracy and Mediacracy*. http://www.pehe.cz/Members/redaktor/populism-in-the-age-of-mediocracy-and-mediacracy. Accessed on 03/11/2009.

Perrig-Chiello, P. and Darbellay, F. (2002). Interdisciplinarité et Analyse des Discours. In: Perrig-Chiello, P. and Darbellay, F. (Eds.), *Qu'est-ce l'interdisciplinarité? Les nouveaux défis de l'enseignement*. Lausanne: Editions Réalités Sociales, 91–113.

Petersen, A.C. (2006). *Simulating Nature. A Philosophical Study of Computer-Simulation Uncertainties and Their Role in Climate Science and Policy Advice*. Apeldoorn, Antwerpen: Het Spinhuis.

Petts, J. (1997). The public-expert interface in local waste management decisions: expertise, credibility, and process. *Public Understanding of Science*, 6, 359–382.

Petts, J. and Brooks, C. (2006). Expert conceptualizations of the role of lay knowledge in environmental decisionmaking: challenges for deliberative democracy. *Environment and Planning A*, 38, 1045–1059.

Philips, K. (1975). *Mediacracy: American Parties and Politics in the Communications Age*. Garden City: Doubleday and Company Inc.

Pielke, R.A. (2007). *The Honest Broker: Making Sense of Science in Policy and Politics.* Cambridge (UK): Cambridge University Press.

Pierre, J. and Peters, G. (2000). *Governance, Politics and the State.* New York: St. Martin's Press.

Pohl, C. (2008). From science to policy through transdisciplinary research. *Environmental Science and Policy*, 11, 46–53.

Pohl, C. and Hirsch Hadorn, G. (2007). *Principles for Designing Transciplinary Research, Proposed by the Swiss Academies of Arts and Sciences.* München: Oekom.

Pohl, C. and Hirsch Hadorn, G. (2008). Methodological challenges of transdisciplinary research. *Natures Sciences Sociétés*, 16(1), 111–121.

Pollitt, C. and Bouckaert, G. (2000). *Public Management Reform. A Comparative Analysis.* Oxford: Oxford University Press.

Pollitt, Ch., Van Thiel, S. and Homburg, V. (2007). *New Public Management in Europe. Adaptation and Alternatives.* Basingstoke: Palgrave MacMillan.

Popper, F. (1970). *The President's Commissions.* New York: Twentieth Century Fund.

Porter, M.E. (1998). Clusters and the new economics of competition. *Harvard Business Review*, November–December 1993, 77–90.

Powell, W.W. (1990). Neither market nor hierarchy. *Research in Organizational Behavior*, 12, 295–336.

Prahalad, C.K. and Ramaswamy, V. (2004). *The Future of Competition: Co-creating Unique Value with Customers.* Boston: Harvard Business School Press.

Pralle, S.B. (2003). Venue shopping, political strategy, and policy change. The internationalization of Canadian forest advocacy. *Journal of Public Policy*, 23(3), 233–260.

Pralle, S.B. (2006). Timing and sequence in agenda-setting and policy change: a comparative study of lawn care pesticide politics in Canada and the US. *Journal of European Public Policy*, 13(7), 987–1005.

Prior, M. (2007). *Post-Broadcast Democracy: How Media Choice Increases Inequality in Political Involvement and Polarizes Elections.* New York: Cambridge University Press.

Pröpper, I.M.A.M. (1989). *Argumentatie en machtsuitoefening in onderzoeken beleid; evaluatieonderzoek naar de Wet Investeringsrekening en het gebruik ervan in het beleidsproces.* Enschede: Business Faculty, University of Twente.

Putters, K. (2004). *Spelen met doorwerking: Over de werking van doorwerking van de adviezen van de adviescolleges in het Nederlands openbaar bestuur.* Tilburg: University of Tilburg and Berenschot Consultancy.

Putters, K. et al. (2004). Spelen met doorwerking: Over de werking van doorwerking van de adviezen van de adviescolleges in het Nederlands openbaar bestuur. Universiteit van Tilburg en Berenschot, Tilburg.

Ramanathan, V. (2007). Role of Black Carbon in Global and Regional Climate Change. Testimonial to the U.S. House Committee on Oversight and Government Reform on 18/10/2007. http://www-ramanathan.ucsd.edu/on_global_dimming.html

Ramanathan, V., Justice, C.O., Carberry, J.B., Dickinson, R.B., Hoffman, E.E. et al. (2009). *Restructuring Federal Climate Research to Meet the Challenges of Climate Change*. Washington, D.C.: National Academies Press.

Rathenau-Institute. (2009). *Energietransitie begint in de regio* (Energy transition starts in the region). Den Haag: Rathenau-Instituut.

Ravetz, J. (1999). What is post-normal science? *Futures*, 31(4), 647–653.

Rawls, J. (2001). *Justice as Fairness. A Restatement.* Cambridge: Belknap Press.

Reason, P. and Bradbury, H. (Eds.) (1990). *Handbook for Action Research: Participative Inquiry and Practice.* London: Sage.

Regeer, B.J. (in press). *Evaluating the development of strategies to deal with persistent problems. Changes in knowledge production for sustainable agriculture and urban development.*

Regeer, B.J. and Bunders, J. (2007). *Kenniscocreatie: samenspel tussen wetenschap & praktijk.* The Hague: RMNO.

Regeer, B.J. and Bunders, J. (2009). *Knowledge Co-creation: Interaction Between Science and Society. A transdisciplinary Approach to Complex Societal Issues.* RMNO: The Hague.

Reinders, A. (1996). *Media en communicatie in Curaçao.* Berlicum: ABC Advies.

Reuters (2009). "Mom admits to "Balloon Boy" hoax: court record". Press release 23/10/2009, http://www.reuters.com/article/newsOne/idUSTRE59M5J720091023.

Rhodes, R.A.W. (1997). *Understanding Governance.* Buckingham: Open University Press.

Rinaudo, J.D. and Garin, P. (2005). The benefits of combining lay and expert input for water-management planning at the watershed level. *Water Policy*, 7, 279–293.

Rip, A., Schot, J.W. and Misa, T.J. (1995). Constructive technology assessment: a new paradigm for managing technology in society. In: Rip, A., Schot, J.W. and Misa, T.J. (Eds.), *Managing Technology in Society. The Approach of Constructive Technology Assessment.* Londen, New York: Pinter Publishers, 1–12.

RMNO (1990). *Duurzame ontwikkeling. Een verkenning van de consequenties voor wetenschapsbeoefening en onderzoek.* The Hague: RMNO.

RMNO. (2003). Omgaan met kennis in transities (Managing knowledge in transitions).

RMNO. (2005). *Interdisciplinarity and Policy Relevance in Research Programmes.* A Position Paper. June 2005.

RMNO. (2007). Kennis co-creatie (Knowledge Co-Creation). Den Haag: RMNO.

RMNO. (2008). Social cost benefit analyses for environmental policy-making.

RMNO. (2009). Innovatie en duurzame ontwikkeling, Deelrapportage over "duurzame ontwikkeling in onderzoek en onderwijs" (Innovation and sustainable development. Part of the report "Sustainable Development in Research and Education", 2009).

Roberts, A. (1996). Why the Brownlow Committee failed: neutrality and partisanship in the early years of public administration. *Administration and Society*, 28(1), 3–38.

Robertson, M.M. (2006). The nature that capital can see: science, state and market in the commodification of ecosystem services. *Environment and Planning D: Society and Space*, 24, 367–378.

Robson, M. (2009). How Teenagers Consume Media: the report that shook the City. *The Guardian*, 13/07/2009, http://www.guardian.co.uk/business/2009/jul/13/teenage-media-habits-morgan-stanley/print. Accessed on 18/10/2009.

Roelofsen, A., Broerse, J.E.W., De Cock Buning, T. and Bunders, J.F.G.(2008). Exploring the future of ecological genomics: integrating CTA with vision assessment. *Technological Forecasting and Social Change*, 75(3), 334–355.

Rollwagen, I., Hofmann J. and Schneider S. (2006). Criteria for improving the business impact of foresight at Deutsche Bank: Lessons learnt in mapping trends: Second International Seville Seminar on Future-Oriented Technology Analysis: Impact of FTA Approaches on Policy and Decision-Making – SEVILLE 28-29 SEPTEMBER 2006. Available from http://forera.jrc.ec.europa.eu/fta/intro.html

Rooney, D., Hearn, G., Mandeville, T. and Joseph, R. (2003). *Public Policy in Knowledge-Based Economies. Foundations and Frameworks.* Cheltenham: Edward Elgar.

Rutten, H. and Van Oosten, H.J. (eds) (1999). *Innoveren met ambitie – Kansen voor agrosector, groene ruimte en vissector.* The Hague: NLRO.

Sabatier, P. (1988). *An Advocacy Coalition Framework of Policy Change and the Role of Policy-Oriented Learning Therein.* Boulder: Westview Press.

Sabatier, P. (1998). The advocacy coalition framework: revisions and relevance for Europe. *Journal of European Public Policy*, 5(1), 89–130.

Salter, L. and Slaco, D. (1981). *Public Inquiries in Canada.* Ottawa: Science Council of Canada.

Sarewitz, D. and Pielke Jr, R.A. (2007). The neglected heart of science policy: reconciling supply of and demand for science. *Environmental Science and Policy*, 10, 5–16.

Sarink, H., Bunders J. and Mabelis, H. (Eds.) (1991). *Biotechnologie en wereldvoedselproductie: discusiees over perspectieven en sturingsmechanismen.* The Hague: NOTA.

Schectman, J. (2009). Iran's twitter revolution? Maybe not yet. *Business Week,* 17/07/2009, http://www.businessweek.com/technology/content/jun2009/tc20090617_803990.htm. Accessed on 05/11/2009.

Scheuer, J. (2007). Media, democracy, and the left; seeing the bigger picture. *Dissent*, Fall, 7–10.

Schneider, S.M. and Foot, K.A. (2006). Web campaigning by US presidential primary candidates in 2000 and 2004. In: Williams, A.P. and Tedesco, J.C. (Eds). *The Internet Election: Perspectives On the Web in Campaign 2004*. Lanham: Rowman and Littlefield, 21–36.

Schneidewind, U. (2009). *Nachhaltige Wissenschaft. Plädoyer für einen Klimawandel im deutschen Wissenschafts- und Hochschulsystem*. Marburg: Metropolis.

Scholten, P. (2008). *Constructing Immigrant Policies. Research Policy Relations and Immigrant Integration in The Netherlands (1970–2004)*. Enschede: Dissertation University of Twente.

Scholz, R.W. (2010/in press). *Environmental Literacy in Science and Society: From Knowledge to Decision*. Cambridge (UK): Cambridge University Press.

Scholz, R.W. and Stauffacher, M. (2007). Managing transition in clusters: area development negotiations as a tool for sustaining traditional industries in a Swiss prealpine region. *Environment and Planning A*, 39, 2518–2539.

Scholz, R.W. and Tietje, O. (2002). *Embedded Case Study Methods: Integrating Quantitative and Qualitative Knowledge*. Thousand Oaks: Sage.

Scholz, R.W., Bösch, S., Oswald, J., Stauffacher, M. and Balmer, M.E. (Eds.) (2001). *Zukunft Schiene 1 – Okoeffizientes Handeln der SBB*. Zurich: Rüegger.

Scholz, R.W., Koller, T., Mieg, H.A. and Schmidlin, C. (Eds.) (1995). *Perspektive "Grosses Moos": Wege zu einer nachhaltigen Landwirtschaft. ETH-UNS Fallstudie 1994*. Zürich: ETH.

Scholz, R.W., Lang, D.J., Wiek, A., Walter, A.I. and Stauffacher, M. (2006). Transdisciplinary case studies as a means of sustainability learning: historical framework and theory. *International Journal of Sustainability in Higher Education*, 7(3), 226–251.

Scholz, R.W., Stauffacher, M., Bösch, S., Krütli, P. and Wiek, A. (Eds.) (2007). *Entscheidungsprozesse Wellenberg – Lagerung radioaktiver Abfälle in der Schweiz.* ETH-UNS Fallstudie 2006. Zürich: Rüegger.

Schon, D.A. and Rein, M. (1994). *Frame Reflection: Toward the Resolution of Intractable Policy Controversies*. New York: Basic Books.

Schot, J.W. and Rip, A. (1997). The Past and the Future of Constructive Technology Assessment. *Technological Forecasting and Social Change*, 54(2–3), 251–268.

Schulz, M. and Van Twist, M. (2009). *Overrun by Rabbits? Governing by Commission in the Netherlands*. Paper for the EGPA Conference in Malta.

Schulz, M., Van Twist, M. and Geveke, H. (2006). *Besturen in commissie: een onderzoek naar de rol van commissies in het openbaar bestuur*. The Hague: SDU.

Schulz, M., Van Twist, M. and Geveke, H. (2008). Besturen in commissie: verklaring van een fenomeen. *BandM*, 35, 94–106.

Scott, J. (1998). *Seeing Like a State: How Certain Schemes to Improve the Human Condition Have Failed.* New Haven, London: Yale University Press.

Searle, J. R. (1983). *Intentionality: an Essay in the Philosphy of Mind.* Cambridge: Cambridge University Press.

Searle, J. R. (1996). *The Construction of Social Reality.* London: Penguin Books.

SER (Social and Economic Council). (2006). Co-financing of the Common Agricultural Policy. www.ser.nl

SER. (2008). Waarden van de landbouw (Values in Agriculture). www.ser.nl.

Sen, A.K. (1977). Rational fools: a critique of the behavioural foundations of economic theory. *Philosophy and Public Affairs*, 6, 317–344, reprinted in Sen (1982). *Choice, Welfare and Measurement.* Oxford: Blackwell, 84–106.

Sen, A.K. (1985). *Commodities and Capabilities* (Hennipman Lecture). Amsterdam: North-Holland.

Sen, A.K. (1987). *On Ethics and Economics.* Oxford: Blackwell.

Sen, A.K. (1999). *Development as Freedom.* New York: Alfred A. Knopf.

Sent, E.M. (2004). Behavioral economics: how psychology made its (limited) way back into economics. *History of Political Economy*, 36, 735–760.

Shapin, S. and Schaffer, S. (1985). *Leviathan and the Air-pump: Hobbes, Boyle and the Experimental Life*. Princeton, Oxford: Princeton University Press.

Sheppard, S.R.J. and Meitner, M. (2004). *Using Multi-Criteria Analysis and Visualisation for Sustainable Forest Management Planning with Stakeholder Groups*, Vancouver: University of British Columbia.

Shirkey, C. (2008). *Here Comes Everybody: How Change Happens When People Come Together.* New York: Penguin.

Shleifer, A. (1998). State versus private ownership. *Journal of Economic Perspectives*, 12, 133–150.

Simon, H. (1976). From substantive to procedural rationality. In: S. Latsis (Ed.), *Method and Appraisal in Economics*. Cambridge: University Press, 129–148.

Smeets, P. (2009). Expeditie Agroparken. Ontwerpend onderzoek naar metropolitane landbouw en duurzame ontwikkeling. Wageningen: Wageningen Universiteit.

Smits, R. and Leyten, A. (1991). *Technology Assessment: waakhond of speurhond? Naar een integraal technologiebeleid.* Zeist: Kerckebosch.

Sørensen, E. (2006). Metagovernance: the changing roles of politicians in processes of democratic governance. *The American Review of Public Administration*, 36(1), 98–114.

Sprinz, D. (2008). Long-term policy problems: definition, origin, and responses. In Wayman, F., Williamson, P. and Bueno de Mesquita, B. (Eds.), *Prediction:*

Breakthrough in Science, Markets, and Politics. Ann Arbor: University of Michigan Press.

Stake, R.E. (1995). *The Art of Case Study Research*. Thousand Oaks: Sage.

Star, L.S. and Griesemer J.R. (1989). Institutional ecology, 'transitions' and boundary objects: amateurs and professionals in Berkeley's Museum of Vertebrate Zoology. *Social Studies of Science*, 19(3), 387–420.

Stauffacher, M., Flüeler, T., Krütli, P. and Scholz, R.W. (2008). Analytic and dynamic approach to collaboration: a transdisciplinary case study on sustainable landscape development in a Swiss prealpine region. *Systemic Practice and Action Research*, 21, 409–422.

Stauffacher, M., Walter, A. I., Lang, D. J., Wiek, A. and Scholz, R. W. (2006). Learning to research environmental problems from a functional socio-cultural constructivism perspective: the transdisciplinary case study approach. *International Journal of Sustainability in Higher Education*, 7(3), 252–275.

Steane, P. (2008). Public management reforms in Australia and New Zealand. *Public Management Review*, 10, 453–465.

Steketee, H. (2004). De relatie tussen media en politiek is destructief. *NRC Handelsblad* (Dutch newspaper), 09/07/2004.

Stern, N. (2006). *Review on the Economics of Climate Change*. London: HM Treasury.

Stiglitz, J. (2002). Information and the change in the paradigm in economics (Nobel Lecture). *American Economic Review*, 92, 460–501.

Stigson, B., Babu, S., Bordewijk, J., O'Donnell, P., Haavisto, P. et al. (2009). *Peer Review on Sustainable Development Policies in Germany*. Berlin: RNE.

Strassheim, H. (2007). Kulturen der Expertise und politischen Wissensproduktion im Wandel: vergleichende Beobachtungen. In: Gosewinkel, D. and Schuppert, F.G. (Eds.), *Politische Kultur im Wandel von Staatlichkeit*. Berlin: Edition Sigma, 281–301.

Streeck, W. and Schmitter, P.C. (1985). Community, market, state – and associations? *European Sociological Review*, 1(2), 119–138.

Surowiecki, J. (2004). *The Wisdom of Crowds: Why the Many are Smarter than the Few and How Collective Wisdom Shapes Business, Economics, Society and Nations*. London, New York: Little Brown, Anchor Books.

Sutton, P. (2004). *Nature, Environment and Society*. Houndmills: Palgrave Macmillan

Tapscott, D. and Williams, A. D. (2007). *Wikinomics: How Mass Collaboration Changes Everything*. New York: Penguin Group.

Tapscott, D. and Williams, A. (2008). *Wikinomics: How Mass Collaboration Changes Everything*. New York: Penguin.

Teisman, G. (2000). Models for research into decision-making processes: on phases, streams and decision-making rounds. *Public Administration*, 78(4), 937–956.

Teisman, G.R, Van Buuren, M.W. and Gerrits, L. (2009). *Managing Complex Governance Systems*. New York: Routledge.

Tenbensel, T. (2005). Multiple modes of governance. *Public Management Review*, 7(2), 267–288.

Ten Heuvelhof, E.F. and Van Twist, M.J.W. (2007). Hoe de 'wisdom of crowds' kan doorwerken in Den Haag: het Burgerforum Kiesstelsel als 'critical case'. *Bestuurswetenschappen*, 5, 10–25.

Termeer, C.J.A.M. (2009). Barriers to new modes of horizontal governance. *Public Management Review*, 11(3), 299–316.

Termeer, C.J.A.M. and Kessener, B. (2007). Revitalizing stagnated policy processes: Using the configuration approach for research and interventions. *Journal of Applied Behavioral Science*, 43(2), 256–272.

Termeer, C.J.A.M., Lieshout, M. v., Breeman, G. E. and Pot, W.D. (2009). *Politieke besluitvorming over het Landbouwontwikkelingsgebied Witveldweg in de Gemeente Horst aan de Maas*. Wageningen: Leerstoelgroep Bestuurskunde, Wageningen Universiteit.

Thompson, G. (2003). *Between Hierarchies and Markets: The Logic and Limits of Network Forms of Organization.* Oxford: Oxford University Press.

Thompson, G., Frances, G., Levacic, R. and Mitchell, J. (Eds.) (1991). *Markets, Hierarchies and Networks: The Coordination of Social Life.* London: Sage.

Thompson, M., Ellis, R. and Wildavsky, A. (1990). *Cultural Theory.* Boulder: Westview.

Thompson Klein, J. (1996). *Crossing Boundaries: Knowledge, Disciplinarities and Inter disciplinarities.* Charlottesville: University of Virginia Press.

Thompson Klein, J. (Ed.), Grossenbacher-Mansuy, W., Häberli, R., Bill, A., Scholz, R.W. et al. (2001). *Transdisciplinarity: Joint Problem Solving among Science, Technology, and Society. An Effective Way for Managing Complexity.* Basel: Birkhauser.

Thrift. (2006). *Re-animating the Space of Thought: Transformation of spacial and temporal description in the twenty-first century.* Paper presented at the DIME Conference Communities of Practice, Durham, UK.

Tirole, J. (1994). The internal organization of government. *Oxford Economic Papers*, 46, 1–29.

Tissen, R.J. and Lekanne Deprez, F.R.E. (2008). Towards a spatial theory of organizations. NRG Working Paper, February 2008 (08-04).

Tissen, R.J. and Van Rijn, S. (2007). Building creative cities: towards 'industry-based' knowledge management in urban vision development processes. Proceedings of the 8th European Conference on Knowledge Management, 2007(2), 1048–1053.

Tissen, R.J., Andriessen, D. and Lekanne Deprez, F.R.E. (2000). *The Knowledge Dividend.* London: Financial Times/Prentice Hall.

Trakhtenberg, A. (2005). Quality of democracy and quality of mass-media: Being different or backward? *Perspective on European Politics and Society*, 6(2), 271–282.

Tromp, H. (2006). *De strijd om de echte Vincent van Gogh. De kunstexpert als brenger van een onwelkome boodschap:* 1900–1970. Amsterdam: Mets and Schilt.

Turnhout, E. (2009). The effectiveness of boundary objects: the case of ecological indicators. *Science and Public Policy*, 36, 403–412.

Turnhout, E., Broekhans, B. and Arts, B. (in prep. a). Data or deliberation, clean waters or involved citizens? A critical assessment of the EU Water Framework. Under review at *Environmental Politics.*

Turnhout, E., Hisschemöller, M. and Eijs-ackers, H. (2008). Science in Wadden Sea Policy: from accommodation to advocacy. *Environmental Science and Policy*, 11, 227–239.

Turnhout, E., Van Bommel, S. and Aarts, N. (2008). Maakbare burgers? Participatie, betrokkenheid en burgerschap in de Drentsche Aa. In: Alberts, G., Blankesteijn, M., Broekhans, B. and Van Tilborgh, Y. (Eds.), *Jaarboek Kennissamenleving Deel 4: Burger in Uitvoering*. Amsterdam: Aksant, 69–93.

Turnhout, E., Van Bommel, S. and Aarts, N. (in prep. b). Creating citizens: performing citizenship in participatory environmental governance. Under review at *Ecology and Society.*

Vaes, G., Willems, P., Swartenbroekx, P., Kramer, K., De Lange, W. et al. (2009). Science-policy interfacing in support of the Water Framework Directive implementation. *Water Science and Technology*, 60, 47–54.

Van Asselt, M.B.A., Rotmans, J. and Rothman D. (2005). *Scenario Innovation, Experiences from a European Experimental Garden.* London: Taylor and Francis, ISBN 90-5809-684-X.

Van Buuren, A. and Edelenbos, J. (2004). Conflicting knowledge: why is knowledge production such a problem? *Science and Public Policy*, 31(4), 289–299.

Van Buuren, M.W. (2006). *Competente besluitvorming: het management van meervoudige kennis in ruimtelijke ontwikkelingsprocessen.* The Hague: Lemma.

Van Buuren, M.W. (2009). Knowledge for governance, governance of knowledge. Inclusive knowledge management in collaborative governance processes. *International Public Management Journal*, 12(2), 208–235.

Van Buuren, M.W., Gerrits, L. and Marks, P. (2009). Public policy-making and the management of co-evolution. In: Teisman, G. et al., 154–171.

Van den Anker, M.J.J. and Van den Hoogenboom, A.B. (1997). *Schijn bedriegt. Overheid, bedrijfsleven en gelegenheidsstructuren voor milieucriminaliteit op de hergebruikersmarkt.* The Hague: Vuga.

Vandenbroucke, F. (2001). *Social Justice and Individual Ethics in an Open Society.* Berlin: Springer.

Van der Arend, S.H. (2007). *Pleitbezorgers, procesmanagers en participanten: Interactief beleid en de rolverdeling tussen overheid en burgers in de Nederlandse democratie.* Utrecht: Dissertation Utrecht University.

Van der Duin, P. et al. (2007). *Knowing Tomorrow.* Delft: Eburon Academic Publishers. ISBN 978-9059722293.

Van der Heijden, J. (2005) (Ed.), *Recombinatie van overheid en samenleving, denken over innovatieve beleidsvorming.* Delft: Eburon.

Van Dongen, H.J., De Laat, W.A.M. and Maas, A.J.J.A. (1996). *Een kwestie van verschil (A Matter of Difference), Conflicthantering en onderhandeling in een configuratieve integratietheorie.* Delft: Eburon.

Van Eeten, M. (1999a). Dialogues of the deaf'on science in policy controversies. *Science and Public Policy*, 26(3), 185–192.

Van Eeten, M.J.G. (1999b). *Dialogues of the Deaf: Defining New Agendas for Environmental Deadlocks.* Delft: Eburon.

Van Gunsteren, H.R. (1998). *A Theory of Citizenship.* Boulder: Westview Press.

Van Gunsteren, H.R. (2006). *Vertrouwen in democratie* (*Trust in Democracy*). Amsterdam: Van Gennep.

Van Mansfeld, M.J.M. (2003). The need for knowledge brokers. In: Tress, B., Tress, G., Van der Valk, A.J.J. and Fry, G. (Eds.), *Interdisciplinary and Transdisciplinary Landscape Studies: Potential and Limitations.* Wageningen: Alterra.

Van Montfort, C.J. (2008). *Besturen van het onbekende.* The Hague: Lemma.

Van Poelje, G.A. (1967). *Het nieuwe burgerschap: Commissies, raden en wat dies meer zij.* Alphen aan de Rijn: Samson.

Van Schendelen, R. (2004). *Opheldering van schaduwmacht: commentaar op de nota-Duyvendak*, published on request by the permanent commission of the Netherlands House of Representatives for the Interior and Kingdom Relations.

Van Schendelen, R. (2005). Republikeinse openbreking van adviescommissies. In: Duyvendak, W., De Jong, P., Pauw, B. and Van Schendelen, R. (Eds.), *Schaduwmacht in de schijnwerpers: adviescommissies in politiek.* The Hague: SDU, 57–72.

Van Schie, N. and Bouma, J.J. (2008). The concept of covaluation: institutionalizing the involvement of local (public) values in regional planning on water. *Competition and Regulation in Network Industries*, 9(4), 363–396.

Van Slyke, D.M. (2007). Agents or stewards: using theory to understand the government-nonprofit social service contracting relationship. *Journal of Public Administration Research and Theory*, 17, 157–187.

Van Twist, M., Van der Steen, M., Karré, P. and Peeters, R. (2009). *Het nieuwe tussen: een conceptuele en empirische verkenning van vernieuwingen in de organisatie van de rijksdienst.* The Hague: NSOB.

Van Twist, M., Verheul, W.J. and Van der Steen, M. (2008). *Ondernemerschap en grensverleggende praktijken.* The Hague: InAxis.

Van Twist, M.J.W. (1994/1995). *Verbale vernieuwing: aantekeningen over de kunst van bestuurskunde.* The Hague: VUGA.

Van Winden, W., Van den Berg, L. and Pol, P. (2007). European cities in the knowledge economy: towards a typology. *Urban Studies*, 44(3), 525–549.

Verhoeven, I. (2009). *Burgers tegen beleid. Een analyse van dynamiek in politieke betrokkenheid.* Amsterdam: Uitgeverij Aksant.

Vernon, R.V. and Mansergh, N. (Eds.) (1940). *Advisory Bodies: A Study of Their Uses in Relation to Central Government* 1919–1939. London: Allen and Unwin.

Von Mutius, B. (Ed.) (2008). *Die andere Intelligenz. Wie wir morgen denken werden. Ein Almanach neuer Denkansätze aus Wissenschaft.* Gesellschaft und Kultur. Stuttgart: Klett-Cotta.

Voβ, J.P., Kemp, R. and Bauknecht, D. (2006). Reflexive governance: a view on an emerging path. In: Voβ, J.P., Bauknecht, D. and Kemp, R. (Eds.), *Reflexive Governance for Sustainable Development.* Cheltenham: Edward Elgar, 419–437.

Voogt, A.A. (1991). Managing of social cognitive configurations in a multiple context. In R.J. in 't Veld, L. Schaap, C.J.A.M. Termeer and M.J.W. Van Twist (Eds.), *Autopoiesis and Configuration Theory: New Approaches to Societal Steering.* Dordrecht/Boston/London: Kluwer.

Walker, B., Holling, C.S., Carpenter, S.R. and Kinzig, A. (2004). Resilience, adaptability and transformability in social-ecological systems. *Ecology and Society*, 9(2), 5.

Walter, A., Helgenberger, S., Wiek, A. and Scholz, R.W. (2007). Measuring societal effects of transdisciplinary research projects: design and application of an evaluation method. *Evaluation and Program Planning*, 30, 325–338.

Weber, L. (1979). *L'Analyse économique des dépenses publiques* (The Economic Analysis of Public Expenditure). Paris: Presses Universitaires de France.

Webler, T. and Tuler S. (2000). Fairness and competence in citizen participation: theoretical reflections from a case study. *Administration and Society*, 32(5), 566–595.

Weick, K. (1979). *The Social Psychology of Organizing.* New York: Random House.

Weick, K. (1995). *Sensemaking in Organizations.* Thousand Oaks: Sage.

Weick, K. and Westley, F. (1996). Organizational learning: affirming an oxymoron. In S.R. Clegg, C. Hardy and W.R. Nord (Eds.), *Handbook of Organization Studies.* London: Sage.

Weick, K.E. and Sutcliffe, K.M. (2001). *Managing the Unexpected: Assuring High Performance in an Age of Complexity.* San Francisco: Jossey-Bass.

Weinberg, A. (1972). Science and trans-science. *Minerva*, 33, 209–222.

Weingart, P. (1999). Scientific expertise and political accountability: paradoxes of science in politics. *Science and Public Policy*, 26, 151–161.

Weiss, C. (1991). Policy research: data, ideas or arguments? In Wagner, P., Hirschon Weiss, C., Wittrock, B. and Wollman, H. (Eds.), *Social Sciences and Modern Stated: National Experiences and Theoretical Crossroads*. Cambridge (UK): Cambridge University Press, 307–331.

Wenger, E.C. (1998). *Communities of Practice: Learning, Meaning, and Identity*. Cambridge (UK): Cambridge University Press.

Weterings, R. and Opschoor, J. B. (1994). *Towards Environmental Performance Indicators Base Don the Notion of Environmental Space*. Rijswijk: RMNO.

Wheare, K.C. (1955). *Government by Committee: An Essay on the British Constitution*. Oxford: Oxford University Press.

Williamson, O. (1985). *The Economic Institutions of Capitalism*. New York: Free Press.

Wilsdon, J. and Willis, R. (2004). *See-Through Science – Why Public Engagement Needs to Move Upstream*. London: DEMOS.

Wolfson, D.J. (2005). *Transactie als bestuurlijke vernieuwing* (Situational Contracting in Public Sector Reform) WRR-Verkenning nr. 9. Amsterdam: Amsterdam University Press.

Wolfson, D.J. (2008). *Gelijkheid in een pluriforme samenleving* (Equality in a Plural Society). Amsterdam: KNAW Press.

Wolfson, D.J. (2010). Situational contracting as a mode of governance. *Public Management Review* (forthcoming).

Woodhouse, E. and Nieusma, D. (2001). Democratic expertise: integrating knowledge, power, and participation. In: Hisschemöller, M., Hoppe, R., Dunn, W. and Ravetz, J. (Eds.), Knowledge, Power, and Participation in Environmental Policy Analysis. *Policy Studies Review Annual* 2001 (12). New Brunswick: Transaction, 73–96.

Woolgar, S. (2000). Social basis of interactive social science. *Science and Public Policy*, 27(3), 165–173.

Wraith, R.E. and Lamb, G.B. (1971). *Public Inquiries as an Instrument of Government*. London: Allen and Unwin.

WRR (1994). *Duurzame risico's: een blijvend gegeven*. The Hague: WRR.

WRR (2006). *Lerende overheid. Een pleidooi voor probleemgerichte politiek*. Amsterdam: Amsterdam University Press.

WRR (2008). *Innovatie vernieuwd. Opening in viervoud*. The Hague: WRR.

Wynne, B. (1991). Knowledges in context: science. *Technology, and Human Values*, 16, 111–121.

Wynne, B. (1996). May the sheep safely graze? A reflexive view of the expert-lay knowledge divide. In: Lash, S., Szerszynski, B., Wynne, B. (Eds.), *Risk, Environment and Modernity, Towards a New Ecology*. London, Thousand Oaks, New Delhi: Sage.

Wynne, B. (2006). Public engagement as a means of restoring public trust in science – hitting the notes, but missing the music? *Community Genetics,* 9, 211–220.

Wynne, B. (2007). Risky delusions: misunderstanding science and misperforming publics in the GE crops issue. In: Taylor, I. and Barrett, K. (Eds.), *Genetic Engineering: Decision Making Under Uncertainty*. Vancouver: University of British Columbia Press.

Yanow, D. (2003). Accessing local knowledge. In M. Hajer and H. Wagenaar (Eds.), *Deliberative Policy Analysis. Understanding Governance in the Network Society*. Cambridge: Cambridge University Press.

Yearley, S. (2000). Making systematic sense of public discontents with expert knowledge: two analytical approaches and a case study. *Public Understanding of Science*, 9, 105–122.

Yin, R.K. (1984). *Case Study Research: Design and Methods*. Beverly Hills: Sage.

Zeiss, R. and Groenewegen, P. (2009). Engaging boundary objects in OMS and STS? Exploring the subtleties of layered engagement. *Organisation*, 16, 81–100.

Zweekhorst, M.B.M. (2004). *Institutionalising an Interactive Approach to Technological Innocation. The Case of the Grameen Krishi Foundation.* Amsterdam: Thesis VU University.

Index

The manufacturer's authorised representative in the EU is Springer
Nature Customer Service Centre GmbH, Europaplatz 3, 69115 Heidelberg,
Germany. If you have any concerns regarding our products, please
contact ProductSafety@springernature.com

Printed and bound by CPI Group (UK) Ltd, Croydon, CR0 4YY
30/09/2026
02225570-0015